KU-078-573

CONTENTS AT A GLANCE

PHP Solutions: Dynamic Web Design Made Easy

David Powers

friendsof

DESIGNER TO DESIGNER™

an Apress® company

PHP Solutions:
Dynamic Web Design Made Easy

Credits

Lead Editor
Chris Mills

Senior Production Editor
Laura Cheu

Technical Reviewer
Samuel Wright

Compositor
Molly Sharp

Editorial Board
Steve Anglin, Ewan Buckingham, Gary Cornell, Jason Gilmore, Jonathan Gennick, Jonathan Hassell, James Huddleston, Chris Mills, Matthew Moodie, Dominic Shakeshaft, Jim Sumser, Keir Thomas, Matt Wade

Artist
April Milne

Proofreader
Liz Welch

Senior Project Manager
Kylie Johnston

Indexer
John Collin

Copy Edit Manager
Nicole Flores

Interior and Cover Designer
Kurt Krames

Copy Editors
Nicole Flores, Ami Knox

Manufacturing Director
Tom Debolski

Assistant Production Director
Kari Brooks-Copony

Cover Photography
David Powers

CONTENTS

Chapter 4: Lightening Your Workload with Includes 89

Chapter 11: Getting Started with a Database **285**

Chapter 12: Creating a Dynamic Online Gallery **319**

Chapter 13: Managing Content 341

Chapter 14: Solutions to Common PHP/MySQL Problems 381

ABOUT THE AUTHOR

David Powers is a professional writer who has been involved in electronic media for more than 30 years, first with BBC radio and television and more recently with the Internet. This is the seventh book he has written or co-authored for friends of ED/Apress, including the highly successful *Foundation PHP for Dreamweaver 8* (ISBN: 1-59059-569-6) and *Foundation PHP 5 for Flash* (ISBN: 1-59059-466-5). He is an Adobe Community Expert for Dreamweaver, and provides regular support and advice on PHP and other aspects of web development in several online forums, including friends of ED at www.friendsofed.com/forums.

What started as a mild interest in computing was transformed almost overnight into a passion, when David was posted to Japan in 1987 as BBC correspondent in Tokyo. With no corporate IT department just down the hallway, he was forced to learn how to fix everything himself. When not tinkering with the innards of his computer, he was reporting for BBC TV and radio on the rise and collapse of the Japanese bubble economy. Since leaving the BBC to work independently, he has built up an online bilingual database of economic and political analysis for Japanese clients of an international consultancy.

When not pounding the keyboard writing books or dreaming of new ways of using PHP and other programming languages, David enjoys nothing better than visiting his favorite sushi restaurant. He has also translated several plays from Japanese.

ABOUT THE TECHNICAL REVIEWER

Samuel Wright is a technical writer and web programmer living near Oxford, England. He is interested in using computers to facilitate routine tasks, and he enjoys learning about new technologies and writing about them. The downside to these interests is spending long hours wrestling with abstruse writing software.

Samuel graduated from the University of Manchester Institute of Science and Technology (UMIST) with a degree in physics, and he has held various positions since. He is currently employed full time at Celoxica as a technical writer.

Samuel runs a music webzine, Lykoszine (www.lykoszine.co.uk), and spends much of his time listening to as much heavy music as he can get his hands on. His remaining time is spent reading, juggling, and hiking.

ABOUT THE COVER IMAGE

The photo on the front cover is a picture I took of the stone water basin behind the monks' quarters at Ryoanji temple in Kyoto, Japan. Ryoanji is perhaps best known for its rock garden—15 stones in a sea of white gravel. It's designated by UNESCO as a World Heritage Site, but was once infamously described by the British travel writer A. A. Gill as "an impractical joke, medieval builder's rubbish." Although I've visited Ryoanji on several occasions, when I went there in early winter 2005, the garden wall was being restored, so for once it did really look like a builder's yard. Instead of contemplating the rocks and gravel, I spent my time admiring this simple, but beautiful water basin.

But why put it on the cover of a book about PHP? Well, apart from the fact that it's a nice photograph, the crystal clear water trickling into the basin through the bamboo pipe symbolizes for me a constant flow of fresh ideas, a fount of knowledge, just like the Internet. Viewed from above, the water basin also has a fascinating inscription (illustrated alongside).

Read clockwise from the left side, the characters mean *arrow*, *five*, *short-tailed bird*. The final character, at the bottom, has no meaning on its own—and that's the clue. In combination with the square opening of the basin, it forms the character for *sufficient*. In fact, the mouth of the basin is an integral part of the inscription. Each character combines with it to form a completely different one.

Once you unlock the secret, it forms the following sentence: *ware tada taru wo shiru*. Roughly translated, this means "I know only satisfaction" or "I am content with what I have."

吾唯足知

This is an important concept in Zen philosophy—knowledge for its own sake is sufficient. A person who learns to become content is rich in spirit, even if not in material terms. The more you think about it, the deeper its meaning becomes. Just like the rock garden—if all you can see is a pile of rubble, you have missed the point.

However, the subtitle of this book is not *Zen and the Art of Website Maintenance* (apologies to Robert M. Pirsig). I want this book to teach you practical skills. At the same time, the inscription on this water basin embodies an important message that applies very much to creating dynamic websites with PHP. The solution to a problem may not always be immediately obvious, but creative thinking will often lead you to the answer. There is no single "right" way to build a dynamic website. The more you experiment, the more inventive your solutions are likely to become.

INTRODUCTION

Dynamic Web Design Made Easy—that's a pretty bold claim. How easy is easy?

It's not like an instant cake mix: just add water and stir. Dynamic web design is—well—dynamic. Every website is different, so it's impossible to grab a script, paste it into a web page, and expect it to work. Building dynamic sites involves diving into the code and adjusting it to your own requirements. If that thought makes you break out in a cold sweat, just relax for a moment. PHP is not difficult, and I've written this book very much with the non-programmer in mind.

I've done so because I don't come from a computing background myself. In fact, I went to school in the days before pocket calculators were invented, never mind personal computers. As a result, I don't assume that you drank in knowledge of arrays, loops, and conditional statements with your mother's milk. Everything is explained in plain, straightforward language, and I've highlighted points where things may go wrong, with advice on how to solve the problem. At the same time, if you're working with computers and websites, you're bound to have a certain level of technical knowledge and skill. So I don't talk down to you either.

Over the years, I've read a lot of books about PHP and MySQL. The one thing that's missing from all of them is any concept of visual design. So I decided to be different. I picked a handful of the best photographs I took on a visit to Japan in late 2005 and incorporated them into a site called Japan Journey (http://foundationphp.com/phpsolutions/journey/), which features throughout the book. I wanted to show that sites powered by PHP don't have to look boring; in fact, they shouldn't—visual appeal is an essential part of any website. All the pages are built in standards-compliant XHTML and styled with Cascading Style Sheets (CSS). However, the main focus remains firmly on working with PHP and MySQL, teaching you how to add a wealth of dynamic features to a website.

Some of the things you'll learn by working through this book include the following:

- Displaying random images of different sizes
- Uploading images and automatically making copies that conform to a maximum size
- Creating an online photo gallery
- Building a navigation system to page through a long set of database results

- Displaying a summary of a long article and linking to the full text
- Protecting parts of your site with user authentication

You'll also learn how to process user input from every type of form element—text fields, drop-down menus, check boxes, and so forth. Most important of all, you'll see how a few simple checks can guard your websites and databases from malicious attack.

In this book, I've followed the same technique that has proved successful in *Foundation PHP 5 for Flash* and *Foundation PHP for Dreamweaver 8*. Each chapter takes you through a series of stages in a single project, with each stage building on the previous one. By working through the chapter, you get the full picture of how everything fits together. You can later refer back to the individual stages to refresh your memory about a particular technique. Although this isn't a reference book, Chapter 3 is a primer on PHP syntax, and some chapters contain short reference sections—notably Chapter 7 (reading from and writing to files), Chapter 9 (PHP sessions), Chapter 11 (MySQL data types and connection commands), and Chapter 13 (the four essential SQL commands).

So, to return to the original question: how easy is easy? I have done my best to ease your path, but there is no snake oil or magic potion. It will require some effort on your part. Don't attempt to do everything at once. Add new dynamic features to your site a few at a time. Get to understand how they work, and your efforts will be amply rewarded. Adding PHP and MySQL to your skills will enable you to build websites that offer much richer content and an interactive user experience.

It's been great fun writing this book, and the process has been smoothed all the way by the editorial team at friends of ED/Apress led admirably—as ever—by Chris Mills, the man with the psychedelic stuffed chicken (www.flickr.com/photos/chrismills/124635002/). Special thanks go also to Samuel Wright for his helpful technical review, Kylie Johnston for keeping the project on an even keel, Nicole Flores and Ami Knox for their sensitive copy editing, Laura Cheu for overseeing the process of turning my words and pictures into the book you're now reading, and everybody else who toiled behind the scenes.

My greatest thanks of all go to you for buying this book. What do you mean you haven't bought it yet? Rush over to the checkout counter and buy it now. Then let the fun begin. If you enjoy what you're doing, then everything becomes easy.

1 WHAT IS PHP—AND WHY SHOULD I CARE?

What this chapter covers:

- Understanding what PHP can do
- Is PHP difficult?
- Is PHP safe?
- Using the download files

One of the first things most people want to know about PHP is what the initials stand for. Then they wish they had never asked. Officially, PHP stands for **PHP: Hypertext Preprocessor**. It's an ugly name that gives the impression that it's strictly for nerds or propellerheads. Nothing could be further from the truth.

PHP is a scripting language that brings websites to life in the following ways:

- Sending feedback from your website directly to your mailbox
- Sending email with attachments
- Uploading files to a web page
- Watermarking images
- Generating thumbnails from larger images
- Displaying and updating information dynamically
- Using a database to display and store information
- Making websites searchable
- And much more . . .

PHP is easy to learn; it's platform-neutral, so the same code runs on Windows, Mac OS X, and Linux; and all the software you need to develop with PHP is open source and therefore free. There was a brief debate on the PHP General mailing list (http://news.php.net/php.general) in early 2006 about changing what PHP stands for. Small wonder, then, that it drew the comment that people who use PHP are Positively Happy People. The aim of this book is to help you become one too.

PHP started out as Personal Home Page in 1995, but it was decided to change the name a couple of years later, as it was felt that Personal Home Page sounded like something for hobbyists, and didn't do justice to the range of sophisticated features that had been added. Since then, PHP has developed even further, adding extensive support for object-oriented programming (OOP) in PHP 5. One of the language's great attractions, though, is that it remains true to its roots. You can start writing useful scripts very quickly without the need to learn lots of theory, yet be confident in the knowledge that you're using a technology with the capability to develop industrial-strength applications. Although PHP supports OOP, it's not an object-oriented language, and the scripts in this book concentrate on simpler techniques that are quick and easy to implement. If they help you to achieve what you want, great; if they inspire you to take your knowledge of PHP to the next level, even better.

Make no mistake, though. Using simple techniques doesn't mean the solutions you'll find in these pages aren't powerful. They are.

Embracing the power of code

If you're the sort of web designer or developer who uses a visual design tool, such as Dreamweaver, GoLive, or FrontPage, and never looks at the underlying code, it's time to rethink your approach. You're rapidly becoming an endangered species—and not the furry or cuddly sort that environmentalists will campaign to save from extinction. Good-looking design is definitely a top priority—and always will be—but it's no longer enough on its own. Designers need to have a solid grasp of the underlying structure of their pages. That means a knowledge of Hypertext Markup Language (HTML)—or its more recent incarnation, Extensible Hypertext Markup Language (XHTML)—and Cascading Style Sheets (CSS).

The CSS Zen Garden, cultivated by Dave Shea, played a pivotal role in convincing designers of the power of code. The underlying XHTML of every page showcased at www.csszengarden.com is identical, but as Figure 1-1 shows, the CSS produces stunningly different results. You don't need to be a CSS superhero, but as long as you have a good understanding of the basics of XHTML and CSS, you're ready to take your web design skills to the next stage by adding PHP to your arsenal.

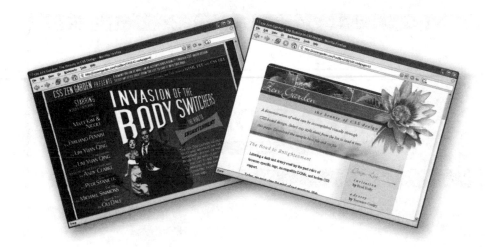

Figure 1-1. CSS Zen Garden has opened the eyes of web designers to the importance of code.

Creating pages that think for themselves

PHP is a **server-side language**. That means it runs on the web server, unlike CSS or JavaScript, which run on the client side (that is, the computer of the person visiting your site). This gives you much greater control. As long as the code works on your server, everyone receives the same output. For instance, Chapter 4 shows you how to create a random image generator with PHP. You can do the same thing with JavaScript, but what visitors to your site actually see depends on two things: JavaScript being enabled in their web browser, and the browser they are using understanding the version of JavaScript you have used. With PHP, this doesn't matter, because the dynamic process takes place entirely on the server and creates the XHTML needed to display the page with a random choice of image. The server chooses the image filename and inserts it into the <img> tag before sending the page to the browser. You can even use images of different sizes, because the PHP code detects the dimensions of the image and inserts the correct width and height attributes.

What PHP does is enable you to introduce logic into your web pages. Chapter 3 covers this subject in detail, but this logic is based on alternatives. If it's Wednesday, show Wednesday's TV schedules . . . If the person who logs in has administrator privileges, display the admin menu; otherwise, deny access . . . that sort of thing.

PHP bases some decisions on information that it gleans from the server: the date, the time, the day of the week, information held in the page's URL, and so on. At other times, the decisions are based on user input, which PHP extracts from XHTML forms. As a result, you can create an infinite variety of output from a single script. For example, if you visit my blog at http://foundationphp.com/blog/ (see Figure 1-2), and click various internal links, what you see is always the same page, but with different content. Admittedly, I tend to write always about the same kinds of subjects, but that's my fault, not PHP's.

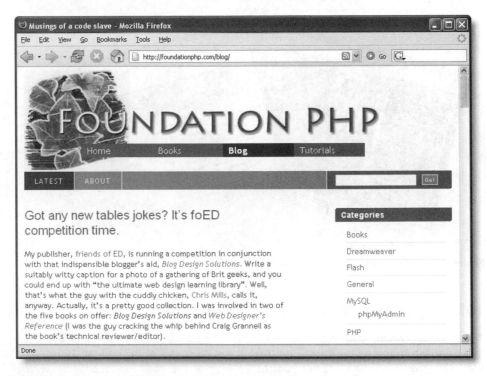

Figure 1-2. Blogs are a good example of sites ideally suited to PHP.

Another website that I have created and maintained for several years, a subscription-only Japanese-language site (see Figure 1-3), is driven entirely by PHP. The navigation menu appears on every page of the site, but it's contained in a completely separate file, so if it ever needs updating, I need to change only one page. Even though the menu is always generated by the same page, a little bit of PHP magic automatically highlights the correct button for the current page. You'll learn how to move an existing navigation bar to an external file and implement automatic highlighting in Chapter 4.

Because the site is subscription-only, users need to log in at the top right of the page to see the content, more than 14,000 articles in Japanese and English stored in a searchable database. When I log in, though, I get to see much more than anyone else: my security setting gives me administrator status, which enables me to insert new articles, edit existing ones, and register new users. You won't be building anything quite so ambitious in this book, but Chapters 9 through 15 teach you how to control access to your site with PHP sessions, as well as how to create a content management system with PHP and the MySQL relational database management system. Don't worry if you haven't worked with MySQL before; Chapter 10 shows you how to install it. Like PHP, it's open source and free for most users.

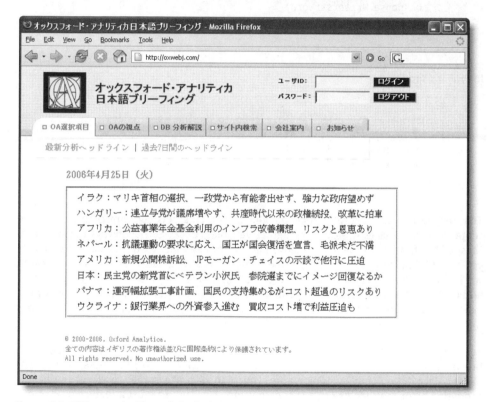

Figure 1-3. PHP not only drives all the logic behind this online database, but also restricts access to subscribers.

Other important uses for PHP in a website are sending email and uploading files, subjects covered in Chapters 5 and 6. By the time you finish this book, you'll wonder how you ever managed without PHP.

So how difficult is it going to be?

How hard is PHP to use and learn?

PHP isn't rocket science, but at the same time, don't expect to become an expert in five minutes. If you're a design-oriented person, you may find it takes time to get used to the way PHP is written. What I like about it very much is that it's succinct. For instance, in classic ASP, to display each word of a sentence on a separate line, you have to type out all this:

```
<%@ Language=VBScript %>
<% Option Explicit %>
<%
  Dim strSentence, arrWords, strWord
  strSentence = "ASP uses far more code to do the same as PHP"
  arrWords = Split(strSentence, " ", -1, 1)
  For Each strWord in arrWords
    Response.Write(strWord)
    Response.Write("<br />")
  Next
%>
```

In PHP, it's simply

```
<?php
$sentence = 'ASP uses far more code to do the same as PHP';
$words = explode(' ', $sentence);
foreach ($words as $word) {
  echo "$word<br />";
  }
?>
```

That may not seem a big difference, but the extra typing gets very tiresome over a long script. PHP also makes it easy to recognize variables, because they always begin with $. Most of the functions have very intuitive names. For example, mysql_connect() connects you to a MySQL database. Even when the names look strange at first sight, you can often work out where they came from. In the preceding example, explode() "blows apart" text and converts it into an array of its component parts. Don't worry if you don't know what variables, functions, or arrays are: they're all explained in Chapter 3, along with the other main things you need to know about the basics of PHP.

Perhaps the biggest shock to newcomers is that PHP is far less tolerant of mistakes than browsers are with XHTML. If you omit a closing tag in XHTML, most browsers will still render the page. If you omit a closing quote, semicolon, or brace in PHP, you'll get an uncompromising error message like that shown in Figure 1-4. This isn't just a feature of PHP, but of all server-side technologies, including ASP, ASP.NET, and ColdFusion. It's why you need to have a reasonable understanding of XHTML and CSS before embarking on PHP. If the underlying structure of your web pages is shaky to start with, your learning curve with PHP will be considerably steeper.

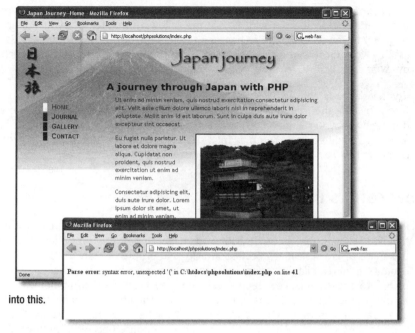

A missing
parenthesis
turns this . . .

into this.

Figure 1-4. Server-side languages like PHP are intolerant of most coding errors.

PHP isn't like XHTML: you can't choose from a range of PHP editors that generate all the code for you automatically. Dreamweaver does have considerable support for PHP, and it automates a lot of code generation, mainly for integrating web pages with the MySQL database. Even so, most of the techniques in this book still need to be coded by hand in Dreamweaver. For more details of what Dreamweaver can do with PHP, see my book *Foundation PHP for Dreamweaver 8* (friends of ED, ISBN: 1-59059-569-6).

Can I just copy and paste the code?

There's nothing wrong with copying the code in this book. That's what it's there for. Copying is the way we all learn as children, but most of us progress from the copycat stage by asking questions and beginning to experiment on our own. Rather than attempt to teach you PHP by going through a series of boring exercises that have no immediate value to your web pages, I've structured this book so that you jump straight into applying your newfound knowledge to practical projects. At the same time, I explain what the code is for and why it's there. Even if you don't understand exactly how it all works, this should give you sufficient knowledge to know which parts of the code to adapt to your own needs and which parts are best left alone.

If you're completely new to PHP, I suggest that you read at least the first six chapters in the order they appear. Chapter 3 covers all the basics of writing PHP. The first half of the chapter offers a bird's-eye view of the language and is probably all that you need to read before moving on to work with PHP in the following chapter. But you should come back regularly to the second half of Chapter 3 to fill in the details of PHP syntax. It's also a good idea to work through the PHP Solutions in each chapter in order, because each one builds on what goes before.

If you've already got the basics of PHP under your belt, you'll be able to hop about more freely, picking the solutions that are of more immediate interest to you. However, I recommend that you still read each chapter in its entirety. One of the features of this book is its emphasis on security. You may miss some important information if you read only part of a chapter.

How safe is PHP?

PHP is like the electricity or kitchen knives in your home: handled properly, it's very safe; handled irresponsibly, it can do a lot of damage. One of the inspirations for this book was the spate of email header injection attacks that erupted in late 2005. This type of attack exploits a vulnerability in a popular technique and enables the attacker to turn an online form into a spam relay. Few people were immune. I certainly wasn't, but once I was alerted to the problem, I plugged the hole and stopped the attacks in their tracks. However, day after day, people were sending frantic pleas for help to online forums. Even when they were told how to deal with the problem, their response became even more frantic. Many admitted they didn't know the first thing about any of the code they were using in their websites. For someone building websites as a hobby, this might be understandable, but many of these people were "professionals" who had built sites on behalf of clients. The clients were naturally unhappy when their mailboxes started filling with spam. They were no doubt even unhappier when their domains were suspended by hosting companies fed up with insecure scripts on their servers.

The moral of this story is not that PHP is unsafe; nor does everyone need to become a security expert to use PHP. What is important is to understand the basic principle of PHP safety: *always check user input before processing it*. You'll find that to be a constant theme throughout this book. Most security risks can be eliminated with very little effort. The other important thing is to know enough about scripts that you're using, so that if a problem arises, you can implement any remedies suggested to you by the author of the script or another expert.

How to use this book

PHP books tend to fall into three broad categories: beginner's tutorials, cookbooks for experienced users, and project-based books. This book tries to steer a middle course. It assumes no prior knowledge of PHP or MySQL, but is intended to be of equal value to designers and developers who already have some experience of these technologies. The approach I have taken is to explain each section of code in sufficient detail so that readers of all levels should be able to follow. However, the basic reference material is concentrated in Chapter 3, so more advanced readers shouldn't find themselves needing to wade through stuff they already know.

Because the book is aimed at web designers, most of the material centers on the Japan Journey site shown in Figure 1-4 (you can also view it online at http://foundationphp.com/phpsolutions/site). It's not intended to be a book-long case study that you're expected to build chapter by chapter. Most PHP books concentrate solely on code and pay zero attention to design, so the idea is to show you that pages built with PHP don't need to look ugly. You also see how to integrate PHP into an existing website. The emphasis is on enhancing your sites rather than building complex PHP applications from scratch.

Using the download files

PHP sites need to be located where the scripts can be processed by the web server. Normally, this means keeping them in a folder inside the Apache document root or an IIS virtual directory. Full instructions for setting up a local test environment are given in the next chapter. If you follow the recommendations there, Windows users should create a folder called C:\htdocs\phpsolutions if using Apache or create a virtual directory called phpsolutions in IIS. On Mac OS X, the phpsolutions folder should be located inside the Sites subfolder of your home folder.

A ZIP file containing the code for this book is available for download at www.friendsofed.com—it contains the following four folders:

- assets: CSS for the Japan Journey site and other pages
- downloads: All the source files arranged by chapter
- images: The images used on the Japan Journey site and other pages
- includes: Originally empty

Copy these four folders and their contents to the phpsolutions folder. When working with the example files in Chapter 3, view them in your browser by typing the following URL into the browser address bar on Windows (using the actual filename instead of *filename*.php):

http://localhost/phpsolutions/downloads/ch03/*filename*.php

On Mac OS X, use the following URL (using your own Mac username instead of *username* and the actual filename instead of *filename*.php):

http://localhost/~*username*/phpsolutions/downloads/ch03/*filename*.php

Most of the code for Chapter 4 and beyond should be copied from the appropriate sub-folder of the downloads folder into the main phpsolutions folder (the Japan Journey site root). Where a page undergoes several changes in the course of a chapter, I have numbered the different versions like this: index01.php, index02.php, and so on. When copying a file into the site root, remove the number from the filename, so index02.php becomes index.php. If you are using a program like Dreamweaver, which prompts you to update links when moving files from one folder to another, do *not* update them. The files are all designed to pick up the correct images and stylesheets when located in the site root. I have done this so that you can use a file comparison utility to compare your code with mine (instructions for how to do this are in the next chapter).

The download files for each chapter contain a complete set of all files, apart from the images and stylesheets, which are common to all chapters. This means you can safely move back and forth through the book and always have the right files to work with. Each chapter gives instructions about which files to use and whether they need to be copied to a particular folder. The URL for the Japan Journey site on Windows is

    http://localhost/phpsolutions/index.php

On Mac OS X the URL is

    http://localhost/~*username*/phpsolutions/index.php

The layout of the Japan Journey site is controlled by CSS. Since this is a book about PHP, it doesn't go into details about the style rules or classes, although the stylesheets are fully commented. To brush up on your CSS skills, take a look at *Web Designer's Reference: An Integrated Approach to Web Design with XHTML and CSS* by Craig Grannell (friends of ED, ISBN: 1-59059-430-4) and *CSS Mastery: Advanced Web Standards Solutions* by Andy Budd (friends of ED, ISBN: 1-59059-614-5).

A note about versions

New versions of open source software are often released at a fast and furious pace. Most of the time, the new versions are just bug fixes, and the basic software is installed and operates in exactly the same way as in the previous versions. Sometimes, though, what should be a minor version upgrade results in significant changes that can confuse newcomers. This book is based on the following versions:

- Apache 2.2.3 and Apache 2.0.59 (Windows), Apache 1.3.33 (Mac)
- PHP 5.2.0 Release Candidate 4 (Windows), PHP 5.1.6 (Mac)
- MySQL 5.0.24
- phpMyAdmin 2.8.2.4

New versions will inevitably come out during the lifetime of this book. My advice is to install the most recent version available for your operating system. As this book was about to go to press, the PHP development team was in the final stages of testing PHP 5.2.0, the first official version compatible with Apache 2.2 on Windows. However, Mac OS X still ships with the Apache 1.3 series as the default installation. Quite honestly, the 1.3 series is more than adequate for a local testing environment.

By the time you read this, the Windows version of PHP should support Apache 2.2, but in case of an unforeseen hitch, the instructions in the next chapter cover both Apache 2.0 and 2.2. If there are any significant changes to the installation or operation of PHP, MySQL, or phpMyAdmin, they will be posted on the friends of ED website at www.friendsofed.com or my website at http://foundationphp.com/phpsolutions.

Some people go to great lengths to find old versions of PHP or MySQL so that they can install the same setup as their hosting company. This is totally unnecessary. If anything, you should be pressuring your hosting company to upgrade to the latest versions. Not only do they have more features, but also they are usually safer. Nevertheless, this book has been written with both backward and forward compatibility in mind. Except where noted, all the code in this book should run on PHP 4.3.1 and MySQL 3.23.32 or later. I have also deliberately avoided using any code that is likely to break in PHP 6.

So, let's get on with it . . .

This chapter has provided only a brief overview of what PHP can do to add dynamic features to your websites and what you can expect from the rest of this book. The first stage in working with PHP is to set up a testing environment. The next chapter covers the process in detail for both Windows and Mac OS X.

What this chapter covers:

- Determining what you need
- Deciding whether to create a local testing setup
- Using a ready-made package
- Doing it yourself—setting up Apache and PHP on Windows and Mac OS X
- Getting PHP to work with IIS on Windows
- Making sure PHP has the right settings

Now that you've decided to use PHP to enrich your web pages, you need to make sure that you have everything you need to get on with the rest of this book. Although you can test everything on your remote server, it's usually more convenient to test PHP pages on your local computer. Everything you need to install is free. In this chapter, I'll explain the various options and give instructions for both Windows and Mac OS X.

What you need to write and test PHP pages

PHP is written in plain text, so you don't need any special authoring software. However, your life will be a lot easier if you choose a good script editor. I'll offer some advice on what to look for. The other thing you need is a web server capable of understanding PHP.

Checking whether your website supports PHP

The easiest way to find out whether your website supports PHP is to ask your hosting company. The other way to find out is to upload a PHP page to your website and see if it works. Even if you know that your site supports PHP, do the following test to confirm which version is running.

Checking the PHP version on your server

1. Open Notepad or TextEdit and type the following code into a blank page:

   ```
   <?php echo phpversion(); ?>
   ```

2. Save the file as phptest.php. It's important to make sure that your operating system doesn't add a .txt filename extension after the .php. Mac users should also make sure that TextEdit doesn't save the file in Rich Text Format (RTF). If you're at all unsure, use phptest.php from the download files for this chapter.

3. Upload phptest.php to your website in the same way you would an HTML page, and then type the URL into a browser. If you see a three-part number like 5.2.0 displayed onscreen, you're in business: PHP is enabled. The number tells you which

version of PHP is running on your server. *You need a minimum of 4.3.1 to use the code in this book.*

If you get a message that says something like Parse error, it means PHP is supported, but that you have made a mistake in typing the file. Use the download version instead.

If you just see the original code, it means PHP is not supported.

Hosting companies have been incredibly slow to update from PHP 4, frequently citing "lack of demand." If your server is still running PHP 4, contact your host and tell them you want PHP 5 (or PHP 6 if that's the current version by the time you read this). Although you can do a lot of really cool things with PHP 4, the newer versions are faster, have more features, and are more secure. If your host refuses to upgrade, it may be time to move to a new one. Equally, if you saw the raw code, you need to move to a new server. Try to find one that offers a minimum of PHP 5.

Choosing a good script editor for PHP

Although PHP isn't difficult to learn, if there's a mistake in your code, your page will probably never make it as far as the browser, and all you'll see is an error message. So, although you *can* write PHP in Notepad or TextEdit, you're much better off with a script editor that has at least the first three of the following features:

- **Line numbering**: Most good script editors allow you to toggle on and off the display of line numbers. Being able to find a specific line quickly makes troubleshooting a lot simpler.
- **A "balance braces" feature**: PHP uses parentheses (()), square brackets ([ ]), and curly braces ({}), which must always be in matching pairs. It's easy to forget to close a pair. All good script editors have a feature that finds the matching parenthesis, bracket, or brace.
- **PHP syntax coloring**: Some script editors highlight code in different colors. If your code is in an unexpected color, it's a sure sign that you've made a typing mistake.
- **PHP code hints**: This is mainly of interest to more advanced users, but some editors automatically display tooltips with reminders of how a particular piece of code works.

The following section describes some of the script editors you might like to consider.

Dreamweaver: Visual display of PHP output

My personal choice for writing PHP code, Dreamweaver (www.adobe.com/products/dreamweaver/), has all of the features just listed. It also has the advantage of strong support for CSS and valid XHTML, making it an ideal editor for designers who want to add interactive elements to their web pages. As Figure 2-1 shows, Dreamweaver is capable of displaying the output of your PHP code in Design view, making it easier to envisage how your final page will look.

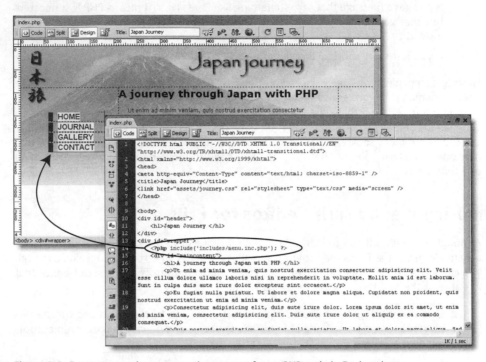

Figure 2-1. Dreamweaver lets you see the output of your PHP code in Design view.

The Coding toolbar puts several useful tools, including the balance braces feature, alongside the code you're working on. And pressing Ctrl+Space anywhere in a PHP code block displays code hints for just about every PHP function you can imagine.

> *Dreamweaver can also generate a lot of PHP code for you automatically. This book is designed to be software-neutral, so it doesn't cover automatic code generation. For that, see my book* Foundation PHP for Dreamweaver 8 *(friends of ED, ISBN: 1-59059-569-6).*

GoLive CS2: Some useful features

GoLive (www.adobe.com/products/golive/) is commonly regarded as the HTML editor for designers who tremble at the mere thought of code, but it does offer quick access to the underlying code (just click the Source tab at the top of the document window). GoLive doesn't have any special PHP features, but its syntax coloring treats PHP more than adequately, and line numbering is displayed by default in Source view. The balance braces feature is hidden, but it works quite well once you find it: double-click an opening or closing brace or parenthesis (but not square bracket) and content is highlighted up to the matching brace.

EditPlus 2: Versatile text-only editor for Windows

If you prefer to hew your code in a text-only environment, EditPlus 2 (www.editplus.com) is an excellent choice. It comes with a lot of built-in features, but you can extend the program with custom syntax files. One set that I find particularly useful is www.editplus.com/files/php504.zip. It specifies syntax coloring and automates many routine tasks. EditPlus 2 is available only for Windows.

BBEdit and TextMate: Script editors for Mac OS X

BBEdit (www.barebones.com/products/bbedit/index.shtml) is the granddaddy of Mac text editors. It's excellent for working with XHTML. Although it has line numbering, syntax coloring, and a balance braces feature, it doesn't have any special PHP features. A much cheaper alternative is TextMate (http://macromates.com), which does have extensive support for PHP through a user-contributed "bundle."

Checking your scripts with a file comparison utility

You're bound to make mistakes, particularly in the early stages. Often, you'll find that the problem is just a missing comma, semicolon, or quotation mark, but spotting the culprit can be the devil's own work in a page full of code. To help you with the learning process, you can download all the code for this book from www.friendsofed.com/downloads.html. Even so, comparing my files with yours can be time-consuming, not to mention tedious. File comparison utilities to the rescue!

A file comparison utility automatically compares two files line by line, highlighting any differences. Figure 2-2 shows the results of comparing two versions of the same file in the Windows program Beyond Compare, using the option to show just the differences. The section at the bottom of the screenshot shows the same line from each file one on top of the other, and highlights any differences. Using a file comparison utility with the download files will save you hours of fruitless searching.

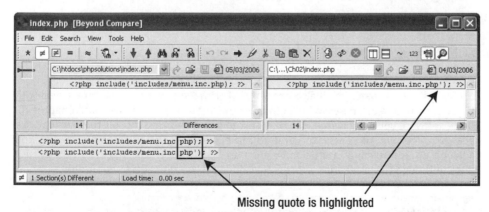

Missing quote is highlighted

Figure 2-2. A file comparison utility makes light work of finding differences between your code and the download files.

I have found the following file comparison utilities to be reliable:

- Windows

  - **Beyond Compare** (www.scootersoftware.com): An excellent tool. Try it free for 30 days. Thereafter it requires an individual license ($30 at the time of this writing).

  - **WinMerge** (http://winmerge.sourceforge.net): A good open source tool. Free.

- Mac OS X

  - **TextWrangler** and **BBEdit** (both from www.barebones.com) contain good file comparison utilities. TextWrangler is a free, cut-down version of BBEdit.

Deciding where to test your pages

Unlike ordinary web pages, you can't just double-click PHP pages in Windows Explorer or Finder on a Mac and view them in your browser. They need to be **parsed**—processed—through a web server that supports PHP. If your hosting company supports PHP, you can just upload your files to your website and test them there. However, you need to upload the file every time you make a change. In the early days, you'll probably find you have to do this often because of some minor mistake in your code. As you become more experienced, you'll still need to upload files frequently because you'll want to experiment with different ideas.

If you want to get working with PHP straight away, by all means use your remote server as a test bed. However, I'm sure you'll soon discover the need to set up a local PHP test environment. The rest of this chapter is devoted to showing you how to do it, with separate instructions for Windows and Mac OS X.

What you need for a local test environment

To test PHP pages on your local computer, you need to install the following:

- A web server (Apache or IIS)
- PHP

To work with a database, you'll also need MySQL. However, you can do a great deal with PHP even without a database, so I plan to leave the installation of MySQL until Chapter 10. All the software you need is free. The only cost to you is the time it takes to download the necessary files, plus, of course, the time to make sure everything is set up correctly. You could be up and running in little more than an hour. However, I urge you not to rush things. Although the installation process isn't difficult, you do need to get it right.

> *If you already have a web server and PHP on your local computer, there's no need to reinstall. Just check the section at the end of the chapter titled "Checking your PHP settings (Windows and Mac)."*

Individual programs or an all-in-one package?

If you're using Mac OS X, the decision is simple: Apache is already installed, so you just need to switch it on, and both PHP and MySQL are available as Mac packages. Individual installation is the most sensible way to go. Jump ahead to the section titled "Setting up on Mac OS X" later in this chapter.

Windows users need to do a bit more work to get everything up and running, so there's a strong temptation to opt for an all-in-one package. Two, in particular, have a good reputation as being stable and easy to install: XAMMP (www.apachefriends.org/en) and WAMP (www.en.wampserver.com). However, before opting for the "easy" route, you should consider the following notice on the official PHP site at www.php.net/manual/en/install.windows.php:

Warning
There are several all-in-one installers over the Internet, but none of those are endorsed by PHP.net, as we believe that the manual installation is the best choice to have your system secure and optimised.

I have no experience of working with XAMMP or WAMP, so I will offer no further advice on either of them. The instructions in the rest of this chapter concentrate on installing the official versions of all the software.

Setting up on Windows

These instructions have been tested on Windows 2000, XP Home, and XP Pro. Make sure that you're logged on as an Administrator.

New versions of software are being released all the time. Check this book's page at www.friendsofed.com for updates. Changes relevant to Windows Vista will also be posted there.

Getting Windows to display filename extensions

By default, most Windows computers hide the three- or four-letter filename extension, such as .doc or .html, so all you see in dialog boxes and Windows Explorer is thisfile instead of thisfile.doc or thisfile.html. The ability to see these filename extensions is essential for working with PHP.

If you haven't already enabled the display of filename extensions, open Start ➤ My Computer (it's a desktop icon on Windows 2000). Then from the menu at the top of the window, choose Tools ➤ Folder Options ➤ View. Uncheck the box marked Hide extensions for known file types. Click OK.

I recommend that you leave your computer permanently at this setting because it is more secure—you can tell if a virus writer has attached an EXE or SCR executable file to an innocent-looking document.

Choosing a web server for Windows

As noted earlier, you need a web server to process and display PHP pages. A web server is a piece of software that normally runs in the background, taking up very few resources, waiting for requests. The web server of choice for PHP is Apache and that is what you should install, as described in the next section.

PHP can also run on Microsoft Internet Information Services (IIS). If IIS is already installed and running, skip ahead to the section titled "Setting up PHP on Windows."

Installing Apache on Windows

These instructions assume that you have never installed Apache on your computer before. The most recent series, Apache 2.2, is not compatible with Windows versions of PHP earlier than PHP 5.2.0. If you plan to use an earlier version of PHP, install Apache 2.0. The screenshots in this section are based on Apache 2.0, but the installation procedure is identical for both Apache 2.2 and 2.0.

1. Go to http://httpd.apache.org/download.cgi and select the file marked Win32 Binary (MSI Installer) for the Apache series that you want to install. If there's no link to the Windows binary, click Other files, and then follow the links for binaries and win32.

2. Apache comes in a Windows installer package. Close all open programs and temporarily disable virus-scanning software. Double-click the Apache installer package icon.

3. A wizard takes you through the installation process. The only part that needs special attention is the Server Information screen (see Figure 2-3), in which you enter the default settings for your web server.

   In the Network Domain and Server Name fields, enter localhost; in the last field, enter an email address. The localhost address tells Apache you will be using it on your own computer. The email address does not need to be a genuine one; it has no bearing on the way the program runs and is normally of relevance only on a live production server.

4. Select the option labeled for All Users, on Port 80, as a Service. Apache will run in the background, and you don't need to worry about starting it. Click Next.

5. In the remaining dialog boxes, leave the default options unchanged and click Next. In the final dialog box, click Install to finish the Apache installation.

6. The process is quite quick, but don't be alarmed if you see a Command Prompt window open and close several times. This is perfectly normal. If a software firewall is installed, you will probably see a warning message asking you whether to block Apache. You must allow communication with Apache. Otherwise it won't work.

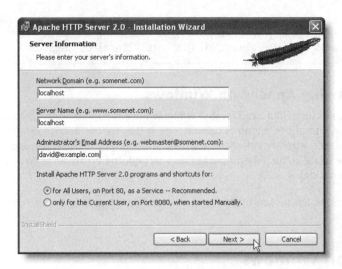

Figure 2-3. Filling out the Server Information dialog box during installation of Apache

7. After the program has been installed, open a browser and type http://localhost/ into the address bar. If all has gone well, you should see the test page shown in Figure 2-4 (Apache 2.2 displays a test page that simply says "It works!").

8. If you get an error message, it probably means that the Apache server is not running. Start up the server, as described in the next section, and try again. If you still get problems, check `C:\Program Files\Apache Software Foundation\Apache2.2\logs\error.log` or `C:\Program Files\Apache Group\Apache2\logs\error.log`. A common cause of failure is that another program, such as Skype, is already using port 80. If that happens, move the other program to a different port, or reinstall Apache, and select the Port 8080 option in step 4.

Figure 2-4. Confirmation that Apache 2.0 is running successfully on Windows

> *If you install Apache on port 8080, you need to start Apache manually and add a colon followed by the port number after* localhost, *like this:* http://localhost:8080/.

Starting and stopping Apache on Windows

Apache places a tiny icon (it looks like a red feather with a white circle) in the tray (or notification area) at the right end of the Windows taskbar. This is the Apache Service Monitor, which shows you at a glance whether Apache is running. If it's running, there is a green, right-facing arrow in the white circle. When Apache has stopped, the arrow turns to a red dot (see screenshots alongside).

Click the icon once with the *left* mouse button to reveal a menu to start, stop, or restart Apache.

Setting up PHP on Windows

The files for PHP come in two versions: a ZIP file for manual installation, and a Windows installer. Up to PHP 5.1, the Windows installer offered an extremely limited setup and was not recommended. However, just as this book was about to go to press, the PHP development team announced plans to create a new Windows installer capable of automating the installation of a full-featured PHP setup on either Apache or IIS. The new installer is expected to be available from PHP 5.2.0 onward.

At the time of this writing, it's not clear whether the installer is intended to become the recommended method of installation. Check my website at http://foundationphp.com/phpsolutions/updates.php for more up-to-date information. The following instructions show you how to install PHP manually from the ZIP file. Although this takes a little longer, it has the advantage of not making any changes to your Windows registry. The process involves four stages, as follows:

1. Download the PHP files and unzip them to a folder on your hard disk.
2. Edit a text file called php.ini that Windows uses to configure PHP on startup.
3. Add PHP to your Windows PATH.
4. Edit the settings for Apache or IIS so that the web server knows what to do with PHP files.

Downloading and configuring PHP

If you have an old installation of PHP, you must first remove any PHP-related files from your main Windows folder (C:\WINDOWS or C:\WINNT, depending on your system) and the system32 subfolder. Deleting the contents of the Windows system folders is not to be undertaken lightly, so I suggest that you cut and paste them to a temporary folder. Then, if anything goes wrong, you can easily restore them.

The PHP files you need to remove are php.ini (in the main Windows folder) and php4ts.dll or php5ts.dll in the system32 subfolder. You should also remove any other PHP-related DLL files from the system32 subfolder. They are easy to recognize because they all begin with php. If there's a copy of `libmysql.dll` in your Windows system folder, remove that, too.

1. Go to `www.php.net/downloads.php` and select the Windows binaries ZIP file for the latest stable version of PHP. Even if your hosting company is running an older version of PHP, I suggest downloading the latest version of PHP to avoid problems when you install MySQL in Chapter 10. When you click the download link, you will be presented with a list of mirror sites. Choose one and download the ZIP file to a temporary folder on your hard disk.

2. Unzip the contents of the ZIP file to a new folder called `C:\php`. The php folder should contain several other folders, as well as about 30 files.

> *The precise name or location of the folder isn't important, but it makes sense to use* php *or* phpx, *where x is the PHP version number. If you choose a location different from* C:\php, *you need to substitute the name of your new folder in all later steps. Don't put the PHP files in a folder that contains spaces in either its name or pathname, because it can create problems with Apache.*

3. In the php folder, locate the file called `php.ini-dist`, make a copy of it, and rename the copy `php.ini`. (There has been talk of giving `php.ini-dist` a more meaningful name, such as `php.ini-development`, so the name may have changed by the time you read this.) As soon as you rename the file, its associated icon in Windows Explorer will change, as shown alongside, indicating that it's an INI file that Windows will use to configure PHP each time you start up your web server.

php.ini

4. Open `php.ini` in any text editor. Notepad will do, but it's better to use a script editor that displays line numbers (such as one listed in the section "Choosing a good script editor for PHP" earlier in the chapter)—because finding the relevant sections will be a lot easier.

5. Scroll down to the following lines in the Error Handling and Logging section (the wording may differ slightly, but you should be able to find them by searching for error_reporting):

Notice how most lines begin with a semicolon. This indicates that they are comments and will be ignored by Windows. Only the final line in the screenshot (indicated by a marker alongside the number on line 292) begins without a semicolon, and this is the one you need to amend. Change it so that it looks like this:

```
278  ;    - Show all errors, except for notices and coding standards warnings
279  ;
280  ;error_reporting = E_ALL & ~E_NOTICE
281  ;
282  ;    - Show all errors, except for notices
283  ;
284  ;error_reporting = E_ALL & ~E_NOTICE | E_STRICT
285  ;
286  ;    - Show only errors
287  ;
288  ;error_reporting = E_COMPILE_ERROR|E_ERROR|E_CORE_ERROR
289  ;
290  ;    - Show all errors except for notices and coding standards warnings
291  ;
292  error_reporting  =  E_ALL & ~E_NOTICE
293
```

```
error_reporting = E_ALL
```

This sets error reporting to a higher level, which helps ensure your PHP is robust.

> *The line numbers and markers in the screenshots are generated by the script editor and are not part of* php.ini. *Use the screenshots and line numbers in this section only as a general guide. The contents of* php.ini *undergo constant revision, so your version may look slightly different. The important thing is to use the settings recommended in the text.*

6. Scroll down to the Paths and Directories section. Locate the following (around line 460):

```
extension_dir = "./"
```

Change it to

```
extension_dir = "C:\php\ext\"
```

This is where PHP will look for any extensions. This assumes you extracted the PHP files to the recommended location. If you chose a different one, change the path accordingly.

7. Scroll further down until you come to Dynamic Extensions. You will see a long list titled Windows Extensions (around line 563), all of them commented out. These extensions add extra features to the core functionality of PHP. You can enable any of them at any time simply by removing the semicolon from the beginning of the line for the extension you want, saving php.ini, and restarting Apache or IIS.

Locate the following (around line 569):

```
;extension=php_mbstring.dll
```

Enable the extension by removing the semicolon from the beginning of the line like this:

```
extension=php_mbstring.dll
```

This enables support for Unicode. Even if you never plan to use anything other than English, it's required to work with the latest versions of MySQL.

8. About eight lines further down, locate the following:

```
;extension=php_gd2.dll
```

Remove the semicolon from the beginning of the line. This will allow you to use PHP's image manipulation functions (see Chapters 4 and 8).

9. About 12 lines further down, locate the line containing php_mysql.dll. Copy and paste it on the line immediately below. Remove the semicolon from the beginning of both lines and amend the second line so they look like this:

```
extension=php_mysql.dll
extension=php_mysqli.dll
```

10. Add the following lines immediately beneath those in the previous step:

extension=php_pdo.dll
extension=php_pdo_mysql.dll

The four lines in this step and the previous one enable all the MySQL-specific functions that will be used in Chapters 11 to 15.

11. In the Module Settings section immediately following the list of extensions, look for the code shown alongside. Change the line shown in the screenshot as line 623 to the name of the SMTP server you normally use for sending email.

```
621  [mail function]
622  ; For Win32 only.
623  SMTP = localhost
624  smtp_port = 25
625
626  ; For Win32 only.
627  ;sendmail_from = me@example.com
628
```

If your email address is, for instance, david@example.com, your outgoing address is most probably smtp.example.com. In that case, you would change the line like this:

SMTP = **smtp.example.com**

> *Changes to the settings in this step and the following one are intended to make it possible to test the mail application in Chapter 5 on your local computer. However, it won't work if your ISP's SMTP server requires a username and password every time you connect (as happens with Gmail and other webmail services). Also, some ISPs reject mail that comes from an unidentified domain. In such circumstances, you will need to upload the files to your remote server to test them.*

12. Remove the semicolon from the beginning of the command shown on line 627, and put your own email address in place of me@example.com:

sendmail_from = **david@example.com**

This puts your correct email address in the From: field of emails sent through PHP.

13. The final change you need to make to php.ini is considerably further down (around line 884). Locate the following:

;session.save_path = "/tmp"

Remove the semicolon from the beginning of the line, and change the setting in quotes to your computer's Temp folder. On most Windows computers, this will be C:\WINDOWS\Temp:

session.save_path = **"C:\WINDOWS\Temp"**

14. Save php.ini, and close it. Leave it inside the C:\php folder.

Adding PHP to your Windows startup procedure

The installation of PHP is complete, but you still need to tell Windows where to find all the necessary files whenever you switch on your computer.

1. Open the Windows Control Panel (Start ➤ Settings ➤ Control Panel or Start ➤ Control Panel). **Double-click the** System **icon. Select the** Advanced **tab and click** Environment Variables, **as shown in the following screenshot.**

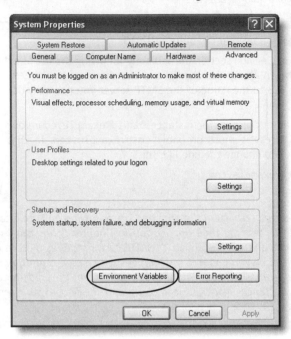

2. In the System variables **pane at the bottom of the dialog box that opens, highlight** Path **as shown and click** Edit.

3. A smaller dialog box opens. Click inside the Variable value field and move your cursor to the end of the existing value. Type a semicolon followed by the name of the PHP folder you created in step 2 of the previous section (;C:\php). As shown in the screenshot, there should be no spaces between the value just entered and the existing value or in the new pathname.

4. Click OK. With the Environment Variables dialog box still open, click New in the System variables pane. Another small dialog box opens, in which you enter the details of the new system variable. In the Variable name field, type PHPRC. In the Variable value field, enter the path of the PHP folder (C:\php).

5. Click OK to close all the dialog boxes. The next time you restart your computer, Windows will know where to find all the necessary files to run PHP. However, before restarting your computer, you still need to make some changes to your web server so that it knows how to handle PHP files. If you are using Apache, continue with the next section. If you are using IIS, skip ahead to the section titled "Configuring IIS to work with PHP."

Configuring Apache to work with PHP

Now that all the configuration settings have been made for PHP, you need to make some adjustments to the main configuration file for Apache.

> *Note that all the pathnames in the Apache configuration file use* forward *slashes instead of the Windows convention of backward slashes. So,* c:\php *becomes* c:/php. *Any path- or filenames that contain spaces must be enclosed in quotes.*

1. The Apache configuration file httpd.conf is located in C:\Program Files\Apache Software Foundation\Apache2.2\conf (for Apache 2.0, it's in C:\Program Files\Apache Group\Apache2\conf). Use Windows Explorer to locate the file and open it in a script editor. Like php.ini, httpd.conf is a very long file composed mainly of comments, which in this case can be distinguished by a pound or hash sign (#) at the beginning of the line.

2. Scroll down until you find a long list of items that begin with LoadModule (many of them will be commented out). At the end of the list, add the following on a new line, (for Apache 2.2):

```
LoadModule php5_module c:/php/php5apache2_2.dll
```

```
113   #LoadModule vhost_alias_module modules/mod_vhost_alias.so
114   #LoadModule ssl_module modules/mod_ssl.so
115
116   LoadModule php5_module c:/php/php5apache2_2.dll
```

If you are using Apache 2.0, this list is about 60 lines further down. Apache 2.0 uses a different DLL file, so the command should look like this:

```
LoadModule php5_module c:/php/php5apache2.dll
```

3. Scroll down again until you find the section shown in the following screenshot:

```
150   #
151   DocumentRoot "C:/Program Files/Apache Software Foundation/Apache2.2/htdocs"
152
153   #
154   # Each directory to which Apache has access can be configured with respect
155   # to which services and features are allowed and/or disabled in that
156   # directory (and its subdirectories).
157   #
158   # First, we configure the "default" to be a very restrictive set of
159   # features.
160   #
161   <Directory />
162       Options FollowSymLinks
163       AllowOverride None
164       Order deny,allow
165       Deny from all
166       Satisfy all
167   </Directory>
168
169   #
170   # Note that from this point forward you must specifically allow
171   # particular features to be enabled - so if something's not working as
172   # you might expect, make sure that you have specifically enabled it
173   # below.
174   #
175
176   #
177   # This should be changed to whatever you set DocumentRoot to.
178   #
179   <Directory "C:/Program Files/Apache Software Foundation/Apache2.2/htdocs">
180       #
```

Apache automatically looks for all web pages in the **server root** (or DocumentRoot as Apache calls it). This is so it can process the scripts and send the right information to both the database and the browser. The two lines indicated by a marker next to the line number (lines 151 and 179 in the screenshot) are where you specify the location of the server root. In a browser this becomes the equivalent of http://localhost/. (In Apache 2.0, this section is around lines 230 and 255, and the server root points to a slightly different address.)

Because this is where all your web files will be stored, it's not a good idea to keep them in the same place as your program files. Whenever I set up a new computer, I always create a dedicated folder called htdocs at the top level of my C drive, and I put all my websites in subfolders of htdocs. I chose that name because it's the traditional name used by Apache for the server root folder. Change both lines to indicate the same location, like this:

```
DocumentRoot "C:/htdocs"
#
# Omitted section
#
<Directory "C:/htdocs">
```

4. Scroll down a bit further until you come to the following command (around line 214):

```
DirectoryIndex index.html
```

This setting tells web servers what to display by default if a URL doesn't end with a filename, but contains only a folder name or the domain name (for instance, www.friendsofed.com). Apache will choose the first available page from a space-separated list. The purpose of this book is to work with PHP, so add index.php.

```
DirectoryIndex index.html index.php
```

In Apache 2.0, this command is around line 323 and includes `index.html.var`. Just add index.php at the end of the line as above.

5. Close to the end of `httpd.conf`, you'll find a section that includes several commands that begin with AddType. Add the following line in that section on a line of its own, as shown (in Apache 2.0, this section is around line 760):

```
AddType application/x-httpd-php .php
```

```
383     #
384     AddType application/x-compress .Z
385     AddType application/x-gzip .gz .tgz
386
387     AddType application/x-httpd-php .php
388
```

6. Save and close `httpd.conf`.

7. You now need to restart your computer so that the changes made to the Windows PATH and startup procedure can take effect. Apache should start automatically, unless you selected the manual option earlier. If everything starts normally, skip ahead to the section titled "Testing PHP on Windows." If you see an error message, read on.

8. If there are any mistakes in `httpd.conf`, Apache will refuse to start. Depending on the version you have installed, you might get a helpful message in a Command Prompt window that tells you what the problem is and which line of `httpd.conf` it occurred on. Reopen `httpd.conf` and correct the error (probably a typo). On the other hand, Windows might display a very unhelpful message simply telling you that the operation has failed.

Check the Apache error log (C:\Program Files\Apache Software Foundation\ Apache2.2\logs\error.log or C:\Program Files\Apache Group\Apache2\logs\ error.log) for clues about the problem. Alternatively, open a Command Prompt window. Inside the Command Prompt window, change to the Apache program folder by typing the following and pressing Enter:

```
cd c:\program files\apache software foundation\apache2.2\bin
```

For Apache 2.0, use this:

```
cd c:\program files\apache group\apache2\bin
```

Then type this (followed by Enter):

```
apache
```

The reason for the failure should appear onscreen, usually with a line number pin-pointing the problem in httpd.conf. After you correct httpd.conf, resave the file and restart Apache using the Apache Service Monitor. Assuming everything goes OK this time, skip ahead to "Testing PHP on Windows."

> *If you type* apache *in the Command Prompt window and nothing appears to happen, it doesn't mean that Apache has hung. It indicates that Apache has started normally. However, while Apache is running, it doesn't return you to the command line; and if you close the window, Apache will crash. To close Apache gracefully, open another Command Prompt window, change the directory to the* apache2.2\bin *or* apache2\bin *folder, and type the following command:*
>
> ```
> apache -k shutdown
> ```
>
> *You can then restart Apache using the Apache Service Monitor.*

Configuring IIS to work with PHP

These instructions assume that you are familiar with IIS basics, and already have it installed and running on your computer. You should also have completed the sections titled "Downloading and configuring PHP" and "Adding PHP to your Windows startup procedure."

1. Open the Internet Information Services panel (Start ➤ Control Panel ➤ Administrative Tools ➤ Internet Information Services).

2. Expand the folder tree in the left panel, and highlight Default Web Site, as shown in the screenshot. Right-click, and select Properties from the context menu.

3. In the Default Web Site Properties dialog box, select the Home Directory tab, and set Execute Permissions to Scripts only, as shown at the top of the next page. Then click Configuration.

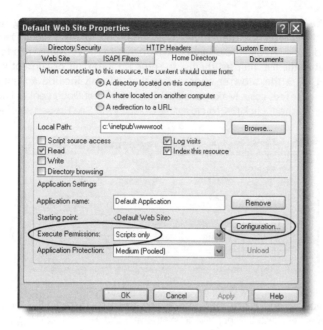

4. The Application Configuration dialog box opens. Select the Mappings tab, and click Add.

5. In the Add/Edit Application Extension Mapping dialog box that opens, enter the full path to php5isapi.dll in the Executable field. If you used the default location for the PHP files recommended earlier, this will be C:\php\php5isapi.dll. Enter .php in the Extension field. **Don't forget the period at the front of the extension**—this is very important. Make sure that Script engine is checked, and leave the other settings unchanged. Click OK twice to return to the Default Web Site Properties dialog box.

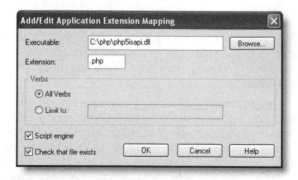

If you click the Browse *button to navigate to the location of your PHP files in step 5, make sure that the drop-down menu labeled* Files of type *at the bottom of the* Open *dialog box is set to* Dynamic Link libraries (*.dll) *or* All files (*.*). *Otherwise, you won't be able to locate the correct file.*

6. Select the Documents tab of the Default Web Site Properties dialog box, and click Add. In the dialog box that opens, type index.php in the Default Document Name field, and click OK. Use the up and down arrows to move index.php to the position you want in the list. IIS uses the list to serve up a default document whenever you enter a URL in the browser address bar that doesn't include a filename (such as www.friendsofed.com). Make sure that Enable Default Document is checked. When you have finished, click OK to close the Default Web Site Properties dialog box.

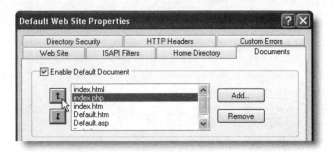

7. Before your changes can take effect, you need to restart IIS. Open the Services panel (Start ➤ Control Panel ➤ Administrative Tools ➤ Services). Highlight IIS Admin, and click Restart the service. Test PHP as described in the next section.

Testing PHP on Windows

Now comes the moment of truth: checking whether you have installed everything correctly. If you have followed the instructions carefully, everything should be OK.

1. Open a script editor and type the following code into a blank file (there should be nothing else in the page):

```
<?php phpinfo(); ?>
```

2. Save the file as index.php in your server root folder. If you have set up Apache as recommended in this chapter, this is C:\htdocs (create a new folder with that name, if you haven't already done so). If you are using IIS, save the file in C:\Inetpub\wwwroot.

3. Open a browser and type http://localhost/index.php in the address bar. (If your web server is running on a nonstandard port, such as 8080, add a colon followed by the port number after localhost, like this: http://localhost:8080/index.php.) You should see a page similar to the one shown in Figure 2-5. Welcome to the world of PHP! The mass of information displayed by index.php may appear overwhelming at the moment, but you should always display this page whenever you need to find out anything about your PHP setup. Assuming everything went OK, skip to the section titled "Checking your PHP settings (Windows and Mac)" at the end of the chapter.

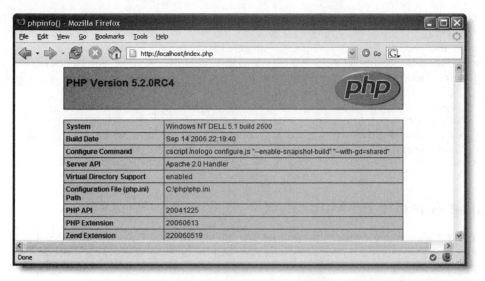

Figure 2-5. The phpinfo() command confirms that PHP is installed and displays useful information about your setup.

Troubleshooting

Use the following checklist if you get error messages or fail to see the page shown in Figure 2-5:

- Test an ordinary HTML web page in the same location. If both fail to display, check that your web server is running. If just the PHP page fails to display, retrace your steps through the sections on installing PHP.

- IIS doesn't always recognize PHP after a simple restart, but rebooting the computer usually does the trick.

- If you see an error message that the mysqli extension cannot be loaded, this usually indicates that an old version of a file called libmysql.dll has been installed in C:\WINDOWS\system32 by another program. Copy the version from C:\php to C:\WINDOWS\system32 and restart your web server.

Setting up on Mac OS X

After leafing through so many pages of Windows instructions, you'll be pleased to know that this section is considerably shorter. It's shorter because Apache is preinstalled on Mac OS X. PHP is also preinstalled, but the default version is lacking in features and isn't very easy to set up. Fortunately, an excellent Mac package is available for free download and will provide you with a full-featured, up-to-date version of PHP 5.

Most of the setup is done through the familiar Mac interface, but you need to edit some configuration files. Although these are ordinary text files, they are normally hidden, so you can't use TextEdit to work with them. I suggest that you use BBEdit or TextWrangler. As mentioned earlier, TextWrangler is a cut-down version of BBEdit, which you can download free from www.barebones.com/products/textwrangler/.

> These instructions do not cover Mac OS X Server, which uses a different version of Apache. I have assumed that if you have the skill to run the server version of OS X, you should be able to handle the configuration without further assistance.

Using Apache on Mac OS X

The default version of Apache that comes preinstalled with Mac OS X is Apache 1.3. It's an excellent web server and does everything you need for developing PHP pages. Because it's preinstalled, all you need to do is switch it on. First, make sure that you're logged into Mac OS X with Administrative privileges.

Starting and stopping Apache

1. Open System Preferences and select Sharing in Internet & Network.

2. In the dialog box that opens, click the lock in the bottom-left corner, if necessary, to allow you to make changes, and enter your password when prompted. Highlight Personal Web Sharing on the Services tab, as shown in Figure 2-6, and then click the Start button on the right. A message will appear, informing you that personal web sharing is starting up. After personal web sharing is running, the label on the button changes to Stop. Use this button to stop and restart Apache whenever you install a new version of PHP or make any changes to the configuration files. Click the lock again if you want to prevent accidental changes.

Figure 2-6. The Apache web server on a Mac is switched on and off in the Sharing section of System Preferences.

2

3. Open your favorite browser and type http://localhost/~*username*/ into the address bar, substituting your own Mac username for *username*. You should see a page like that shown in Figure 2-7, confirming that Apache is running. That's all there is to it.

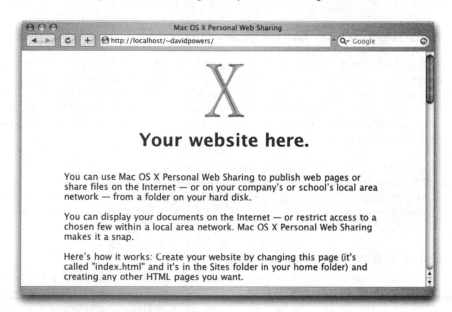

Figure 2-7.
Confirmation that Apache is running successfully on Mac OS X

> *Sometimes, Macs seem to develop a personality of their own. If you have a local network, you might discover that the* localhost *part of the URL changes to something like* deathstar.local *or whatever you have called your computer. For testing on the same machine,* localhost *is much shorter to type. After you use* localhost *a few times, your Mac will probably give up trying to be so clever and accept the shorter version. You can also use* 127.0.0.1 *as a synonym for* localhost.

Where to locate your web files

As the message in Figure 2-7 indicates, the place to store all your web files is in the Sites folder in your home folder. You need to keep them there because Apache needs to process PHP scripts before it can display the output in your browser. Unlike ordinary web pages, you can't just double-click them in Finder and expect them to pop up in your default browser. To view a page that uses PHP on your local computer, you must enter the correct URL in the browser address bar in the same way as you access a site on the Internet.

The address for the top level of your Sites folder is http://localhost/~*username*/. Any subfolders are accessed by adding the folder name to the end of the URL.

If you're the only person using the computer, you might prefer to locate all your files in Macintosh HD:Library:WebServer:Documents. It works exactly the same way, but instead of needing to include a tilde (~) followed by your username in the URL every time, you use just http://localhost/ as the address. If you test it now, you will see the same screen as shown in Figure 2-4. It makes no difference whether you use the central location or your own Sites folder. Choose whichever is more convenient for you.

Installing PHP on Mac OS X

Rather than attempt to activate the preinstalled version of PHP, a tedious job at the best of times, I suggest you use a precompiled Mac package created by Marc Liyanage (www.entropy.ch). You get a full-featured version of PHP that works "straight out of the box." If you run into problems, there's a searchable support forum on Marc's website, on which answers tend to be fast and accurate. It should be your first port of call in case of installation problems.

> *PHP relies heavily on the availability of external code libraries. It is essential that you have installed all the latest Apple system software updates before proceeding. Click the Apple menu and select* Software Update. *Install any security and OS X system updates.*

Using a Mac package for PHP

1. Marc Liyanage creates different packages for Apache 1.3 and Apache 2. The default installation in Mac OS X at the time of this writing is Apache 1.3, but it's important to check whether it's the same in your case. In Finder, open the Utilities folder in Applications and launch Terminal.

2. A window like the one shown here opens.

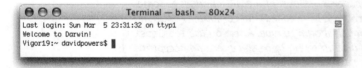

All instructions to the computer are inserted as written commands at what's known as the **shell prompt**. This is the final line in the screenshot and it looks something like this:

Vigor19:~ davidpowers$

The first part (before the colon) is the name of your Macintosh hard disk. The tilde (~) is the Unix shorthand for your home directory (or folder). It should be followed by your username and a dollar sign. As you navigate around the hard disk, your location is indicated in place of ~. All commands in Terminal are followed by Return.

3. To find out which version of Apache is running on your Mac, type the following command:

httpd -v

After pressing Return, you should see a window similar to the one shown here.

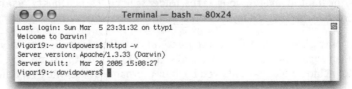

This window tells you the version of Apache and the date it was built. You need the first two numbers of the server version—in this case, 1.3—to ensure that you download the correct PHP package.

4. Go to www.entropy.ch/software/macosx/php/, scroll about halfway down the page, and select the Universal Binary for PHP 5 that also matches the version of Apache running on your computer. Marc Liyanage maintains PHP packages only for the current version of Mac OS X (currently 10.4). If you're using an older version, you'll have to settle for PHP 4 (assuming the link hasn't been removed by the time you read this).

Read any installation instructions on the site because they contain the most up-to-date information about special requirements or restrictions.

5. The Universal Binary is contained in a compressed file named entropy-php-5.x.x.tar.gz. Double-click the file to extract its contents, and then double-click the entropy-php.mpkg icon it places your desktop. Follow the instructions onscreen to install PHP.

6. Your upgraded version of PHP is ready for use, but first you need to make a minor change to the PHP configuration file php.ini.

Configuring PHP to display errors on Mac OS X

Marc Liyanage's package uses a version of php.ini that turns off the display of error messages. When using PHP for development, it's essential to see what's gone wrong and why.

1. Open BBEdit or TextWrangler. From the File menu, choose Open Hidden, and navigate to Macintosh HD:usr:local:php5:lib:php.ini. Because php.ini is a protected file, you need to select All Files from the Enable drop-down menu at the top of the Open dialog box, shown here. Click Open.

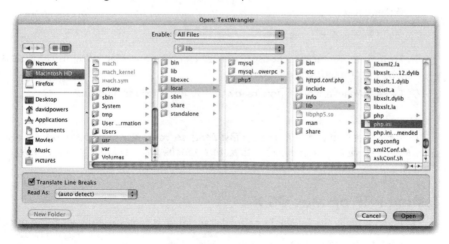

2. When php.ini opens in your text editor, you'll see that it's a long text file and that most lines begin with a semicolon. This means they are comments; the configuration commands are on lines that don't have a semicolon at the beginning.

To make it easier to identify the correct place in the files you edit, choose Preferences from the BBEdit or TextWrangler menu, and then select Text Status Display. Make sure that the Show Line Numbers check box is selected, and close the Preferences dialog box.

3. At the top left of the toolbar, an icon showing a pencil with a line through it indicates that this is a read-only file. Click the pencil icon. You will see the prompt shown here.

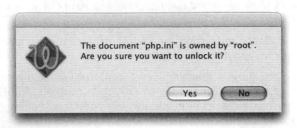

4. Click Yes and locate the following command around line 353 (use the line number only as a guide—it might be different in a later version of PHP):

```
display_errors = Off
```

Change it to this

```
display_errors = On
```

5. About ten lines further down, locate the following command:

```
log_errors = On
```

Change it to

```
log_errors = Off
```

6. From the File menu, choose Save, and enter your Mac administrator password when prompted. Close php.ini.

7. Restart Apache. You're now ready to test your PHP installation.

> If you ever need to make further adjustments to your PHP configuration, follow the same procedure to edit php.ini, and restart Apache for the changes to take effect.

Testing PHP on Mac OS X

1. Open a blank file in BBEdit or TextWrangler, and type the following line of code:

```
<?php phpinfo(); ?>
```

2. Save the file in the Sites subfolder of your home folder as index.php.

3. Open a browser and enter the following URL in the address bar:

```
http://localhost/~username/index.php
```

Use the name of your Mac Home folder (the one identified by a little house icon in the Finder sidebar) in place of *username*.

4. Press Return. You should see a screen similar to that shown in Figure 2-8. This screen not only confirms that PHP is installed and running, but also provides masses of detail about the way the installation has been configured. This is the page you will always be asked to display if you ever need to check why PHP doesn't work as expected.

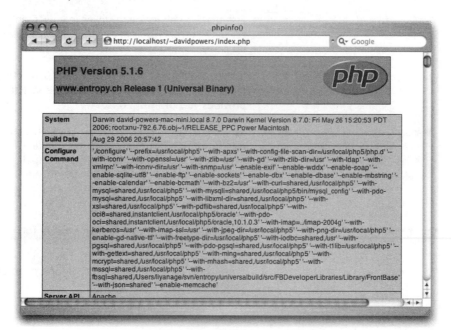

Figure 2-8. The precompiled PHP package created by Marc Liyanage comes with an impressive range of features.

Checking your PHP settings (Windows and Mac)

The screen full of information produced by phpinfo(), as shown in Figures 2-5 and 2-8, tells you just about everything you need to know about your PHP setup in a very user-friendly format. The following is a quick guide to help you check whether your installation is set up correctly to work through the rest of this book.

The section at the top of the page contains two vital pieces of information: the PHP version number and the path to php.ini. You should be using a minimum of PHP 4.3.1, and preferably PHP 5 or later.

The value of Configuration File (php.ini) Path tells you the location of the file your computer is reading at startup. Frequently Windows users complain that changes to php.ini have no effect. This usually means an old version has been left in the Windows system folder and is taking precedence. Remove the redundant file, and restart your web server.

The main settings are displayed in a long list titled PHP Core. In most cases, the default settings are fine. Table 2-1 lists the settings that you need to check for this book, together with the recommended values.

Table 2-1. Recommended PHP configuration settings

Directive	Local value	Remarks
display_errors	On	Essential for debugging mistakes in your scripts. If set to Off, errors result in a completely blank screen, leaving you clueless as to the possible cause.
error_reporting	See remarks	Displayed as a number. Since PHP 5.2.0, a setting in php.ini of E_ALL is 6143. The same setting in previous versions displays 2047.
extension_dir	See remarks	This is mainly of importance to Windows users. It tells Windows where to find the DLL files for extensions that expand the core functionality of PHP. If you installed PHP 5 to the location recommended in this chapter, this should be C:\php\ext\.
file_uploads	On	Self-explanatory. Allows you to use PHP for uploading files.
log_errors	Off	With display_errors set on, you don't need to fill your hard disk with an error log.

The rest of the configuration page shows you which PHP extensions are enabled. Mac users will have many more listed than the average Windows user because extensions need to be built in at compile time on the Mac. Windows users can turn extensions on and off very quickly by editing the Dynamic Extensions section of php.ini and restarting their web server.

To work with this book, you need the following extensions enabled:

- gd
- mbstring
- mysql
- mysqli
- pdo_mysql (optional)
- session

> *Your computer reads the PHP configuration file only when the web server first starts up, so changes to php.ini require Apache or IIS to be restarted for them to take effect.*

What's next?

Now that you've got a working test bed for PHP, you're no doubt raring to go. The last thing I want to do is dampen any enthusiasm, but before using any PHP in a live website, it's important to have a basic understanding of the basic rules of the language. So before jumping into the really cool stuff, the next chapter explains how to write PHP. Don't skip it—it's really important stuff. You may also be pleasantly surprised at how few rules there are.

2

What this chapter covers:

- Understanding how PHP is structured
- Embedding PHP in a web page
- Storing data in variables and arrays
- Getting PHP to make decisions
- Looping through repetitive tasks
- Using functions for preset tasks
- Displaying PHP output
- Understanding PHP error messages

If you're the sort of person who runs screaming at the sight of code, this is probably going to be the scariest chapter in the book, but it's an important one—and I've tried to make it as user-friendly as possible. The reason for putting the rules of PHP in one chapter is to make it easier for you to dip into other parts of the book and use just the bits that you want. If there's anything you don't understand, you can come back to the relevant part of this chapter to look up the details. That way, you can concentrate on what you need to know without having to wade through dozens of pages that aren't of immediate interest to you.

With that in mind, I've divided this chapter into two parts: the first section offers a quick overview of how PHP works and gives you the basic rules; the second section goes into more detail. Depending on your style of working, you can read just the first section and come back to the more detailed parts later, or you can read the chapter straight through. However, don't attempt to memorize everything at one sitting. The best way to learn anything is by doing it. Coming back to the second part of the chapter for a little information at a time is likely to be much more effective.

If you're already familiar with PHP, you may just want to skim through the main headings to see what this chapter contains and brush up your knowledge on any aspects that you're a bit hazy about.

PHP: The big picture

When you load a PHP page into a browser, it looks no different from an ordinary web page. But before it reaches your browser, quite a lot goes on behind the scenes to generate the page's dynamic content. In most cases, this frenetic activity takes only a few microseconds, so you rarely notice any delay. At first glance, PHP code can look quite intimidating, but once you understand the basics, you'll discover that the structure is remarkably simple. If you have worked with any other computer language, such as JavaScript, ActionScript, or ASP, you'll find they have a lot in common.

Every PHP page *must* have the following:

- The correct filename extension, usually .php
- Opening and closing PHP tags surrounding each block of PHP code

A typical PHP page will use some or all of the following elements:

- Variables to act as placeholders for unknown or changing values
- Arrays to hold multiple values
- Conditional statements to make decisions
- Loops to perform repetitive tasks
- Functions to perform preset tasks

Let's take a quick look at each of these in turn.

Telling the server to process PHP

PHP is a **server-side language**. This means that the web server processes your PHP code and sends only the results—usually as XHTML—to the browser. Because all the action is on the server, you need to tell it that your pages contain PHP code. This involves two simple steps, namely:

- Give every page a PHP filename extension—the default is .php. Do not use anything other than .php unless you are told to specifically by your hosting company.
- Enclose all PHP code within PHP tags.

The opening tag is <?php and the closing tag is ?>. It doesn't matter whether you put the tags on the same line as surrounding code, but when inserting more than one line of PHP, it's a good idea to put the opening and closing tags on separate lines for the sake of clarity.

```
<?php
// some PHP code
?>
```

You may come across <? as an alternative short version of the opening tag. However, <? doesn't work on all servers. Stick with <?php, which is guaranteed to work.

> To save space, many of the examples in this book omit the opening and closing PHP tags. You must always use them when writing your own scripts or embedding PHP into a web page.

Embedding PHP in a web page

PHP is an **embedded** language. This means that you can insert blocks of PHP code inside ordinary web pages. When somebody visits your site and requests a PHP page, the server sends it to the PHP engine, which reads the page from top to bottom looking for PHP tags. XHTML passes through untouched, but whenever the PHP engine encounters a <?php tag, it starts processing your code and continues until it reaches the closing ?> tag. If the PHP code produces any output, it's inserted at that point. Then any remaining XHTML passes through until another <?php tag is encountered.

> *You can have as many PHP code blocks as you like on a page, but they cannot be nested inside each other.*

Figure 3-1 shows a block of PHP code embedded in an ordinary web page and what it looks like in a browser and page source view after it has been passed through the PHP engine. The code calculates the current year, checks whether it's different from a fixed year (represented by $startYear in line 32 of the code on the left of the figure), and displays the appropriate year range in a copyright statement. As you can see from the page source view at the bottom right of the figure, there's no trace of PHP in what's sent to the browser. The only clue that PHP has been used to generate that part of the page lies in the whitespace between the date range and the surrounding text, but that doesn't affect the way it's displayed because browsers ignore anything more than a single space in XHTML.

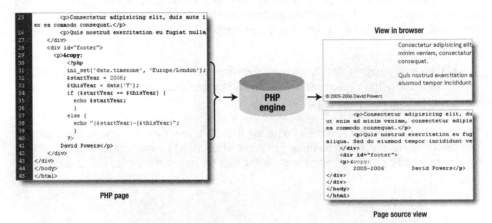

Figure 3-1. Output from PHP is normally displayed in the same place as it is embedded in the XHTML code.

> *PHP doesn't always produce direct output for the browser. It may, for instance, check the contents of form input before sending an email message or inserting information into a database. So some code blocks are placed above or below the main XHTML code. Code that produces direct output, however, always goes where you want the output to be displayed.*

Using variables to represent changing values

The code in Figure 3-1 probably looks like an awfully long-winded way to display a range of years. Surely it's much simpler to just type out the actual dates? Yes, it is, but the PHP solution saves you time in the long run. Instead of you needing to update the copyright statement every year, the PHP code does it automatically. You write the code once and forget it. What's more, as you'll see in the next chapter, if you need to amend the code, it's possible to do so by updating only one page, and the changes are reflected on every page of your site.

This ability to display the correct year automatically relies on two key aspects of PHP: **variables** and **functions**. As the name suggests, functions do things; they perform preset tasks, such as getting the current date and converting it into human-readable form. I'll cover functions a little later, so let's take variables first. The script in Figure 3-1 contains two variables: $startYear and $thisYear.

> A **variable** *is simply a name that you give to something that may change or that you don't know in advance. Variables in PHP always begin with $ (a dollar sign).*

Although the concept of variables sounds abstract, we use variables all the time in everyday life. When you meet somebody for the first time, one of the first things you ask is "What's your name?" It doesn't matter whether the person you've just met is Tom, Dick, or Harry, we use the word "name" in the same way as PHP uses variables. The word "name" remains constant, but the value we store in it varies for different people. Similarly, with your bank account, money goes in and out all of the time (mostly out, it seems), but as Figure 3-2 shows, it doesn't matter whether you're scraping the bottom of the barrel or as rich as Croesus, the amount available at any particular time is always referred to as the balance.

Figure 3-2. The balance on your bank statement is an everyday example of a variable—the name stays the same, even though the value may change from day to day.

So, name and balance are everyday variables. Just put a dollar sign in front of them, and you have two ready-made PHP variables, like this:

```
$name
$balance
```

Simple.

Naming variables

You can choose just about anything you like as the name for a variable, as long as you keep the following rules in mind:

- Variables always begin with a dollar sign ($).
- The first character after the dollar sign cannot be a number.
- No spaces or punctuation are allowed, except for the underscore (_).
- Variable names are case-sensitive: $startYear and $startyear are not the same.

When choosing names for variables, it makes sense to choose something that tells you what it's for. The variables you've seen so far—$startYear, $thisYear, $name, and $balance—are good examples. Even if you don't understand how the code works, a variable's name should give some indication as to what it's about. Because you can't use spaces in variable names, it's a good idea to capitalize the first letter of the second or subsequent words when combining them (sometimes called **camel case**). Alternatively, you can use an underscore ($start_year, $this_year, etc.). Technically speaking, you can use an underscore as the first character after the dollar sign, but it's not a good idea. PHP predefined variables (e.g., the superglobal arrays described a little later in this chapter) begin with an underscore, so there's a danger that you may accidentally choose the same name and cause problems for your script.

Don't try to save time by using really short variables. Using $sy, $ty, $n, and $b instead of the more descriptive ones makes code harder to understand—and that makes it hard to write. More important, it makes errors more difficult to spot.

> Although you have considerable freedom in the choice of variable names, you can't use $this, *because it has a special meaning in PHP object-oriented programming. It's also advisable to avoid using any of the keywords listed at* www.php.net/manual/en/ reserved.php.

Assigning values to variables

Variables get their values from a variety of sources, including the following:

- User input through online forms
- A database
- An external source, such as a news feed or XML file
- The result of a calculation
- Direct inclusion in the PHP code

Wherever the value comes from, it's always assigned in the same way with an equal sign (=), like this:

```
$variable = value;
```

The variable goes on the left of the equal sign, and the value goes on the right. Because it assigns a value, the equal sign is called the **assignment operator**. Note that the line of code ends with a semicolon. This is an important point that I'll come to after this quick warning.

Familiarity with the equal sign from childhood makes it difficult to get out of the habit of thinking that it means "is equal to." However, PHP uses two equal signs (==) to signify equality. This is one of the biggest causes of beginner mistakes—and it often catches more experienced developers, too. The difference between = and == is covered in more detail later in this chapter.

3

Ending commands with a semicolon

PHP is written as a series of commands or statements. Each **statement** normally tells the PHP engine to perform a particular action, and it must always be followed by a semicolon, like this:

```
<?php
do this;
now do something else;
finally, do that;
?>
```

As with all rules, there is an exception: you can omit the semicolon if there's only one statement in the code block. However, *don't do it*. Get into the habit of always using a semicolon at the end of every PHP statement. PHP is not like JavaScript or ActionScript. It won't automatically assume there should be a semicolon at the end of a line if you omit it. This has a nice side effect: you can spread long statements over several lines and lay out your code for ease of reading. PHP, like XHTML, ignores whitespace in code. Instead, it relies on semicolons to indicate where one command ends and the next one begins.

Using a semicolon at the end of a PHP statement (or command) is always right. A missing semicolon will bring your page to a grinding halt.

Commenting scripts

PHP treats everything between the opening and closing PHP tags as statements to be executed, unless you tell it not to do so by marking a section of code as a comment. The following three reasons explain why you may want to do this:

- To insert a reminder of what the script does
- To insert a placeholder for code to be added later
- To disable a section of code temporarily

When a script is fresh in your mind, it may seem unnecessary to insert anything that isn't going to be processed. However, if you need to revise the script several months later, you'll find comments much easier to read than trying to follow the code on its own.

During testing, it's often useful to prevent a line of code, or even a whole section, from running. Because PHP ignores anything marked as a comment, this is a useful way of turning code on and off.

There are three ways of adding comments: two for single-line comments and one for comments that stretch over several lines.

Single-line comments

The most common method of adding a single-line comment is to precede it with two forward slashes, like this:

```
// this is a comment and will be ignored by the PHP engine
```

PHP ignores everything from the double slashes to the end of the line, so you can also place comments alongside code (but only to the right):

```
$startYear = 2006; // this is a valid comment
```

Instead of two slashes, you can use the hash or pound sign (#). Because # stands out prominently when several are used together, this style of commenting is used mainly to indicate sections of a longer script, like this:

```
##################
## Menu section ##
##################
```

Multiline comments

If you want a comment to stretch over several lines, you can use the same style of comments as in Cascading Style Sheets (CSS). Anything between /* and */ is treated as a comment, no matter how many lines are used, like this:

```
/* This is a comment that stretches
   over several lines. It uses the
   same beginning and end markers
   as in CSS. */
```

Multiline comments are particularly useful when testing or troubleshooting, as they can be used to disable long sections of script without the need to delete them.

A combination of good comments and well-chosen variable names makes code easier to understand and maintain.

Using arrays to store multiple values

In common with other computing languages, PHP lets you store multiple values in a special type of variable called an **array**. The simple way of thinking about arrays is that they're like a shopping list. Although each item might be different, you can refer to them collectively by a single name. Figure 3-3 demonstrates this concept: the variable $shoppingList refers collectively to all five items—wine, fish, bread, grapes, and cheese.

Figure 3-3. Arrays are variables that store multiple items, just like a shopping list.

Individual items—or **array elements**—are identified by means of a number in square brackets immediately following the variable name. PHP assigns the number automatically, but it's important to note that the numbering always begins at 0. So the first item in the array, wine, is referred to as $shoppingList[0], not $shoppingList[1]. And although there are five items, the last one (cheese) is $shoppingList[4]. The number is referred to as the array **key** or **index**, and this type of array is called an **indexed array**.

PHP uses another type of array, in which the key is a word (or any combination of letters and numbers). For instance, an array containing details of this book might look like this:

```
$book['title'] = 'PHP Solutions: Dynamic Web Design Made Easy';
$book['author'] = 'David Powers';
$book['publisher'] = 'friends of ED';
$book['ISBN'] = '1-59059-731-1';
```

This type of array is called an **associative array**. Note that the array key is enclosed in quotes (single or double, it doesn't matter). It mustn't contain any spaces or punctuation, except for the underscore.

Arrays are an important—and useful—part of PHP. You'll use them a lot, starting with the next chapter, when you'll store details of images in an array to display a random image on a web page. Arrays are also used extensively with a database, as you fetch the results of a search in a series of arrays.

You can learn the various ways of creating arrays in the second half of this chapter.

PHP's built-in superglobal arrays

PHP has several built-in arrays that are automatically populated with really useful information. They are called **superglobal arrays**, and all begin with a dollar sign followed by an underscore. Two that you will meet frequently are $_POST and $_GET. They contain information passed from forms through the post and get methods, respectively. The superglobals are all associative arrays, and the keys of $_POST and $_GET are automatically derived from the names of form elements.

Let's say you have a text input field called address in a form; PHP automatically creates an array element called $_POST['address'] when the form is submitted by the post method or $_GET['address'] if you use the get method. As Figure 3-4 shows, $_POST['address'] contains whatever value a visitor enters in the text field, enabling you to display it onscreen, insert it in a database, send it to your email inbox, or do whatever you want with it.

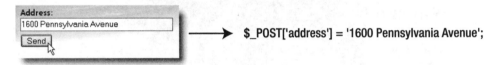

Figure 3-4. You can retrieve the values of user input through the $_POST array, which is created automatically when a form is submitted using the post method.

The main superglobal arrays that you'll work with in this book are as follows:

- **$_POST**: This contains values sent through the post method. You'll encounter it in most chapters, beginning with Chapter 5, where you'll use it to send the content of an online feedback form by email to your inbox.
- **$_GET**: This contains values sent through a URL query string. You'll use it frequently in Chapters 12 through 14 to pass information to a database.
- **$_SERVER**: This contains information stored by the web server, such as filename, pathname, hostname, etc. You'll see it in action in Chapters 4, 12, and 13.
- **$_FILES**: This contains details of file uploads, which are covered in Chapter 6.
- **$_SESSION**: This stores information that you want to preserve so that it's available to other pages. It's used to create a simple login system in Chapters 9 and 15.

Don't forget that PHP is case-sensitive. All superglobal array names are written in uppercase. $_Post or $_Get, for example, won't work.

Understanding when to use quotes

If you look closely at the PHP code block in Figure 3-1, you'll notice that the value assigned to the first variable isn't enclosed in quotes. It looks like this:

```
$startYear = 2006;
```

Yet all the examples in "Using arrays to store multiple values" *did* use quotes, like this:

```
$book['title'] = 'PHP Solutions: Dynamic Web Design Made Easy';
```

The simple rules are as follows:

- **Numbers**: No quotes
- **Text**: Requires quotes

As a general principle, it doesn't matter whether you use single or double quotes around text—or a **string**, as text is called in PHP and other computer languages. The situation is actually a bit more complex than that, as explained in the second half of this chapter, because there's a subtle difference in the way single and double quotes are treated by the PHP engine.

> The word "string" is borrowed from computer and mathematical science, where it means a sequence of simple objects—in this case, the characters in text.

The important thing to remember for now is that *quotes must always be in matching pairs.* This means you need to be careful about including apostrophes in a single-quoted string or double quotes in a double-quoted string. Take a look at the following line of code:

```
$book['description'] = 'This is David's sixth book on PHP.';
```

At first glance, there seems nothing wrong with it. However, the PHP engine sees things differently from the human eye, as Figure 3-5 demonstrates.

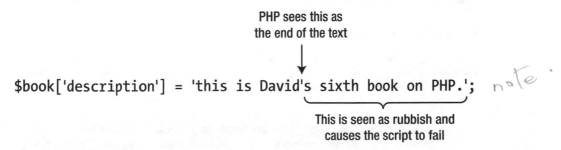

Figure 3-5. An apostrophe inside a single-quoted string confuses the PHP engine.

There are two ways around this problem:

- Use double quotes if the text includes any apostrophes.
- Precede apostrophes with a backslash (this is known as **escaping**).

So, either of the following is acceptable:

```
$book['description'] = "This is David's sixth book on PHP.";
$book['description'] = 'This is David\'s sixth book on PHP.';
```

The same applies with double quotes in a double-quoted string (although with the rules reversed). The following code causes a problem:

```
$play = "Shakespeare's "Macbeth"";
```

In this case the apostrophe is fine, because it doesn't conflict with the double quotes, but the opening quotes in front of Macbeth bring the string to a premature end. To solve the problem, either of the following is acceptable:

```
$play = 'Shakespeare\'s "Macbeth"';
$play = "Shakespeare's \"Macbeth\"";
```

In the first example, the entire string has been enclosed in single quotes. This gets around the problem of the double quotes surrounding Macbeth, but introduces the need to escape the apostrophe in Shakespeare's. The apostrophe presents no problem in a double-quoted string, but the double quotes around Macbeth both need to be escaped. So, to summarize:

- Single quotes and apostrophes are fine inside a double-quoted string.
- Double quotes are fine inside a single-quoted string.
- Anything else must be escaped with a backslash.

> *The key is to remember that the outermost quotes must match. There is more on this important subject in the second half of this chapter, including a technique that avoids the need to give special treatment to quotes.*

Special cases: true, false, and null

Although text should be enclosed in quotes, three special cases—true, false, and null—should never be enclosed in quotes unless you want to treat them as genuine text (or strings). The first two mean what you would expect; the last one, null, means "nothing" or "no value."

> *Technically speaking,* true *and* false *are* **Boolean values**. *The name comes from a nineteenth-century mathematician, George Boole, who devised a system of logical operations that subsequently became the basis of much modern-day computing. It's a complicated subject, but you can find out more at* http://en.wikipedia.org/wiki/ Boolean_logic. *For most people, it's sufficient to know that Boolean means* true *or* false.

As the next section explains, PHP makes decisions on the basis of whether something evaluates to true or false. Putting quotes around false has surprising consequences. The following code:

```
$OK = false;
```

does exactly what you expect: it makes $OK false. Now take a look at this:

```
$OK = 'false';
```

This does exactly the opposite of what you might expect: it makes $OK true! Why? Because the quotes around false turn it into a string, and PHP treats strings as true. (There's a more detailed explanation in "The truth according to PHP" in the second half of this chapter.)

The other thing to note about true, false, and null is that they are *case-insensitive*. The following examples are all valid:

```
$OK = TRUE;
$OK = tRuE;
$OK = true;
```

So, to recap: PHP treats true, false, and null as special cases.

- Don't enclose them in quotes.
- They are case-insensitive.

Making decisions

Decisions, decisions, decisions . . . Life is full of decisions. So is PHP. They give it the ability to display different output according to circumstances. Decision making in PHP uses **conditional statements**. The most common of these uses if and closely follows the structure of normal language. In real life, you may be faced with the following decision (admittedly not very often if you live in Britain):

```
If the weather's hot, I'll go to the beach.
```

In PHP pseudo-code, the same decision looks like this:

```
if (the weather's hot) {
  I'll go to the beach;
  }
```

The condition being tested goes inside parentheses, and the resulting action goes between curly braces. This is the basic decision-making pattern:

```
if (condition is true) {
  // code to be executed if condition is true
  }
```

> *Confusion alert: I mentioned earlier that statements must always be followed by a semi-colon. This applies only to the statements (or commands) inside the curly braces. Although called a conditional* statement, *this decision-making pattern is one of PHP's control structures, and it shouldn't be followed by a semicolon. Think of the semicolon as a command that means "do it." The curly braces surround the command statements and keep them together as a group.*

The code inside the curly braces is executed *only* if the condition is true. If it's false, PHP ignores everything between the braces and moves on to the next section of code. How PHP determines whether a condition is true or false is described in the following section.

Sometimes, the if statement is all you need, but you often want a default action to be invoked. To do this, use else, like this:

```
if (condition is true) {
  // code to be executed if condition is true
  }
else {
  // default code to run if condition is false
  }
```

What if you want more alternatives? One way is to add more if statements. PHP will test them, and as long as you finish with else, at least one block of code will run. However, it's important to realize that *all* if statements will be tested, and the code will be run in every single one where the condition equates to true. If you want only one code block to be executed, use elseif like this:

```
if (condition is true) {
  // code to be executed if first condition is true
  }
elseif (second condition is true) {
  // code to be executed if first condition fails
  // but second condition is true
else {
  // default code to run if both conditions are false
  }
```

You can use as many elseif clauses in a conditional statement as you like. It's important to note that *only the first one* that equates to true will be executed; all others will be ignored, even if they're also true. This means you need to build conditional statements in the order of priority that you want them to be evaluated. It's strictly a first-come, first-served hierarchy.

> *Although* elseif *is normally written as one word, you can use* else if *as separate words.*

An alternative decision-making structure, the switch statement, is described in the second half of this chapter.

Making comparisons

Conditional statements are interested in only one thing: whether the condition being tested equates to true. If it's not true, it must be false. There's no room for half-measures or maybes. Conditions often depend on the comparison of two values. Is this bigger than that? Are they both the same? And so on.

To test for equality, PHP uses two equal signs (==) like this:

```
if ($status == 'administrator') {
  // send to admin page
  }
else {
  // refuse entry to admin area
  }
```

> *Don't use a single equal sign in the first line like this:*
>
> ```
>     if ($status = 'administrator') {
> ```
>
> *Doing so will open the admin area of your website to everyone. Why? Because this automatically sets the value of $status to administrator; it doesn't compare the two values. To compare values, you must use two equal signs. It's an easy mistake to make, but one with potentially disastrous consequences.*

Size comparisons are performed using the mathematical symbols for less than (<) and greater than (>). Let's say you're checking the size of a file before allowing it to be uploaded to your server. You could set a maximum size of 50KB like this:

```
if ($bytes > 51200) {
  // display error message and abandon upload
  }
else {
  // continue upload
  }
```

You can test for two or more conditions simultaneously. Details are in the second half of this chapter.

Using indenting and whitespace for clarity

Indenting code helps to keep statements in logical groups, making it easier to understand the flow of the script. There are no fixed rules; PHP ignores any whitespace inside code, so you can adopt any style you like. The important thing is to be consistent so that you can spot anything that looks out of place.

The limited width of the printed page means that I normally use just two spaces to indent code in this book, but most people find that tabbing four or five spaces makes for the most readable code. Perhaps the biggest difference in styles lies in the way individual developers arrange curly braces. I align the closing brace with the block of code it concludes. Other writers use this style:

```
if ($bytes > 51200) {
    // display error message and abandon upload
} else {
    // continue upload
}
```

Yet others use this style:

```
if ($bytes > 51200)
    {
        // display error message and abandon upload
    }
else
    {
        // continue upload
    }
```

Choose whichever style you're most comfortable with. As long as it's consistent and easy to read, that's all that matters.

Using loops for repetitive tasks

Loops are huge time-savers because they perform the same task over and over again, yet involve very little code. They're frequently used with arrays and database results. You can step through each item one at a time looking for matches or performing a specific task. Loops are particularly powerful in combination with conditional statements, allowing you to perform operations selectively on a large amount of data in a single sweep. Loops are best understood by working with them in a real situation, but details of all looping structures, together with examples, are in the second half of this chapter.

Using functions for preset tasks

As I mentioned earlier, **functions** do things . . . lots of things, mind-bogglingly so in PHP. The last time I counted, PHP had nearly 3,000 built-in functions, and more have been added since. Don't worry: you'll only ever need to use a handful, but it's reassuring to know that PHP is a full-featured language capable of industrial-strength applications.

The functions you'll be using in this book do really useful things, such as get the height and width of an image, create thumbnails from existing images, query a database, send email, and much, much more. You can identify functions in PHP code because they're always followed by a pair of parentheses. Sometimes the parentheses are empty, as in the case of phpversion(), which you used in phptest.php in the previous chapter. Often, though, the parentheses contain variables, numbers, or strings, like this line of code from the script in Figure 3-1:

```
$thisYear = date('Y');
```

This calculates the current year and stores it in the variable $thisYear. It works by feeding the string 'Y' to the built-in PHP function date(). Placing a value between the parentheses like this is known as **passing an argument** to a function. The function takes the value in the argument and processes it to produce (or **return**) the result. For instance, if you pass the string 'M' as an argument to date() instead of 'Y', it will return the current month as a three-letter abbreviation (e.g., Mar, Apr, May). As the following example shows, you capture the result of a function by assigning it to a suitably named variable:

```
$thisMonth = date('M');
```

The date() function is covered in depth in Chapter 14.

Some functions take more than one argument. When this happens, separate the arguments with commas inside the parentheses, like this:

```
$mailSent = mail($to, $subject, $message);
```

It doesn't take a genius to work out that this sends an email to the address stored in the first argument, with the subject line stored in the second argument, and the message stored in the third one. You'll see how this function works in Chapter 5.

> You'll often come across the term "parameter" in place of "argument." There is a technical difference between the two words, but for all practical purposes, they are interchangeable.

As if the 3,000-odd built-in functions weren't enough, PHP lets you build your own custom functions. Even if you don't relish the idea of creating your own, throughout this book you'll use some that I have made. You use them in exactly the same way.

Displaying PHP output

There's not much point in all this wizardry going on behind the scenes unless you can display the results in your web page. There are two ways of doing this in PHP: using echo or print. There are some subtle differences between the two, but they are so subtle, you can regard them as identical. I prefer echo for the simple reason that it's one fewer letter to type.

You can use echo with variables, numbers, and strings. Simply put it in front of whatever you want to display, like this:

```
$name = 'David';
echo $name;    // displays David
echo 5;        // displays 5
echo 'David';  // displays David
```

The important thing to remember about echo and print, when using them with a variable, is that they work only with variables that contain a single value. You cannot use them to display the contents of an array or of a database result. This is where loops are so useful: you use echo or print inside the loop to display each element individually. You will see plenty of examples of this in action throughout the rest of the book.

You may see scripts that use parentheses with echo and print, like this:

```
echo('David'); // displays David
```

The parentheses make absolutely no difference. Unless you enjoy typing purely for the sake of it, I suggest you leave them out.

Joining strings together

PHP has a rather unusual way of joining strings (text). Although many other computer languages use the plus sign (+), PHP uses a period, dot, or full stop (.) like this:

```
$firstName = 'David';
$lastName = 'Powers';
echo $firstName.$lastName; // displays DavidPowers
```

As the comment in the final line of code indicates, when two strings are joined like this, PHP leaves no gap between them. Don't be fooled into thinking that adding a space after the period will do the trick. It won't. You can put as much space on either side of the period as you like; the result will always be the same, because PHP ignores whitespace in code. You must either include a space in one of the strings or insert the space as a string in its own right, like this:

```
echo $firstName.' '.$lastName; // displays David Powers
```

> The period—or **concatenation operator**, to give it its correct name—can be difficult to spot among a lot of other code. Make sure the font size in your script editor is large enough to read without straining to see the difference between periods and commas.

Working with numbers

PHP can do a lot with numbers—from simple addition to complex math. The second half of this chapter contains details of the arithmetic operators you can use with PHP. All you need to remember at the moment is that numbers mustn't contain any punctuation other than a decimal point. PHP will choke if you feed it numbers that contain commas (or anything else) as the thousands separator.

Understanding PHP error messages

There's one final thing you need to know about before savoring the delights of PHP: error messages. They're an unfortunate fact of life, but it helps a great deal if you understand what they're trying to tell you. The following illustration shows the structure of a typical error message.

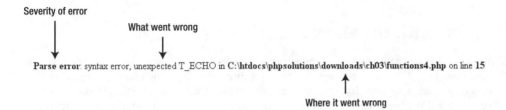

The first thing to realize about PHP error messages is that they report the line where PHP discovered a problem. Most newcomers—quite naturally—assume that's where they've got to look for their mistake. Wrong . . .

What PHP is telling you most of the time is that something unexpected has happened. In other words, the mistake lies *before* that point. The preceding error message means that PHP discovered an echo command where there shouldn't have been one. (Error messages always prefix PHP elements with T_, which stands for token. Just ignore it.)

Instead of worrying what might be wrong with the echo command (probably nothing), start working backward, looking for anything that might be missing. Usually, it's a semicolon or closing quote on a previous line.

There are four main categories of error, presented here in descending order of importance:

- **Fatal error**: Any XHTML output preceding the error will be displayed, but once the error is encountered—as the name suggests—everything else is killed stone dead. A fatal error is normally caused by referring to a nonexistent file or function.

- **Parse error**: This means there's a mistake in your code, such as mismatched quotes, or a missing semicolon or closing brace. Like a fatal error, it stops the script in its tracks and doesn't even allow any XHTML output to be displayed.

- **Warning**: This alerts you to a serious problem, such as a missing include file. (Include files are the subject of Chapter 4.) However, the error is not serious enough to prevent the rest of the script from being executed.

- **Notice**: This advises you about relatively minor issues, such as the use of deprecated code or a nondeclared variable. Although this type of error won't stop your page from displaying (and you can turn off the display of notices), you should always try to eliminate them. Any error is a threat to your output.

*There is a fifth type of error: **strict**, which was introduced in PHP 5.0.0, mainly for the benefit of advanced developers. Strict error messages warn you about the use of deprecated code or techniques that aren't recommended. As of this writing, strict error messages are not displayed by default, but there are plans to change this as a prelude to removing outdated parts of the language. The idea is to warn you that anything that generates a strict error in PHP 6 will generate a fatal error in the next major version, PHP 7. This policy is in the early stages of development, so it may change, but if you see a strict error message, ignore it at your peril. None of the code in this book generates strict error messages in the version of PHP current at the time of this writing (5.1.4).*

Now, on with the show . . .

Your head is probably reeling by now, but—believe it or not—you have covered all the fundamentals of PHP. Of course, there are a lot more details, many of which are described in the reference section that follows. However, rather than plowing straight on, I suggest you take a short break and then move on to the next chapter. Come back to the next section when you've gained some practical experience of working with PHP, as it will make much more sense then. Also, the idea of this book is to put PHP to work and provide real solutions for your websites. The projects in each chapter use progressively more advanced techniques, so if you're new to PHP, cut your teeth on them first before plunging into working with a database.

PHP: A quick reference

This part of the chapter is intended to provide a quick source of information on PHP basics. It makes no attempt to cover every aspect of PHP syntax. For that, you should refer to the PHP documentation at www.php.net/manual/en or a more detailed reference book, such as *Beginning PHP and MySQL 5: From Novice to Professional, Second Edition* by W. Jason Gilmore (Apress, ISBN: 1-59059-552-1).

Using PHP in an existing website

There is no problem mixing .html and .php pages in the same website. However, PHP code will be processed only in files that have the .php filename extension, so it's a good idea to give the same extension to all your pages, even if they don't all contain dynamic features. That way, you have the flexibility to add PHP to pages without breaking existing links or losing search engine rankings.

Data types in PHP

PHP is what's known as a **weakly typed** language. What this means in practice is that, unlike some other computer languages (e.g., Java or C#), PHP doesn't care what type of data you store in a variable.

Most of the time, this is very convenient, although it does mean that you need to be careful with user input. You may expect a user to enter a number in a form, but PHP won't object if it encounters a word instead. Checking user input carefully is one of the major themes of later chapters.

Even though PHP is weakly typed, it uses the following eight data types:

- **Integer**: This is a whole number, such as 1, 25, 42, or 2006. Integers must not contain any commas or other punctuation as thousand-separators. You can also use hexadecimal numbers, which should be preceded by 0x (e.g., 0xFFFFFF, 0x000000).

- **Floating-point number**: This is a number that contains a decimal point, such as 9.99, 98.6, or 2.1. Like integers, floating-point numbers must not contain thousand-separators. (This type is also referred to as **float** or **double**.)

- **String**: A string is text of any length. It can be as short as zero characters (an empty string), and it has no upper limit.

- **Boolean**: This type has only two values: true or false. See "The truth according to PHP" later in this chapter for details of what PHP regards as true and false.

- **Array**: An array is a variable that is capable of storing multiple values, although it may contain none at all (an empty array). Arrays can hold any data type, including other arrays. An array of arrays is called a **multidimensional array**. See "Creating arrays" later in this chapter for details of how to populate an array with values.

- **Object**: PHP has powerful object-oriented capabilities, which are mainly of interest to advanced users. Objects are covered only briefly in this book when connecting to a database with the MySQL Improved extension or PHP Data Objects (PDO).

- **Resource**: When PHP connects to an external data source, such as a file or database, it stores a reference to it as a resource.

- NULL: This is a special data type that indicates that a variable has no value.

An important side effect of PHP's weak typing is that, if you enclose an integer or floating-point number in quotes, PHP automatically converts it from a string to a number, allowing you to perform calculations without the need for any special handling. This is different from JavaScript and ActionScript, and it can have unexpected consequences. When PHP sees the plus sign (+), it assumes that you want to perform addition, and it tries to convert strings to integers or floating-point numbers, as in the following example (the code is in data_conversion1.php in the download files for this chapter):

```
$fruit = '2 apples';
$veg = ' 2 carrots';
echo $fruit + $veg;   // displays 4
```

PHP sees that both $fruit and $veg begin with a number, so it extracts the number and ignores the rest. However, if the string doesn't begin with a number, PHP converts it to 0, as shown in this example (the code is in data_conversion2.php):

```
$fruit = '2 apples';
$veg = ' and 2 carrots';
echo $fruit + $veg;   // displays 2
```

3

Weak typing is a mixed blessing. It makes PHP very easy for beginners, but it means you often need to check that a variable contains the correct data type before using it.

Doing calculations with PHP

PHP is highly adept at working with numbers and can perform a wide variety of calculations, from simple arithmetic to complex math. This reference section covers only the standard arithmetic operators. See www.php.net/manual/en/ref.math.php for details of the mathematical functions and constants supported by PHP.

Arithmetic operators

The standard arithmetic operators all work the way you would expect, although some of them look slightly different from those you learned at school. For instance, an asterisk (*) is used as the multiplication sign, and a forward slash (/) is used to indicate division.

Table 3-1 shows examples of how the standard arithmetic operators work. To demonstrate their effect, the following variables have been set:

```
$x = 20;
$y = 10;
$z = 4.5;
```

Table 3-1. Arithmetic operators in PHP

Operation	Operator	Example	Result
Addition	+	$x + $y	30
Subtraction	-	$x - $y	10
Multiplication	*	$x * $y	200
Division	/	$x / $y	2
Modulo division	%	$x % $z	2
Increment (adds 1)	++	$x++	21
Decrement (subtracts 1)	--	$y--	9

The modulo operator returns the remainder of a division, as follows:

```
26 % 5     // result is 1
26 % 27    // result is 26
10 % 2     // result is 0
```

A practical use of the modulo operator is to work out whether a number is odd or even. $number % 2 will always produce 0 or 1. If the result is 0, there is no remainder, so the number must be even.

The increment (++) and decrement (--) operators can come either before or after the variable. When they come before the variable, 1 is added to or subtracted from the value before any further calculation is carried out. When they come after the variable, the main calculation is carried out first, and then 1 is either added or subtracted. Since the dollar sign is an integral part of the variable name, the increment and decrement operators go before the dollar sign when used in front:

```
++$x
--$y
```

Determining the order of calculations

Calculations in PHP follow exactly the same rules as standard arithmetic. Table 3-2 summarizes the precedence of arithmetic operators.

Table 3-2. Precedence of arithmetic operators

Precedence	Group	Operators	Rule
Highest	Parentheses	()	Operations contained within parentheses are evaluated first. If these expressions are nested, the innermost is evaluated foremost.
Next	Multiplication and division	* / %	These operators are evaluated next. If an expression contains two or more operators, they are evaluated from left to right.
Lowest	Addition and subtraction	+ -	These are the final operators to be evaluated in an expression. If an expression contains two or more operators, they are evaluated from left to right.

If in doubt, use parentheses all the time to group the parts of a calculation that you want to make sure are performed as a single unit.

Combining calculations and assignment

PHP offers a shorthand way of performing a calculation on a variable and assigning the result back to the same variable through **combined assignment operators**. The main ones are listed in Table 3-3.

Table 3-3. Combined arithmetic assignment operators used in PHP

Operator	Example	Equivalent to
+=	$a += $b	$a = $a + $b
-=	$a -= $b	$a = $a - $b
*=	$a *= $b	$a = $a * $b
/=	$a /= $b	$a = $a / $b
%=	$a %= $b	$a = $a % $b

Adding to an existing string

The same convenient shorthand allows you to add new material to the end of an existing string by combining a period and an equal sign, like this:

```
$hamlet = 'To be';
$hamlet .= ' or not to be';
```

Note that you need to create a space at the beginning of the additional text unless you want both strings to run on without a break. This shorthand, known as the **combined concatenation operator**, is extremely useful when combining many strings, such as you need to do when building the content of an email message or looping through the results of a database search.

> *The period in front of the equal sign is easily overlooked when copying code. When you see the same variable repeated at the beginning of a series of statements, it's often a sure sign that you need to use .= instead of = on its own.*

All you ever wanted to know about quotes—and more

Handling quotes within any computer language—not just PHP—can be fraught with difficulties because computers always take the first matching quote as marking the end of a string. Structured Query Language (SQL)—the language used to communicate with databases—also uses strings. Since your strings may include apostrophes, the combination of single and double quotes isn't enough. Moreover, PHP gives variables and escape sequences (certain characters preceded by a backslash) special treatment inside double quotes.

As if that weren't enough to cope with, PHP has a feature called magic quotes. It was originally designed to make life simpler for beginners, but is now deemed to cause more problems than it solves, and has been completely phased out of PHP 6.

Over the next few pages, I'll unravel this maze and make sense of it all for you.

How PHP treats variables inside strings

Choosing whether to use double quotes or single quotes around strings might just seem like a question of personal preference, but there's an important difference in the way that PHP handles them.

- Anything between single quotes is treated literally as text.
- Double quotes act as a signal to process variables and special characters known as escape sequences.

Take a look at the following examples to see what this means. In the first example (the code is in quotes1.php), $name is assigned a value and then used in a single-quoted string. As you can see from the screenshot alongside the code, $name is treated like normal text.

```
$name = 'Dolly';
// Single quotes: $name is treated as literal text
echo 'Hello, $name';
```

Hello, $name

If you replace the single quotes in the final line with double ones (see quotes2.php), $name is processed and its value is displayed onscreen.

```
$name = 'Dolly';
// Double quotes: $name is processed
echo "Hello, $name";
```

Hello, Dolly

> *In both examples, the string in the first line is in single quotes. This has no effect on the outcome. What causes the variable to be processed is the fact that it's inside a double-quoted string, not how the variable originally got its value.*

Because double quotes are so useful in this way, a lot of people use double quotes all the time. Technically speaking, using double quotes when you don't need to process any variables is inefficient, but the difference it's likely to make in the speed of your script is infinitesimal. My personal style is to use single quotes unless my string contains variables, but feel free to follow whichever style you find more convenient.

Using escape sequences inside double quotes

Double quotes have another important effect: they treat **escape sequences** in a special way. All escape sequences are formed by placing a backslash in front of a character. Most of them are designed to avoid conflicts with characters that are used with variables, but three of them have special meanings: \n inserts a new line character, \r inserts a carriage return, and \t inserts a tab. Table 3-4 lists the main escape sequences supported by PHP.

Table 3-4. The main PHP escape sequences

Escape sequence	Character represented in double-quoted string
\"	Double quote
\n	New line
\r	Carriage return
\t	Tab
\\	Backslash
\$	Dollar sign
\{	Opening curly brace
\}	Closing curly brace
\[	Opening square bracket
\]	Closing square bracket

> *The escape sequences listed in Table 3-4, with the exception of \\, work only in double-quoted strings. If you use them in a single-quoted string, they will be treated as a literal backslash followed by the second character.*

Avoiding the need to escape quotes with heredoc syntax

Using a backslash to escape one or two quotation marks isn't a great burden, but I frequently see examples of code where backslashes seem to have run riot. It must be difficult to type, and it's certainly difficult to read. However, it's totally unnecessary. The PHP **heredoc syntax** offers a relatively simple method of assigning text to a variable without the need for any special handling of quotes.

> *The name "heredoc" is derived from here-document, a technique used in Unix and Perl programming to pass large amounts of text to a command.*

Assigning a string to a variable using heredoc involves the following steps:

1. Type the assignment operator, followed by <<< and an identifier. The identifier can be any combination of letters, numbers, and the underscore, as long as it doesn't begin with a number.

2. Begin the string on a new line. It can include both single and double quotes. Any variables will be processed in the same way as in a double-quoted string.

3. Place the identifier on a new line after the end of the string. Nothing else should be on the same line, except for a final semicolon. Moreover, the identifier *must* be at the beginning of the line; it *cannot* be indented.

It's a lot easier when you see it in practice. The following simple example can be found in heredoc.php in the download files for this chapter:

```
$fish = 'whiting';
$mockTurtle = <<< Gryphon
"Will you walk a little faster?" said a $fish to a snail.
"There's a porpoise close behind us, and he's treading on my tail."
Gryphon;
echo $mockTurtle;
```

In this example, Gryphon is the identifier. The string begins on the next line, and *the double quotes are treated as part of the string*. Everything is included until you reach the identifier at the beginning of a new line. As you can see from the following screenshot, the heredoc displays the double quotes and processes the $fish variable.

To achieve the same effect without using the heredoc syntax, you need to add the double quotes and escape them like this:

```
$fish = 'whiting';
$mockTurtle = "\"Will you walk a little faster?\" said a $fish to a ➡
snail.
\"There's a porpoise close behind us, and he's treading on my tail.\""
echo $mockTurtle;
```

This is only a short example. The heredoc syntax is mainly of value when you have a long string and/or lots of quotes.

Unraveling the magic quotes tangle

Several years ago, the developers of PHP decided it would be a lot easier to handle quotes if input from online forms and certain other sources were escaped automatically with a backslash, so they invented **magic quotes**. In some respects, it was good magic; it went a long way toward solving some security problems for beginners. Unfortunately, it created new problems, most notably the proliferation of backslashes in the middle of dynamically generated text.

After a lot of heated argument, it was finally decided to remove magic quotes from PHP 6. Although magic quotes are enabled by default in earlier versions of PHP, server administrators have the option to turn them off. So the only sensible approach to this period of change is a strategy that assumes magic quotes are off, but removes backslashes if the server still inserts them.

To find out whether your remote server has magic quotes on or off, upload a PHP page containing the single-line script <?php phpinfo(); ?> that you used in the previous chapter to display your PHP configuration. Load the page into a browser, and check the PHP Core section near the top. Find the line indicated in the following screenshot. If the value of magic_quotes_gpc is Off, you can run all the scripts in this book without taking further measures. You should also change the setting of magic_quotes_gpc to Off in php.ini in your local testing environment.

Check this line ──────▶

log_errors	Off	Off
log_errors_max_len	1024	1024
magic_quotes_gpc	On	On
magic_quotes_runtime	Off	Off
magic_quotes_sybase	Off	Off
mail.force_extra_parameters	no value	no value

> *For security reasons, it's advisable to delete the* phpinfo() *page or move it to a password-protected folder after checking your remote server's settings. Leaving the script on a publicly accessible page exposes details about your site that malicious users might try to exploit.*

If the value of magic_quotes_gpc is On, you need to use the following custom-built function, nukeMagicQuotes(), which I have adapted from a solution in the PHP online documentation. It checks the value of magic quotes and strips out any backslashes if necessary, leaving you with clean data.

```
function nukeMagicQuotes() {
  if (get_magic_quotes_gpc()) {
    function stripslashes_deep($value) {
      $value = is_array($value) ? array_map('stripslashes_deep', ➥
$value) : stripslashes($value);
      return $value;
    }
    $_POST = array_map('stripslashes_deep', $_POST);
    $_GET = array_map('stripslashes_deep', $_GET);
```

```
        $_COOKIE = array_map('stripslashes_deep', $_COOKIE);
    }
}
```

The code for this function is included in corefuncs.php in the download files for this book. To use the function, add the following code immediately after the opening PHP tag on any page where it is needed:

```
include('path/to/file/corefuncs.php');
nukeMagicQuotes();
```

The value of *path/to/file* should be a relative path to corefuncs.php. Alternatively, use the technique described in PHP Solution 4-8 in the next chapter to establish a full path to the file. Using a dynamically generated full path allows you to use the same code in any page, regardless of its position in the site folder hierarchy.

> *The* nukeMagicQuotes() *function is not the ideal solution, because it involves removing the magic quotes, rather than preventing them from being inserted in the first place. However, it is the only universally applicable one. It also has the advantage that your pages will continue to run smoothly even if the server administrator decides to turn off magic quotes.*

Creating arrays

As explained earlier, there are two types of arrays: indexed arrays, which use numbers to identify each element, and associative arrays, which use strings. You can build both types by assigning a value directly to each element. Let's take another look at the $book associative array:

```
$book['title'] = 'PHP Solutions: Dynamic Web Design Made Easy';
$book['author'] = 'David Powers';
$book['publisher'] = 'friends of ED';
$book['ISBN'] = '1-59059-731-1';
```

To build an indexed array the direct way, use numbers instead of strings. Indexed arrays are numbered from 0, so to build the $shoppingList array depicted in Figure 3-3, you declare it like this:

```
$shoppingList[0] = 'wine';
$shoppingList[1] = 'fish';
$shoppingList[2] = 'bread';
$shoppingList[3] = 'grapes';
$shoppingList[4] = 'cheese';
```

Although both are perfectly valid ways of creating arrays, it's a nuisance to have to type out the variable name each time, so there's a much shorter way of doing it. The method is slightly different for each type of array.

Using array() to build an indexed array

Instead of declaring each array element individually, you declare the variable name once, and assign all the elements by passing them as a comma-separated list to array(), like this:

```
$shoppingList = array('wine', 'fish', 'bread', 'grapes', 'cheese');
```

> The comma must go outside the quotes, unlike American typographic practice. For ease of reading, I have inserted a space following each comma, but it's not necessary to do so.

PHP numbers each array element automatically, beginning from 0, so this creates exactly the same array as if you had numbered them individually. To add a new element to the end of the array, use a pair of empty square brackets like this:

```
$shoppingList[] = 'coffee';
```

PHP simply uses the next number available, so this becomes $shoppingList[5].

Using array() to build an associative array

The shorthand way of creating an associative array uses the => operator (an equal sign followed by a greater-than sign) to assign a value to each array key. The basic structure looks like this:

```
$arrayName = array('key1' => 'element1', 'key2' => 'element2');
```

So, this is the shorthand way to build the $book array:

```
$book = array('title'     => 'PHP Solutions: Dynamic Web Design ➥
                             Made Easy',
             'author'    => 'David Powers',
             'publisher' => 'friends of ED',
             'ISBN'      => '1-59059-731-1');
```

It's not essential to align the => operators like this, but it makes code easier to read and maintain.

Using array() to create an empty array

There are two reasons you might want to create an empty array, as follows:

- To create an array so that it's ready to have elements added to it inside a loop (this is known as **initializing** an array)
- To clear all elements from an existing array

To create an empty array, simply use array() with nothing between the parentheses, like this:

```
$shoppingList = array();
```

The $shoppingList array now contains no elements. If you add a new one using $shoppingList[], it will automatically start numbering again at 0.

Multidimensional arrays

Array elements can store any data type, including other arrays. For instance, the $book array holds details of only one book. It might be more convenient to create an array of arrays—in other words, a multidimensional array—containing details of several books, like this:

```
$books = array(
  array(
    'title'     => 'PHP Solutions: Dynamic Web Design Made Easy',
    'author'    => 'David Powers',
    'publisher' => 'friends of ED',
    'ISBN'      => '1-59059-731-1'),
  array(
    'title'     => 'Beginning PHP and MySQL 5',
    'author'    => 'W. Jason Gilmore',
    'publisher' => 'Apress',
    'ISBN'      => '1-59059-552-1')
  );
```

This example shows associative arrays nested inside an indexed array, but multidimensional arrays can nest either type. To refer to a specific element use the key of both arrays, for example:

```
$books[1]['author']  // value is 'W. Jason Gilmore'
```

Working with multidimensional arrays isn't as difficult as it first looks. The secret is to use a loop to get to the nested array. Then you can work with it in the same way as an ordinary array. This is how you handle the results of a database search, which is normally contained in a multidimensional array.

Using print_r() to inspect an array

To inspect the content of an array during testing, pass the array to print_r() like this (see inspect_array2.php):

```
print_r($books);
```

The following screenshot shows how PHP displays a multidimensional array; load inspect_array1.php into a browser to see how print_r() outputs the contents of an ordinary array. Often, it helps to switch to Source view to inspect the details, as browsers ignore indenting in the underlying output.

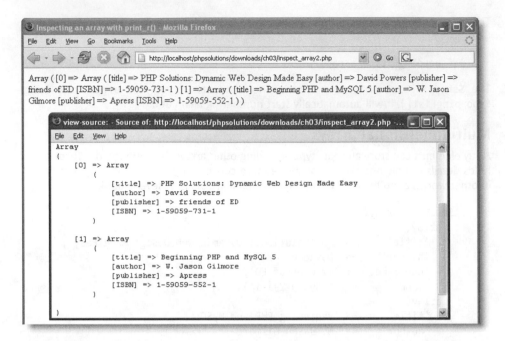

> *Always use* print_r() *to inspect arrays;* echo *and* print *don't work. To display the contents of an array in a web page, use a* foreach *loop, as described later in the chapter.*

The truth according to PHP

Decision making in PHP conditional statements is based on the mutually exclusive Boolean values, true and false. If the condition equates to true, the code within the conditional block is executed. If false, it's ignored. Whether a condition is true or false is determined in one of the following ways:

- A variable set explicitly to one of the Boolean values
- A value PHP interprets implicitly as true or false
- The comparison of two non-Boolean values

Explicit Boolean values

This is straightforward. If a variable is assigned the value true or false, and then used in a conditional statement, the decision is based on that value. As stated in the first half of this chapter, true and false are case-insensitive and must not be enclosed in quotes, for example:

```
$OK = false;
if ($OK) {
  // do something
  }
```

The code inside the conditional statement won't be executed, because $OK is false.

Implicit Boolean values

Using implicit Boolean values provides a convenient shorthand, although it has the disadvantage—at least to beginners—of being less clear. Implicit Boolean values rely on PHP's relatively narrow definition of what it regards as false, namely:

- The case-insensitive keywords false and null
- Zero as an integer (0), a floating-point number (0.0), or a string ('0' or "0")
- An empty string (single or double quotes with no space between them)
- An empty array
- An object with no values or functions

Everything else is true.

> *This definition explains why* "false" *(in quotes) is interpreted by PHP as* true.

Making decisions by comparing two values

Most true/false decisions are based on a comparison of two values using **comparison operators**. Decisions are based on whether two values are equal, whether one is greater than the other, and so on. Table 3-5 lists the comparison operators used in PHP.

Table 3-5. PHP comparison operators used for decision making

Symbol	Name	Use
==	Equality	Returns true if the values are equal; otherwise, returns false.
!=	Inequality	Returns true if the values are different; otherwise, returns false.
===	Identical	Determines whether both values are identical. To be considered identical, they must not only have the same value, but also be of the same data type (e.g., both floating-point numbers).

Continues

Table 3-5. *Continued*

Symbol	Name	Use
!==	Not identical	Determines whether the values are not identical (according to the same criteria as the previous operator).
>	Greater than	Determines whether the value on the left is greater than the one on the right.
>=	Greater than or equal to	Determines whether the value on the left is greater than or equal to the one on the right.
<	Less than	Determines whether the value on the left is less than the one on the right.
<=	Less than or equal to	Determines whether the value on the left is less than or equal to the one on the right.

> *When comparing two values, you must always use the equality operator (==), the identical operator (===), or their negative equivalents (!= and !==). A single equal sign assigns a value; it doesn't perform comparisons.*

Testing more than one condition

Frequently, comparing two values is not enough. PHP allows you to set a series of conditions using **logical operators** to specify whether all, or just some, need to be fulfilled.

The most important logical operators in PHP are listed in Table 3-6. **Negation**—testing that the opposite of something is true—is also considered a logical operator, although it applies to individual conditions rather than a series.

Table 3-6. The main logical operators used for decision making in PHP

Symbol	Name	Use
&&	Logical AND	Evaluates to true if both conditions are true
||	Logical OR	Evaluates to true if either is true; otherwise, returns false
!	Negation	Tests whether something is not true

Technically speaking, there is no limit to the number of conditions that can be tested. Each condition is considered in turn from left to right, and as soon as a defining point is reached, no further testing is carried out. When using &&, every condition must be fulfilled, so testing stops as soon as one turns out to be false. Similarly, when using ||, only one condition needs to be fulfilled, so testing stops as soon as one turns out to be true.

```
$a = 10;
$b = 25;
if ($a > 5 && $b > 20) // returns true
if ($a > 5 || $b > 30) // returns true, $b never tested
```

The implication of this is that when you need all conditions to be met, you should design your tests with the condition most likely to return false as the first to be evaluated. When you need just one condition to be fulfilled, place the one most likely to return true first. If you want a particular set of conditions considered as a group, enclose them in parentheses.

```
if (($a > 5 && $a < 8) || ($b > 20 && $b < 40))
```

> *PHP also uses AND in place of && and OR in place of ||. However, they aren't exact equivalents. To avoid problems, it's advisable to stick with && and ||.*

Using the switch statement for decision chains

The switch statement offers an alternative to if... else for decision making. The basic structure looks like this:

```
switch(variable being tested) {
  case value1:
    statements to be executed
    break;
  case value2:
    statements to be executed
    break;
  default:
    statements to be executed
}
```

The case keyword indicates possible matching values for the variable passed to switch(). When a match is made, every subsequent line of code is executed until the break keyword is encountered, at which point the switch statement comes to an end. A simple example follows:

```
switch($myVar) {
  case 1:
    echo '$myVar is 1';
    break;
  case 'apple':
    echo '$myVar is apple';
    break;
  default:
    echo '$myVar is neither 1 nor apple';
}
```

The main points to note about switch are as follows:

- The expression following the case keyword must be a number or a string.
- You can't use comparison operators with case. So case > 100: isn't allowed.
- Each block of statements should normally end with break, unless you specifically want to continue executing code within the switch statement.
- You can group several instances of the case keyword together to apply the same block of code to them.
- If no match is made, any statements following the default keyword will be executed. If no default has been set, the switch statement will exit silently and continue with the next block of code.

Using the conditional operator

The **conditional operator** (?:) is a shorthand method of representing a simple conditional statement. The basic syntax looks like this:

```
condition ? value if true : value if false;
```

Here is an example of it in use:

```
$age = 17;
$fareType = $age > 16 ? 'adult' : 'child';
```

The second line tests the value of $age. If it's greater than 16, $fareType is set to adult, otherwise $fareType is set to child. The equivalent code using if... else looks like this:

```
if ($age > 16) {
  $fareType = 'adult';
  }
else {
  $fareType = 'child';
  }
```

The if... else version is easier to read, but the conditional operator is more compact. Most beginners hate this shorthand, but once you get to know it, you'll realize how convenient it can be. Because it uses three operands, it's sometimes called the **ternary operator**.

Creating loops

As the name suggests, a **loop** is a section of code that is repeated over and over again until a certain condition is met. Loops are often controlled by setting a variable to count the number of iterations. By increasing the variable by one each time, the loop comes to a halt when the variable gets to a preset number. The other way loops are controlled is by running through each item of an array. When there are no more items to process, the loop stops.

Loops frequently contain conditional statements, so although they're very simple in structure, they can be used to create code that processes data in often sophisticated ways.

Loops using while and do... while

The simplest type of loop is called a while loop. Its basic structure looks like this:

```
while (condition is true) {
  do something
  }
```

The following code displays every number from 1 through 100 in a browser (you can test it in while.php in the download files for this chapter). It begins by setting a variable ($i) to 1, and then using the variable as a counter to control the loop, as well as display the current number onscreen.

```
$i = 1;  // set counter
while ($i <= 100) {
  echo "$i<br />";
  $i++; // increase counter by 1
  }
```

A variation of the while loop uses the keyword do and follows this basic pattern:

```
do {
  code to be executed
  } while (condition to be tested);
```

The only difference between a do... while loop and a while loop is that the code within the do block is executed at least once, even if the condition is never true. The following code (in dowhile.php) displays the value of $i once, even though it's greater than the maximum expected.

```
$i = 1000;
do {
  echo "$i<br />";
  $i++; // increase counter by 1
  } while ($i <= 100);
```

The danger with while and do... while loops is forgetting to set a condition that brings the loop to an end, or setting an impossible condition. When this happens, you create an infinite loop that either freezes your computer or causes the browser to crash.

The versatile for loop

The for loop is less prone to generating an infinite loop because you are required to declare all the conditions of the loop in the first line. The for loop uses the following basic pattern:

```
for (initialize counter; test; increment) {
  code to be executed
  }
```

The following code does exactly the same as the previous while loop, displaying every number from 1 to 100 (see forloop.php):

```
for ($i = 1; $i <= 100; $i++) {
  echo "$i<br />";
  }
```

The three expressions inside the parentheses control the action of the loop (note that they are separated by semicolons, not commas):

- The first expression shows the starting point. You can use any variable you like, but the convention is to use $i. When more than one counter is needed, $j and $k are frequently used.

- The second expression is a test that determines whether the loop should continue to run. This can be a fixed number, a variable, or an expression that calculates a value.

- The third expression shows the method of stepping through the loop. Most of the time, you will want to go through a loop one step at a time, so using the increment (++) or decrement (--) operator is convenient. There is nothing stopping you from using bigger steps. For instance, replacing $i++ with $i+=10 in the previous example would display 1, 11, 21, 31, and so on.

Looping through arrays with foreach

The final type of loop in PHP is used exclusively with arrays. It takes two forms, both of which use temporary variables to handle each array element. If you only need to do something with the value of each array element, the foreach loop takes the following form:

```
foreach (array_name as temporary_variable) {
  do something with temporary_variable
  }
```

The following example loops through the $shoppingList array and displays the name of each item, as shown in the screenshot (see shopping_list.php):

```
$shoppingList = array('wine', 'fish', ➥
'bread', 'grapes', 'cheese');
foreach ($shoppingList as $item) {
  echo $item.'<br />';
  }
```

Although the preceding example uses an indexed array, you can also use it with an associative array. However, the alternative form of the foreach loop is of more use with associative arrays, because it gives access to both the key and value of each array element. It takes this slightly different form:

```
foreach (array_name as key_variable => value_variable) {
  do something with key_variable and value_variable
  }
```

This next example uses the $book associative array from the "Creating arrays" section earlier in the chapter and incorporates the key and value of each element into a simple string, as shown in the screenshot (see book.php):

```
foreach ($book as $key => $value) {
    echo "The value of $key is $value<br />";
    }
```

3

> The foreach *keyword is one word. Inserting a space between* for *and* each *doesn't work.*

Breaking out of a loop

To bring a loop prematurely to an end when a certain condition is met, insert the break keyword inside a conditional statement. As soon as the script encounters break, it exits the loop.

To skip an iteration of the loop when a certain condition is met, use the continue keyword. Instead of exiting, it returns to the top of the loop and executes the next iteration.

Modularizing code with functions

Functions offer a convenient way of running frequently performed operations. In addition to the large number of built-in functions, PHP lets you create your own. The advantages are that you write the code only once, rather than needing to retype it everywhere you need it. This not only speeds up your development time, but also makes your code easier to read and maintain. If there's a problem with the code in your function, you update it in just one place rather than hunting through your entire site. Moreover, functions usually speed up the processing of your pages.

Building your own functions in PHP is very easy. You simply wrap a block of code in a pair of curly braces and use the function keyword to name your new function. The function name is always followed by a pair of parentheses. The following—admittedly trivial—example demonstrates the basic structure of a custom-built function (see functions1.php in the download files for this chapter):

```
function sayHi() {
    echo 'Hi!';
    }
```

Simply putting sayHi(); in a PHP code block results in Hi! being displayed onscreen. This type of function is like a drone: it always performs exactly the same operation. For functions to be responsive to circumstances, you need to pass values to them as arguments (or parameters).

Passing values to functions

Let's say you want to adapt the sayHi() function so that it displays someone's name. You do this by inserting a variable between the parentheses in the function declaration. The same variable is then used inside the function to display whatever value is passed to the function. To pass more than one variable to a function, separate them with commas inside the opening parentheses. This is how the revised function looks (see functions2.php):

```php
function sayHi($name) {
  echo "Hi, $name!";
  }
```

You can now use this function inside a page to display the value of any variable passed to sayHi(). For instance, if you have an online form that saves someone's name in a variable called $visitor, and Chris visits your site, you give him the sort of personal greeting shown alongside by putting sayHi($visitor); in your page.

A downside of PHP's weak typing is that if Chris is being particularly uncooperative, he might type 5 into the form instead of his name, giving you not quite the type of high five you might have been expecting.

This illustrates why it's so important to check user input before using it in any critical situation.

It's also important to understand that variables inside a function remain exclusive to the function. This example should illustrate the point (see functions3.php):

```php
function doubleIt($number) {
  $number *= 2;
  echo "$number<br />";
  }
$number = 4;
doubleIt($number);
echo $number;
```

If you view the output of this code in a browser, you may get a very different result from what you expect. The function takes a number, doubles it, and displays it onscreen. Line 5 of the script assigns the value 4 to $number. The next line calls the function and passes it $number as an argument. The function processes $number and displays 8. After the function comes to an end, $number is displayed onscreen by echo. This time, it will be 4 and not 8.

This example demonstrates that the variable $number that has been declared inside the function is limited in **scope** to the function itself. The variable called $number in the main script is totally unrelated to the one inside the function. To avoid confusion, it's a good idea to use variable names in the rest of your script that are different from those used inside functions. This isn't always possible, so it's useful to know that functions work like little black boxes and don't normally have any direct impact on the values of variables in the rest of the script.

Returning values from functions

There's more than one way to get a function to change the value of a variable passed to it as an argument, but the most important method is to use the return keyword, and to assign the result either to the same variable or to another one. This can be demonstrated by amending the doubleIt() function like this:

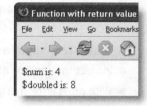

```
function doubleIt($number) {
  return $number *= 2;
  }
$num = 4;
$doubled = doubleIt($num);
echo "\$num is: $num<br />";
echo "\$doubled is: $doubled";
```

You can test this code in functions4.php. The result is shown in the screenshot alongside the code. This time, I have used different names for the variables to avoid confusing them. I have also assigned the result of doubleIt($num) to a new variable. The benefit of doing this is that I now have available both the original value and the result of the calculation. You won't always want to keep the original value, but it can be very useful at times.

Where to locate custom-built functions

If your custom-built function is in the same page as it's being used, it doesn't matter where you declare the function; it can be either before or after it's used. It's a good idea, however, to store functions together, either at the top or the bottom of a page. This makes them easier to find and maintain.

Functions that are used in more than one page are best stored in an external file and included in each page. Including external files with include() and require() is covered in detail in Chapter 4. When functions are stored in external files, you must include the external file *before* calling any of its functions.

PHP quick checklist

This chapter contains a lot of information that is impossible to absorb in one sitting, but hopefully the first half has given you a broad overview of how PHP works. Here's a reminder of some of the main points:

- Always give PHP pages the correct filename extension, normally .php.
- Enclose all PHP script between the correct tags: <?php and ?>.
- Avoid the short form of the opening tag: <?. Using <?php is more reliable.
- PHP variables begin with $ followed by a letter or the underscore character.

- Choose meaningful variable names and remember they're case-sensitive.
- Use comments to remind you what your script does.
- Remember that numbers don't require quotes, but strings (text) do.
- You can use single or double quotes, but the outer pair must match.
- Use a backslash to escape quotes of the same type inside a string.
- To store related items together, use an array.
- Use conditional statements, such as `if` and `if... else`, for decision making.
- Simplify repetitive tasks with loops.
- Use functions to perform preset tasks.
- Display PHP output with `echo` or `print`.
- Inspect the content of arrays with `print_r()`.
- With most error messages, work *backward* from the position indicated.
- Keep smiling—and remember that PHP is *not* difficult.

4 LIGHTENING YOUR WORKLOAD WITH INCLUDES

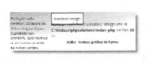

What this chapter covers:

- Using PHP includes for common page elements
- Protecting sensitive information in include files
- Automating a "you are here" menu link
- Generating a page's title from its filename
- Automatically updating a copyright notice
- Displaying random images complete with captions
- Using the error control operator
- Using absolute pathnames with PHP includes

One of the great payoffs of using PHP is that it can save you a lot of repetitive work. Figure 4-1 shows how four elements of a static web page benefit from a little PHP magic.

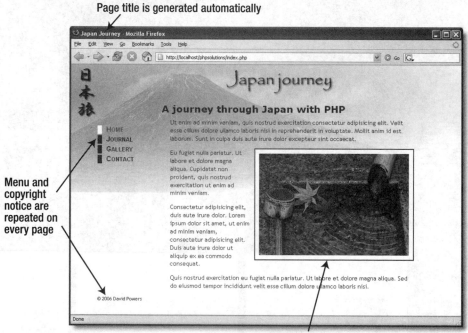

Figure 4-1. Identifying elements of a static web page that could be improved with PHP

The menu and copyright notice appear on each page. Wouldn't it be wonderful if you could make changes to just one page and see them propagate throughout the site in the same way as with CSS? You can with PHP includes. You can even get the menu to display the correct style to indicate which page the visitor is on. Similar PHP wizardry automatically changes the date on the copyright notice and the text in the page title. PHP can also add variety by displaying a random image. JavaScript solutions fail if JavaScript is disabled, but with PHP your script is guaranteed to work all the time. The images don't all need to be the same size; PHP inserts the correct width and height attributes in your <img> tag. And with a little extra scripting, you can add a caption to each image.

As you work through this chapter you'll learn how PHP includes work, where PHP looks for include files, and how to prevent errors when an include file can't be found.

Including code from other files

The ability to include code from other files is a core part of PHP. All that's necessary is to use one of PHP's include commands and tell the server where to find the file.

Introducing the PHP include commands

PHP has four commands that can be used to include code from an external file, namely:

- include()
- include_once()
- require()
- require_once()

They all do basically the same thing, so why have four?

Normally, include() is the only command you need. The fundamental difference is that include() attempts to continue processing a script, even if the include file is missing, whereas require() is used in the sense of mandatory: if the file is missing, the PHP engine stops processing and throws a fatal error. The purpose of include_once() and require_once() is to ensure that the external file doesn't reset any variables that may have been assigned a new value elsewhere. Since you normally include an external file only once in a script, these commands are rarely necessary. However, using them does no harm.

To show you how to include code from an external file, let's convert the page shown in Figure 4-1. Because the menu and footer appear on every page of the Japan Journey site, they're prime candidates for include files. Here's the code for the body of the page with the menu and footer highlighted in bold.

```
<body>
<div id="header">
  <h1>Japan Journey </h1>
</div>
<div id="wrapper">
  <ul id="nav">
    <li><a href="index.php" id="here">Home</a></li>
    <li><a href="journal.php">Journal</a></li>
    <li><a href="gallery.php">Gallery</a></li>
    <li><a href="contact.php">Contact</a></li>
  </ul>
```

4

```
        <div id="maincontent">
          <h1>A journey through Japan with PHP </h1>
          <p>Ut enim ad minim veniam, quis nostrud . . .</p>
          <div id="pictureWrapper">
            <img src="images/water_basin.jpg" alt="Water basin at Ryoanji ➥
temple" width="350" height="237" class="picBorder" />
          </div>
          <p>Eu fugiat nulla pariatur. Ut labore et dolore . . .</p>
          <p>Consectetur adipisicing elit, duis aute irure . . .</p>
          <p>Quis nostrud exercitation eu fugiat nulla . . .</p>
        </div>
        <div id="footer">
        <p>&copy; 2006 David Powers</p>
        </div>
    </div>
    </body>
```

PHP Solution 4-1: Moving the navigation menu and footer to include files

1. Copy index01.php from the download files for this chapter to the phpsolutions site root, and rename it index.php. If you are using a program like Dreamweaver that offers to update the page links, *don't* update them. The relative links in the download file are correct. Check that the CSS and images are displaying properly by loading index.php into a browser. It should look the same as Figure 4-1.

2. Copy journal.php, gallery.php, and contact.php from the download files to your site root folder. These pages won't display correctly in a browser yet because the necessary include files still haven't been created. That'll soon change.

3. In index.php, highlight the nav unordered list as shown in bold in the previous listing, and cut (Ctrl+X/Cmd+X) it to your computer clipboard.

4. Create a new file called menu.inc.php in the includes folder. Remove any code inserted by your editing program; *the file must be completely blank*.

5. Paste (Ctrl+V/Cmd+V) the code from your clipboard into menu.inc.php and save the file. The contents of menu.inc.php should look like this:

```
<ul id="nav">
  <li><a href="index.php" id="here">Home</a></li>
  <li><a href="journal.php">Journal</a></li>
  <li><a href="gallery.php">Gallery</a></li>
  <li><a href="contact.php">Contact</a></li>
</ul>
```

> *Don't worry that your new file doesn't have a DOCTYPE declaration or any <html>, <head>, or <body> tags. The other pages that include the contents of this file will supply those elements.*

6. Open `index.php`, and insert the following in the space left by the nav unordered list:

```php
<?php include('includes/menu.inc.php'); ?>
```

7. Save `index.php` and load the page into a browser. It should look exactly the same as before. Although the menu and the rest of the page are coming from different files, PHP merges them before sending any output to the browser.

8. Do the same with the footer `<div>`. Cut the lines highlighted in bold in the original listing, and paste them into a blank file called `footer.inc.php` in the `includes` folder. Then insert the command to include the new file in the gap left by the footer `<div>`:

```php
<?php include('includes/footer.inc.php'); ?>
```

9. Save all pages and load `index.php` into a browser. Again, it should look identical to the original page. If you navigate to other pages in the site, the menu and footer should appear on every page. The code in the include files is now serving all pages.

10. To prove that the menu is being drawn from a single file, change one of the links in `menu.inc.php` like this, for example:

```html
<li><a href="journal.php">Blog</a></li>
```

11. Save `menu.inc.php` and view the site again. The change is reflected on all pages. You can check your code against `index02.php`, `menu.inc01.php`, and `footer.inc01.php`.

As Figure 4-2 shows, there's a problem with the code at the moment. Even when you navigate away from the home page, the style that indicates which page you're on doesn't change (it's controlled by the here ID in the `<a>` tag). Fortunately, that's easily fixed with a little PHP conditional logic.

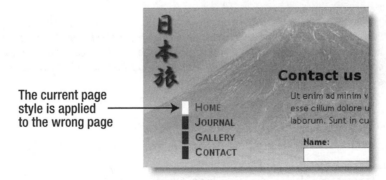

The current page style is applied to the wrong page

Figure 4-2. Moving the navigation menu to an external file makes maintenance easier, but you need some conditional logic to apply the correct style to the current page.

Before doing that, let's take a look at some important aspects of working with include files in PHP.

Choosing the right filename extension for includes

Both of the include files you created in the preceding section have what may seem rather unusual filenames with two extensions, .inc and .php, strung together. The truth is that it doesn't matter what you use as a filename extension; PHP simply includes the content of the file and treats it as part of the main page. A common convention is to use .inc for all include files. However, this potentially exposes you to a major security risk because most servers treat .inc files as plain text. Let's say an include file contains the username and password to your database, and you store the file with an .inc filename extension within your website's root folder. Anyone who discovers the name of the file can simply type the URL in a browser address bar, and the browser will obligingly display all your secret details!

On the other hand, any file with a .php extension is automatically sent to the PHP engine for parsing before it's sent to the browser. So, *as long as your secret information is inside a PHP code block and in a file with a .php extension*, it won't be exposed. That's why it's now widely recommended to use .inc.php as a double extension for PHP includes. The .inc part reminds you that it's an include file, but servers are only interested in the .php on the end, which ensures that all PHP code is correctly parsed.

PHP Solution 4-2: Testing the security of includes

Use index.php and menu.inc.php from the previous section. Alternatively, use index02.php and menu.inc01.php from the download files for this chapter. If you use the download files, remove the 02 and 01 from the filenames before using them.

1. Rename menu.inc.php as menu.inc and change the code in index.php so that the include command refers to menu.inc instead of menu.inc.php, like this:

```php
<?php include('includes/menu.inc'); ?>
```

> *Even if you normally use absolute pathnames in your websites (ones that begin with a forward slash), use a relative pathname on this occasion. PHP include commands don't normally work with absolute pathnames. I'll show you how to get around this restriction later in the chapter.*

2. Load index.php into a browser. You should see no difference.

3. Amend the code inside menu.inc to store a password inside a PHP variable like this:

```html
<ul id="nav">
  <li><a href="index.php" id="here">Home</a></li>
  <?php $password = 'topSecret'; ?>
  <li><a href="journal.php">Journal</a></li>
  <li><a href="gallery.php">Gallery</a></li>
  <li><a href="contact.php">Contact</a></li>
</ul>
```

4. Click the Reload button in your browser. As Figure 4-3 shows, the navigation menu still displays correctly. What's more, if you view the page's source code in the

browser, the password remains hidden. Although the include file doesn't have a .php filename extension, its contents have been merged with index.php, and both files are treated as a single entity.

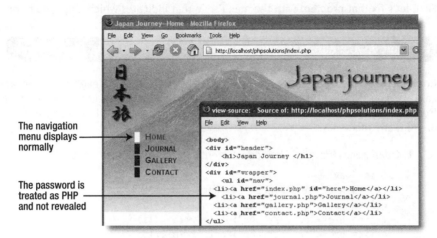

Figure 4-3. PHP code inside an include file is parsed before the page is sent to the browser.

5. Now type the URL for menu.inc in the browser address bar. It should be http://localhost/phpsolutions/includes/menu.inc (adjust the URL if your include file is in a different location). Load the file into your browser. This time, you'll see something very different, as shown in Figure 4-4.

Figure 4-4. A file with an .inc filename extension is treated as plain text when accessed directly.

Neither the server nor the browser knows how to deal with an .inc file, so the entire contents are displayed onscreen: raw XHTML, your secret password, everything . . .

6. Change the name of the include file back to menu.inc.php, and load it directly into your browser by adding .php to the end of the URL you used in the previous step. This time, you should see an unordered list of links, as shown alongside. Inspect the browser's source view. It should look similar to the navigation section in Figure 4-3. *The PHP isn't exposed.*

7. Change the include command inside index.php back to its original setting like this:

```php
<?php include('includes/menu.inc.php'); ?>
```

Using PHP to identify the current page

I'll have more to say about security issues surrounding include files later in the chapter. First, let's fix that problem with the menu style that indicates which page you're on.

PHP Solution 4-3: Automatically setting a style to indicate the current page

Continue working with the same files. Alternatively, use index02.php, contact.php, gallery.php, journal.php, includes/menu.inc01.php, and includes/footer.inc01.php from the download files for this chapter. If using the download files, remove the 01 and 02 from any filenames.

1. Open menu.inc.php. The code currently looks like this:

```
<ul id="nav">
  <li><a href="index.php" id="here">Home</a></li>
  <li><a href="journal.php">Journal</a></li>
  <li><a href="gallery.php">Gallery</a></li>
  <li><a href="contact.php">Contact</a></li>
</ul>
```

The style to indicate the current page is controlled by the **id="here"** highlighted in line 3. What you need is a way of getting PHP to insert id="here" into the journal.php <a> tag *if* the current page is journal.php, into the gallery.php <a> tag *if* the page is gallery.php, and into the contact.php <a> tag *if* the page is contact.php.

Hopefully, you have got the hint by now—you need an if statement (see the section on conditional statements, "Making decisions," in Chapter 3) in each <a> tag. Line 3 needs to look like this:

```
<li><a href="index.php" <?php if ($currentPage == 'index.php') { ➡
echo 'id="here"'; } ?>>Home</a></li>
```

The other links should be amended in a similar way. But how does $currentPage get its value? You need some way of finding out the filename of the current page.

2. Leave menu.inc.php to one side for the moment and create a new PHP page called scriptname.php. Insert the following code between a pair of PHP tags (alternatively, just use scriptname1.php in the download files for this chapter):

```
echo $_SERVER['SCRIPT_NAME'];
```

3. Save scriptname.php and view it in a browser. On a Windows system, you should see something like the following screenshot. (The download file contains the code for this step and the next, together with text indicating which is which.)

On Mac OS X, you should see something similar to this:

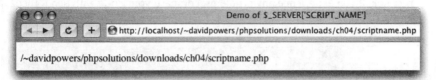

$_SERVER['SCRIPT_NAME'] comes from one of PHP's built-in superglobal arrays, and it always gives you the absolute (site root–relative) pathname for the current page. As you can see from the two screenshots, it works the same regardless of the server's operating system. What you need now is a way of extracting just the filename.

4. Amend the code in the previous step like this:

```
echo basename($_SERVER['SCRIPT_NAME']);
```

5. Save scriptname.php and click the Reload button in your browser. You should now see just the filename: scriptname.php. If you get a parse error message instead, make sure that you have included the closing parenthesis just before the final semicolon.

The built-in PHP function basename() takes the pathname of a file and extracts the filename. So, there you have it—a way of finding the filename of the current page.

6. Amend the code in menu.inc.php like this (the changes are highlighted in bold):

```
<?php $currentPage = basename($_SERVER['SCRIPT_NAME']); ?>
<ul id="nav">
  <li><a href="index.php" <?php if ($currentPage == ➡
'index.php') {echo 'id="here"';} ?>>Home</a></li>
  <li><a href="journal.php" <?php if ($currentPage == ➡
'journal.php') {echo 'id="here"';} ?>>Journal</a></li>
  <li><a href="gallery.php" <?php if ($currentPage == ➡
'gallery.php') {echo 'id="here"';} ?>>Gallery</a></li>
  <li><a href="contact.php" <?php if ($currentPage == ➡
'contact.php') {echo 'id="here"';} ?>>Contact</a></li>
</ul>
```

> *Make sure that you get the combination of single and double quotes correct. The value of attributes, such as id, must be enclosed in quotes for valid XHTML. Since I've used double quotes around here, I've wrapped the string 'id="here"' in single quotes. I could have written "id=\"here\"", but a mixture of single and double quotes is easier to read.*

7. Save menu.inc.php and load index.php into a browser. The menu should look no different from before. Use the menu to navigate to other pages. This time, as shown in Figure 4-5, the border alongside the current page should be white, indicating your location within the site. If you inspect the page's source view in the browser, you'll see that the here ID has been automatically inserted into the correct link. If you experience any problems, compare your code with menu.inc02.php in the download files.

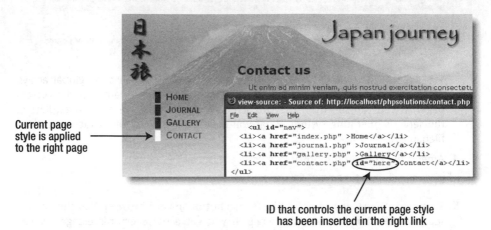

Current page style is applied to the right page

ID that controls the current page style has been inserted in the right link

Figure 4-5. With the help of some simple conditional code, the include file produces different output for each page.

Now that you know how to find the filename of the current page, you might also find it useful to automate the <title> tag of each page. This works only if you use filenames that tell you something about the page's contents, but since that's a good practice anyway, it's not really a restriction.

PHP Solution 4-4: Automatically generating a page's title from its filename

Although the following steps use the Japan Journey website, you can try this out with any page.

1. The basename() function used in the previous solution takes an optional second argument: a string containing the filename extension. Create a new PHP file and insert the following code between a pair of PHP tags (the code is in scriptname2.php):

   ```
   echo basename($_SERVER['SCRIPT_NAME'], '.php');
   ```

   > Note that when passing more than one argument to a function, you separate the arguments with commas.

2. Save the page with any name you like (as long as it has a .php filename extension), and load it into a browser. It should display the name of the file stripped of the .php extension. The download file displays scriptname2.

You now have the basis for automatically creating the page title for every page in your site, using basename(), $_SERVER['SCRIPT_NAME'], and an include file.

3. Create a new PHP file called title.inc.php and save it in the includes folder.

4. Strip out any code inserted by your script editor, and type in the following code (the finished code for title.inc.php is in the ch04/includes folder of the download files):

```php
<?php
$title = basename($_SERVER['SCRIPT_NAME'], '.php');
?>
```

This finds the filename of the current page, strips the .php filename extension, and assigns the result to a variable called $title.

> *The code for this include file must be enclosed in PHP tags. This is because the whole file needs to be treated as PHP. Unlike the menu, it won't be displayed directly inside other pages.*

5. Open a PHP page in your script editor. If you're using the Japan Journey site, use contact.php. Include title.inc.php by typing this above the DOCTYPE declaration:

```php
<?php include('includes/title.inc.php'); ?>
```

6. Amend the <title> tag like this:

```
<title>Japan Journey<?php echo "&#8212;{$title}"; ?></title>
```

This uses echo to display — (the numerical entity for an em dash) followed by the value of $title. Because the string is enclosed in *double* quotes, PHP displays the value of $title (see "All you ever wanted to know about quotes—and more" in Chapter 3 for an explanation of how PHP treats variables inside double quotes).

The variable $title has also been enclosed in curly braces because there is no space between the em dash and $title. Although not always necessary, it's a good idea to enclose variables in braces when using them without any whitespace in a double-quoted string, as it makes the variable clear to you and the PHP engine.

The first few lines of your page should look like this:

```
1  <?php include('includes/title.inc.php'); ?>
2  <!DOCTYPE html PUBLIC "-//W3C//DTD XHTML 1.0 Transitional//EN"
   "http://www.w3.org/TR/xhtml1/DTD/xhtml1-transitional.dtd">
3  <html xmlns="http://www.w3.org/1999/xhtml">
4  <head>
5  <meta http-equiv="Content-Type" content="text/html; charset=iso-8859-1" />
6  <title>Japan Journey<?php echo "&#8212;{$title}"; ?></title>
```

> *If you've been using CSS for a while, you'll know that putting anything above the* DOCTYPE *declaration forces browsers into quirks mode. However, this doesn't apply to PHP code, as long as it doesn't send any output to the browser. The code in* title.inc.php *only assigns a value to* $title, *so the* DOCTYPE *declaration remains the first thing that the browser sees, and any CSS is displayed in standards-compliant mode.*

7. Save both pages and load the web page into a browser. Figure 4-6 shows how the change is reflected in contact.php.

The changing part of the page title is derived dynamically from the filename

Figure 4-6. Once you extract the filename, it's possible to create the page title dynamically.

8. Not bad, but what if you prefer an initial capital letter for the part of the title derived from the filename? Nothing could be simpler. PHP has a neat little function called ucfirst(), which does exactly that (the name is easy to remember once you realize that uc stands for "uppercase"). Add another line to the code in step 4 like this:

```php
<?php
$title = basename($_SERVER['SCRIPT_NAME'], '.php');
$title = ucfirst($title);
?>
```

When confronted by something like this, some people start breaking out into a sweat, convinced that programming is a black art that is the work of the devil—or at least of a warped mind. Actually, it's quite simple: the first line of code after the PHP tag gets the filename, strips the .php off the end, and stores it as $title. The next line takes the value of $title, passes it to ucfirst() to capitalize the first letter, and stores the result back in $title. So, if the filename is contact.php, $title starts out as contact, but by the end of the following line it has become Contact.

> *You can shorten the code by combining both lines into one like this:*
>
> ```php
> $title = ucfirst(basename($_SERVER['SCRIPT_NAME'], '.php'));
> ```
>
> *When you nest functions like this, PHP processes the innermost one first and passes the result to the outer function. It makes your code shorter, but it's not so easy to read.*

100

9. A drawback with this technique is that filenames consist of only one word—at least they should. If you've picked up bad habits from Windows and Mac OS X permitting spaces in filenames, get out of them immediately. Spaces are not allowed in URLs, which is why most web design software replaces spaces with %20. You can get around this problem, though, by using an underscore. Change the name of the file you're working with so that it uses two words separated by an underscore. For example, change contact.php to contact_us.php.

10. Change the code in title.inc.php like this:

```php
<?php
$title = basename($_SERVER['SCRIPT_NAME'], '.php');
$title = str_replace('_', ' ', $title);
$title = ucwords($title);
?>
```

The middle line uses a function called str_replace() to look for every underscore and replace it with a space. The function takes three arguments:

■ The character you want to replace (you can also search for multiple characters)

■ The replacement character or characters

■ The string where you want the changes to be made

You can also use str_replace() to remove character(s) by using an empty string (a pair of quotes with nothing between them) as the second argument. This replaces the string in the first argument with nothing, effectively removing it.

The other change is in the final line of code. Instead of ucfirst(), it uses the related function ucwords(), which gives each word an initial cap.

11. Save title.inc.php and load into a browser the file that you renamed in step 9. Figure 4-7 shows the result with contact_us.php.

The PHP function str_replace() removes the underscore, while ucwords() capitalizes the initial letter of each word

Figure 4-7. With the help of str_replace(), you can even create titles that contain more than one word.

12. Change back the name of the file so that it no longer has an underscore. Reload the file into a browser. You'll see that the script in title.inc.php still works. There are no underscores to replace, so str_replace() leaves the value of $title untouched, and ucwords() converts the first letter to uppercase, even though there's only one word.

4

13. What happens, though, if you have page names that don't make good titles? The home page of the Japan Journey site is called index.php. As the following screenshot shows, applying the current solution to this page doesn't seem quite right.

There are two solutions: either don't apply this technique to such pages or use a conditional statement (an if statement) to handle special cases. For instance, to display Home instead of Index, amend the code in title.inc.php like this:

```php
<?php
$title = basename($_SERVER['SCRIPT_NAME'], '.php');
$title = str_replace('_', ' ', $title);
if ($title == 'index') {
  $title = 'home';
  }
$title = ucwords($title);
?>
```

The first line of the conditional statement uses two equal signs to check the value of $title. The following line uses a single equal sign to assign the new value to $title. If the page is called anything other than index.php, the line inside the curly braces is ignored, and $title keeps its original value.

> *PHP is case-sensitive, so this solution works only if* index *is all lowercase. To do a case-insensitive comparison, change the fourth line of the preceding code like this:*
>
> ```php
> if (strtolower($title) == 'index') {
> ```
>
> *The function* strtolower() *converts a* **str***ing* **to lower***case—hence its name— and is frequently used to make case-insensitive comparisons. The conversion to lowercase is not permanent, because* strtolower($title) *isn't assigned to a variable; it's only used to make the comparison. To make a change permanent, you need to assign the result back to a variable as in the final line, when* ucwords($title) *is assigned back to* $title.
>
> *To convert a string to uppercase, use* strtoupper().

14. Save title.inc.php and reload index.php into a browser. The page title now looks more natural, as shown in the following screenshot.

15. Navigate back to contact.php, and you'll see that the page title is still derived correctly from the page name.

16. There's one final refinement you should make. The PHP code inside the <title> tag relies on the existence of the variable $title, which won't be set if there's a problem with the include file. Before attempting to display the contents of a variable that comes from an external source, it's always a good idea to check that it exists, using a function called isset(). Wrap the echo command inside a conditional statement, and test for the variable's existence like this:

```
<title>Japan Journey<?php if (isset($title)) {echo "&#8212;{$title}";} ➡
?></title>
```

If $title doesn't exist, the echo command will be ignored, leaving just the default site title, Japan Journey. You can check your code against an updated version of index.php in index03.php in the download files.

4

Creating pages with changing content

So far, we've looked at using PHP to generate different output depending on the page's filename. The next two solutions generate content that changes independently: a copyright notice that updates the year automatically on January 1 and a random image generator.

PHP Solution 4-5: Automatically updating a copyright notice

Continue working with the files from the previous solution. Alternatively, use index02.php and includes/footer.inc01.php from the download files for this chapter. If using the download files, remove the numbers from the filenames when moving them into your working site.

1. Open footer.inc.php. It contains the following XHTML:

```
<div id="footer">
  <p>&copy; 2006 David Powers</p>
</div>
```

The advantage of using an include file is that you can update the copyright notice throughout the site by changing this one file. However, it would be much more efficient to increment the year automatically, doing away with the need for updates altogether.

2. The PHP date() function takes care of that very neatly. Change the code like this:

```
<div id="footer">
  <p>&copy;
  <?php
  ini_set('date.timezone', 'Europe/London');
  echo date('Y');
  ?>
  David Powers</p>
</div>
```

Chapter 14 explains dates in PHP and MySQL in detail, but let's take a quick look at what's happening here. The core part of the code is this line:

```php
echo date('Y');
```

This displays the year using four digits. Make sure you use an uppercase Y. If you use a lowercase y instead, only the final two digits of the year will be displayed.

The reason for the preceding line is because of changes to the way that PHP handles dates. Since PHP 5.1.0, PHP requires a valid time-zone setting. This should be set in php.ini, but if your hosting company forgets to do this, you may end up with ugly error messages in your page. Using ini_set() in a script like this is good insurance against this happening. It also allows you to override the hosting company setting, so this is particularly convenient if your host is in a different time zone from your own. I live in London, so the second argument for ini_set() is 'Europe/London'. Check the time zone for where you live at www.php.net/manual/en/timezones.php.

> The date.timezone *setting works only in PHP 5.1.0 and above. However,* ini_set() *silently ignores any settings it doesn't recognize, so you can use this setting safely on older versions of PHP.*

3. Save footer.inc.php and load index.php into a browser. The copyright notice at the foot of the page should look the same as before—unless, of course, you're reading this in 2007 or later, in which case the current year will be displayed.

4. Copyright notices normally cover a range of years, indicating when a site was first launched. To improve the copyright notice, you need to know two things: the start year and the current year. If both years are the same, you need to display only the current year; if they're different, you need to display both with a hyphen between them. It's a simple if... else situation. Change the code in footer.inc.php like this:

```php
<div id="footer">
  <p>&copy;
  <?php
  ini_set('date.timezone', 'Europe/London');
  $startYear = 2006;
  $thisYear = date('Y');
  if ($startYear == $thisYear) {
    echo $startYear;
    }
  else {
    echo "{$startYear}-{$thisYear}";
    }
  ?>
  David Powers</p>
</div>
```

As in PHP Solution 4-4, I've used curly braces around the variables in line 11 because they're in a double-quoted string that contains no whitespace. Since hyphens aren't permitted in variable names, this is one of the cases where you could omit the curly braces. However, their presence makes the code easier to read.

5. Save `footer.inc.php` and reload `index.php` in a browser. Experiment by changing the value of $startYear and alternating between uppercase and lowercase y in the date() function to see the different output, as shown in the following image.

```
$thisYear = date('Y');
```
© 2005-2006 David Powers

```
$thisYear = date('y');
```
© 2005-06 David Powers

These values and the name of the copyright owner are the only things you need to change, and you have a fully automated copyright notice. The finished code for the footer include file is in `footer.inc02.php`.

PHP Solution 4-6: Displaying a random image

Displaying a random image is very easy. All you need is a list of available images, which you store in an indexed array (see "Creating arrays" in Chapter 3). Since indexed arrays are numbered from 0, you can select one of the images by generating a random number between 0 and one less than the length of the array. All accomplished in a few lines of code . . .

Continue using the same files. Alternatively, use `index03.php` from the download files and rename it `index.php`. Since `index03.php` uses `menu.inc.php`, `title.inc.php`, and `footer.inc.php`, make sure all three files are in your includes folder. The images are already in the images folder.

1. Create a blank PHP page in the includes folder and name it `random_image.php`. Insert the following code (it's also in `includes/random_image01.php` in the download files):

```php
<?php
$images = array('kinkakuji', 'maiko', 'maiko_phone', 'monk',
  'fountains', 'ryoanji', 'menu', 'basin');
$i = rand(0, count($images)-1);
$selectedImage = "images/{$images[$i]}.jpg";
?>
```

This is the complete script: an array of image names minus the `.jpg` filename extension (there's no need to repeat shared information—they're all JPEG), a random number generator, and a string that builds the correct pathname for the selected file.

To generate a random number within a range, you pass the minimum and maximum numbers as arguments to the function `rand()`. Since there are eight images in the array, you need a number between 0 and 7. The simple way to do this would be to use `rand(0, 7)`. Simple, but inefficient . . . Every time you change the $images array, you need to count how many elements it contains and change the maximum

4

number passed to rand(). It's much easier to get PHP to count them for you, and that's exactly what the count() function does: it counts the number of elements in an array. You need a number one less than the number of elements in the array, so the second argument passed to rand() becomes count($images)-1, and the result is stored in $i.

> *If you're new to PHP, you may find it hard to understand expressions like* $i = rand(0, count($images)-1). *All that's happening is that you're passing an expression to* rand(), *rather than the actual number. If it makes it easier for you to follow the logic of the code, rewrite it like this:*
>
> ```
> $numImages = count($images); // $numImages is 8
> $max = $numImages - 1;        // $max is 7
> $i = rand(0, $max);           // $i = rand(0, 7)
> ```

The random number is used in the final line to build the correct pathname for the selected file. The variable $images[$i] is embedded in a double-quoted string with no whitespace separating it from surrounding characters, so it's enclosed in curly braces. Arrays start at 0, so if the random number is 1, $selectedImage is images/maiko.jpg.

2. Open index.php and include random_image.php by inserting the command in the same code block as title.inc.php like this:

```
<?php include('includes/title.inc.php');
    include('includes/random_image.php'); ?>
```

Since random_image.php doesn't send any direct output to the browser, it's quite safe to put it above the DOCTYPE without forcing browsers into quirks mode.

3. Scroll down inside index.php and locate the code that displays the image in the maincontent <div>. It looks like this:

```
<div id="pictureWrapper">
  <img src="images/basin.jpg" alt="Water basin at Ryoanji temple" ➥
width="350" height="237" class="picBorder" />
</div>
```

4. Instead of using images/basin.jpg as a fixed image, replace it with $selectedImage. All the images have different dimensions, so delete the width and height attributes, and use a generic alt attribute. The code in step 3 should now look like this:

```
<div id="pictureWrapper">
  <img src="<?php echo $selectedImage; ?>" alt="Random image" ➥
class="picBorder" />
</div>
```

5. Save both `random_image.php` and `index.php`, and load `index.php` into a browser. The image should now be chosen at random. Click the Reload button in your browser, and you should see a variety of images, as shown in Figure 4-8.

You can check your code for `index.php` against `index04.php` in the download files. The code for `random_image.php` is in `random_image01.php`.

Figure 4-8. Storing image names in an indexed array makes it easy to display a random image.

This is a simple and effective way of displaying a random image, but it would be much better if you could add a caption and set the width and height attributes for different sized images dynamically.

PHP Solution 4-7: Adding a caption to the random image

As I explained in Chapter 3, arrays can hold any type of data, including other arrays. To store more than one piece of information about an image, each image in the original `$images` array needs to be represented by a separate array. Each subarray has two elements: the filename and a caption. In graphical terms, it looks like this (for space reasons, only the first two items are displayed as arrays):

In the original array, $images[1] is the picture of the two trainee geishas. In the multidimensional array, it still represents the same photo, but the filename is now stored in the subarray as $images[1]['file'] and the description as $images[1]['caption']. Since the images are different sizes, you may be thinking it would be a good idea to store their width and height too. It's not necessary, because PHP can generate the details dynamically with a function called, appropriately enough, getimagesize().

This PHP solution builds on the previous one, so continue working with the same files.

1. Open random_image.php and change the code like this:

```php
<?php
$images = array(
  array('file'    => 'kinkakuji',
        'caption' => 'The Golden Pavilion in Kyoto'),
  array('file'    => 'maiko',
        'caption' => 'Maiko&#8212;trainee geishas in Kyoto'),
  array('file'    => 'maiko_phone',
        'caption' => 'Every maiko should have one&#8212;a mobile, ➥
of course'),
  array('file'    => 'monk',
        'caption' => 'Monk begging for alms in Kyoto'),
  array('file'    => 'fountains',
        'caption' => 'Fountains in central Tokyo'),
  array('file'    => 'ryoanji',
        'caption' => 'Autumn leaves at Ryoanji temple, Kyoto'),
  array('file'    => 'menu',
        'caption' => 'Menu outside restaurant in Pontocho, Kyoto'),
  array('file'    => 'basin',
        'caption' => 'Water basin at Ryoanji temple, Kyoto')
  );
$i = rand(0, count($images)-1);
$selectedImage = "images/{$images[$i]['file']}.jpg";
$caption = $images[$i]['caption'];
?>
```

Although the code looks complicated, it's an ordinary indexed array that contains eight items, each of which is an associative array containing definitions for 'file' and 'caption'. The definition of the multidimensional array forms a single statement, so there are no semicolons until line 19. The closing parenthesis on that line matches the opening one on line 2. All the array elements in between are separated by commas. The deep indenting isn't necessary, but it makes the code a lot easier to read.

The variable used to select the image also needs to be changed, because $images[$i] no longer contains a string, but an array. To get the correct filename for the image, you need to use $images[$i]['file']. The caption for the selected image is contained in $images[$i]['caption'] and stored in a shorter variable.

2. You now need to amend the code in index.php to display the caption like this:

```
<div id="pictureWrapper">
  <img src="<?php echo $selectedImage; ?>" alt="Random image" ➥
class="picBorder" />
  <p id="caption"><?php echo $caption; ?></p>
</div>
```

3. Save index.php and random_image.php, and load index.php into a browser. Most images will look fine, but there's an ugly gap to the right of the image of the trainee geisha with a mobile phone, as shown in Figure 4-9. Fortunately, this is easily fixed.

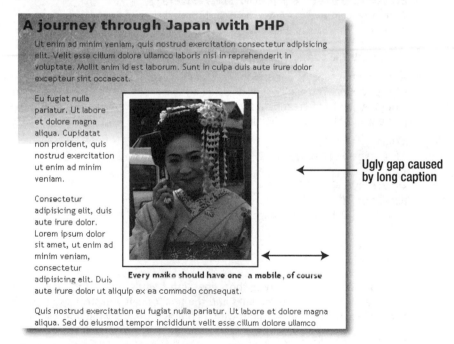

Figure 4-9. The long caption shifts the image too far left.

4. Add the following code to random_image.php just before the closing PHP tag:

```
if (file_exists($selectedImage) && is_readable($selectedImage)) {
  $imageSize = getimagesize($selectedImage);
  }
```

The if statement uses two functions, file_exists() and is_readable(), to make sure $selectedImage not only exists, but also that it's accessible (it may be corrupted or have the wrong permissions). These functions return Boolean values (true or false), so they can be used directly as part of the conditional statement.

The single line inside the if statement uses the function getimagesize() to get the image's dimensions. The function returns an array containing four elements. By assigning the result to $imageSize, you can extract the following information:

- $imageSize[0]: The width of the image in pixels
- $imageSize[1]: The height of the image in pixels
- $imageSize[2]: A number indicating the type of file (see Chapter 8 for details)
- $imageSize[3]: A string containing the height and width for use in an <img> tag

The first and last items in this array are just what you need to solve the problem shown in Figure 4-9.

5. First of all, let's fix the code in step 2. Change it like this:

```
<div id="pictureWrapper">
  <img src="<?php echo $selectedImage; ?>" alt="Random image" ➥
class="picBorder" <?php echo $imageSize[3]; ?> />
  <p id="caption"><?php echo $caption; ?></p>
</div>
```

This inserts the correct width and height attributes inside the <img> tag.

6. Although this sets the dimensions for the image, you still need to control the width of the caption. You can't use PHP inside an external stylesheet, but there's nothing stopping you from creating a style block in the <head> of index.php. Put this code just before the closing </head> tag:

```
<?php
if (isset($imageSize)) {
?>
<style type="text/css">
p#caption {
  width: <?php echo $imageSize[0]; ?>px;
  }
</style>
<?php } ?>
```

This code consists of only nine short lines, but there's quite a lot going on in there. Let's start with the first three lines and the final one. If you strip away the PHP tags and replace the middle five lines with a comment, this is what you end up with:

```
if (isset($imageSize)) {
  // do something if $imageSize has been set
  }
```

In other words, if the variable $imageSize *hasn't* been **set** (defined), the PHP engine will ignore everything between the curly braces. It doesn't matter that most of the code between the braces is XHTML and CSS. If $imageSize hasn't been set, the PHP engine skips to the closing brace, and the intervening code isn't sent to the browser.

> *Many inexperienced PHP coders wrongly believe that they need to use* echo *or* print *to create XHTML output inside a conditional statement. As long as the opening and closing braces match, you can use PHP to hide or display sections of XHTML like this. It's a lot neater and involves a lot less typing than using* echo *all the time.*

If $imageSize has been set, the style block is created, and $imageSize[0] is used to set the correct width for the paragraph that contains the caption.

7. Save random_image.php and index.php, and reload index.php into a browser. Click the Reload button until the image of the trainee geisha with the mobile phone appears. This time, it should look like Figure 4-10. If you view the source code in the browser, you will see that the style rule changes automatically for each image. The correct width and height attributes should also be inside the <img> tag.

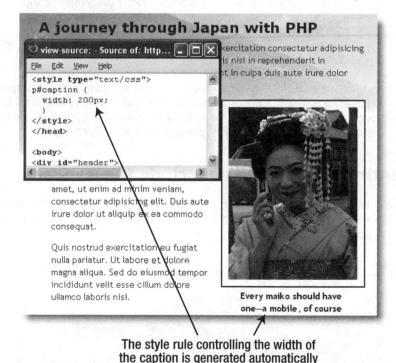

The style rule controlling the width of the caption is generated automatically

Figure 4-10. The ugly gap is removed by creating a style rule directly related to the image size.

8. There's just one final refinement we need to make. The code in random_image.php and in step 6 prevents errors if the selected image can't be found, but we've left the most important section of the code completely devoid of similar checks. Temporarily change the name of one of the images, either in random_image.php or in your images folder. Reload index.php several times. Eventually, you should see an error message like the following, making your site look very unprofessional.

9. The conditional statement at the foot of random_image.php sets $imageSize only if the selected image both exists and is readable, so if $imageSize has been set, you know it's all systems go. Add the opening and closing blocks of a conditional statement around the <div> that displays the image in index.php like this:

```
<?php if (isset($imageSize)) { ?>
<div id="pictureWrapper">
  <img src="<?php echo $selectedImage; ?>" alt="Random image"
class="picBorder" <?php echo $imageSize[3]; ?> />
  <p id="caption"><?php echo $caption; ?></p>
</div>
<?php } ?>
```

Images that exist will display normally, but you'll avoid any embarrassing error messages in case of a missing or corrupt file—a much more professional look. Don't forget to restore the name of the image you changed in the previous step. You can check your code against index05.php and random_image02.php.

Preventing errors when an include file is missing

A danger with using includes is that the include file may be corrupted or accidentally deleted from the server. Or you might type the filename or pathname incorrectly. Figure 4-11 shows what happened when I mistyped the name of random_image.php. It's not a pretty sight.

Figure 4-11. Unless you take preventive measures, a missing include file results in ugly error messages.

The two warning messages about the missing (or misnamed) file are helpful in a development context, as they tell you exactly what the problem is. In a live website, though, they not only look unprofessional, but also reveal potentially useful information about your site structure to malicious users.

It's quite simple to prevent this sort of mess from appearing onscreen. The quick and easy way is to use the PHP **error control operator** (@), which suppresses error messages associated with the line of code in which it's used. You place the error control operator either at the beginning of the line or directly in front of the function or command that you think might generate an error. So the error messages shown in Figure 4-11 could be eliminated like this:

```
@ include('includes/randomimage.php');
```

The error control operator is extremely useful, but without error messages, you're often left with no idea why a script isn't working. Insert it only after you are sure everything's OK. When troubleshooting, the @ mark should be the first thing you remove. Put it back after you have identified the problem. The error control operator affects only the current line. You need to use it in every line that might generate an error message.

A more sophisticated approach involves the following two steps:

- Always check that a file exists and is readable before attempting to include it.
- Always check the existence of variables or functions defined in external files before attempting to use them.

PHP Solution 4-7 ("Adding a caption to the random image") implemented both steps: first using file_exists() and is_readable() to check whether an image is accessible, and then using isset() to test whether a variable exists. So the errors in Figure 4-11 could be eliminated like this:

```
$file = 'includes/randomimage.php'
if (file_exists($file) && is_readable($file)) {
  include($file);
  }
```

Storing the name of the include file in a variable avoids the need to retype its pathname three times. It also means you need to correct the spelling mistake in only one place.

To check whether a custom-built function has been defined, pass the name of the function as a string to function_exists() like this:

```
if (function_exists('myFunction')) {myFunction();}
```

The name of the function being tested must be in quotes and without the final parentheses.

```
function_exists('myFunction')    // correct
function_exists(myFunction())    // wrong
```

Choosing where to locate your include files

A useful feature of PHP include files is they can be located anywhere, as long as the page with the include command knows where to find them. Include files don't even need to be inside your web server root. This means that you can protect include files that contain sensitive information, such as passwords, in a private directory (folder) that cannot be accessed through a browser. So, if your hosting company provides a storage area outside your server root, you should seriously consider locating some, if not all, of your include files there.

The include command expects either a relative path or a fully qualified path. This causes problems for developers who prefer to use absolute paths (beginning with a forward slash) that are relative to the site root (sometimes known as **site root–relative links**). There are two ways to get around this restriction.

PHP Solution 4-8: Using includes with absolute pathnames

The simplest way to use absolute pathnames with an include command is to use one of the predefined superglobal variables, $_SERVER['DOCUMENT_ROOT']. This variable automatically finds the full pathname to your website's server root, so you can use it in combination with an absolute path to build a fully qualified path. For example, if your site is hosted on a Linux server, the value of $_SERVER['DOCUMENT_ROOT'] might be /home/mydomain/htdocs, so $_SERVER['DOCUMENT_ROOT'].'/includes/filename.php' always translates to /home/mydomain/htdocs/includes/filename.php, and it can be used anywhere within your site's folder hierarchy.

Unfortunately, some servers don't support $_SERVER['DOCUMENT_ROOT'], so you need to find out first whether you can use it.

1. Create a PHP file and insert the following code (or use document_root.php):

```
if (isset($_SERVER['DOCUMENT_ROOT'])) {
  echo 'Supported. The server root is '.$_SERVER['DOCUMENT_ROOT'];
  }
else {
  echo "\$_SERVER['DOCUMENT_ROOT'] is not supported";
  }
```

2. Upload the file to your remote server and load it into a browser. If you see a message displaying the pathname of the server root, you can include files at any level in your site hierarchy like this:

```
include($_SERVER['DOCUMENT_ROOT'].'/includes/filename.php');
```

3. If $_SERVER['DOCUMENT_ROOT'] isn't supported, you need to create a variable manually to define the correct path. If you are using a Windows server, define the server root pathname using forward slashes like this:

```
$docRoot = 'C:/Inetpub/wwwroot/mydomain';
```

You can then build a fully qualified pathname using $docRoot in the same way as $_SERVER['DOCUMENT_ROOT'].

Security considerations with includes

Include files are a very powerful feature of PHP. With that power come some serious security risks. As long as the external file is accessible, PHP includes it and incorporates any code into the main script. But, as mentioned in the previous section, include files can be located anywhere—even on a different website. *Never use includes from a remote server.* Even if you control the remote server yourself, it's possible for a malicious attacker to spoof the address. Because of the security risks involved, some hosting companies turn off the ability to include files from other servers.

Summary

This chapter has plunged you headlong into the world of PHP, using includes, arrays, and multidimensional arrays. It has shown you how to extract the name of the current page and get the dimensions of an image. If it's your first experience with PHP, your head may be reeling. Don't worry. Once you get used to the basic structures, you will find them being used over and over again, and familiarity will help you overcome any initial confusion.

4

5 **BRINGING FORMS TO LIFE**

What this chapter covers:

- Gathering user input and sending it by email
- Displaying errors without losing user input
- Checking user input for security risks

Forms lie at the very heart of working with PHP. You use forms for logging in to restricted pages, registering new users, placing orders with online stores, entering and updating information in a database, sending feedback . . . The list goes on. The same principles lie behind all these uses, so the knowledge you gain from this chapter will have practical value in most PHP applications. To demonstrate how to process information from a form, I'm going to show you how to gather feedback from visitors to your site and send it to your mailbox. Unfortunately, user input can lay your site open to malicious attacks. The PHP Solutions in this chapter show you how to filter out or block anything suspicious or dangerous. It doesn't take a lot of effort to keep marauders at bay.

How PHP gathers information from a form

The Japan Journey website contains a feedback form (see Figure 5-1). I've kept it deliberately simple to start with, but will add other elements—such as radio buttons, check boxes, and drop-down menus—later. Although XHTML contains all the necessary tags to construct a form, it doesn't provide any means to process the form when submitted. For that, you need a server-side solution, such as PHP.

Figure 5-1. Activating a feedback form is one of the most popular uses of PHP.

First, let's take a look at the XHTML code used to build the form (it's in contact.php in the download files for this chapter):

```
<form id="feedback" method="post" action="">
  <p>
    <label for="name">Name:</label>
    <input name="name" id="name" type="text" class="formbox" />
  </p>
  <p>
    <label for="email">Email:</label>
    <input name="email" id="email" type="text" class="formbox" />
  </p>
  <p>
    <label for="comments">Comments:</label>
    <textarea name="comments" id="comments" cols="60" rows="8"> ➡
</textarea>
  </p>
  <p>
    <input name="send" id="send" type="submit" value="Send message" />
  </p>
</form>
```

The first thing to notice about this code is that the <input> and <textarea> tags contain both name and id attributes set to the same value. The reason for this duplication is that XHTML, CSS, and JavaScript all refer to the id attribute. Form processing scripts, however, rely on the name attribute. So, although the id attribute is optional, you *must* use the name attribute for each element that you want to be processed.

> *The XHTML 1.0 specification (www.w3.org/TR/xhtml1) lists a number of elements, including <form>, for which the* name *attribute has been deprecated. This applies only to the* <form> *tag. The* name *attribute remains valid for* <input>, <select>, *and* <textarea>.

Two other things to notice are the method and action attributes inside the opening <form> tag. The method attribute determines how the form sends data to the processing script. It can be set to either post or get. The action attribute tells the browser where to send the data for processing when the submit button is clicked. If the value is left empty, as here, the page attempts to process the form itself.

Understanding the difference between post and get

The best way to demonstrate the difference between the post and get methods is with a real form. The download files for this chapter contain a complete set of files for the Japan Journey site with all the script from the last chapter incorporated in them. Make sure that the includes folder contains footer.inc.php and menu.inc.php. Copy contact01.php to your working site, and rename it contact.php.

1. Locate the opening `<form>` tag in contact.php, and change the value of the method attribute from post to get like this:

`<form id="feedback" method="`**get**`" action="">`

2. Save contact.php and load the page in a browser. Type your name, email, and a short message into the form, and click Send message.

3. Look in the browser address bar. You should see the contents of the form attached to the end of the URL like this:

If you break up the URL, it looks like this:

```
http://localhost/phpsolutions/contact.php
?name=David+Powers
&email=david%40example.com
&comments=I+hope+you+get+this.+%3B%29
&send=Send+message
```

Each line after the basic URL begins with the name attribute of one of the form elements, followed by an equal sign and the contents of the input fields. URLs cannot contain spaces or certain characters (such as my smiley), so the browser encodes them as hexadecimal values, a process known as **URL encoding** (for a full list of values, see www.w3schools.com/tags/ref_urlencode.asp).

The first name attribute is preceded by a question mark (?) and the others by an ampersand (&). You'll see this type of URL when using search engines, which helps explain why everything after the question mark is known as a **query string**.

4. Go back into the code of contact.php, and change method back to post, like this:

`<form id="feedback" method="`**post**`" action="">`

5. Save contact.php, and reload the page in your browser. Type another message, and click Send message. Your message should disappear, but nothing else happens. So where has it gone? It hasn't been lost, but you haven't done anything to process it yet.

6. In contact.php, add the following code immediately below the closing </form> tag:

```
<pre>
<?php if ($_POST) {print_r($_POST);} ?>
</pre>
```

This displays the contents of the $_POST superglobal array if any post data has been sent. As explained in Chapter 3, the print_r() function allows you to inspect the contents of arrays; the <pre> tags simply make the output easier to read.

7. Save the page, and click the Refresh button in your browser. You will probably see a warning similar to the following. This tells you that the data will be resent, which is exactly what you want. Click OK or Send depending on your browser.

8. The code from step 6 should now display the contents of your message below the form as shown in Figure 5-2. Everything has been stored in one of PHP's superglobal arrays, $_POST, which contains data sent using the post method. The name attribute of each form element is used as the array key, making it easy to retrieve the content.

```
              Send message

                  Array
    (
        [name] => David Powers
        [email] => david@example.com
        [comments] => So what does post do then?
        [send] => Send message
    )
```

Figure 5-2. Data from a form is stored as an associative array, with each element identified by its name attribute.

As you have just seen, the get method sends your data in a very exposed way, making it vulnerable to alteration. Also, some browsers limit the maximum length of a URL, so it can be used only for small amounts of data. The post method is more secure and can be used for much larger amounts of data. By default, PHP permits up to 8MB of post data, although hosting companies may set a smaller limit.

Because of these advantages, you should normally use the post method with forms. The get method is used mainly in conjunction with database searches, and has the advantage that you can bookmark a search result because all the data is in the URL. We'll return to the get method later in the book, but the rest of this chapter concentrates on the post method and its associated superglobal array, $_POST.

> *Although the* post *method is more secure than* get, *you shouldn't assume that it's 100% safe. For secure transmission, you need to use encryption or the Secure Sockets Layer (SSL).*

Keeping safe with PHP superglobals

While I'm on the subject of security, it's worth explaining the background to the PHP superglobal arrays, which include $_POST and $_GET. The $_POST array contains data sent using the post method. So it should come as no surprise that data sent by the get method is in the $_GET array.

Before the release of PHP 4.2.0 in April 2002, you didn't need to worry about using special arrays to access data submitted from a form. If the name of the form element was email, all that was necessary was to stick a dollar sign on the front, like this: $email. Bingo, you had instant access to the data. It was incredibly convenient. Unfortunately, it also left a gaping security hole. All that an attacker needed to do was view the source of your web page and pass values to your script through a query string.

When the loophole was closed, millions of PHP scripts stopped working. Inexperienced web developers were up in arms, and harassed hosting companies changed a setting called register_globals in php.ini to restore a little peace to their lives. You will find lots of "advice" on the Internet to turn register_globals on in php.ini, because it will make your life easier. This is completely misguided. Turning on register_globals is foolish for the following reasons:

- It's totally insecure.
- There is no way to override the setting for individual scripts. If your hosting company turns register_globals off, any scripts that rely on it will break.
- The register_globals setting has been removed completely from PHP 6. Scripts that rely on register_globals won't work, period.

It's very easy to write scripts that don't rely on register_globals, so it's not the major burden that some people imply. It just requires putting the name of the form element in quotes between square brackets after $_POST or $_GET, depending on the form's method attribute. So email becomes $_POST['email'] if sent by the post method, and $_GET['email'] if sent by the get method. That's all there is to it.

You may come across scripts that use $_REQUEST, which avoids the need to distinguish between $_POST or $_GET. It's less secure. Always use $_POST or $_GET instead.

Old scripts may use $HTTP_POST_VARS or $HTTP_GET_VARS, which have exactly the same meaning as $_POST and $_GET. The longer versions have been removed from PHP 6. Use $_POST and $_GET instead.

Sending email

The PHP `mail()` function takes up to five arguments, all of them strings, as follows:

- The address(es) of the recipient(s)
- The subject line
- The message body
- A list of other email headers
- Additional parameters

The first three arguments are required. Email addresses in the first argument can be in either of the following formats:

```
'user@example.com'
'Some Guy <user2@example.com>'
```

To send to more than one address, use a comma-separated string like this:

```
'user@example.com, another@example.com, Some Guy <user2@example.com>'
```

The second argument is a string containing the subject line. The third argument is the message body, which must be presented as a single string, regardless of how long it is. I'll explain how the fourth argument works later. Most people are unlikely to need the fifth argument, although some hosting companies now make it a requirement. It ensures that the email is sent by a trusted user, and it normally consists of -f followed (without a space) by your own email address, all enclosed in quotes. Check your hosting company's instructions to see whether this is required and the exact format it should take.

It's important to understand that `mail()` isn't an email program. It passes the address, subject line, message, and any additional email headers to the web server's mail transport agent (MTA). PHP's responsibility ends there. It has no way of knowing if the email is delivered to its intended destination.

> *Email doesn't always arrive when testing* `mail()` *in a local testing environment. Normally, this has nothing to do with your configuration, but with your service provider's security policies. If email fails to arrive, upload the script to your remote server and test it there.*

Removing unwanted backslashes from form input

As explained in "Unraveling the magic quotes tangle" in Chapter 3, many PHP servers automatically insert backslashes in front of quotes when a form is submitted. You need to remove these backslashes.

PHP Solution 5-1: Eliminating magic quotes

Continue working with the file from the previous exercise. Alternatively, use contact02.php from the download files for this chapter. Copy it to your working site and rename it contact.php.

1. Load contact.php into a browser. Enter some text. It doesn't matter what it is, as long as it contains an apostrophe or some double quotes. Click Send message.

2. Check the contents of the $_POST array at the bottom of the screen. If magic quotes are on, you will see something like Figure 5-3. A backslash has been inserted in front of all single and double quotes (apostrophes are treated the same as single quotes). If magic quotes are off, you will see no change from your original text.

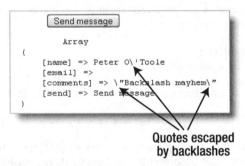

**Quotes escaped
by backslashes**

Figure 5-3. PHP magic quotes automatically insert a backslash in front of quotes when a form is submitted.

3. It's the setting on your remote server that matters, not what you see locally. Refer to Chapter 3 for instructions on how to check whether your remote server uses magic quotes. If it doesn't, make sure they are turned off in your local testing setup, and move on to PHP Solution 5-2. If in doubt, continue with the remaining steps. You can safely use the nukeMagicQuotes() function even if magic quotes have been disabled.

4. If your remote server uses magic quotes, copy includes/corefuncs.php from the download files for this chapter to the includes folder in your working site, and add the following code shown in bold to the end of the code block at the top of contact.php:

```php
<?php
include('includes/title.inc.php');
include('includes/corefuncs.php');
```

```
if (function_exists('nukeMagicQuotes')) {
  nukeMagicQuotes();
  }
?>
```

The file corefuncs.php contains the function nukeMagicQuotes(). To prevent errors if corefuncs.php can't be accessed, the call to nukeMagicQuotes() is wrapped in a conditional statement using function_exists() as described in the last chapter.

5. Save contact.php and click the Reload button in your browser. Confirm that you want to resend the post data. The $_POST array should now be clear of backslashes, as shown in Figure 5-4. You can check your code with contact03.php.

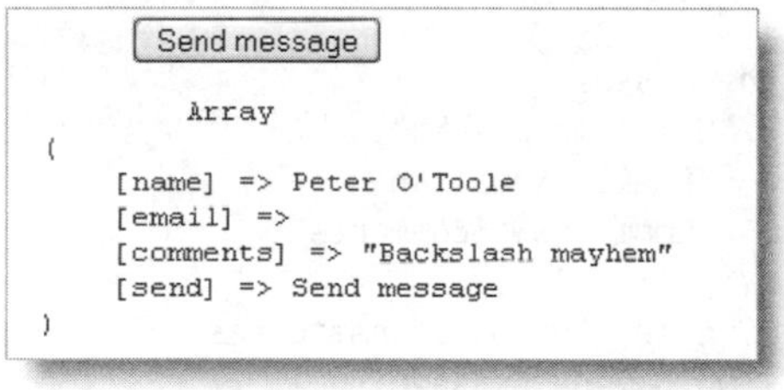

```
      Send message
            Array
      (
          [name] => Peter O'Toole
          [email] =>
          [comments] => "Backslash mayhem"
          [send] => Send message
      )
```

Figure 5-4. The nukeMagicQuotes() function cleans up the $_POST array ready for use in an email.

Processing and acknowledging the message

You can now build the message body with the contents of the $_POST array and email it to your inbox. You also need some way of informing the user that the message has been sent or if there is a problem. Rather than redirect the user to a different page, the following PHP Solution displays the result on the same page. I've adopted this approach because an improved version later in the chapter redisplays the user's input if any required fields are missing. Once the final version of the form is complete, you can redirect the user to a separate acknowledgment page by adding only two lines of code.

PHP Solution 5-2: Sending email from the feedback form

Continue using the same files. Alternatively, use contact03.php from the download files.

1. Now that you have finished testing the $_POST array, delete the following three lines of code that were used to display its contents (they're just after the closing </form> tag):

```
<pre>
<?php if ($_POST) {print_r($_POST);} ?>
</pre>
```

2. Add the code to process and send the email. It goes immediately before the closing PHP tag of the code block above the DOCTYPE declaration. (If your remote server uses magic quotes, this means immediately after the code you entered in step 3 of PHP Solution 5-1.) The new code looks like this:

```php
// process the email
if (array_key_exists('send', $_POST)) {
  $to = 'me@example.com'; // use your own email address
  $subject = 'Feedback from Japan Journey site';

  // process the $_POST variables
  $name = $_POST['name'];
  $email = $_POST['email'];
  $comments = $_POST['comments'];

  // build the message
  $message = "Name: $name\n\n";
  $message .= "Email: $email\n\n";
  $message .= "Comments: $comments";

  // limit line length to 70 characters
  $message = wordwrap($message, 70);

  // send it
  $mailSent = mail($to, $subject, $message);
}
```

This entire section of code is wrapped in an if statement, which uses the function array_key_exists(). If you refer to Figures 5-3 and 5-4, you'll see that the last element in the $_POST array looks like this:

[send] => Send message

This is the name attribute of the form's submit button and the label shown on the button. You don't normally need either of these as part of the email message, but passing the name of the submit button and $_POST to array_key_exists() is a foolproof way of checking that a form has been submitted. When the page first loads, there's no way that the submit button can have been clicked, so its name isn't present in the $_POST array. As a result, array_key_exists('send', $_POST) equates to false, and everything inside the if statement is ignored. However, as soon as the button is clicked, the page reloads, array_key_exists('send', $_POST) equates to true, and the email script is processed.

The code that does the processing consists of five stages. The first two lines assign your email address to $to and the subject line of the email to $subject.

The next section labeled "process the $_POST variables" reassigns $_POST['name'], $_POST['email'], and $_POST['comments'] to ordinary variables. This makes them easier to handle when you subject them to security checks or style the email later.

Next, you build the body of the email message, which must consist of a single string. By using double quotes, you can embed the variables in the string and use \n to insert new line characters (see Table 3-4 in Chapter 3). Once the message body is complete, it's passed to the `wordwrap()` function, which takes two arguments: a string and an integer that sets the maximum length of each line. Although most mail systems will accept longer lines, it's recommended to limit each line to 70 characters.

After the message has been built and formatted, the recipient's address, the subject line, and the body of the message are passed to the `mail()` function. The function returns a Boolean value indicating whether it succeeded in passing the email to the MTA. So, it's useful to capture that value as $mailSent. You can then use $mailSent to redirect the user to another page or change the contents of the current one.

3. For the time being, let's keep everything in the same page, because the rest of the chapter will add further refinements to the basic script. Scroll down and insert the following code just after the page's main heading (new code is highlighted in bold):

```
<h1>Contact us</h1>
<?php
if ($_POST && !$mailSent) {
?>
  <p class="warning">Sorry, there was a problem sending your message.
Please try later.</p>
<?php
  }
elseif ($_POST && $mailSent) {
?>
  <p><strong>Your message has been sent. Thank you for your feedback.
</strong></p>
<?php } ?>
<p>Ut enim ad minim veniam . . .</p>
```

This is a straightforward `if... elseif` conditional statement, but it may look odd if you're not used to seeing scripts that mix XHTML with PHP logic. What's happening can be summarized like this:

```
<h1>Contact us</h1>
<?php
if ($_POST && !$mailSent) {
  // display a failure message
  }
elseif ($_POST && $mailSent) {
  // display an acknowledgment
  }
?>
<p>Ut enim ad minim veniam . . .</p>
```

> As noted before, many developers mistakenly think that you need to use echo or print to display XHTML inside a PHP block. It's more efficient to switch back to XHTML, except for very short pieces of code. Doing so avoids the need to worry about escaping quotes. Just make sure that you balance your opening and closing braces correctly.

Both parts of the conditional statement check the Boolean values of $_POST and $mailSent. Although the $_POST array is always set, it doesn't contain any values unless the form has been submitted. Since PHP treats an empty array as false (see "The truth according to PHP" in Chapter 3), you can use $_POST on its own to test whether a form has been submitted. So the code in both parts of this conditional statement is ignored when the page first loads.

If the form has been submitted, $_POST equates to true, so the next condition is tested. The exclamation mark in front of $mailSent is the negative operator, making it the equivalent of *not* $mailSent. So, if the email hasn't been sent, both parts of the test are true, and the XHTML containing the error message is displayed. However, if $mailSent is true, the XHTML containing the acknowledgment is displayed instead.

4. Save contact.php and load it into a browser. Type something into each text field, and click Send message. If everything went well, you should see the following message:

Contact us

Your message has been sent. Thank you for your feedback.

Ut enim ad minim veniam, quis nostrud exercitation consectetur adipisicing elit. Velit esse cillum dolore ullamco laboris nisi in reprehenderit in voluptate. Mollit anim id est laborum. Sunt in culpa duis aute irure dolor excepteur sint occaecat.

Not long afterward, you should receive the content of your message as an email. If the email fails to arrive, test contact.php on your remote server. Sometimes email sent from a local test environment is rejected by ISPs, particularly if the SMTP server requires a username and password each time you connect. If that happens, conduct all further tests that involve sending mail on your remote server.

5. The acknowledgment shown in the preceding screenshot is controlled by the if... elseif conditional statement that you entered in step 3. To prove this, use the site menu to go to another page, and return to contact.php. (If you're not using the full site, click inside the browser address bar and press Enter/Return. If you use the browser's Reload button, select the option *not* to resend the post data.) The acknowledgment should disappear. Your page is becoming truly interactive.

6. The way to test the failure message is to disable the mail() function temporarily. Comment out the mail() function and hard-code a false value for $mailSent like this:

```
// send it
$mailSent = false; // mail($to, $subject, $message);
```

7. Save contact.php and try to send another message. This time you should see the failure message as shown in the following screenshot.

> **Contact us**
>
> Sorry, there was a problem sending your message. Please try later.
>
> Ut enim ad minim veniam, quis nostrud exercitation consectetur adipisicing elit. Velit esse cillum dolore ullamco laboris nisi in reprehenderit in voluptate. Mollit anim id est laborum. Sunt in culpa duis aute irure dolor excepteur sint occaecat.

8. Again, navigate to a different page and return. The failure message disappears when you come back. Revert the code in step 6 to its original state, so that you can send email again. You can check your code against contact04.php in the download files.

The form contains only 3 input fields, but even if it had 30, the process is the same: extract the contents of each field from the $_POST array, and combine them into a single string. Once you've built the message, simply pass the recipient's address, subject, and message to the mail() function.

Although this is a good start, the feedback form needs a lot of improvement. There's nothing to stop users from sending a blank email. You also need to check the validity of input to make sure that your site isn't exploited by a spam relay. The rest of the chapter shows you how to make these improvements, plus how to use other form elements: drop-down menus, radio buttons, and check boxes.

Validating user input

Most visual editors, like Dreamweaver or GoLive, have features that check whether required fields have been filled in. Dreamweaver performs the checks when the submit button is clicked; GoLive does it when the focus moves to another field. Both rely on JavaScript and perform the checks on the user's computer before the form is submitted to the server. This is called **client-side validation**. It's useful because it's almost instantaneous and can alert the user to a problem without making an unnecessary round-trip to the server. However, you should never rely on client-side validation alone because it's too easy to sidestep. All a malicious user has to do is turn off JavaScript in the browser, and your checks are rendered useless. So it's important to check user input on the server side with PHP, too.

> *Just because client-side validation with JavaScript can be sidestepped doesn't mean it's not worthwhile doing, as it saves time and bandwidth. However, it's probably not worth performing very detailed checks. Just verifying that each required field has a value may be all you need.*

Making sure required fields aren't blank

When required fields are left blank, you don't get the information you need, and the user may never get a reply, particularly if contact details have been omitted.

PHP Solution 5-3: Checking required fields

Continue using the same files. Alternatively, use contact04.php from the download files. The completed code for this section is in contact05.php.

1. Start by creating two arrays: one listing the name attribute of each field in the form and the other listing all *required* fields. Also, initialize an empty array to store the names of required fields that have not been completed. For the sake of this demonstration, make the email field optional, so that only the name and comments fields are required. Add the following code just before the section that processes the $_POST variables:

```
$subject = 'Feedback from Japan Journey site';

// list expected fields
$expected = array('name', 'email', 'comments');
// set required fields
$required = array('name', 'comments');
// create empty array for any missing fields
$missing = array();

// process the $_POST variables
```

2. In PHP Solution 5-2, the $_POST variables were assigned manually to variables that use the same name as the $_POST array key. For example, $_POST['email'] became $email. With three fields, manual assignment is fine, but it becomes a major chore if you have a dozen or more fields. Let's kill two birds with one stone by checking the required fields and automating the naming of the variables at the same time. Replace the three lines of code beneath the $_POST variables comment as follows:

```
// process the $_POST variables
foreach ($_POST as $key => $value) {
  // assign to temporary variable and strip whitespace if not an array
  $temp = is_array($value) ? $value : trim($value);
  // if empty and required, add to $missing array
  if (empty($temp) && in_array($key, $required)) {
    array_push($missing, $key);
    }
  // otherwise, assign to a variable of the same name as $key
  elseif (in_array($key, $expected)) {
    ${$key} = $temp;
    }
}

// build the message
```

If studying PHP code makes your brain hurt, you don't need to worry about how this works. As long as you create the $expected, $required, and $missing arrays in the previous step, you can just copy and paste the code for use in any form. So what does it do? In simple terms, this foreach loop goes through the $_POST array, strips out any whitespace from user input, and assigns its contents to a variable with the same name (so $_POST['email'] becomes $email, and so on). If a required field is left blank, its name attribute is added to the $missing array.

> *Why is the $expected array necessary? It's to prevent an attacker from injecting other variables in the $_POST array in an attempt to overwrite your default values. By processing only those variables that you expect, your form is much more secure. Any spurious values are ignored.*

3. You want to build the body of the email message and send it only if all required fields have been filled in. Since $missing starts off as an empty array, nothing is added to it if all required fields are completed, so empty($missing) is true. Wrap the rest of the script in the opening PHP code block like this:

```
// go ahead only if all required fields OK
if (empty($missing)) {

  // build the message
  $message = "Name: $name\n\n";
  $message .= "Email: $email\n\n";
  $message .= "Comments: $comments";

  // limit line length to 70 characters
  $message = wordwrap($message, 70);

  // send it
  $mailSent = mail($to, $subject, $message);
  if ($mailSent) {
    // $missing is no longer needed if the email is sent, so unset it
    unset($missing);
    }
  }
}
```

This ensures that the mail is sent only if nothing has been added to $missing. However, $missing will be used to control the display in the main body of the page, so you need to get rid of it if the mail is successfully sent. This is done by using unset(), which destroys a variable and any value it contains.

4. Let's turn now to the main body of the page. You need to display a warning if anything is missing. Amend the conditional statement at the top of the page content like this:

```
<h1>Contact us</h1>
<?php
if ($_POST && isset($missing)) {
?>
  <p class="warning">Please complete the missing item(s) indicated.</p>
<?php
  }
elseif ($_POST && !$mailSent) {
?>
  <p class="warning">Sorry, there was a problem sending your message.
Please try later.</p>
<?php
  }
elseif ($_POST && $mailSent) {
?>
  <p><strong>Your message has been sent. Thank you for your feedback.
</strong></p>
<?php } ?>
<p>Ut enim ad minim veniam . . . </p>
```

This simply adds a new condition to the block. It's important to note that I've placed it as the first condition. The $mailSent variable won't even be set if any required fields have been omitted, so you must test for $missing first. The second and third conditions are impossible if isset($missing) equates to true.

5. To make sure it works so far, save contact.php and load it in a browser. Click Send message without filling in any of the fields. You should see the message about missing items that you added in the previous step.

6. To display a suitable message alongside each missing required field, add a PHP code block to display a warning as a <span> inside the <label> tag like this:

```
<label for="name">Name: <?php
if (isset($missing) && in_array('name', $missing)) { ?>
<span class="warning">Please enter your name</span><?php } ?>
</label>
```

Since the $missing array is created only after the form has been submitted, you need to check first with isset() that it exists. If it doesn't exist—such as when the page first loads or if the email has been sent successfully—the <span> is never displayed. If $missing does exist, the second condition checks if the $missing array contains the value name. If it does, the <span> is displayed as shown in Figure 5-5.

7. Insert a similar warning for the comments field like this:

```
<label for="comments">Comments: <?php
if (isset($missing) && in_array('comments', $missing)) { ?>
<span class="warning">Please enter your comments</span><?php } ?>
</label>
```

The PHP code is the same except for the value you are looking for in the $missing array. It's the same as the name attribute for the form element.

8. Save contact.php and test the page again, first by entering nothing into any of the fields. The page should look like Figure 5-5.

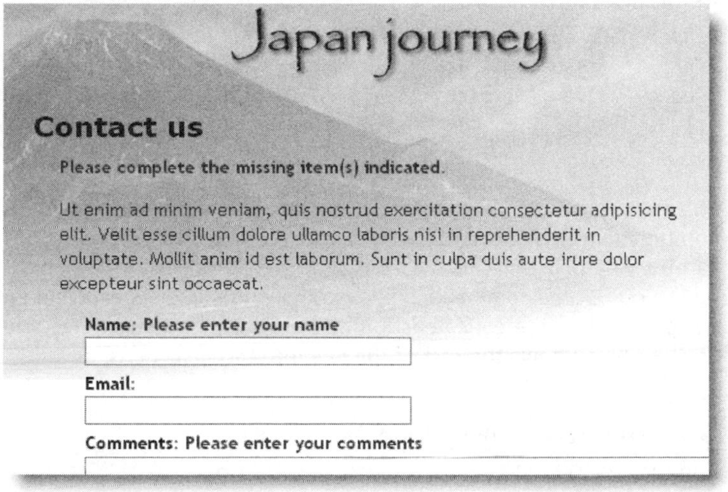

Figure 5-5. By validating user input, you can prevent the email from being sent and display suitable warnings.

Then try sending a message with all fields filled in. The page should work as before, and you should receive an email in your inbox. If you have any problems, compare your code with contact05.php.

All you need to do to change the required fields is change the names in the $required array and add a suitable alert inside the <label> tag of the appropriate input element inside the form. It's easy to do, because you always use the name attribute of the form input element. Try making the email field required, too. You can see the solution in contact06.php in the download files.

Preserving user input when a form is incomplete

Imagine you have just spent ten minutes filling in a form. You click the submit button, and back comes the response that a required field is missing. It's infuriating if you have to fill in every field all over again. Since the content of each field is in the $_POST array, it's easy to redisplay it when an error occurs.

Continue working with the same file. Alternatively, use contact06.php from the download files.

1. When the page first loads, or the email is successfully sent, you don't want anything to appear in the input fields. But you do want to redisplay the content if a required field is missing. So that's the key: if the $missing variable exists, you want the content of each field to be redisplayed. You can set default text for a text input field by setting the value attribute of the <input> tag, so amend the <input> tag for name like this:

```
<input name="name" id="name" type="text" class="formbox"
<?php if (isset($missing)) {
  echo 'value="'.htmlentities($_POST['name']).'"';
  } ?>
/>
```

This PHP code block is quite short, but the line inside the curly braces contains a combination of quotes and periods that are likely to catch you out if you're not careful. The first thing to realize is that there's only one semicolon—right at the end—so the echo command applies to the whole line. As explained in Chapter 3, a period is called the concatenation operator, which joins strings and variables. So you can break down the rest of the line into three sections, as follows:

- `'value="'.`
- `htmlentities($_POST['name'])`
- `.'"'`

The first section outputs value=" as text and uses the concatenation operator to join it to the next section, which passes $_POST['name'] to a function called htmlentities(). I'll explain what the function does in a moment, but the third section uses the concatenation operator again to join the next section, which consists solely of a double quote. So, if $missing has been set, and $_POST['name'] contains Joe, you'll end up with this inside the <input> tag:

```
<input name="name" id="name" type="text" class="formbox" value="Joe" />
```

This is the type of situation where you need to keep careful track of double and single quotes. The double quotes are part of the string value="", so each part of the string needs to be enclosed in single quotes. Because the closing double quote stands on its own in the script, it's easy to forget, but it will play havoc with the form when displayed in a browser.

So, what's the htmlentities() function for? Again, it's all to do with handling quotes and apostrophes. As the function name suggests, it converts certain characters to their equivalent HTML entity. The one you're concerned with here is the double quote. Let's say Elvis really is still alive and decides to send feedback through the form. If you use $_POST['name'] on its own, Figure 5-6 shows what happens when a required field is omitted and you don't use htmlentities().

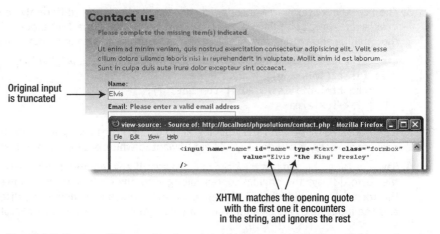

Original input
is truncated

XHTML matches the opening quote
with the first one it encounters
in the string, and ignores the rest

Figure 5-6. Quotes within user input need special treatment before form fields can be
redisplayed.

Passing the content of the $_POST array element to the htmlentities(), however,
converts the double quotes in the middle of the string to ". And, as Figure 5-7
shows, the content is no longer truncated. What's cool about this is that the HTML
entity " is converted back to double quotes when the form is resubmitted. As
a result, there's no need for any further conversion before the email can be sent.

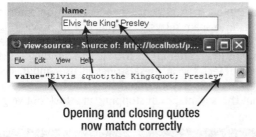

Opening and closing quotes
now match correctly

Figure 5-7. The problem is solved by passing the value to htmlentities() before it's
displayed.

> *By default,* htmlentities() *leaves single quotes untouched. Since I chose to
> wrap the* value *attribute in double quotes, this doesn't matter. To convert single
> quotes to an HTML entity as well, pass* ENT_QUOTES *(all uppercase) as a second
> argument to* htmlentities() *like this:*
>
> htmlentities($_POST['name'], ENT_QUOTES)

2. Amend the email input field in the same way, using $_POST['email'] instead of
$_POST['name'].

3. The comments text area needs to be handled slightly differently because <textarea> tags don't have a value attribute. You place the PHP block between the opening and closing tags of the text area like this (new code is shown in bold):

```
<textarea name="comments" id="comments" cols="60" rows="8"><?php
  if (isset($missing)) {
    echo htmlentities($_POST['comments']);
  } ?></textarea>
```

It's important to position the opening and closing PHP tags right up against the <textarea> tags. If you don't, you'll get unwanted whitespace inside the text area.

4. Save contact.php and test the page in a browser. If any required fields are omitted, the form displays the original content along with any error messages. However, if the form is correctly filled in, the email is sent, an acknowledgment is displayed, and the input fields are cleared. You can check your code with contact07.php.

> Using this technique prevents a form reset button from clearing any fields that have been changed by the PHP script. This is a minor inconvenience in comparison with the greater usability offered by preserving existing content when an incomplete form is submitted.

Filtering out potential attacks

A particularly nasty exploit known as email header injection emerged in mid-2005. It seeks to turn online forms into spam relays. A simple way of preventing this is to look for the strings "Content-Type:", "Cc:", and "Bcc:", as these are email headers that the attacker injects into your script in an attempt to trick it into sending HTML email with copies to many people. If you detect any of these strings in user input, it's a pretty safe bet that you're the target of an attack, so you should block the message. An innocent message may also be blocked, but the advantages of stopping an attack outweigh that small risk.

PHP Solution 5-5: Blocking emails that contain specific phrases

Continue working with the same page. Alternatively, use contact07.php from the download files.

1. As you know, PHP conditional statements rely on a true/false test to determine whether to execute a section of code. So the way to filter out suspect phrases is to create a Boolean variable that is switched to true as soon as one of those phrases is detected. The detection is done using a search pattern or **regular expression**. Insert the code for both of these just above the section that processes the $_POST variables:

```
// create empty array for any missing fields
$missing = array();
```

```
    // assume that there is nothing suspect
    $suspect = false;
    // create a pattern to locate suspect phrases
    $pattern = '/Content-Type:|Bcc:|Cc:/i';

    // process the $_POST variables
```

The string assigned to $pattern will be used to perform a case-insensitive search for any of the following: "Content-Type:", "Bcc:", or "Cc:". It's written in a format called Perl-compatible regular expression (PCRE). The search pattern is enclosed in a pair of forward slashes, and the i after the final slash makes the pattern case-insensitive.

> This is a very simple example, but regular expressions (regex) are a complex subject that can reduce grown men to tears. Fortunately, you can find a lot of tried and tested regular expressions that you can simply drop into your own scripts. Two good places to look are http://regexlib.com and *Regular Expression Recipes: A Problem–Solution Approach* by Nathan A. Good (Apress, ISBN: 1-59059-441-X).
>
> In addition to PCRE, you will probably also come across Portable Operating System Interface (POSIX) regular expressions. They tend to be easier to read, but they are slower and less powerful than PCRE. The easy way to tell whether a PHP script uses PCRE or POSIX is to look at the function used with the regex. All PCRE functions begin with preg_, while POSIX functions begin with ereg. To prevent your scripts from breaking in future, always use PCRE regular expressions, because there are plans to drop the ereg functions from the default configuration of PHP 6.

2. You can now use the PCRE stored in $pattern to filter out any suspect user input from the $_POST array. At the moment, each element of the $_POST array contains only a string. However, multiple-choice form elements, such as check boxes, return an array of results. So you need to tunnel down any subarrays and check the content of each element separately. That's precisely what the following custom-built function isSuspect() does. Insert it immediately after the $pattern variable from step 1.

```
// create a pattern to locate suspect phrases
$pattern = '/Content-Type:|Bcc:|Cc:/i';

// function to check for suspect phrases
function isSuspect($val, $pattern, &$suspect) {
  // if the variable is an array, loop through each element
  // and pass it recursively back to the same function
  if (is_array($val)) {
    foreach ($val as $item) {
      isSuspect($item, $pattern, $suspect);
      }
    }
```

```
    else {
      // if one of the suspect phrases is found, set Boolean to true
      if (preg_match($pattern, $val)) {
        $suspect = true;
        }
      }
    }
```

The isSuspect() function is another piece of code that you may want to just copy and paste without delving too deeply into how it works. The important thing to notice is that the third argument has an ampersand (&) in front of it (&$suspect). This means that any changes made to the variable passed as the third argument to isSuspect() will affect the value of that variable elsewhere in the script. The other feature of this function is that it's what's known as a **recursive function**. It keeps on calling itself until it finds a value that it can compare against the regex.

3. Don't worry if that last paragraph makes your brain hurt. Calling the function is very easy. You just pass it three values: the $_POST array, the pattern, and the $suspect Boolean variable. Insert the following code immediately after the code in the previous step:

```
// check the $_POST array and any subarrays for suspect content
isSuspect($_POST, $pattern, $suspect);
```

> Note that you don't put an ampersand in front of $suspect *this time. The amper-sand is required only when you define the function in step 2, not when you call it.*

4. If any suspect phrases are detected, the value of $suspect changes to true, so you need to set $mailSent to false and delete the $missing array to prevent the email from being sent, and to display an appropriate message in the form. There's also no point in processing the $_POST array any further. Wrap the code that processes the $_POST variables in the second half of an if... else statement like this:

```
if ($suspect) {
  $mailSent = false;
  unset($missing);
  }
else {
  // process the $_POST variables
  foreach ($_POST as $key => $value) {
    // assign to temporary variable and strip whitespace if not an array
    $temp = is_array($value) ? $value : trim($value);
    // if empty and required, add to $missing array
    if (empty($temp) && in_array($key, $required)) {
      array_push($missing, $key);
      }
    // otherwise, assign to a variable of the same name as $key
    elseif (in_array($key, $expected)) {
      ${$key} = $temp;
```

```
      }
    }
  }
```

Don't forget the extra curly brace to close the `else` statement.

5. Just one final change is required to the section of code that builds and sends the email. If suspect content is detected, you don't want that code to run, so amend the condition in the opening `if` statement like this:

```
// go ahead only if not suspect and all required fields OK
if (!$suspect && empty($missing)) {
  // build the message
```

6. Save contact.php, and test the form. It should send normal messages, but block any message that contains any of the suspect phrases. Because the `if` statement in step 4 sets $mailSent to false and unsets $missing, the code in the main body of the page displays the same message that's displayed if there's a genuine problem with the server. A neutral, nonprovocative message reveals nothing that might assist an attacker. It also avoids offending anyone who may have innocently used a suspect phrase. You can check your code against contact08.php in the download files.

Safely including the user's address in email headers

Up to now, I've avoided using one of the most useful features of the PHP mail() function: the ability to add extra email headers with the optional fourth argument. A popular use of extra headers is to incorporate the user's email address into a Reply-To header, which enables you to reply directly to incoming messages by clicking the Reply button in your email program. It's convenient, but it provides a wide open door for an attacker to supply a spurious set of headers. With PHP Solution 5-5 in place, you can block attacks, but safely pass filtered email addresses to the mail() function.

You can find a full list of email headers at www.faqs.org/rfcs/rfc2076, but some of the most well-known and useful ones enable you to send copies of an email to other addresses (Cc and Bcc), or to change the encoding (often essential for languages other than Western European ones). Each new header, except the final one, must be on a separate line terminated by a carriage return and new line character. This means using the \r and \n escape sequences in double-quoted strings.

Let's say you want to send copies of messages to other departments, plus a copy to another address that you don't want the others to see. Email sent by mail() is often identified as coming from nobody@yourdomain (or whatever username is assigned to the web server), so it's also a good idea to add a more user-friendly "From" address. This is how you build those additional email headers and pass them to mail():

```
$additionalHeaders = "From: Japan Journey<feedback@example.com>\r\n";
$additionalHeaders .= "Cc: sales@example.com, finance@example.com\r\n";
$additionalHeaders .= 'Bcc: secretplanning@example.com';

$mailSent = mail($to, $subject, $message, $additionalHeaders);
```

If you want to send the email in an encoding other than iso-8859-1 (English and Western European), you need to set the Content-Type header. For Unicode (UTF-8), set it like this:

```
$additionalHeaders = "Content-Type: text/plain; charset=utf-8\r\n";
```

The web page that the form is embedded in must use the same encoding (usually set in a <meta> tag).

Hard-coded additional headers like this present no security risk, but anything that comes from user input must be filtered before it's used. So, let's take a look at incorporating the user's email address into a Reply-To header. Although PHP Solution 5-5 should sanitize any user input, it's worth subjecting the email field to a more rigorous check.

PHP Solution 5-6: Automating the reply address

Continue working with the same page. Alternatively, use contact08.php from the download files.

1. Although I suggested at the end of PHP Solution 5-3 that you add the email field to the $required array, there may be occasions when you don't want to make it required. So, it makes more sense to keep the code to validate the email address separate from the main loop that processes the $_POST array.

   - If email is required, but has been left blank, the loop will have already added email to the $missing array, so the message won't get sent anyway.

   - If it's not a required field, you need to check $email only if it contains something. So you need to wrap the validation code in an if statement that uses !empty(). An exclamation mark is the negative operator, so you read this as "not empty."

   Insert the code shown in bold immediately after the loop that processes the $_POST array. It contains a complex line, so you may prefer to copy it from contact09.php.

   ```
       // otherwise, assign to a variable of the same name as $key
       elseif (in_array($key, $expected)) {
         ${$key} = $temp;
         }
       }
     }

   // validate the email address
   if (!empty($email)) {
     // regex to ensure no illegal characters in email address
     $checkEmail = '/^[^@]+@[^\s\r\n\'";,@%]+$/';
     // reject the email address if it doesn't match
     if (!preg_match($checkEmail, $email)) {
       array_push($missing, 'email');
       }
     }
   ```

```
// go ahead only if not suspect and all required fields OK
if (!$suspect && empty($missing)) {
```

Designing a regular expression to recognize a valid-looking email address is notoriously difficult, and many that you find in books or on the Internet reject valid email addresses. Instead of striving for perfection, $checkEmail simply checks for an @ mark surrounded by at least one character on either side.

More important, it rejects any attempt to append spurious email headers. If the contents of $email don't match the regex, email is added to the $missing array. I decided not to create a special variable to indicate a suspected attack because the user may have innocently mistyped the email address. Moreover, it keeps the logic of the code simple. If the $missing array contains any elements, the message isn't sent, which is the whole point: you've stopped the attack.

2. You now need to add the additional headers to the section of the script that sends the email. Place them immediately above the call to the mail() function like this:

```
// limit line length to 70 characters
$message = wordwrap($message, 70);

// create additional headers
$additionalHeaders = 'From: Japan Journey<feedback@example.com>';
if (!empty($email)) {
  $additionalHeaders .= "\r\nReply-To: $email";
  }

// send it
$mailSent = mail($to, $subject, $message, $additionalHeaders);
```

If you don't want email to be a required field, there's no point in using a nonexistent value in the Reply-To header, so I have wrapped it in a conditional statement. Since you have no way of telling whether the Reply-To header will be created, it makes sense to put the carriage return and new line characters at the beginning of the second header. It doesn't matter whether you put them at the end of one header or the start of the next one, as long as a carriage return and new line separates each header. For instance, if you wanted to add a Cc header, you could do it like this:

```
$additionalHeaders = "From: Japan Journey<feedback@example.com>\r\n";
$additionalHeaders .= 'Cc: admin@example.com';
if (!empty($email)) {
  $additionalHeaders .= "\r\nReply-To: $email";
  }
```

Or like this:

```
$additionalHeaders = 'From: Japan Journey<feedback@example.com>';
$additionalHeaders .= "\r\nCc: admin@example.com";
if (!empty($email)) {
  $additionalHeaders .= "\r\nReply-To: $email";
  }
```

Finally, don't forget to add $additionalHeaders as the fourth argument to mail().

5

3. Save `contact.php` and test the form. When you receive the email, click the Reply button in your email program, and you should see the address that you entered in the form automatically entered in the recipient's address field. You can check your code against `contact09.php` in the download files.

Handling multiple-choice form elements

You now have the basic knowledge to process user input from an online form and email it to your inbox, but to keep things simple, the form in `contact.php` uses only text input fields and a text area. To work successfully with forms, you also need to know how to handle multiple-choice elements, namely:

- Radio buttons
- Check boxes
- Drop-down option menus
- Multiple-choice lists

Figure 5-8 shows `contact.php` with an example of each type added to the original design. The principle behind them is exactly the same as the text input fields you have been working with: the name attribute of the form element is used as the key in the $_POST array. However, check boxes and multiple-choice lists store the selected values as an array, so you need to adapt the code slightly to capture all the values.

Let's look briefly at each type of form element. Rather than go through each step in detail, I'll just highlight the important points. The completed code for the rest of the chapter is in `contact10.php`.

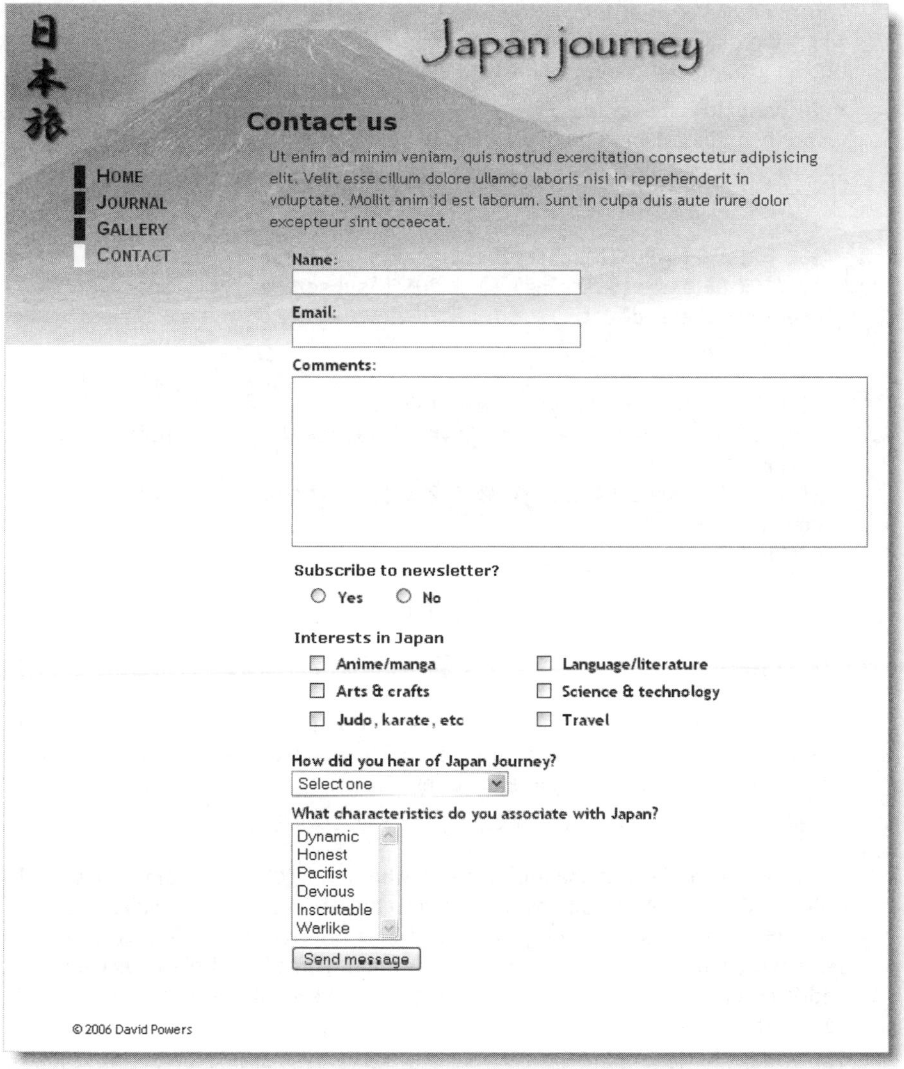

Figure 5-8. The feedback form with examples of each type of form element

PHP Solution 5-7: Getting data from radio button groups

Radio button groups allow you to pick only one value. This makes it easy to retrieve the selected one.

1. All buttons in the same group must share the same name attribute, so the $_POST array contains the value attribute of whichever radio button is selected. If no button is selected, the radio button group's $_POST array element remains unset. This is different from the behavior of text input fields, which are always included in the $_POST array, even if they contain nothing.

You need to take this into account in the code that preserves the selected value when a required field is omitted. The following listing shows the subscribe radio button group from contact.php, with all the PHP code highlighted in bold:

```
<fieldset id="subscribe">
<h2>Subscribe to newsletter?</h2>
<p>
  <input name="subscribe" type="radio" value="Yes" id="subscribe-yes"
  <?php
  $OK = isset($_POST['subscribe']) ? true : false;
  if ($OK && isset($missing) && $_POST['subscribe'] == 'Yes') { ?>
  checked="checked"
  <?php } ?>
  />
  <label for="subscribe-yes">Yes</label>
  <input name="subscribe" type="radio" value="No" id="subscribe-no"
  <?php
  if ($OK && isset($missing) && $_POST['subscribe'] == 'No') { ?>
  checked="checked"
  <?php } ?>
  />
  <label for="subscribe-no">No</label>
  </p>
</fieldset>
```

The checked attribute in both buttons is wrapped in an if statement, which checks three conditions, all of which must be true. The value of the first condition, $OK, is determined by the following line of code:

```
$OK = isset($_POST['subscribe']) ? true : false;
```

This uses the conditional operator to check whether $_POST['subscribe'] is set. The only reason for this line is to avoid having to type isset($_POST['subscribe']) in both if statements. With only two buttons in the radio group, this may hardly seem worthwhile, but I've used the same technique in all multiple-choice elements, and it certainly makes things easier when you have six items in a group, as is the case with the check boxes and multiple-choice list.

The other two conditions inside the if statements check whether $missing has been set and the value of $_POST['subscribe'].

2. When building the body of the email message, you also need to take into account that $_POST['subscribe'] may not exist. Otherwise, you could end up with unprofessional error messages onscreen. Again, using the conditional operator offers the most succinct way of doing this. The following code goes in the section that prepares the message prior to sending it:

```
// go ahead only if not suspect and all required fields OK
if (!$suspect && empty($missing)) {
  // set default values for variables that might not exist
  $subscribe = isset($subscribe) ? $subscribe : 'Nothing selected';
```

If $subscribe exists, the value is simply passed to the same variable. If it doesn't exist, it's set to the string Nothing selected. You can now safely use $subscribe within the body of the message.

PHP Solution 5-8: Getting data from check boxes

Check boxes are similar to radio button groups, except that they permit multiple selections. This affects how you name a check box group and extract the selected values.

1. The following listing shows the code for the check boxes in contact.php. To save space, just the first two check boxes are shown. The name attribute and PHP sections of code are highlighted in bold.

```
<fieldset id="interests">
<h2>Interests in Japan</h2>
<div>
  <p>
    <input type="checkbox" name="interests[]" value="Anime/manga" ➥
id="anime"
    <?php
    $OK = isset($_POST['interests']) ? true : false;
    if ($OK && isset($missing) && in_array('Anime/manga', ➥
$_POST['interests'])) { ?>
    checked="checked"
    <?php } ?>
    />
    <label for="anime">Anime/manga</label>
  </p>
  <p>
    <input type="checkbox" name="interests[]" value="Arts & crafts" ➥
id="art"
    <?php
    if ($OK && isset($missing) && in_array('Arts & crafts', ➥
$_POST['interests'])) { ?>
    checked="checked"
    <?php } ?>
    />
    <label for="art">Arts &amp; crafts</label>
  </p>
. . .
</div>
</fieldset>
```

The really important thing to note about this code is the empty pair of square brackets following the name attribute of each check box. This tells PHP to treat interests as an array. If you omit the brackets, $_POST['interests'] contains the value of only the first check box selected; all others are ignored.

The PHP code inside each check box element performs the same role as in the radio button group, wrapping the checked attribute in a conditional statement. The first two conditions are the same as for a radio button, but the third condition uses the in_array() function to check whether the value associated with that check box is in the $_POST['interests'] subarray. If it is, it means the check box was selected.

As with radio buttons, if no check box is selected, the $_POST['interests'] element is not even created. So the code for the first check box contains the following:

```
$OK = isset($_POST['interests']) ? true : false;
```

This uses the same $OK variable as the radio button group, but that's not a problem, since you've finished with $_POST['subscribe']. So it's safe to reuse $OK.

2. Because the check box array might never be created, you need to set a default value before attempting to build the body of the email. This time, rather than a string, it needs to be presented as an array like this:

```
// set default values for variables that might not exist
$subscribe = isset($subscribe) ? $subscribe : 'Nothing selected';
$interests = isset($interests) ? $interests : array('None selected');
```

3. To extract the values of the check box array, you can use a foreach loop or the implode() function. This oddly named function joins array elements. It takes two arguments: a string to be used as a separator and the array. So, implode(', ', $interests) joins the elements of $interests as a comma-separated string.

PHP Solution 5-9: Getting data from a drop-down option menu

Drop-down option menus created with the <select> tag are similar to radio button groups in that they normally allow the user to pick only one option from several. Where they differ is one item is always selected in a drop-down menu, even if it's only the first item inviting the user to select one of the others. As a result, this means that the $_POST array always contains an element referring to a menu, whereas a radio button group is ignored unless a default value is preset.

1. The following code shows the first two items from the drop-down menu in contact.php with the PHP code highlighted in bold. As with all multiple-choice elements, the PHP code wraps the attribute that indicates which item has been chosen. Although this attribute is called checked in radio buttons and check boxes, it's called selected in <select> menus and lists. It's important to use the correct attribute to redisplay the selection if the form is submitted with required items missing. When the page first loads, the $_POST array contains no elements, so you can select the first <option> by testing for !$_POST. Once the form is submitted, the $_POST array always contains an element from a drop-down menu, so you don't need to test for its existence.

```
<p>
  <label for="select">How did you hear of Japan Journey?</label>
  <select name="howhear" id="howhear">
    <option value="No reply"
    <?php
    if (!$_POST || $_POST['howhear'] == 'No reply') { ?>
    selected="selected"
    <?php } ?>
    >Select one</option>
    <option value="foED"
```

```php
<?php
if (isset($missing) && $_POST['howhear'] == 'foED') { ?>
selected="selected"
<?php } ?>
>friends of ED</option>
. . .
   </select>
</p>
```

2. Because there is always an element in the $_POST array for a drop-down menu, it doesn't require any special handling in the code that builds the body of the email.

PHP Solution 5-10: Getting data from a multiple-choice list

Multiple-choice lists are similar to check boxes: they allow the user to choose zero or more items, so the result is stored in an array. If no items are selected, the $_POST array contains no reference to the list, so you need to take that into consideration both in the form and when processing the message.

1. The following code shows the first two items from the multiple choice list in contact.php with the name attribute and PHP code highlighted in bold. Note that the name attribute needs a pair of square brackets on the end to store the results as an array. The code works in an identical way to the check boxes in PHP Solution 5-8.

```php
<p>
  <label for="select">What characteristics do you associate with ➡
Japan?</label>
  <select name="characteristics[]" size="6" multiple="multiple" ➡
id="characteristics">
    <option value="Dynamic"
    <?php
    $OK = isset($_POST['characteristics']) ? true : false;
    if ($OK && isset($missing) && in_array('Dynamic', ➡
$_POST['characteristics'])) { ?>
    selected="selected"
    <?php } ?>
    >Dynamic</option>
    <option value="Honest"
    <?php
    if ($OK && isset($missing) && in_array('Honest', ➡
$_POST['characteristics'])) { ?>
    selected="selected"
    <?php } ?>
    >Honest</option>
. . .
   </select>
</p>
```

2. In the code that processes the message, set a default value for a multiple-choice list in the same way as for an array of check boxes.

```
$interests = isset($interests) ? $interests : array('None selected');
$characteristics = isset($characteristics) ? $characteristics : ➥
array('None selected');
```

3. When building the body of the message, use a foreach loop to iterate through the subarray, or use implode() to create a comma-separated string like this:

```
$message .= 'Characteristics associated with Japan: '.implode(', ', ➥
$characteristics);
```

A complete script using all form elements is in contact10.php in the download files for this chapter.

Redirecting to another page

Throughout this chapter, everything has been kept within the same page, even if the message is sent successfully. If you prefer to redirect the visitor to a separate acknowledgment page, locate this section of code at the end of the message processing section:

```
// send it
$mailSent = mail($to, $subject, $message, $additionalHeaders);
if ($mailSent) {
   // $missing is no longer needed if the email is sent, so unset it
   unset($missing);
   }
 }
}
```

Change it like this:

```
// send it
$mailSent = mail($to, $subject, $message, $additionalHeaders);
if ($mailSent) {
   // redirect the page with a fully qualified URL
   header('Location: http://www.example.com/thanks.php');
   exit;
   }
 }
}
```

The HTTP/1.1 protocol stipulates a fully qualified URL for a redirect command, although most browsers will perform the redirect correctly with a relative pathname.

When using the header() function, you must be very careful that no output is sent to the browser before PHP attempts to call it. If, when testing your page, you see an error message warning you that headers have already been sent, check there are no new lines or other whitespace ahead of the opening PHP tag. Also check any include files for white-space and new lines before the opening PHP tag and after the closing one. The error is fre-quently triggered by a single new line after the closing tag of an include file.

Summary

What began as a slender 50 lines of XHTML and PHP at the beginning of the chapter has grown by nearly 300 lines, of which about 100 process the form content ready for sending by email. This may seem like a lot if you have a phobia about code, but the most impor-tant sections of code (in PHP Solutions 5-5 and 5-6) filter out suspect input and should never need changing. Once you have built the script above the DOCTYPE declaration, you can copy and paste it into any form or use an include file.

The only parts that need tweaking are the $expected and $required arrays and the sec-tion that builds the body of the email message. In order to concentrate on the mechanics of working with forms, I have kept the body of the message plain and simple. However, once you have extracted the form contents into variables, such as $name, $email, and so on, you can incorporate them into an email message any way you like.

I've also avoided talking about HTML email because the mail() function handles only plain text email. The PHP online manual at www.php.net/manual/en/function.mail.php shows a way of sending HTML mail by adding an additional header. However, it's not a good idea, as HTML mail should always contain an alternative text version for email programs that don't accept HTML. If you want to send HTML mail or attachments, I suggest that you use the PHPMailer class. It's open source and is available for free from http://phpmailer.sourceforge.net/. The site has a tutorial showing you how to use it.

As you'll see in later chapters, online forms lie at the heart of just about everything you do with PHP. They're the gateway between the browser and the web server. You'll come back time and again to the techniques that you have learned in this chapter.

5

What this chapter covers:

- Understanding how PHP handles file uploads
- Restricting the size and type of uploads
- Preventing files from being overwritten
- Organizing uploads into specific folders
- Handling multiple uploads

PHP's ability to handle forms isn't restricted to text. It can also be used to upload files to a server. In theory, this opens up great possibilities. For instance, you could build a real estate website where clients could upload pictures of their properties, or a site for all your friends and relatives to upload their holiday photos. However, just because you can do it, doesn't necessarily mean that you should. Allowing others to upload material to your website could expose you to all sorts of problems. You need to make sure that images are the right size, that they're of suitable quality, and that they don't contain any illegal material. You also need to ensure that uploads don't contain malicious scripts. In other words, you need to protect your website just as carefully as your own computer.

Fortunately, the way that PHP handles file uploads makes it relatively simple to restrict the type and size of files accepted. What it cannot do is check the suitability of the content. It's therefore always a good idea to implement a strategy that prevents indecent or illegal material from being automatically displayed on your site. One way is to store uploaded material in a nonpublic directory until it has been approved. Another way is to restrict uploads to registered and trusted users by placing the upload form in a password-protected area. A combination of both approaches is even more secure.

> *User registration and authentication are covered in Chapters 9 and 15. Until you know how to restrict access to pages with PHP, I recommend that you use the PHP Solutions described in this chapter only in a password-protected directory if deployed on a public website. Most hosting companies provide simple password protection through the site's control panel.*

Before you dive into the scripts, you'll next look at how PHP handles file uploads, which should make the scripts easier to understand when you come to them.

How PHP handles file uploads

The term "upload" means moving a file from one computer to another, but as far as PHP is concerned, all that's happening is that a file is being moved from one location to another. This means you can test all the scripts in this chapter on your local computer without the need to upload files to a remote server.

PHP supports file uploads by default, but hosting companies can restrict the size of uploads or disable them altogether. Before going any further, it's a good idea to check the settings on your remote server.

Checking whether your server supports uploads

All the information that you need is displayed in the main PHP configuration page that you can display by creating a PHP page with the following script and uploading it by FTP to your remote server:

```php
<?php phpinfo(); ?>
```

Load the page into a browser, and locate the section shown in the screenshot to the right.

Scroll down until you find file_uploads. If the Local Value column contains On, you're ready to go, but you should also check the other configuration settings listed in Table 6-1.

Configuration

PHP Core

Directive	Local Value	Master Value
allow_call_time_pass_reference	On	On
allow_url_fopen	On	On
always_populate_raw_post_data	Off	Off
arg_separator.input	&	&
arg_separator.output	&	&
	Off	

Table 6-1. PHP configuration settings that affect file uploads

Directive	Default value	Description
max_execution_time	30	The maximum number of seconds that a PHP script can run. If the script takes longer, PHP generates a fatal error.
max_input_time	60	The maximum number of seconds that a PHP script is allowed to parse the $_POST and $_GET arrays, and file uploads. Very large uploads are likely to run out of time.
post_max_size	8M	The maximum permitted size of all $_POST data, *including* file uploads. Although the default is 8MB, hosting companies may impose a smaller limit.
upload_tmp_dir		This is where PHP stores uploaded files until your script moves them to a permanent location. If no value is defined in php.ini, PHP uses the system default temporary directory.
upload_max_filesize	2M	The maximum permitted size of a single upload file. Although the default is 2MB, hosting companies may impose a smaller limit. A number on its own indicates the number of bytes permitted. A number followed by K indicates the number of kilobytes permitted.

6

The default limits set by PHP are quite generous, but you need to make sure that you don't exceed any limits set by your hosting company; if you do, scripts that are otherwise perfect will fail. It's important to note the limit imposed by post_max_size. Even though the default values theoretically permit the simultaneous upload of four 2MB files, the upload is likely to fail because the content of the $_POST array would bring the total to more than 8MB.

If the Local Value of file_uploads is Off, uploads have been disabled. There is nothing you can do about it, other than ask your hosting company if it offers a package with file uploading enabled. Your only alternatives are to move to a different host or to use a different solution, such as uploading files by FTP.

> *After using* phpinfo() *to check your remote server's settings, it's a good idea to remove the script or put it in a password-protected directory.*

Adding a file upload field to a form

Adding a file upload field to an XHTML form is easy. Just add enctype="multipart/form-data" to the opening <form> tag, and set the type attribute of an <input> element to file. The following code is a simple example of an upload form (it's in upload01.php in the download files for this chapter):

```
<form action="" method="post" enctype="multipart/form-data" ➥
name="uploadImage" id="uploadImage">
  <p>
    <label for="image">Upload image:</label>
    <input type="file" name="image" id="image" />
  </p>
  <p>
    <input type="submit" name="upload" id="upload" value="Upload" />
  </p>
</form>
```

In most browsers, this code inserts a text input field with a Browse button alongside, as shown in Figure 6-1. However, as the figure shows, not only does Safari label the button differently, but also it doesn't permit direct input of the filename; users are obliged to click Choose File to navigate to the local file. This doesn't affect the operation of an upload form, but you need to take it into consideration when designing the layout.

Most browsers give users a choice of typing in the filename directly or using the Browse button to find it

Safari doesn't allow direct filename input

Figure 6-1. Browsers automatically add a button to enable users to select a file ready for uploading.

Understanding the $_FILES array

What confuses many people is that their file seems to vanish after it has been uploaded. This is because you can't refer to an uploaded file in the $_POST array in the same way as with text input. PHP transmits the details of uploaded files in a separate superglobal array called, not unreasonably, $_FILES. Moreover, files are uploaded to a temporary folder and are deleted unless you explicitly move them to the desired location. Although this sounds like a nuisance, it's done for a very good reason: you can subject the file to security checks before accepting the upload.

The best way to understand how the $_FILES array works is to see it in action. If you have installed a local test environment, you can test everything on your computer. It works in exactly the same way as uploading a file to a remote server.

Inspecting the $_FILES array

1. Create a new folder called uploads in the phpsolutions site root. Create a new PHP file called upload.php in the uploads folder, and insert the code from the previous section. Alternatively, copy upload01.php from the download files for this chapter, and rename the file upload.php.

2. Insert the following code right after the closing </form> tag (it's also in upload02.php):

```
</form>
<pre>
<?php
if (array_key_exists('upload', $_POST)) {
  print_r($_FILES);
  }
?>
</pre>
</body>
```

This uses the array_key_exists() function that you met in the previous chapter. It checks whether the $_POST array contains upload, the name attribute of the submit button. If it does, you know the form has been submitted, so you can use print_r() to inspect the $_FILES array. The <pre> tags make the output easier to read.

3. Save upload.php and load it into a browser. It should look like Figure 6-1.

4. Click the Browse (or Choose File) button, and select a file on your hard disk. Click Open (or Choose on a Mac) to close the file selection dialog box, and then click Upload. On Windows, you should see something similar to Figure 6-2 on the next page. A Mac should display the same information, although the value of tmp_name will probably be something like /var/tmp/phpAVSylw.

6

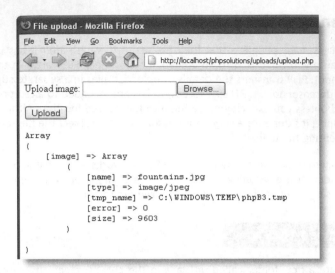

Figure 6-2. The $_FILES array contains five important pieces of information about an uploaded file.

You can see that the $_FILES array is actually a multidimensional array. The key (or name) of the top-level array comes from the name attribute of the file input field—in this case, image. The image subarray consists of five elements, namely

- name: The original name of the uploaded file
- type: The uploaded file's MIME type
- tmp_name: The location of the uploaded file
- error: An integer indicating any problems with the upload (see Table 6-2)
- size: The size of the uploaded file in bytes

5. On Windows, open Explorer, and navigate to C:\WINDOWS\TEMP or the location indicated in tmp_name.

On a Mac, open Terminal (it's in Applications:Utilities), and type the following commands, both followed by pressing Return:

```
cd /var/tmp
ls -l
```

Don't waste time searching for the temporary file: it won't be there. It really is temporary. If you don't do anything with it immediately after uploading, PHP discards it. It's a highly efficient way of doing things, because it means your server doesn't get clogged up with files that are no longer needed. I'll explain shortly how to handle a file upload, but first let's continue our exploration of the $_FILES array.

6. Click Upload again without selecting a file to upload. The contents of the $_FILES array should now look like this:

```
Array
(
    [image] => Array
        (
            [name] =>
            [type] =>
            [tmp_name] =>
            [error] => 4
            [size] => 0
        )
)
```

So, even if no file is uploaded, you know that the $_FILES array still exists, but that each element of the image subarray, except for error and size, is empty. An error level of 0, as seen in Figure 6-2, indicates a successful upload; 4 indicates that the form was submitted with no file selected. Table 6-2 lists all the error levels.

7. As one final experiment with the $_FILES array, click the Browse or Choose File button, and navigate to a program file. Click the Upload button. On a Mac, you will probably get an error message, but on Windows, the form will happily attempt to upload the program and display the type as application/x-msdownload. This is a warning that it's important to check the MIME type before allowing the upload process to be completed.

Table 6-2. Meaning of the different error levels in the $_FILES array

Error level	Meaning
0	Upload successful
1	File exceeds maximum upload size specified in php.ini (default 2MB)
2	File exceeds size specified by MAX_FILE_SIZE embedded in the form (see PHP Solution 6-3)
3	File only partially uploaded
4	Form submitted with no file specified
5	Currently not defined
6	No temporary folder (PHP 4.3.10 and 5.0.3 and above)
7	Cannot write file to disk (PHP 5.1.0 and above)

6

Establishing an upload directory

Another frequent source of confusion is the question of file ownership and how PHP runs on a web server. If you're testing in Windows, an upload script that has been working perfectly may confront you with a message like this when you transfer it to your remote server:

```
Warning:  move_uploaded_file(/home/user/htdocs/testarea/kinkakuji.jpg)
[function.move-uploaded-file]: failed to open stream: Permission
denied in /home/user/htdocs/testarea/upload_test.php on line 3
```

Most people react with total bemusement to this message. Why is permission denied? It's my own website, after all. The answer is that most hosting companies use Linux servers, which impose strict rules about the ownership of files and directories. Uploading a file creates a new version of the file on the server, so the user needs all three privileges—read, write, and execute. However, in most cases, PHP doesn't run in *your* name, but as the web server—usually nobody or apache. Unless your hosting company has configured PHP to run in your own name, you need to give global access (chmod 777) to every directory to which you want to be able to upload files.

Since 777 is the least secure setting, you need to adopt a cautious approach to file uploads. Begin by testing upload scripts with a setting of 700. If that doesn't work, try 770, and use 777 only as a last resort. Your upload directory doesn't need to be within your site root; it can be anywhere on the server. If your hosting company gives you a private directory outside the site root, the most secure solution is to create a subdirectory for uploads inside the private one. Alternatively, create a directory inside your site root, but don't link to it from any web pages. Give it an innocuous name, such as lastyear.

Creating an upload folder for local testing

It doesn't matter where you create an upload folder in your local test environment, but for the purposes of this book, I suggest that Windows users create a folder called upload_test at the top level of the C drive. There are no permissions issues on Windows, so that's all that you need to do.

I suggest that Mac users create a folder called upload_test within their own home folder. After creating the folder, you need to change the permissions on a Mac in the same way as on Linux. Ctrl-click the folder in Finder, and select Get Info. In the Ownership & Permissions section at the bottom of the Get Info window, click the triangle alongside Details to reveal the permissions for all users, as shown in Figure 6-3. Click the padlock icon to the right of Owner to unlock the settings, and change the setting for Others from Read only to Read & Write. Click the padlock icon again to preserve the new settings, and close the Get Info window. Your upload_test folder is now ready for use.

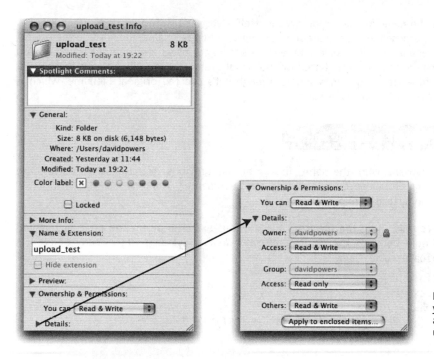

Figure 6-3. On Mac OS X, you need to set global read and write permissions on the upload folder.

Uploading files

With the knowledge from the previous section under your belt, you should now be able to avoid most common mistakes with PHP file uploads.

> All scripts in the rest of this chapter assume that you have created an upload folder in your local testing environment as described in the preceding section. If you are using a remote Linux server for testing, make sure the target directory has the correct permissions.

Moving the temporary file to the upload folder

As the previous exercise demonstrated, the temporary version of an uploaded file has only a fleeting existence. If you don't do anything with the file, it's discarded immediately. You need to tell PHP where to move it and what to call it. You do this with the move_uploaded_file() function, which takes the following two arguments:

- The name of the temporary file
- The full pathname of the file's new location, including the filename itself

Obtaining the name of the temporary file itself is easy: it's stored in the $_FILES array as tmp_name. Because the second argument requires a full pathname, it gives you the opportunity to rename the file. For example, on a site where users are required to log in, you could create a new filename based on individual usernames, combined with the current date and time. To keep things simple, though, let's use the original filename, which is stored in the $_FILES array as name.

PHP Solution 6-1: Basic file upload

Continue working with the same file as in the previous exercise. Alternatively, use upload03.php from the download files for this chapter. The final script for this PHP Solution is in upload04.php.

1. If you are using the file from the previous exercise, delete the code highlighted in bold between the closing </form> and </body> tags (it's already deleted in upload03.php):

```
</form>
<pre>
<?php
if (array_key_exists('upload', $_POST)) {
  print_r($_FILES);
  }
?>
</pre>
</body>
```

2. You now need to move the uploaded file from its temporary location to its permanent one. Insert the following code immediately above the DOCTYPE declaration:

```
<?php
if (array_key_exists('upload', $_POST)) {
  // define constant for upload folder
  define('UPLOAD_DIR', 'path/to/upload_test/');
  // move the file to the upload folder and rename it
  move_uploaded_file($_FILES['image']['tmp_name'], ➥
UPLOAD_DIR.$_FILES['image']['name']);
  }
?>
```

Although the code is quite short, there's a lot going on. The entire code block is enclosed in a conditional statement that checks whether the Upload button has been clicked by checking to see if its key is in the $_POST array.

The define() function in line 4 is used to create a **constant**. Constants are similar to variables, except they're values you don't want to change. The only place you can change a constant is in the original call to define(). Even if you make a second call to define(), the value remains the same. To distinguish them from variables, constants don't begin with a dollar sign, and they're normally written entirely in uppercase.

The define() function takes two arguments: the name of the constant and the value. The first argument, 'UPLOAD_DIR', is the same for everyone. The second argument depends on your operating system and the location of the upload folder.

- If you are using Windows, and you created the upload_test folder at the top level of the C drive, line 4 should look like this:

```
define('UPLOAD_DIR', 'C:/upload_test/');
```

Note that I have used forward slashes instead of the Windows convention of backslashes. You can use either, but forward slashes avoid problems with the trailing slash just before the closing quote. If you use backslashes, the final one needs to be escaped by another backslash, like this:

```
define('UPLOAD_DIR', 'C:\upload_test\\');
```

- If you are using a Mac, and you created the upload_test folder in your home folder, line 4 should look like this (replace *username* with your own Mac username):

```
define('UPLOAD_DIR', '/Users/username/upload_test/');
```

- If you are using a remote server for testing, or when you deploy an upload script on your live website, you need to supply the fully qualified filepath as the second argument. On a Linux server, it will probably be something like this:

```
define('UPLOAD_DIR', '/home/user/private/upload_test/');
```

The final line inside the if statement moves the file with the move_uploaded_file() function. Since $_FILES['image']['name'] contains the name of the original file, the second argument, UPLOAD_DIR.$_FILES['image']['name'], stores the uploaded file under its original name inside the upload folder.

> If a file of the same name already exists in the upload folder, the new file will overwrite it without warning. Later in the chapter, I show some simple techniques to prevent this from happening. PHP Solution 7-4 in the next chapter offers a much more robust solution.
>
> You may come across scripts that use copy() instead of move_uploaded_file(). Without other checks in place, copy() can expose your website to serious security risks. Always use move_uploaded_file(); it's much more secure.

3. Save upload.php and load it into your browser. Click the Browse or Choose File button, and select any image on your computer. Click Open (Choose on a Mac) to display the filename in the form. In browsers other than Safari, the file input field might not be wide enough to display the full path. That's a cosmetic matter that I'll leave you to sort out yourself with CSS. Click the Upload button. If you're testing locally, the form input field should clear almost instantly.

4. Navigate to the upload_test folder, and confirm that a copy of the image you selected is there. If you encounter any problems, check your code against upload04.php. Also check that the correct permissions have been set on the upload folder, if necessary.

If you get no error messages, and cannot find the file, make sure that the image didn't exceed upload_max_filesize (see Table 6-1). Also check that you didn't leave the trailing slash off the end of UPLOAD_DIR. Instead of myfile.jpg in upload_test, you may find upload_testmyfile.jpg one level higher in your disk structure.

Removing spaces from filenames

Windows and Mac OS X allow you to create long filenames with spaces in them. It makes them easier to recognize, but spaces in filenames can wreak havoc on Linux servers. Even if your remote server runs on Windows, you should remove all spaces in the names of files likely to be used in web pages, and replace them with hyphens or underscores. This is easily done with a function called str_replace(), which searches for all occurrences of a string within a string, and replaces them with another. The search string can consist of one or more characters, and the replacement string can be zero or more characters. (Using zero characters in the replacement string—a pair of quotes with nothing between them—effectively removes the search string from the target string.) Although you may not think of a space as being a string, it's just the same as any other character to PHP.

PHP Solution 6-2: Making filenames web-safe

Continue working with the same file. Alternatively use upload04.php from the download files. The finished script is in upload05.php.

1. Add the new code highlighted in bold right after the definition of the upload folder:

```
define('UPLOAD_DIR', 'C:/upload_test/');
// replace any spaces in original filename with underscores
// at the same time, assign to a simpler variable
$file = str_replace(' ', '_', $_FILES['image']['name']);
```

The function str_replace() takes the following three arguments:

- The character or substring that you want to replace—in this case, a space
- The character or substring that you want to insert—in this case, an underscore
- The string that you want to update—in this case, $_FILES['image']['name']

You'll need to make frequent references to the filename later, so it's a good idea to assign the updated filename to a simpler variable, $file, at the same time.

2. You can make use of the shorter variable right away by amending the line that moves the uploaded file as follows:

```
move_uploaded_file($_FILES['image']['tmp_name'], UPLOAD_DIR.$file);
```

3. Save upload.php, and test it with a file that contains spaces in its name, as well as with one with no spaces. As Figure 6-4 shows, the script works with both types, but spaces are replaced by underscores. You can check your code with upload05.php.

Figure 6-4. Spaces should be removed from filenames before storage on a web server.

Rejecting large files

The ability to upload files is not enough on its own: you need to make your form more secure. The first step is to set a maximum size for file uploads. Even if your hosting company sets a lower limit than the 2MB default, you may want to set a much lower limit yourself. At the same time, it's a good idea to make your form more user-friendly by reporting whether the upload was successful. You can do this easily by checking the error level reported by the $_FILES array (see Table 6-2).

PHP Solution 6-3: Setting a size limit and displaying outcome

Continue working with the previous file. Alternatively, use upload05.php from the download files. The final code for this PHP Solution is in upload06.php.

1. In addition to the automatic limits set in the PHP configuration (see Table 6-1), you can also specify a maximum size for an upload file in your XHTML form. Add the following line highlighted in bold immediately before the file input field:

```
<label for="image">Upload image:</label>
<input type="hidden" name="MAX_FILE_SIZE" value="<?php echo ➥
MAX_FILE_SIZE; ?>" />
<input type="file" name="image" id="image" />
```

This is a hidden form field, so it won't be displayed onscreen. However, it is vital that you place it *before* the file input field; otherwise, it won't work. The value attribute sets the maximum size of the upload file in bytes. Instead of specifying a numeric value, I have used a constant, which needs to be defined next.

2. Scroll up to the top of upload.php, and define the value of MAX_FILE_SIZE immediately after the opening PHP tag like this:

```
<?php
// define a constant for the maximum upload size
define ('MAX_FILE_SIZE', 3000);

if (array_key_exists('upload', $_POST)) {
```

I have deliberately chosen a very small size (3,000 bytes) for testing purposes.

3. Save upload.php and load it in a browser. Select a file bigger than 2.9KB to upload. Click the Upload button, and check the upload folder. The file shouldn't be there. If you're in the mood for experimentation, move the MAX_FILE_SIZE hidden field below the file input field, and try it again. This time the file should be copied to your upload folder. Move the hidden field back to its original position before continuing.

The advantage of using MAX_FILE_SIZE is that PHP abandons the upload if the file is bigger than the stipulated value, avoiding unnecessary delay if the file is too big.

4. Unfortunately, users can get around this restriction by faking the value of MAX_FILE_SIZE in the hidden field, so it's important to check the actual size of the file on the server side, too. Add the code shown here in bold immediately after the line that removes spaces from filenames.

```
$file = str_replace(' ', '_', $_FILES['image']['name']);
// convert the maximum size to KB
$max = number_format(MAX_FILE_SIZE/1024, 1).'KB';
// begin by assuming the file is unacceptable
$sizeOK = false;

// check that file is within the permitted size
if ($_FILES['image']['size'] > 0 && $_FILES['image']['size'] <= ➥
MAX_FILE_SIZE) {
  $sizeOK = true;
  }

// move the file to the upload folder and rename it
```

The first line of new code is typical of the concise way PHP is often written:

```
  $max = number_format(MAX_FILE_SIZE/1024, 1).'KB';
```

It converts MAX_FILE_SIZE from bytes to kilobytes and formats it all in one pass. The number_format() function normally takes two arguments: a number that you want nicely formatted with commas as the thousands-separator and the number of decimal places to be displayed. To get the number of kilobytes, you need to divide MAX_FILE_SIZE by 1,024; and PHP takes that calculation as the first argument. It's also perfectly happy for you to tag KB on the end with the concatenation operator (a period). If you find this difficult to follow, the following three lines do exactly the same:

```
$kilobytes = MAX_FILE_SIZE/1024;
$formatted = number_format($kilobytes, 1);
$max = $formatted.'KB';
```

After converting MAX_FILE_SIZE, the script assumes that the file is too big by setting a variable $sizeOK to false. The guilty until proven innocent approach may seem harsh, but it's wise on the Web.

Finally, an if statement checks whether $_FILES['image']['size'] is greater than 0 and less than or equal to MAX_FILE_SIZE. You need to check both conditions, because $_FILES['image']['size'] is set to 0 if PHP detects that the file is larger than the maximum permitted by the hidden field or the server configuration. If the size is within the acceptable range, $sizeOK is set to true.

5. You can now use $sizeOK to control whether the file is moved to the upload folder. PHP Solutions 6-1 and 6-2 assume that the upload is successful, but that may not always be the case. It's a good idea to check the error level (see Table 6-2) reported by the $_FILES array, so you can inform users what happens to their upload.

This means that you need to create a series of nested decisions. One way is to nest lots of if... else statements inside each other. The code is more readable, though, if you use a switch statement (see "Using the switch statement for decision chains" in Chapter 3) in combination with if... else. Amend the remaining part of the PHP code above the DOCTYPE declaration like this (new code is in bold):

```
// check that file is within the permitted size
if ($_FILES['image']['size'] > 0 && $_FILES['image']['size'] <= ➥
MAX_FILE_SIZE) {
    $sizeOK = true;
    }

if ($sizeOK) {
  switch($_FILES['image']['error']) {
    case 0:
      // move the file to the upload folder and rename it
      $success = move_uploaded_file($_FILES['image']['tmp_name'], ➥
UPLOAD_DIR.$file);
      if ($success) {
        $result = "$file uploaded successfully";
        }
      else {
        $result = "Error uploading $file. Please try again.";
        }
      break;
    case 3:
      $result = "Error uploading $file. Please try again.";
    default:
      $result = "System error uploading $file. Contact webmaster.";
    }
  }
elseif ($_FILES['image']['error'] == 4) {
  $result = 'No file selected';
  }
else {
  $result = "$file cannot be uploaded. Maximum size: $max.";
  }
}
?>
```

6

The basic structure here is an if... else statement, which determines whether the size of the uploaded file is acceptable. If it is, the switch statement examines the value of $_FILES['image']['error'].

Error level 0 indicates the file was uploaded successfully, so it's OK to move it to the upload folder. As long as the folder has the correct permissions, and there's sufficient disk space, this operation should succeed. However, move_uploaded_file() returns a Boolean value, so you can verify the outcome of the operation by capturing the result in $success. If $success is true, you can report the successful upload. Otherwise, inform the user of a problem.

Error levels 1 and 2 both indicate that the file exceeds the maximum size. You don't need to check for either of these, because the code in step 4 already takes care of files that are too big. Error level 3 indicates that the upload was incomplete, so a suitable message is stored in $result.

Using default at the end of the switch statement covers any remaining possibilities. Since the $_FILES array reports a size of 0 when no file is selected, $sizeOK remains false, so the switch statement never encounters error level 4, which is handled separately in the elseif clause. That leaves error levels 6 (no temporary folder) and 7 (cannot write file). These are system errors that the user cannot overcome by trying again, so a suitable catchall message is used.

Finally, if the file is too big, a message is prepared, saying that the file can't be uploaded and reporting the maximum permitted size.

6. The common feature of every branch of this decision chain is that a message reporting the outcome of the upload is stored in $result. All that's needed now is to display the contents of $result after the form is submitted. Insert the following code between the opening <body> and <form> tags:

```
<body>
<?php
// if the form has been submitted, display result
if (isset($result)) {
  echo "<p><strong>$result</strong></p>";
  }
?>
<form action="" method="post" enctype="multipart/form-data" ➡
name="uploadImage" id="uploadImage">
```

Since $result is set only after the form has been submitted, this new code block is ignored when the form first loads, but displays the outcome of any upload operation.

7. Let's test the page. Save upload.php and select an image that's bigger than 2.9KB. Click Upload. You should see an error message like the following:

8. Change MAX_FILE_SIZE to something more reasonable—say, 51200 (50KB)—like this:

```
// define a constant for the maximum upload size
define ('MAX_FILE_SIZE', 51200);
```

9. Save output.php and test the file again, making sure you choose an image that's smaller than MAX_FILE_SIZE. This time you should see a message like the one shown to the right.

10. Check inside the upload folder. Your image should be there. You can compare your code with upload06.php if you run into any problems. Change the value of MAX_FILE_SIZE to suit your particular needs.

Accepting only certain types of files

The upload script is now much more robust, but it still doesn't restrict the types of files that users can upload. The script refers to $_FILES['image'], but it's only a name. As it stands, it could be used to upload any type of file, so it's important to check the MIME type and restrict uploads to permitted ones. You can find definitions of recognized MIME types at www.iana.org/assignments/media-types. Table 6-3 lists some of the most commonly used ones. An easy way to find others not on the list is to use upload02.php, and see what value is displayed for $_FILES['image']['type'].

Table 6-3. Commonly used MIME types

Category	MIME type	Description
Documents	application/msword	Microsoft Word document
	application/pdf	PDF document
	text/plain	Plain text
	text/rtf	Rich text format
Images	image/gif	GIF format
	image/jpeg	JPEG format (includes .jpg files)
	image/pjpeg	JPEG format (nonstandard MIME type used by Internet Explorer)
	image/png	PNG format
	image/tiff	TIFF format

6

The way you handle acceptable types is very similar to the preceding PHP Solution. First, you define what is acceptable and assume that the uploaded file is suspect until you have checked its credentials—in other words, the value of $_FILES['image']['type']. Since there are several MIME types for images, you store the acceptable ones in an array and loop through the array until you find one that matches the value in the $_FILES array. If there's a match, a Boolean variable is set to true. If not, the file is rejected.

PHP Solution 6-4: Restricting upload file types

Continue working with the same file. Alternatively, use upload06.php from the download files. The finished script for this PHP Solution is in upload07.php.

1. Start by adding an array of permitted MIME types and a Boolean variable that begins by assuming the type is unacceptable. Insert the code just after the line that converts MAX_FILE_SIZE to kilobytes (new code is shown in bold):

```
// convert the maximum size to KB
$max = number_format(MAX_FILE_SIZE/1024, 1).'KB';
// create an array of permitted MIME types
$permitted = array('image/gif','image/jpeg','image/pjpeg','image/png');
// begin by assuming the file is unacceptable
$sizeOK = false;
$typeOK = false;
```

Although image/pjpeg isn't an official MIME type listed by the Internet Assigned Numbers Authority (IANA), you need to include it in the $permitted array. Otherwise, your form will reject all JPEG files submitted through Internet Explorer.

2. You need to loop through each element in the $permitted array to see if one of them matches $_FILES['image']['type']. Add the code immediately after the conditional statement that checks the size of the file.

```
// check that file is within the permitted size
if ($_FILES['image']['size'] > 0 && $_FILES['image']['size'] <= ➥
MAX_FILE_SIZE) {
  $sizeOK = true;
  }

// check that file is of a permitted MIME type
foreach ($permitted as $type) {
  if ($type == $_FILES['image']['type']) {
    $typeOK = true;
    break;
    }
  }
```

This uses a foreach loop (see "Looping through arrays with foreach" in Chapter 3), which assigns each element of the $permitted array to a temporary variable, $type, and compares it to the uploaded file's MIME type. As soon as it finds a match, it sets $typeOK to true and breaks out of the loop; there's no need to test the others.

> *Don't forget that when comparing values to see if they're the same, you must use two equal signs. If you use just one equal sign, the test will always equate to true (see "Making comparisons" in Chapter 3 if you need reminding why).*

3. You can now use $typeOK to control whether the file is moved to the upload folder. Both $typeOK and $sizeOK must be true for the upload to continue. Immediately after the code you have just entered, amend the if statement like this:

```
if ($sizeOK && $typeOK) {
  switch($_FILES['image']['error']) {
```

4. There's just one final touch needed. Add details of the permitted types to the else statement at the bottom of the script, just before the DOCTYPE declaration.

```
else {
  $result = "$file cannot be uploaded. Maximum size: $max. ➥
Acceptable file types: gif, jpg, png.";
  }
}
```

You could use the values of $typeOK and $sizeOK to create different error messages depending on the reason for the failure, but it's probably more user-friendly to indicate all restrictions at the same time

5. Save upload.php, and test it with a variety of files to make sure that only files of the right type and size get through. Check your code against upload07.php if you encounter any problems.

Preventing files from being overwritten

If you have been testing upload.php regularly through this chapter, by now you probably have quite a few files in the upload folder. If you have only a handful, it's probably because you have been using the same files over and over again. As the script stands, PHP automatically overwrites existing files without warning. That may be exactly what you want. On the other hand, it may be your worst nightmare.

In Chapter 4, you used file_exists() to check the existence of a file. You may be thinking it would be a good idea to use it here and display a message asking the user if the file should be replaced. It's not the solution I'm going to suggest. You can never be 100% sure who is accessing your site, so giving users the opportunity to delete files is something you should approach with the utmost caution.

A very simple way of giving every file a unique name is to combine it with the date and time of upload. PHP bases date calculations on Unix timestamps, which measure the number of seconds since midnight GMT on January 1, 1970. So, by prefixing the existing filename with a Unix timestamp, the likelihood of two files ever having the same name is infinitesimal. Using a timestamp also has the advantage that files are listed in chronological order of receipt. By the way, PHP uses Unix timestamps on all operating systems, including Windows.

6

PHP Solution 6-5: Using a timestamp to create a unique name

Continue working with the same file. Alternatively, use upload07.php from the download files.

1. You create a current timestamp by calling the time() function, which takes no arguments. If you want to apply a timestamp to all filenames, simply add it between the UPLOAD_DIR constant and the filename in the second argument passed to move_uploaded_file() like this:

```
$success = move_uploaded_file($_FILES['image']['tmp_name'], ➥
UPLOAD_DIR.time().$file);
```

Notice that there are periods on either side of time(). This is the concatenation operator, so what you're doing is joining three values together as a single string—in other words, the path and filename.

2. If you want to prefix only potential duplicates with a timestamp, you need to check whether a file of the same name already exists, and then use an if... else construct to take the appropriate action. Amend the first section of the switch statement like this:

```
if ($sizeOK && $typeOK) {
  switch($_FILES['image']['error']) {
    case 0:
      // make sure file of same name does not already exist
      if (!file_exists(UPLOAD_DIR.$file)) {
        // move the file to the upload folder and rename it
        $success = move_uploaded_file($_FILES['image']['tmp_name'], ➥
UPLOAD_DIR.$file);
      }
      else {
        $success = move_uploaded_file($_FILES['image']['tmp_name'], ➥
UPLOAD_DIR.time().$file);
      }
      if ($success) {
        $result = "$file uploaded successfully";
      }
```

3. Save upload.php and test it by uploading the same image twice. As you can see in Figure 6-5, the message displayed in the form still uses the original name, but the duplicate in the upload folder has a timestamp in its filename.

Figure 6-5. Prefixing a filename with a timestamp prevents existing files from being overwritten.

4. If you find the timestamps difficult to understand, you can use the date() function instead to create a more readable date and time. (The date() function and its formatting options are described in detail in Chapter 14.) Change the else statement in the previous step like this:

```
else {
  // get the date and time
  ini_set('date.timezone', 'Europe/London');
  $now = date('Y-m-d-His');
  $success = move_uploaded_file($_FILES['image']['tmp_name'], ➥
UPLOAD_DIR.$now.$file);
  }
```

As explained in Chapter 4, PHP 5.1.0 and above requires a valid time zone when using date(), so it's a good idea to future-proof your code by setting the time zone for your server (see www.php.net/manual/en/timezones.php for a list of valid time zones). The preceding code produces a filename like that on the right in Figure 6-6.

Figure 6-6. Using the date() function makes the date and time easier to read.

You can check your code against upload08.php in the download files.

This is just a simple example of how you can prevent files from being overwritten, which also demonstrates the principle of giving upload files names of your choice, rather than accepting whatever is input by the user. Choosing your own filename also adds an extra level of security, as long as you don't reveal the new name in a message displayed onscreen. PHP Solution 7-4 in the next chapter shows you how to rename files in a consecutive series by appending the next available number to its filename.

Organizing uploads into specific folders

You can take the categorization of upload files a step further by creating a new upload folder (directory) for each user. This assumes that you require users to log in using a user authentication process (see Chapters 9 and 15) and store the username in a session variable.

There's no need to set up the folders in advance; PHP can handle it for you automatically, as long as the new folders are created inside the upload folder.

Moving uploaded files to specific folders involves just three steps, as follows:

1. Getting the name of the specific folder
2. Creating the folder if it doesn't already exist
3. Adding the folder name to the upload path

PHP Solution 6-6: Creating user-specific upload folders

Continue working with the same file. Alternatively, use upload08.php from the download files. The completed script is in upload09.php.

1. In a real application, you would store the user's username in a session variable when logging in, and the upload form would be in a restricted area protected by a PHP session (see PHP Solution 9-4 in Chapter 9). However, for the purposes of this demonstration, the username is hard-coded into the script.

   Insert the following code at the beginning of the switch statement:

   ```
   switch($_FILES['image']['error']) {
     case 0:
       // $username would normally come from a session variable
       $username = 'davidp';
       // if the subfolder doesn't exist yet, create it
       if (!is_dir(UPLOAD_DIR.$username)) {
         mkdir(UPLOAD_DIR.$username);
         }
   ```

   This stores the username as $username and then uses it with the is_dir() function to see whether a subfolder of that name exists in the upload folder. If it doesn't exist, the new folder is created by the mkdir() function.

2. All you need to do now is to add $username to the pathname to the next part of the script, which moves the upload file to its new location. Change the code like this:

```
// check if a file of the same name has been uploaded
if (!file_exists(UPLOAD_DIR.$username.'/'.$file)) {
  // move the file to the upload folder and rename it
  $success = move_uploaded_file($_FILES['image']['tmp_name'], ➥
UPLOAD_DIR.$username.'/'.$file);
  }
else {
  // get the date and time
  ini_set('date.timezone', 'Europe/London');
  $now = date('Y-m-d-His');
  $success = move_uploaded_file($_FILES['image']['tmp_name'], ➥
UPLOAD_DIR.$username.'/'.$now.$file);
  }
```

Note that you need to add a forward slash as a string between the name of the new folder and the filename. Figure 6-7 shows two files uploaded to a user-specific folder, with the duplicate filename prefixed with the date and time of upload.

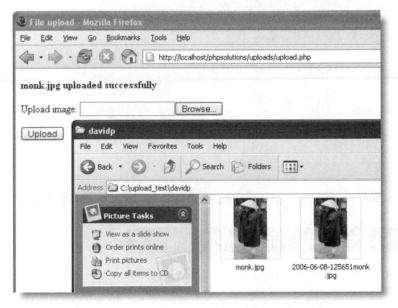

Figure 6-7. PHP can automatically create subfolders to categorize uploads by date or username.

Make sure that the username has been properly authenticated before using it to create a new folder on your server. Never create a new folder name from unfiltered form input, as it may contain invalid characters designed to probe your server's directory structure and overwrite important files. Authentication is covered in Chapters 9 and 15.

Uploading multiple files

Since $_FILES is a multidimensional array, it's capable of handling multiple uploads. You need to create a file input field for each file to be uploaded. If you give each field a different name, you need to handle each file separately. A more efficient way is to give each field the same name followed by a pair of square brackets like this:

```
<input type="file" name="image[]" id="image1" />
```

You can examine how this affects the $_FILES array by using upload_multi01.php in the download files. The result should look something like this (to save space, only the first two subarrays are shown):

```
Array
(
    [image] => Array
        (
            [name] => Array
                (
                    [0] => basin.jpg
                    [1] => monk.jpg
                )
            [type] => Array
                (
                    [0] => image/jpeg
                    [1] => image/jpeg
                )
...
        )
)
```

This makes it easy to use a foreach loop to iterate through the $_FILES array.

PHP Solution 6-7: Processing a multiple file upload

The script for handling a multiple upload is very similar to the one that has been built throughout this chapter. To keep it simple, I have omitted the code from the previous PHP Solution that creates user-specific folders, and based it on upload07.php.

1. The following listing (which you can find in upload_multi02.php) shows the entire PHP block above the DOCTYPE declaration with all the changes highlighted in bold.

```php
<?php
// define a constant for the maximum upload size
define ('MAX_FILE_SIZE', 51200);

if (array_key_exists('upload', $_POST)) {
  // define constant for upload folder
  define('UPLOAD_DIR', 'C:/upload_test/');
```

```php
    // convert the maximum size to KB
    $max = number_format(MAX_FILE_SIZE/1024, 1).'KB';
    // create an array of permitted MIME types
    $permitted = array('image/gif', 'image/jpeg', 'image/pjpeg', ➡
'image/png');

    foreach ($_FILES['image']['name'] as $number => $file) {
      // replace any spaces in the filename with underscores
      $file = str_replace(' ', '_', $file);
      // begin by assuming the file is unacceptable
      $sizeOK = false;
      $typeOK = false;

      // check that file is within the permitted size
      if ($_FILES['image']['size'][$number] > 0 || ➡
$_FILES['image']['size'][$number] <= MAX_FILE_SIZE) {
        $sizeOK = true;
      }

      // check that file is of a permitted MIME type
      foreach ($permitted as $type) {
        if ($type == $_FILES['image']['type'][$number]) {
          $typeOK = true;
        break;
        }
      }

      if ($sizeOK && $typeOK) {
        switch($_FILES['image']['error'][$number]) {
          case 0:
            // check if a file of the same name has been uploaded
            if (!file_exists(UPLOAD_DIR.$file)) {
              // move the file to the upload folder and rename it
              $success = move_uploaded_file($_FILES['image'] ➡
['tmp_name'][$number], UPLOAD_DIR.$file);
              }
            else {
              // get the date and time
              ini_set('date.timezone', 'Europe/London');
              $now = date('Y-m-d-His');
              $success = move_uploaded_file($_FILES['image'] ➡
['tmp_name'][$number], UPLOAD_DIR.$now.$file);
              }
            if ($success) {
              $result[] = "$file uploaded successfully";
              }
            else {
              $result[] = "Error uploading $file. Please try again.";
              }
            break;
```

6

```
        case 3:
          $result[] = "Error uploading $file. Please try again.";
        default:
          $result[] = "System error uploading $file. Contact ➥
webmaster.";
        }
      }
    elseif ($_FILES['image']['error'][$number] == 4) {
      $result[] = 'No file selected';
      }
    else {
      $result[] = "$file cannot be uploaded. Maximum size: $max. ➥
Acceptable file types: gif, jpg, png.";
      }
    }
  }
?>
```

The key line in this code is line 13, which looks like this:

```
foreach ($_FILES['image']['name'] as $number => $file) {
```

When two files are uploaded simultaneously, the name part of the array looks like this:

```
$_FILES['image']['name'][0] = basin.jpg;
$_FILES['image']['name'][1] = monk.jpg;
```

By looping through $_FILES['image']['name'], on the first iteration $number is 0 and $file is basin.jpg. The next time the loop runs, $number is 1 and $file is monk.jpg. This does the same as the following line in the original script:

```
$file = $_FILES['image']['name'];
```

The added bonus is that $number gives you access to the other parts of the $_FILES array. When $number is 0, $_FILES['image']['size'][$number] gives you the size of basin.jpg, and on the second pass through the loop, the size of monk.jpg. Consequently, you need to add [$number] at the end of each reference to the $_FILES array to access the details of the current file.

The only other changes are that the code to remove spaces from filenames is now inside the loop and square brackets have been added to $result to turn it into an array.

2. Since $result is an array, you need to loop through it in the main body of the page to let users know the outcome of each upload. The revised code looks like this:

```
if (isset($result)) {
  echo '<ol>';
  foreach ($result as $item) {
    echo "<strong><li>$item</li></strong>";
    }
  echo '</ol>';
  }
```

This produces a numbered list of results as shown in the screenshot to the right.

Thanks to the use of a foreach loop, this script can handle as many files as you like. However, you need a separate file input field for each file. You should also beware of exceeding any limits imposed by the server configuration as listed in Table 6-1.

Points to watch with file uploads

Uploading files from a web form is easy with PHP. The main causes of failure are not setting the correct permissions on the upload directory or folder, and forgetting to move the uploaded file to its target destination before the end of the script. Letting other people upload files to your server, however, exposes you to risk. In effect, you're allowing visitors the freedom to write to your server's hard disk. It's not something you would allow strangers to do on your own computer, so you should guard access to your upload directory with the same degree of vigilance.

Ideally, uploads should be restricted to registered and trusted users, so the upload form should be in a password-protected part of your site. Also, the upload folder does not need to be inside your site root, so locate it in a private directory whenever possible unless you want uploaded material to be displayed immediately in your web pages. Remember, though, there is no way PHP can check that material is legal or decent, so immediate public display entails risks that go beyond the merely technical. You should also bear the following security points in mind:

- Set a maximum size for uploads both in the web form and on the server side.

- Make sure you're dealing with a genuine uploaded file by using move_uploaded_file() instead of copy(). Otherwise, sensitive files, such as your server's password file, might be copied to a public folder.

- PHP has a function called is_uploaded_file(), which can be used to verify a genuine upload, but move_uploaded_file() is sufficient on its own because it checks the status of a file before moving it.

- Restrict the types of uploaded files by inspecting the MIME type in the $_FILES array.

- Adopt a naming policy, such as adding a timestamp to filenames or using the consecutive series solution in the next chapter, to prevent existing files being overwritten.

- Replace spaces in filenames with underscores or hyphens.

Follow these guidelines, and your upload scripts should remain secure. One final thought: don't forget to inspect your upload folder on a regular basis. Make sure there's nothing in there that shouldn't be, and do some housekeeping from time to time. Even if you limit file upload sizes, you may run out of your allocated space without realizing it.

7 USING PHP TO MANAGE FILES

What this chapter covers:

- Reading and writing files
- Listing the contents of a folder
- Automatically naming the next file in a series
- Opening remote data sources
- Creating a download link

PHP has a huge range of functions designed to work with the server's file system, but finding the right one for the job isn't always easy. This chapter cuts through the tangle to show you some practical uses of these functions, such as reading and writing text files to store small amounts of information without a database. I'll also show you how to create a dropdown menu that lists all images in a folder, automatically name the next file in a series, and prompt a visitor to download an image or PDF file rather than open it in the browser.

As with file uploads in the previous chapter, setting the correct permissions is crucial to success in using many of the file management functions. Unfortunately, hosting companies often impose limits on their use. So, I'll begin with a quick overview of some of the restrictions you need to be aware of.

Checking that PHP has permission to open a file

As you saw in Chapter 4, a PHP script has the ability to open another file and include the content as its own. In a default PHP configuration, the file doesn't even need to be on the same server; as long as PHP can find the file and open it, the contents of both files are merged. This is an extremely powerful concept, which—sadly—is open to misuse. As a result, you must have the right permissions to open a file. This affects not only the file system functions that are the main focus of this chapter, but also any function that opens another file, among them include(), require(), and simplexml_load_file().

As I explained in the previous chapter, PHP runs on most Linux servers as nobody or apache. Consequently, a folder must have minimum access permissions of 755 for scripts to open a file. If you also want your scripts to create or alter files, you normally need to set global access permissions of 777, the least secure setting. If PHP is configured to run in your own name, you can be more restrictive, because your scripts can create and write to files in any folder for which you have read, write, and execute permissions. On a Windows server, you need write permission to create or update a file.

Configuration settings that affect file access

Hosting companies can impose further restrictions on file access through php.ini. To find out what restrictions have been imposed, run <?php phpinfo(); ?> on your website, and check the settings in PHP Core. Table 7-1 lists the settings you need to check and notes changes planned in PHP 6.

Table 7-1. PHP configuration settings that affect file access

Directive	Default value	Description
allow_url_fopen	On	Allows PHP scripts to open public files anywhere on the Internet. Prior to PHP 6, if allow_url_fopen is enabled, remote files can also be used as include files.
allow_url_include	Off	New in PHP 6. Controls the ability to include remote files. Disabled by default.
open_basedir	no value	Restricts accessible files to the specified directory tree. Even if no value is set, restrictions may be set directly in the server configuration.
safe_mode	Off	Mainly restricts the ability to use certain functions (for details, see www.php.net/manual/en/features.safe-mode.functions.php). Removed from PHP 6.
safe_mode_include_dir	no value	If safe_mode is enabled, user and group ID checks are skipped when files are included from the specified directory tree.

Arguably the most important of these settings is allow_url_fopen. If it's disabled, you are prevented from accessing useful external data sources, such as news feeds and public XML documents. Fortunately, you can get around this problem by creating a socket connection, as shown in PHP Solution 7-5. Hopefully, the decision to create a separate allow_url_include directive in PHP 6 will encourage hosting companies to reverse any restrictions on the use of allow_url_fopen.

If the Local Value column displays a setting for open_basedir or safe_mode_include_dir, the meaning depends on whether the value ends with a trailing slash, like this:

> /home/includes/

If it does, it means you are restricted to opening or including files from the specified directory or any of its subdirectories. If the value doesn't have a trailing slash, it acts as a prefix. For example, /home/inc gives you access to /home/inc, /home/includes, /home/incredible, and so on—assuming, of course, that they exist or you have the right to create them.

Creating a file storage folder for local testing

It should be obvious that storing data inside your site root is highly insecure, particularly if you need to set global access permissions on the folder. If you have access to a private folder outside the site root, create your data store as a subfolder and give it the necessary permissions.

181

For the purposes of this chapter, I suggest that Windows users create a folder called private on their C drive. Mac users should create a private folder inside their home folder, and then set Read & Write permissions in Get Info as shown in Figure 6-3 in the previous chapter.

Reading and writing files

The restrictions described in the previous section reduce considerably the attraction of reading and writing files with PHP. Using a database is more convenient and offers greater security. However, that assumes you have access to a database and the necessary knowledge to administer it. So, for relatively small-scale data storage and retrieval, working directly with text files is worth considering. It's also useful to know how PHP interacts with external files, because you can use the same techniques to inspect the contents of a folder or prompt a user to download a file.

Reading files in a single operation

Since PHP 4.3.0, the simplest way to read the entire contents of a text file is to use the file_get_contents() function.

PHP Solution 7-1: Reading a text file into a string

1. Create a text file in your private folder, type some text into it, and save it as filetest01.txt (or use the version in the download files).

2. Create a new folder called filesystem in your phpsolutions site root, and create a PHP file called file_get_contents.php in the new folder. Insert the following code inside a PHP block (the download file file_get_contents01.php shows the code embedded in a web page, but you can use just the PHP for testing purposes):

```
echo file_get_contents('C:/private/filetest01.txt');
```

If you're on a Mac, amend the pathname like this, using your own Mac username:

```
echo file_get_contents('/Users/username/private/filetest01.txt');
```

If you're testing on a remote server, amend the pathname accordingly.

> For brevity, the remaining code examples in this chapter show only the Windows pathname.

3. Save file_get_contents.php and view it in a browser. Depending on what you wrote in filetest01.txt, you should see something like the screenshot to the left.

When testing on your local system, you shouldn't see any error messages, unless you typed the code incorrectly or you did not set the correct permissions on a Mac. However, on a remote system, you may see error messages similar to this:

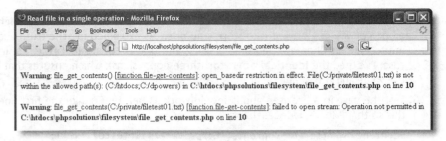

The error messages in the preceding screenshot were created on a local system to demonstrate what happens when open_basedir has been set either in php.ini or on the server. It means that you are trying to access a file outside your permitted file structure. The first error message should indicate the allowed paths. On a Windows server, each path is separated by a semicolon. On Linux, the separator is a colon.

Another possible cause of errors on a remote server is the use of spaces or illegal characters in the names of files or folders. *Never use spaces in filenames on the Web.*

4. At this stage, using file_get_contents() looks no different from using an include command. However, file_get_contents() treats the external file as a string, which means that you can store the contents in a variable and manipulate it in a way that's impossible with an include file. Change file_get_contents.php like this (or use file_get_contents02.php) and load the page into a browser:

```
$contents = file_get_contents('C:/private/filetest01.txt');
// convert contents to uppercase and display
echo strtoupper($contents);
```

The result should look like the screenshot to the right:

Admittedly, this is a trivial example, but it means that you can use any of PHP's string functions to format the contents of an external file or to search for specific information with regular expressions and pattern matching functions.

5. A danger with an external file is that you may not be able to open it: the file might be missing, its name misspelled, or the network connection down. Change the code like this (it's in file_get_contents03.php):

```
$contents = file_get_contents('C:/private/filetest01.txt');
if ($contents === false) {
  echo 'Sorry, there was a problem reading the file.';
  }
else {
  // convert contents to uppercase and display
  echo strtoupper($contents);
  }
```

If the `file_get_contents()` function can't open the file, it returns false. Often, you can test for false by using the negative operator like this:

```
if (!$contents) {
```

The reason I haven't used that shortcut here is because the external file might be empty, or you might want it to store a number. As explained in "The truth according to PHP" in Chapter 3, an empty string and 0 also equate to false. So, in this case, I've used the **identical operator** (three equal signs), which ensures that both the value and the data type are the same.

6. Test the page in a browser, and it should work as before. Change the first line like this so that it loads `filetest02.txt`:

```
$contents = file_get_contents('C:/private/filetest02.txt');
```

The new text file contains the number 0, which should display correctly when you test `file_get_contents.php`. Delete the number in `filetest02.txt`, and reload `file_get_contents.php`. You should get a blank screen, but no error message. This indicates that the file was loaded successfully, but doesn't contain anything.

7. Change the first line in `file_get_contents.php` so that it attempts to load a non-existent file, such as `filetest0.txt`. When you load the page, you should see an ugly error message reporting that `file_get_contents()` "failed to open stream"—in other words, it couldn't open the file.

8. This is an ideal place to use the error control operator (see Chapter 4). Insert an @ mark immediately in front of the call to `file_get_contents()` like this:

```
$contents = @ file_get_contents('C:/private/filetest0.txt');
```

9. Test `file_get_contents.php` in a browser. You should now see only the following custom error message:

Always add the error control operator only after testing the rest of a script. When developing, error messages are your friends. You need to see them to understand why something isn't working the way you expect.

Text files can be used as a **flat-file database**—where each record is stored on a separate line, with a tab, comma, or other delimiter between each field (see http://en.wikipedia.org/wiki/Flat_file_database). When handling this sort of file, it's more convenient to store each line individually in an array ready for processing with a loop. The PHP `file()` function builds the array automatically.

To demonstrate the file() function, let's use filetest03.txt, which contains just two lines as follows:

```
david, codeslave
chris, bigboss
```

This will be used as the basis for a simple login system to be developed further in Chapter 9.

PHP Solution 7-2: Reading a text file into an array

1. Create a PHP file called file.php inside the filesystem folder. Insert the following code (or use file01.php from the download files for this chapter):

```php
<?php
// read the file into an array called $users
$users = file('C:/private/filetest03.txt');
?>
<pre>
<?php print_r($users); ?>
</pre>
```

This draws the contents of filetest03.txt into an array called $users, and then passes it to print_r() to display the contents of the array. The <pre> tags simply make the output easier to read in a browser.

2. Save the page, and load it in a browser. You should see the output shown in the screenshot to the right.

   It doesn't look very exciting, but now that each line is a separate array element, you can loop through the array to process each line individually.

3. You need to use a counter to keep track of each line; a for loop is the most convenient (see "The versatile for loop" in Chapter 3). To find out how many times the loop should run, pass the array to the count() function to get its length. Amend the code in file.php like this (or use file02.php):

```php
<?php
// read the file into an array called $users
$users = file('C:/private/filetest03.txt');

// loop through the array to process each line
for ($i = 0; $i < count($users); $i++) {
  // separate each element and store in a temporary array
  $tmp = explode(', ', $users[$i]);
  // assign each element of the temporary array to a named array key
  $users[$i] = array('name' => $tmp[0], 'password' => $tmp[1]);
  }
?>
<pre>
```

7

```
<?php print_r($users); ?>
</pre>
```

The count() function returns the length of an array, so in this case the value of count($users) is 2. This means the first line of the loop is equivalent to this:

```
for ($i = 0; $i < 2; $i++) {
```

The loop continues running while $i is less than 2. Since arrays are always counted from 0, this means the loop runs twice before stopping.

Inside the loop, the current array element ($users[$i]) is passed to the explode() function, which converts a string into an array by splitting the string each time it encounters a separator. In this case, the separator is defined as a comma followed by a space (', '). However, you can use any character or sequence of characters: using "\t" (see Table 3-4 in Chapter 3) as the first argument to explode() turns a tab-separated string into an array.

The first line in filetest03.txt looks like this:

```
david, codeslave
```

When this line is passed to explode(), the result is saved in $tmp, so $tmp[0] is david, and $tmp[1] is codeslave. The final line inside the loop reassigns $tmp[0] to $users[0]['name'], and $tmp[1] to $users[0]['password'].

The next time the loop runs, $tmp is reused, and $users[1]['name'] becomes chris, and $users[0]['password'] becomes bigboss.

4. Save file.php, and view it in a browser. The result should look like this:

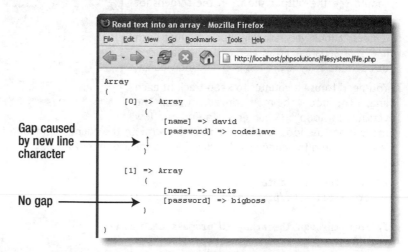

Take a close look at the gap between codeslave and the closing parenthesis of the first subarray. If a line ends in a new line character, the file() function doesn't remove it, so you need to do it yourself. Pass the final item of $tmp to rtrim() to remove the new line character like this:

```
$users[$i] = array('name' => $tmp[0], 'password' => rtrim($tmp[1]));
```

> *If you're working with each line as a whole, pass the entire line to* rtrim().

5. As always, you need to check that the file is accessible before attempting to process its contents, so wrap the main PHP block in a conditional statement like this (see file03.php):

```
$textfile = 'C:/private/filetest03.txt';
if (file_exists($textfile) && is_readable($textfile)) {
  // read the file into an array called $users
  $users = file($textfile);

  // loop through the array to process each line
  for ($i = 0; $i < count($users); $i++) {
    // separate each element and store in a temporary array
    $tmp = explode(', ', $users[$i]);
    // assign each element of the temporary array to a named array key
    $users[$i] = array('name' => $tmp[0], 'password' => ➥
rtrim($tmp[1]));
  }
}
else {
  echo "Can't open $textfile";
}
```

To avoid typing out the file pathname each time, begin by storing it in a variable.

This simple script extracts a useful array of names and associated passwords. You could also use this with a series of sports statistics or any data that follows a regular pattern.

Opening and closing files for read/write operations

The functions we have looked at so far do everything in a single pass. However, PHP also has a set of functions that allow you to open a file, read it and/or write to it, and then close the file. The following are the most important functions used for this type of operation:

- fopen(): Opens a file
- fgets(): Reads the contents of a file, normally one line at a time
- fread(): Reads a specified amount of a file
- fwrite(): Writes to a file
- feof(): Determines whether the end of the file has been reached
- rewind(): Moves an internal pointer back to the top of the file
- fclose(): Closes a file

The first of these, fopen(), is the most difficult to understand, mainly because you need to specify how the file is to be used once it's open: fopen() has one read-only mode, three write-only modes, and four read/write modes. Sometimes, you want to overwrite the existing content. At other times, you may want to append new material. At yet other times, you may want PHP to create a file if it doesn't already exist. The other thing you need to understand is where each mode places the internal pointer when it opens the file. It's like the cursor in a word processor: PHP starts reading or writing from wherever the pointer happens to be when you call fread() or fwrite(). Table 7-2 brings order to the confusion.

Table 7-2. Read/write modes used with fopen()

Type	Mode	Description
Read-only	r	Internal pointer initially placed at beginning of file.
Write-only	w	Existing data deleted before writing. Creates a file if it doesn't already exist.
	a	Append mode. New data added at end of file. Creates a file if it doesn't already exist.
	x	Creates a file only if it doesn't already exist, so no danger of deleting existing data.
Read/write	r+	Read/write operations can take place in either order and begin wherever the internal pointer is at the time. Pointer initially placed at beginning of file. File must already exist for operation to succeed.
	w+	Existing data deleted. Data can be read back after writing. Creates a file if it doesn't already exist.
	a+	Opens a file ready to add new data at end of file. Also permits data to be read back after internal pointer has been moved. Creates a file if it doesn't already exist.
	x+	Creates a new file, but fails if a file of the same name already exists. Data can be read back after writing.

Choose the wrong mode, and you could end up overwriting or deleting valuable data. You also need to be careful about the position of the internal pointer. If the pointer is at the end of the file, and you try to read the contents, you'll end up with nothing. On the other hand, if the pointer is at the beginning of the file, and you start writing, you'll overwrite the equivalent amount of any existing data.

You work with fopen() by passing it the following two arguments:

- The pathname to the file you want to open
- One of the modes listed in Table 7-2 (for a binary file, such as an image, add b)

The fopen() function returns a reference to the open file, which can then be used with any of the other read/write functions. So, this is how you would open a text file for reading:

```
$file = fopen('C:/private/filetest03.txt', 'r');
```

Thereafter, you pass $file as the argument to other functions, such as fgets(), feof(), and fclose().

Things should become clearer with a few practical demonstrations. Rather than building the files yourself, you'll probably find it easier to use the download files. I'll run quickly through each mode.

Reading a file with fopen()

The file fopen_read.php contains the following code:

```php
<?php
// store the pathname of the file
$filename = 'C:/private/filetest03.txt';
// open the file in read-only mode
$file = fopen($filename, 'r');
// read the file and store its contents
$contents = fread($file, filesize($filename));
// close the file
fclose($file);
// display the contents
echo nl2br($contents);
?>
```

If you load this into a browser, you should see the following output:

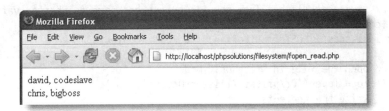

The inline comments in the code explain the process. Unlike file_get_contents(), the function fread() needs to know how much of the file to read. So you need to supply a second argument indicating the number of bytes. This can be useful if you want, say, only the first 100 characters of a text file. However, if you want the whole file, you need to pass the file's pathname to filesize() to get the correct figure.

The nl2br() function in the final line converts new line characters to XHTML <br /> tags.

The other way to read the contents of a file with fopen() is to use the fgets() function, which retrieves one line at a time. This means that you need to use a while loop in combination with feof() to read right through to the end of the file. This is done by replacing this line

```
$contents = fread($file, filesize($filename));
```

with this (the full script is in fopen_readloop.php)

```
// create variable to store the contents
$contents = '';
// loop through each line until end of file
while (!feof($file)) {
  // retrieve next line, and add to $contents
  $contents .= fgets($file);
  }
```

The while loop uses fgets() to retrieve the contents of the file one line at a time—!feof($file) is the same as saying until the end of $file—and stores them in $contents.

It doesn't take a genius to see that both methods are more long-winded than using file() or file_get_contents(). However, you need to use either fread() or fgets() if you want to read the contents of a file at the same time as writing to it.

Replacing content with fopen()

The first of the write-only modes (w) deletes any existing content in a file, so it's useful for working with files that need to be updated frequently. You can test the w mode with fopen_write.php, which has the following PHP code above the DOCTYPE declaration:

```
<?php
// if the form has been submitted, process the input text
if (array_key_exists('putContents', $_POST)) {
  // strip backslashes from the input text and save to shorter variable
  $contents = get_magic_quotes_gpc() ? ➥
stripslashes($_POST['contents']) : $_POST['contents'];

  // open the file in write-only mode
  $file = fopen('C:/private/filetest04.txt', 'w');
  // write the contents
  fwrite($file, $contents);
  // close the file
  fclose($file);
  }
?>
```

There's no need to use a loop this time: you're just writing the value of $contents to the opened file. The function fwrite() takes two arguments: the reference to the file and whatever you want to write to it.

> In other books or scripts on the Internet, you may come across fputs() instead of fwrite(). The two functions are identical: fputs() is a synonym for fwrite().

If you load fopen_write.php into a browser, type something into the text area, and click Write to file, PHP creates filetest04.txt and inserts whatever you typed into the text area. Since this is just a demonstration, I've omitted any checks to make sure that the file was successfully written. Open filetest04.txt to verify that your text has been inserted. Now type something different into the text area and submit the form again. The original content is deleted from filetest04.txt and replaced with the new text. No record is kept of the deleted text. It's gone forever.

Appending content with fopen()

The append mode is one of the most useful ways of using fopen(), because it adds new content at the end, preserving any existing content. The main code in fopen_append.php is the same as fopen_write.php, apart from those elements highlighted here in bold:

```
// open the file in append mode
$file = fopen('C:/private/filetest04.txt', 'a');
// write the contents after inserting new line
fwrite($file, "\r\n$contents");
// close the file
fclose($file);
```

If you load fopen_append.php into a browser and insert some text, it should now be added to the end of the existing text, as shown in the following screenshot.

Notice that I have enclosed $contents in double quotes and preceded it by carriage return and new line characters (\r\n). This makes sure that the new content is added on a fresh line. When using this on Mac OS X or a Linux server, omit the carriage return, and use this instead:

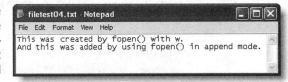

```
fwrite($file, "\n$contents");
```

This is a very easy way of creating a flat-file database. We'll come back to append mode in Chapter 9.

Writing a new file with fopen()

Although it can be useful to have a file created automatically with the same name, it may be exactly the opposite of what you want. To make sure you're not overwriting an existing file, you can use fopen() with x mode. The main code in fopen_exclusive.php looks like this (changes are highlighted in bold):

```
// create a file ready for writing only if it doesn't already exist
$file = fopen('C:/private/filetest05.txt', 'x');
// write the contents
fwrite($file, $contents);
// close the file
fclose($file);
```

If you load fopen_exclusive.php into a browser, type some text, and click Write to file, the content should be written to filetest05.txt in your target folder, as shown in the following screenshot:

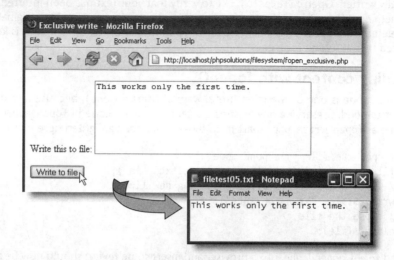

If you try it again, you should get a series of error messages telling you that the file already exists. I'll show you later in the chapter how to use x mode to create a series of consecutively numbered files.

Combined read/write operations with fopen()

By adding a plus sign (+) after any of the previous modes, the file is opened for both reading and writing. You can perform as many read or write operations as you like—and in any order—until the file is closed. The difference between the combined modes is as follows:

- r+: The file must already exist; a new one will not be automatically created. The internal pointer is placed at the beginning, ready for reading existing content.

- w+: Existing content is deleted, so there is nothing to read when the file is first opened.

- a+: The file is opened with the internal pointer at the end, ready to append new material, so the pointer needs to be moved back before anything can be read.

- x+: Always creates a new file, so there's nothing to read when the file is first opened.

Reading is done with fread() or fgets(), and writing with fwrite() exactly the same as before, so I won't go through each mode. What's important is to understand the position of the internal pointer.

Moving the internal pointer

Since reading and writing operations always start wherever the internal pointer happens to be, you normally want it to be at the beginning of the file for reading, and at the end of the file for writing.

To move the pointer to the beginning of a file   Pass the reference to the open file to rewind() like this:

```
rewind($file);
```

To move the pointer to the end of a file   This is a little more complex. You need to use fseek(), which moves the pointer to a location specified by an offset and a PHP constant. The constant that represents the end of the file is SEEK_END, so an offset of 0 bytes places the pointer where you want it. You also need to pass fseek() a reference to the open file, so all three arguments together look like this:

```
fseek($file, 0, SEEK_END);
```

SEEK_END is a constant, so it doesn't need quotes, and it must be in uppercase. This is probably the only way you'll need to use fseek(), but you can also use it to move the internal pointer to a specific position or relative to its current position. For details, see www.php.net/manual/en/function.fseek.php.

The file fopen_pointer.php uses the fopen() r+ mode to demonstrate combining several read and write operations, and the effect of moving the pointer. The main code looks like this:

```php
$filename = 'C:/private/filetest05.txt';
// open a file for reading and writing
$file = fopen($filename, 'r+');

// the pointer is at the beginning, so existing content is overwritten
fwrite($file, $contents);

// read the contents from the current position
$readRest = '';
while (!feof($file)) {
  $readRest .= fgets($file);
  }

// reset internal pointer to the beginning
rewind($file);
// read the contents from the beginning (nasty gotcha here)
$readAll = fread($file, filesize($filename));

// pointer now at the end, so write the form contents again
fwrite($file, $contents);

// read immediately without moving the pointer
$readAgain = '';
while (!feof($file)) {
  $readAgain .= fgets($file);
  }

// close the file
fclose($file);
```

7

193

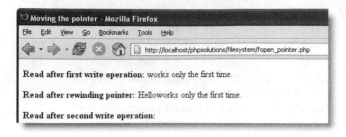

The download file also contains code that displays the values of $readRest, $readAll, and $readAgain to show what happens at each stage of the read/write operations. The existing content in filetest05.txt was This works only the first time. When I typed Hello in fopen_pointer.php and clicked Write to file, I got the results shown to the left.

Opening filetest05.txt revealed the results to the right.

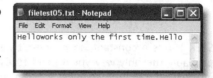

Compare the screenshots to see what happened. Table 7-3 describes the sequence of events.

Table 7-3. Sequence of read/write operations in fopen_pointer.php

Command	Position of pointer	Result
`$file = fopen($filename, 'r+');`	Beginning of file	File opened for processing
`fwrite($file, $contents);`	End of write operation	Form contents overwrites beginning of existing content

`while (!feof($file)) {`
`  $readRest .= fgets($file);`
`}`
	End of file	Remainder of existing content read

`rewind($file);`	Beginning of file	Pointer moved back to beginning of file
`$readAll = fread($file, filesize($filename));`	See text	Content read from beginning of file
`fwrite($file, $contents);`	At end of previous operation	Form contents added at current position of pointer

`while (!feof($file)) {`
`  $readAgain .= fgets($file);`
`}`
	End of file	Nothing read because pointer was already at end of file

`fclose($file);`	Not applicable	File closed and all changes saved

If you study the preceding code, you'll notice that the second read operation uses fread(). It works perfectly with this example, but contains a nasty surprise. Change the code in fopen_pointer.php to add the following line after the external file has been opened (it's commented out in the download version):

```
$file = fopen($filename, 'r+');
fseek($file, 0, SEEK_END);
```

This moves the pointer to the end of the file before the first write operation. Yet, when you run the script, fread() ignores the text added at the end of the file. This is because the external file is still open, so filesize() reads its original size. Consequently, you should always use a while loop with !feof() and fgets() if your read operation takes place after any new content has been written to a file.

> *The changes to a file with read and write operations are saved only when you call* fclose() *or when the script comes to an end. Although PHP saves the file if you forget to use* fclose()*, you should always close the file explicitly. Don't get into bad habits; one day they may cause your code to break and lose valuable data.*

When you create or open a file in a text editor, you can use your mouse to highlight and delete existing content, or position the insertion point exactly where you want. You don't have that luxury with a PHP script, so you need to give it precise instructions. On the other hand, you don't need to be there when the PHP script runs. Once you have designed it, it runs automatically every time.

Exploring the file system

PHP's file system functions can also open directories (folders) and inspect their contents. From a web designer's viewpoint, the most practical applications of this are building a drop-down menu of files and creating a unique name for a new file.

Inspecting a directory the quick way

If your server runs PHP 5 or later, you can use the scandir() function, which returns an array consisting of the files and directories within a specified directory. Just pass the pathname of the directory as a string to scandir(), and store the result in a variable like this:

```
$files = scandir('../images');
```

You can examine the result by using print_r() to display the contents of the array, as shown in the screenshot to the right (the code is in scandir.php in the download files).

```
Array
(
    [0] => .
    [1] => ..
    [2] => .svn
    [3] => Thumbs.db
    [4] => _notes
    [5] => basin.jpg
    [6] => fountains.jpg
    [7] => fuji.jpg
    [8] => kinkakuji.jpg
    [9] => maiko.jpg
    [10] => maiko_phone.jpg
    [11] => menu.jpg
    [12] => monk.jpg
    [13] => ryoanji.jpg
)
```

As you can see from the screenshot on the previous page, the folder doesn't contain only images, so it's necessary to extract them before you can build a drop-down menu. First let's take a look at how to do the same thing in PHP 4.

Opening a directory to inspect its contents

If your server is still running PHP 4, complain to your hosting company (PHP 5 has been a stable release since July 2004), and in the meantime do things the old way. Inspecting a directory is similar to opening a file for reading or writing. It involves the following three steps:

1. Open the directory with opendir().

2. Read the directory's contents with readdir().

3. Close the directory with closedir().

So, instead of the single line of code required in PHP 5 or later, you need this (the code is in opendir.php in the download files):

```
// open the directory
$folder = opendir('../images');
// initialize an array to store the contents
$files = array();
// loop through the directory
while (false !== ($item = readdir($folder))) {
  $files[] = $item;
  }
// close it
closedir($folder);
```

The readdir() function gets one item at a time and uses an internal pointer in the same way as the functions used with fopen(). To build a list of the directory's entire contents, you need to use a while loop and store each result in an array. The condition for the loop is contained in the following line:

```
while (false !== ($item = readdir($folder))) {
```

The readdir() function returns false when it can find no more items, so to prevent the loop from coming to a premature end if it encounters an item named 0, for example, you need to use false with the nonidentical operator (!==).

> Of course, it's unlikely you'll intentionally name an item 0. However, good programmers expect the unexpected. This makes absolutely sure the function works as intended.

Each time the while loop runs, $item stores the name of the next file or folder, which is then added to the $files array. Using this trio of functions isn't difficult, but the one-line scandir() is much simpler.

Building a drop-down menu of files

When you work with a database, you'll find you often need a list of images or other types of files in a particular folder. For instance, you may want to associate a photo with a blog entry or product detail page. Although you can type the name of the image into a text field, you need to make sure that the image is there and that you spell its name correctly. Get PHP to do the hard work for you by building a drop-down menu automatically. It's always up-to-date, and there's no danger of misspelling the name.

I find this so convenient that I have turned the whole process into a function. There are two versions in the download files: one for use with PHP 5 and later, and the other for PHP 4. So, with just two lines of code, you can create a drop-down menu like that shown in Figure 7-1.

Figure 7-1. PHP makes light work of creating a drop-down menu of images in a specific folder.

PHP Solution 7-3: Using the buildFileList() function

1. Create a PHP page called `imagelist.php` in the `filesystem` folder. If you just want to study the code, use either `imagelist_php5.php` or `imagelist_php4.php` from the download files, depending on the version of PHP running on your server.

2. Copy `buildFileList5.php` (for PHP 5) or `buildFileList4.php` (for PHP 4) to your includes folder.

3. Create a form inside imagelist.php, and insert a `<select>` element with just one `<option>` like this:

```
<form id="form1" name="form1" method="post" action="">
<select name="pix" id="pix">
  <option value="">Select an image</option>
</select>
</form>
```

This `<option>` is the only static element in the drop-down menu.

4. Amend the code in the previous step like this (new code is shown in bold):

```
<form id="form1" name="form1" method="post" action="">
<select name="pix" id="pix">
  <option value="">Select an image</option>
<?php
include('../includes/buildFileList5.php');
buildImageList5('../images');
?>
</select>
</form>
```

Make sure that the pathnames to the include file and the images folder are correct for your site's folder structure. If you're using PHP 4, the two lines in the PHP code block need to refer to the PHP 4 version of the function like this:

```
include('../includes/buildFileList4.php');
buildImageList4('../images');
```

> For brevity, I'm not using the techniques in Chapter 4 for checking that the include file exists.

5. Save imagelist.php and load it into a browser. You should see a drop-down menu listing all the images in your images folder, as shown in Figure 7-1. When incorporated into an online form, the filename of the selected image appears in the $_POST array identified by the name attribute of the `<select>` element—in this case, $_POST['pix']. That's all there is to it!

You can adapt this function to display any type of file simply by changing the filename extensions listed in the $fileTypes array (highlighted in bold on line 7 in the following listing). This listing shows the PHP 5 version; the PHP 4 version is identical except for the way it opens and inspects the directory:

```
function buildFileList5($theFolder) {
  // execute code if the folder can be opened, or fail silently
  if ($contents = @ scandir($theFolder)) {
    // initialize an array for matching files
    $found = array();
    // Create an array of file types
```

```
$fileTypes = array('jpg','jpeg','gif','png');
// traverse folder, and add file to $found array if type matches
$found = array();
foreach ($contents as $item) {
  $fileInfo = pathinfo($item);
  if (array_key_exists('extension', $fileInfo) && ➥
in_array($fileInfo['extension'],$fileTypes)) {
    $found[] = $item;
    }
  }


// Check the $found array is not empty
if ($found) {
  // sort in natural, case-insensitive order, and populate menu
  natcasesort($found);
  foreach ($found as $filename) {
    echo "<option value='$filename'>$filename</option>\n";
    }
  }
 }
}
```

How the buildFileList() function works I suspect many readers will be happy just to use the function, but if you're curious as to how it works, here's a brief description to flesh out the inline comments. After the folder has been opened, each item is passed to a PHP function called pathinfo(), which returns an associative array with the following elements:

- dirname: The name of the directory (folder)
- basename: The filename, including extension (or just the name if it's a directory)
- extension: The filename extension (not returned for a directory)

Because the extension element is not returned for a directory, you need to use array_key_exists() before attempting to check its value. The second half of the conditional statement in line 12 uses in_array() to see if the value of extension matches one of the file types that you're looking for. It there's a match, the filename is added to the $found array. It's then just a case of building the <option> elements with a foreach loop, but to add a user-friendly touch, the $found array is first passed to the natcasesort() function, which sorts the filenames in a case-insensitive order.

Automatically creating the next file in a series

In the last chapter I showed you how to create a unique filename by adding a timestamp or using the date() function to generate the date and time in human-readable format. It works, but is hardly ideal. A numbered series, such as file01.txt, file02.txt, and so on, is usually better. The problem is that a PHP script has no way to keep track of a series of numbers between requests to the server. However, by inspecting the contents of a directory, you can use pattern matching to find the highest existing number, and assign the next one in the series.

7

I've turned this into a function called getNextFilename(), which you can find in getNextFilename5.php and getNextFilename4.php in the download files for this chapter. The function takes the following three arguments:

- The pathname of the directory where you want the new file to be created
- The prefix of the filename, which must consist of alphanumeric characters only
- The filename extension (without a leading period)

Let's say you choose comment as the prefix and txt as the filename extension. The getNextFilename() function generates a series of files called comment001.txt, comment002.txt, and so on.

PHP Solution 7-4: Using the getNextFilename() function

1. Copy getNextFilename5.php (or getNextFilename4.php, if your server is running PHP 4) from the download files, and save it in the includes folder.

2. Open fopen_exclusive.php from the download files and save it in the filesystem folder as create_series.php. If you just want to read along, the finished code is in the download version of create_series.php.

3. Include the file that contains the getNextFilename() function for the appropriate version of PHP. You need the function only when the form is submitted, so place it inside the conditional statement at the top of the page like this (again, for brevity, I'm not checking that the include file exists):

```
if (array_key_exists('putContents', $_POST)) {
    include('../includes/getNextFilename5.php');
```

4. Then, after the line that removes backslashes from the form output, amend the rest of the PHP block at the top of the page like this:

```
$dir = 'C:/private';
$filename = getNextFilename5($dir, 'comment', 'txt');
// attempt to create file only if $filename contains a real value
if ($filename) {
  // create a file ready for writing only if it doesn't already exist
  if ($file = @ fopen("$dir/$filename", 'x')) {
    // write the contents
    fwrite($file, $contents);
    // close the file
    fclose($file);
    $result = "$filename created";
  }
  else {
    $result = 'Cannot create file';
  }
}
else {
  $result = 'Invalid folder or filename';
  }
}
```

The first two lines assign the target folder to a variable and call getNextFilename5() (use getNextFilename4() for PHP 4) to generate the next filename in the series. The function runs a number of checks on the three arguments and returns false if any fail. So the next section of code is wrapped in a conditional statement to ensure that the script attempts to create a new file only if a valid filename is obtained.

The call to fopen() is enclosed in another conditional statement. This checks that the file has been successfully created before attempting to write to it. If the file can't be opened, a suitable message is assigned to $result.

The final else clause belongs to the following conditional statement:

```
if ($filename) {
```

So, if getNextFilename() returns false, $result reports the likely reasons for failure.

5. Insert the following PHP code between the opening <body> and <form> tags to display the outcome of the operation after the form has been submitted.

```
<body>
<?php
if (isset($result)) {
  echo "<p>$result</p>";
  }
?>
<form id="writeFile" name="writeFile" method="post" action="">
```

6. Save create_series.php and load it into a browser. Test the page, and you should see the following message, indicating that the first file in the series has been created:

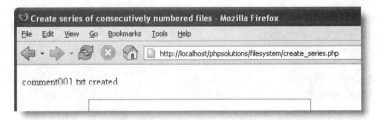

7. Submit the form again. This time the message should read comment002.txt created. Experiment with invalid filename prefixes, such as including a forward slash in the name. Also try selecting a directory that doesn't exist or for which you don't have the necessary permissions.

How the getNextFilename() function works The function builds a Perl-compatible regular expression (PCRE) in line 11, using the values in the second and third arguments, to find the correct series of files and extract the numerical part of matching filenames. The numbers are stored in an array, and the max() function is used to find the highest number, to which 1 is added. If the array is empty, no files have yet been created, so it assigns the number 1. The final part of the function calculates how many leading zeros to add to the number and then builds the filename from its composite parts. A series can contain up to 999 files and still remain in the correct order. The full listing follows:

```php
function getNextFilename($dir, $prefix, $type) {
  // run some security checks on the arguments supplied
  if (!is_dir($dir)) return false;
  if (!preg_match('/^[-._a-z0-9]+$/i', $prefix)) return false;
  $permittedTypes = array('txt','doc','pdf','jpg','jpeg','gif','png');
  if (!in_array(strtolower($type), $permittedTypes)) return false;

  // if the checks are OK, get an array of the directory contents
  $existing = scandir($dir);
  // create a search pattern for files that match the prefix and type
  $pattern = '/^'.$prefix.'(\d+)\.'.$type.'$/i';
  $nums = array();
  // loop through the directory
  // get the numbers from all files that match the pattern
  foreach ($existing as $file) {
    if (preg_match($pattern, $file, $m)) {
      $nums[] = intval($m[1]);
      }
    }
  // find the highest number and increase it by 1
  // if no file yet created, assign it number 1
  $next = $nums ? max($nums)+1 : 1;
  // calculate how many zeros to prefix the number with
  if ($next < 10) {
    $zeros = '00';
    }
  elseif ($next < 100) {
    $zeros = '0';
    }
  else {
    $zeros = '' ;
    }
  // return the next filename in the series
  return "{$prefix}{$zeros}{$next}.{$type}";
}
```

As with the buildFileList() function, I have created an array of acceptable file types (highlighted in bold on line 5 in the preceding code). Although create_series.php is used to create a text file, you can incorporate this function in a file upload script. If you need to change the range of acceptable file types, amend the $permittedTypes array. The function should not need any other alteration. The PHP 4 version is identical except for the way it opens and inspects the directory.

Opening remote data sources

PHP can open publicly available files on other servers just as easily as on the same server. This is particularly useful for accessing XML files or news feeds. All that you need to do is pass the URL as an argument to the function. Unfortunately, as noted earlier, many hosting companies disable the allow_url_fopen setting in PHP. One way to get around this is to use a socket connection instead.

To create a socket connection, use the fsockopen() function, which takes the following five arguments:

- The target domain name
- The port you want to open—for web pages, this is always 80
- A variable to capture an error number if the connection fails
- A variable to capture any error message
- The number of seconds to attempt the connection before timing out

Only the first argument is required, but using all five is a good idea since you can always use the same values, and the error message may help you understand what's gone wrong if the connection fails. The fsockopen() function works in a very similar way to fopen() by opening a file for you to read.

Let's use fsockopen() to access the friends of ED news feed at www.friendsofed.com/news.php.

PHP Solution 7-5: Opening a news feed with fsockopen()

1. Create a PHP file called fsockopen.php in the filesystem folder. If you just want to study the final code, use fsockopen.php in the download files for this chapter.

2. If your script editor automatically inserts a DOCTYPE declaration and XHTML skeleton, remove them. You need to start with a blank page. Insert the following code:

```php
<?php
// create a socket connection
$remote = fsockopen('www.friendsofed.com', 80, $errno, $errstr, 30);

if (!$remote) {
  // if no connection, display the error message and number
  echo "$errstr ($errno)";
  }
else {
  // otherwise communicate with remote server
  }
?>
```

This is the basic skeleton for any socket connection using fsockopen(). The only change you normally need to make is to the first argument, which is the domain name of the site that you want to access. If a connection can't be made, the first half of the conditional statement displays the error message and number. If the error number is 0, it may indicate the socket connections have been disabled on your server. In that event, consult your hosting company.

If a successful connection is made, the else clause is executed. At the moment, it contains just a comment. So let's fix that now.

3. First of all, you need to prepare a request and send it to the remote server. Add the following code after the comment in the else clause:

```
// otherwise communicate with remote server
// prepare the request
$out = "GET /news.php HTTP/1.1\r\n";
$out .= "Host: www.friendsofed.com\r\n";
$out .= "Connection: Close\r\n\r\n";

// send the request
fwrite($remote, $out);
```

The request is stored in $out and consists of the following three elements:

- The page you want, presented in this format:

  GET */path_to_page* HTTP/1.1

  The URL that we plan to open is www.friendsofed.com/news.php, which becomes just /news.php. Note that it begins with a forward slash. If you want the default page of a site, use a forward slash on its own.

- Host, followed by a colon and the domain name.

- An instruction to close the connection after the response has been sent.

Each part of the request must be followed by a carriage return and new line character (\r\n), and the final line by an extra carriage return and new line character (\r\n\r\n). Since these characters are PHP escape sequences, you need to use double quotes (see "Using escape sequences with double quotes" in Chapter 3).

Once you have built the request, send it by passing $out to fwrite() with a reference to the remote connection that you have opened.

4. After sending the request, you need to capture the response in a variable, and then close the socket connection. Add the following code to the else clause immediately below the code in the previous step:

```
// initialize a variable to capture the response
$received = '';
// keep the connection open until the end of the response
while (!feof($remote)) {
  $received .= fgets($remote, 1024);
  }
// close the connection
fclose($remote);
```

This uses feof(), fgets(), and fclose() in the same way as with local files. The only difference is that I have added a second argument to fgets(). This tells the function how many bytes to retrieve at a time. The fgets() function gets one line at a time, but some XML files don't use new lines, so it's more resource-efficient to specify a length.

5. Finally, use echo to display the response from the remote server. Add the following line after the closing curly brace of the conditional statement:

```
echo $received;
```

6. Save fsockopen.php and load it into a browser. As long as you're connected to the Internet, you'll probably see the friends of ED news feed displayed as continuous plain text. To get a better understanding of what you have received, open the browser's source code view. You should see something similar to Figure 7-2.

```
view-source: - Source of: http://localhost/phpsolutions/filesystem/fsockopen.php - Mozilla Fir...
File   Edit   View   Help

HTTP/1.1 200 OK
Date: Sun, 21 May 2006 10:55:40 GMT
Server: Apache/2.0.55 (Unix) mod_ssl/2.0.55 OpenSSL/0.9.7a PHP/5.1.1
X-Powered-By: PHP/5.1.1
Connection: close
Transfer-Encoding: chunked
Content-Type: application/xml

2020
<?xml version="1.0" encoding="iso-3859-1"?>

<rdf:RDF xmlns:dc="http://purl.org/dc/elements/1.1/"
         xmlns:h="http://www.w3.org/1999/xhtml"
                xmlns:hr="http://www.w3.org/2000/08/w3c-synd/#"
                xmlns:rdf="http://www.w3.org/1999/02/22-rdf-syntax-ns#"
         xmlns="http://purl.org/rss/1.0/">
<channel rdf:about="http://www.friendsofed.com">

<title>friends of ED newsfeed</title>
<description> friendsofed.com designer to designer</description>
<link>
http://www.friendsofed.com
</link>
<items></items>
</channel>
<item rdf:about="http://www.friendsofed.com/index.html?859"><title>Bring out the
Gimp</title>
```

Figure 7-2. Remote data sources accessed with fsockopen() include the HTTP headers.

The disadvantage of using fsockopen() to access a remote data source is that you get all the HTTP headers, in addition to the news feed. If you scroll to the bottom of the source code view, you may also see some unwanted characters after the closing XML tag, as shown in the following screenshot:

7. To get rid of the headers and any extraneous characters at the end of the feed, replace the line of code in step 5 with the following:

```
// find beginning and end of news feed
$start = strpos($received, '<?xml');
$endTag = '</rdf:RDF>';
$end = strpos($received, $endTag) + strlen($endTag);
// extract news feed and display
$clean = substr($received, $start, $end-$start);
echo $clean;
```

This uses the `strpos()` function to find the position of the beginning and end of the XML feed. At the time of this writing, the friends of ED news feed is enclosed in `<rdf:RDF>` tags. Other feeds may use different tags, so you need to adjust the value of $endTag accordingly to find the end of the feed. The `strpos()` function returns the position of the first matching character in the substring that you're searching for, so to find the end position, you need to add the number of characters in the end tag. The `strlen()` function is designed to do precisely that, so adding `strlen($endTag)` to the position of the first character of $endTag gives you the end of the feed.

Finally, the `substr()` function extracts the news feed. It takes three arguments: the original string, the position from which you want to start the extraction (the opening XML tag), and the number of characters (calculated in this case by subtracting $start from $end).

8. Save the page and reload it. Switch to your browser's source code view, and you should see the clean XML feed.

You need to use `fsockopen()` only if your hosting company has disabled `allow_url_fopen`. Once you have captured the remote data, you treat it as any other string. The easiest way to handle an XML news feed is with SimpleXML, which is available in PHP 5 and later. To learn more about SimpleXML, visit www.php.net/manual/en/ref.simplexml.php or see *Beginning PHP and MySQL 5: From Novice to Professional* by W. Jason Gilmore (Apress, ISBN: 1-59059-552-1).

> *If using SimpleXML with* `fsockopen()`, *you need to use* `simplexml_load_string()` *instead of* `simplexml_load_file()`.

Creating a download link

A question that crops up regularly in online forums is, How do I create a link to an image (or PDF file) that prompts the user to download it? The quick solution is to convert the file into a compressed format, such as ZIP. This frequently results in a smaller download, but the downside is that inexperienced users may not know how to unzip the file, or they may be using an older operating system that doesn't include an extraction facility. With PHP file system functions, it's easy to create a link that automatically prompts the user to download a file in its original format. The script sends the necessary HTTP headers, opens the file, and outputs its contents as a binary stream.

PHP Solution 7-6: Prompting a user to download an image

1. Create a PHP file called `download.php` in the `filesystem` folder. The full listing is given in the next step. You can also find it in `download.php` in the files for this chapter.

2. Remove any default code created by your script editor, and insert the following code:

```php
<?php
// block any attempt to explore the filesystem
if (isset($_GET['file']) && basename($_GET['file']) == $_GET['file']) {
  $getfile = $_GET['file'];
  }
else {
  $getfile = NULL;
  }
// define error handling
$nogo = 'Sorry, download unavailable. <a href="prompt.php">Back</a>.';

if (!$getfile) {
  // go no further if filename not set
  echo $nogo;
  }
else {
  // define the pathname to the file
  $filepath = 'C:/htdocs/phpsolutions/images/'.$getfile;
  // check that it exists and is readable
  if (file_exists($filepath) && is_readable($filepath)) {
    // get the file's size and send the appropriate headers
    $size = filesize($filepath);
    header('Content-Type: application/octet-stream');
    header('Content-Length: '.$size);
    header('Content-Disposition: attachment; filename='.$getfile);
    header('Content-Transfer-Encoding: binary');
    // open the file in binary read-only mode
    // suppress error messages if the file can't be opened
    $file = @ fopen($filepath, 'rb');
    if ($file) {
      // stream the file and exit the script when complete
      fpassthru($file);
      exit;
      }
    else {
      echo $nogo;
      }
    }
  else {
    echo $nogo;
    }
  }
?>
```

The only two lines that you need to change in this script are highlighted in bold type. The first defines $nogo, a variable that is called whenever something prevents the file from being downloaded. In this script, I have simply created a link to a page called prompt.php, which you will create in the next step. You could, however, use the header() function in combination with Location to divert the user to another page (see "Redirecting to another page" in Chapter 5). The second line that needs to be changed defines the pathname to the folder where the download file is stored.

The script works by taking the name of the file to be downloaded from a query string appended to the URL and saving it as $getfile. Because query strings can be easily tampered with, the opening conditional statement uses basename() to make sure that an attacker cannot request a file, such as one that stores passwords, from another part of your file structure. As explained in Chapter 4, basename() extracts the filename component of a path, so if basename($_GET['file']) is different from $_GET['file'], you know there's an attempt to probe your server, and you can stop the script from going any further by setting $getfile to NULL.

After checking that the requested file exists and is readable, the script gets the file's size, sends the appropriate HTTP headers, and opens the file in binary read-only mode by adding b after the r mode argument. Finally, fpassthru() dumps the file to the output buffer.

3. Test the script by creating another page and add a couple of links to download.php. Add a query string at the end of each link with file= followed by the name a file to be downloaded. You'll find a page called prompt.php in the download files, which contains the following two links:

```
<p><a href="download.php?file=maiko.jpg">Download image 1</a></p>
<p><a href="download.php?file=basin.jpg">Download image 2</a></p>
```

4. Click one of the links, and the browser should present you with a dialog box prompting you to download the file, as shown in Figure 7-3.

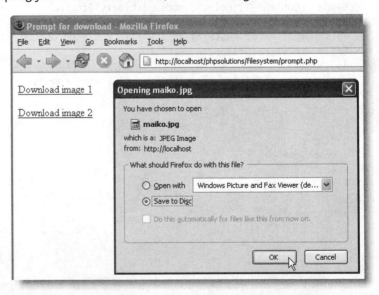

Figure 7-3. The browser prompts the user to download the image, rather than opening it directly.

Click OK, and the file should be saved rather than displayed. Click Cancel to abandon the download. Whichever button you click, the original page remains in the browser window. The only time download.php should load into the browser is if the file cannot be opened. That's why it's important to create a back link through $nogo or send the user to a different page.

I've demonstrated download.php with image files, but it can be used for any type of file because the headers send the file as a binary stream.

> *This script relies on* header() *to send the appropriate HTTP headers to the browser. It is vital to ensure that there are no new lines or whitespace ahead of the opening PHP tag. If you have removed all whitespace and still get an error message saying "headers already sent," your editor may have inserted invisible control characters at the beginning of the file. Try opening your script in a different editor, delete the opening PHP tag, and press the Backspace key several times before retyping the opening tag.*

Summary

The file system functions aren't particularly difficult to use, but there are many subtleties that can turn a seemingly simple task into a complicated one. It's important to check that you have the right permissions. Even when handling files in your own website, PHP needs permission to access any directory where you want to read files or write to them. When dealing with remote data sources, you also need to check that allow_url_fopen hasn't been disabled. Hopefully, this problem will disappear when PHP 6 becomes standard. However, hosting companies are notoriously slow at implementing major upgrades of PHP, so it's useful to know how to work around this issue with fsockopen().

In the next two chapters, we'll put some of the PHP Solutions from this chapter to further practical use when working with images and building a simple user authentication system.

7

8 GENERATING THUMBNAIL IMAGES

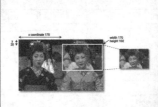

What this chapter covers:

- Scaling an image
- Saving a rescaled image
- Automatically resizing and renaming uploaded images

PHP has an extensive range of functions designed to work with images. You've already met one of them, getimagesize(), in Chapter 4. As well as providing useful information about an image's dimensions, PHP can manipulate images by resizing or rotating them. It can also add text dynamically without affecting the original; it can even create images on the fly.

To give you just a taste of PHP image manipulation, I'm going to show you how to generate a smaller copy of an uploaded image. Most of the time, you'll want to use a dedicated graphics program, such as Photoshop or Fireworks, to generate thumbnail images because it gives you much better quality control. However, automatic thumbnail generation with PHP can be very useful if you want to allow registered users to upload images, but make sure that they conform to a maximum size. You can save just the resized copy, or the copy along with the original.

Checking your server's capabilities

Working with images in PHP relies on the GD extension. Originally GD stood for GIF Draw, but support for GIF files was dropped in favor of JPEG and PNG because of a dispute over a patent. However, the name GD stuck, even though it no longer stands for anything. The problematic patent has now expired and GIF is once again supported, but you need to make sure GD has been enabled on your server and check which features are available.

As in previous chapters, load a page containing <?php phpinfo(); ?> to check the server's configuration. Scroll down until you reach the section shown in the following screenshot (it should be about halfway down the page).

gd	
GD Support	enabled
GD Version	bundled (2.0.28 compatible)
FreeType Support	enabled
FreeType Linkage	with freetype
FreeType Version	2.1.9
T1Lib Support	enabled
GIF Read Support	enabled
GIF Create Support	enabled
JPG Support	enabled
PNG Support	enabled
WBMP Support	enabled
XBM Support	enabled

If you can't find this section, it means that the GD extension isn't enabled, so you won't be able to use any of the scripts in this chapter. Your next move depends on your situation.

- On a hosting company's shared server, there's nothing you can do about it, apart from complain or move to a different host.

- If you're checking your local testing environment on a Windows computer, open php.ini and locate the following line in the list of Windows extensions:

  ;extension=php_gd2.dll

  Remove the semicolon at the start of the line, save php.ini, and restart Apache or IIS. If you still can't see that GD support has been enabled, refer back to Chapter 2. Make sure that the correct version of php.ini is being read, extension_dir is pointing to the correct location, and your Windows path setting includes your PHP folder.

- On a Mac, GD is enabled by default in the package created by Marc Liyanage that I recommended in Chapter 2.

Assuming that GD support is enabled on your server, check the version and the settings for GIF Read Support, GIF Create Support, JPG Support, and PNG Support. GD Version needs to be a minimum of 2. All versions should support JPEG and PNG files, but you need 2.0.28 or later for full GIF support. If the version number is lower than 2.0.28, you will probably be able to read GIF files, but not create them. The scripts in this chapter have been designed to respond appropriately to different levels of support.

> *Strictly for abbreviation/acronym freaks: GIF stands for Graphics Interchange Format, JPEG is the standard created by the Joint Photographic Experts Group, and PNG is short for Portable Network Graphics. Although JPEG is the correct name for the standard, the "E" is frequently dropped, particularly when used as a filename extension.*

8

Manipulating images dynamically

The GD extension allows you to generate images entirely from scratch or work with existing images. Either way, the underlying process always follows four basic steps:

1. Create a resource for the image in the server's memory while it's being processed.

2. Process the image.

3. Display and/or save the image.

4. Remove the image resource from the server's memory.

This process means that you are always working on an image in memory only and not on the original. Unless you save the image to disk before the script terminates, any changes are discarded. Working with images requires a lot of memory, so it's vital to destroy the image resource as soon as it's no longer needed. If a script runs very slowly or crashes, it probably indicates that the original image is too large.

Making a smaller copy of an image

The aim of this chapter is to show you how to resize images automatically on upload. This involves adapting the file upload form from Chapter 6. However, to make it easier to understand how to work with PHP's image manipulation functions, I propose to start by using images already on the server, and merge the resizing script with the upload code only at the final stage.

Getting ready

The starting point is the following simple form, which uses the buildFileList() function from the last chapter to create a drop-down menu of the photos in the images folder. You can find the code in create_thumb01.php in the download files for this chapter. Copy it to a new folder called gd in the phpsolutions site root, and rename it create_thumb.php.

```php
<?php
// execute script only if the form has been submitted
if (array_key_exists('create', $_POST)) {
  // image resizing script goes here
  }
?>
<!DOCTYPE html PUBLIC "-//W3C//DTD XHTML 1.0 Transitional//EN" ➥
"http://www.w3.org/TR/xhtml1/DTD/xhtml1-transitional.dtd">
<html xmlns="http://www.w3.org/1999/xhtml">
<head>
<meta http-equiv="Content-Type" content="text/html; ➥
charset=iso-8859-1" />
<title>Create thumbnail image</title>
</head>

<body>
<form id="form1" name="form1" method="post" action="">
  <p>
    <select name="pix" id="pix">
      <option value="">Select an image</option>
<?php
// if using PHP 4, use buildFileList4.php and buildFileList4()
include('../includes/buildFileList5.php');
buildFileList5('../images');
?>
    </select>
  </p>
  <p>
    <input name="create" id="create" type="submit" ➥
value="Create thumbnail" />
  </p>
</form>
</body>
</html>
```

The page requires buildFileList5.php (or buildFileList4.php, if you're using PHP 4), which should already be in your includes folder from the previous chapter. If you don't have a copy, get it from the download files for Chapter 7. Use buildListFile5() for PHP 5 and buildListFile4() for PHP 4.

When loaded into a browser, the form looks like the screenshot to the right, and the drop-down menu should display the names of the photos in the images folder, as shown in Figure 7-1 in the previous chapter.

Inside the upload_test folder that you created in Chapter 6, create a new folder called thumbs, and make sure it has the necessary permissions for PHP to write to it. Refer back to "Establishing an upload directory" in Chapter 6 if you need to refresh your memory.

Building the script

Once you have created the thumbs folder and checked that the drop-down menu in create_thumb.php is displaying a list of images, you're ready to start.

PHP Solution 8-1: Calculating the scaling ratio

1. If you have been reading the chapters in order, you'll know by now that the conditional statement above the DOCTYPE declaration checks whether the name attribute of the submit button is in the $_POST array. Since the submit button is called create, the script inside the conditional statement runs only if the form has been submitted. Replace the placeholder comment with the following code:

```
if (array_key_exists('create', $_POST)) {
  // define constants
  define('SOURCE_DIR', 'C:/htdocs/phpsolutions/images/');
  define('THUMBS_DIR', 'C:/upload_test/thumbs/');
  define('MAX_WIDTH', 120);
  define('MAX_HEIGHT', 90);
}
```

The new code defines four constants: the folder containing the original images, the folder where the resized images are to be stored, and the maximum width and height you want the thumbnails to be. You could use ordinary variables, but defining constants at the start of a script makes it easy to identify default values and change them at a later stage. Note that the folder pathnames must end with a trailing slash.

> If you're using a remote server or a Mac, replace the pathnames just shown with the correct paths to your images and thumbs folders. The download files also use the pathnames for a Windows local testing environment, so you need to make the changes there, too.

8

2. When the form is submitted, the pix element of the $_POST array contains the name of the image you want to resize. PHP needs to know the full path to the image, so combine the value of the SOURCE_DIR constant with $_POST['pix'], and assign it to a shorter variable like this (the code goes inside the conditional statement immediately after the four constants inserted in the previous step):

```
// get image name and build full pathname
if (!empty($_POST['pix'])) {
  $original = SOURCE_DIR.$_POST['pix'];
  }
else {
  $original = NULL;
  }
```

The static option of the drop-down menu has no value, so you need to check that $_POST['pix'] isn't empty. If it is, $original is set to NULL to prevent the rest of the script from going ahead.

3. Next comes the script to calculate the scaling ratio. Insert the following code after the code in the previous step (still inside the original conditional statement):

```
// abandon processing if no image selected
if (!$original) {
  echo 'No image selected';
  }
// otherwise resize the image
else {
  // begin by getting the details of the original
  list($width, $height, $type) = getimagesize($original);
  // calculate the scaling ratio
  if ($width <= MAX_WIDTH && $height <= MAX_HEIGHT) {
    $ratio = 1;
    }
  elseif ($width > $height) {
    $ratio = MAX_WIDTH/$width;
    }
  else {
    $ratio = MAX_HEIGHT/$height;
    }
  echo "Image selected: $original<br />";
  echo "Original width: $width<br />Original height: $height<br />";
  echo "Image type: $type<br />Scaling ratio: $ratio";
  }
```

Although there should never be any output ahead of the DOCTYPE declaration, echo is being used here simply for testing purposes and will be removed later. When building scripts, it's always a good idea to display the result of a calculation or conditional statement, as it helps confirm you're getting the expected results.

The following line of code needs a little explanation:

```
list($width, $height, $type) = getimagesize($original);
```

As you saw in Chapter 4, getimagesize() returns an array containing four elements. On that occasion, we were interested only in the fourth element: a string containing the width and height of an image, ready to insert into an <img> tag. This time, it's the first three elements we want: the width, height, and image type.

The list() construct lets you assign array elements directly to variables. The array elements are assigned to the variables in the same order. So, the first variable ($width) gets the first element of the array produced by getimagesize($original)—in other words, the image's width. The second variable ($height) gets the height of the image, and so on. If you pass fewer variables to list() than the number of array elements, any surplus ones are ignored.

The calculation of the scaling ratio is a simple arithmetic calculation. If the width and height of the original image are smaller or equal to the maximum, you don't want to scale the image. So the ratio is set to 1. Otherwise, you divide the maximum by the larger of the two dimensions. If the image is square, the ratio is determined by dividing the maximum height by the height of the original.

4. Save create_thumb.php and load it in a browser. Click Create thumbnail without selecting an image. You should see No image selected at the top of the screen. Then pick an image from the drop-down menu, and test the page again. You should see something like the screenshot to the right.

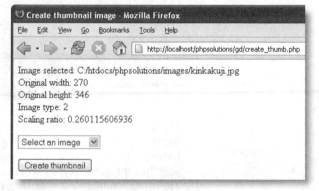

Try several different images. The scaling ratio should change for images of different dimensions. All the photos in the images folder are JPEG files, so Image type should always be 2.

Compare your code with create_thumb02.php in the download files, if necessary.

The getimagesize() function returns the image type as a number. You can find a full list at www.php.net/manual/en/function.getimagesize.php. The ones of interest to web developers are the first three, as follows:

- 1 GIF
- 2 JPEG
- 3 PNG

The GD image functions handle each type of image differently, so these numbers will be used to create the script's branching logic.

PHP Solution 8-2: Creating a scaled-down copy

Continue working with the same file. Alternatively, use create_thumb02.php from the download files. The finished script for this section is in create_thumb03.php.

1. You no longer need to display the results onscreen, so change the first echo command in step 3 of the previous section like this:

```
if (!$original) {
  $result = 'No image selected';
}
```

2. Delete the three echo commands at the end of the code in step 3, and replace them with the following code:

```
  else {
    $ratio = MAX_HEIGHT/$height;
  }
  // strip the extension off the image filename
  $imagetypes = array('/\.gif$/','/\.jpg$/','/\.jpeg$/','/\.png$/');
  $name = preg_replace($imagetypes, '', basename($original));
  }
}
```

> *Don't forget that all the code needs to go inside the original conditional statement that makes sure the script runs only when the form has been submitted. I've included the closing curly brace of that statement in the preceding code as a reminder.*

The first new line of code creates an array of regular expressions to identify the following filename extensions: .gif, .jpg, .jpeg, and .png. The next line uses basename() to extract the filename and passes it to preg_replace(), which searches the $imagetypes array for a match and replaces it with nothing. Let's say $original contains the following pathname:

C:/htdocs/phpsolutions/images/kinkakuji.jpg

By passing it to basename(), it becomes this:

kinkakuji.jpg

Finally, .jpg is removed, leaving you with this:

kinkakuji

This value is stored in $name and can be used to build the name of the resized image.

3. As explained earlier, the first step in working with an image in PHP is to create an image resource in memory. To create a scaled-down copy, you need two image resources: one for the original image and another for the thumbnail image. Let's begin with the original image.

The function used to create an image resource from an existing image depends on the file type. Since you stored that information in $type, you can use a switch statement (see "Using the switch statement for decision chains" in Chapter 3) to select the appropriate function. Insert the following code immediately after the code in the previous step:

```php
$name = preg_replace($imagetypes, '', basename($original));
// create an image resource for the original
switch($type) {
  case 1:
    $source = @ imagecreatefromgif($original);
    if (!$source) {
      $result = 'Cannot process GIF files. Please use JPEG or PNG.';
      }
    break;
  case 2:
    $source = imagecreatefromjpeg($original);
    break;
  case 3:
    $source = imagecreatefrompng($original);
    break;
  default:
    $source = NULL;
    $result = 'Cannot identify file type.';
    }
  }
}
```

The switch statement checks the number stored in $type and creates an image resource called $source using the correct function for the file type. All servers should support imagecreatefromjpeg() and imagecreatefrompng(), but a server using an older version of GD might not support imagecreatefromgif(). That's why I have used the error control operator (see "Preventing errors when an include file is missing" in Chapter 4) if $type is 1 (a GIF file). If the server can't handle GIF files, $source will be false, so a suitable error message is stored in $result. A different error message is created if $type is not 1, 2, or 3.

4. After making sure that the image resource for the original is OK, you can go ahead and create the thumbnail. Insert the following code immediately after the switch statement from the previous step:

```php
    $result = 'Cannot identify file type.';
    }
  }
// make sure the image resource is OK
if (!$source) {
  $result = 'Problem copying original';
  }
else {
  // calculate the dimensions of the thumbnail
  $thumb_width = round($width * $ratio);
  $thumb_height = round($height * $ratio);
  // create an image resource for the thumbnail
  $thumb = imagecreatetruecolor($thumb_width, $thumb_height);
```

8

```
            // create the resized copy
            // save the resized copy
            // remove the image resources from memory
        }
    }
}
```

If $source is false, there must be a problem with copying the original, so there's no point in continuing. However, if a valid image resource exists, the else statement is executed. It begins by multiplying the width and height of the original by the scaling ratio. Because the dimensions of an image must be integers, the calculation is passed to round(), which returns the nearest whole number.

Then you need to create the image resource for the resized copy. This is done by passing the width and height of the thumbnail to imagecreatetruecolor() and storing the resource as $thumb.

Just three more steps remain, as indicated by the three comments at the end of the new code. Before moving on to them, let's pause to see how the copy is actually created.

The function that creates a resized copy of an image is imagecopyresampled(), which takes—wait for it—ten arguments! While this sounds horrendous, the arguments fall into five pairs as follows:

- References to the two image resources—copy first, original second
- The x and y coordinates of where to position the top-left corner of the copied image
- The x and y coordinates of the top-left corner of the original
- The width and height of the copy
- The width and height of the area to copy from the original

The only time you need to worry about the x and y coordinates is when you want to extract a specific area, rather than copy the whole image. The coordinates are measured in pixels from the top left of the image. Figure 8-1 shows the effect of the following code:

```
imagecopyresampled($thumb, $source, 0, 0, 170, 20, $thumb_width, ➥
$thumb_height, 170, 102);
```

The x coordinate of the original image is set at 170 pixels from the top left, and the y coordinate is at 20 pixels. By setting the width and height of the original to 170 and 102, respectively, PHP copies only the area outlined in white. Although this is impressive, you can probably already see a problem: you need to view the image first to find the best area to extract and get the correct coordinates. Although you could use a pixel ruler, it's messy. You get a much more satisfactory result in a graphics program, such as Photoshop, where you can crop and rescale the image quickly and accurately.

Figure 8-1. The x and y coordinates can be used to extract part of an image.

Consequently, when using PHP to create a thumbnail, the x and y coordinates aren't really relevant. You simply set all four coordinates to the top-left corner (0), and use the actual width and height of the original image. This makes a thumbnail of the entire image. So let's get back to the code.

5. Insert the following line of code immediately beneath the first of the three comments that you inserted at the end of the previous step:

```
// create the resized copy
imagecopyresampled($thumb, $source, 0, 0, 0, 0, $thumb_width, ➥
$thumb_height, $width, $height);
```

Note that you don't need to assign the result of `imagecopyresampled()` to a variable; $thumb now contains the scaled-down image, but you still need to save it to a file.

6. The functions that save an image to file need to know the file type. So this means using another `switch` statement to select the appropriate function: `imagegif()`, `imagejpeg()`, or `imagepng()`. Each function takes the following two arguments:

- The image resource being held in memory
- The pathname of the file you want to save the image to

You can build the pathname with `THUMBS_DIR`, followed by $name (the original filename minus the extension), plus `_thb.gif`, `_thb.jpg`, or `_thb.png`, as appropriate. This results in the thumbnail for `kinkakuji.jpg` being saved in the thumbs subfolder as `kinkakuji_thb.jpg`.

The function that creates JPEG files takes a third, optional argument: an integer between 0 and 100 to indicate the quality of the image. JPEG compresses the image, so a lower number produces a smaller file size, but of lower quality. If you omit the third argument, the default is 75. Except when saving a GIF in JPEG format, it's a good idea to specify 100. You can always reduce the quality later if the file is too big, but you can't restore picture quality once it's been reduced.

8

Place this code under the second comment:

```
// save the resized copy
switch($type) {
  case 1:
    if (function_exists('imagegif')) {
      $success = imagegif($thumb, THUMBS_DIR.$name.'_thb.gif');
      $thumb_name = $name.'_thb.gif';
      }
    else {
      $success = imagejpeg($thumb, THUMBS_DIR.$name.'_thb.jpg', 50);
      $thumb_name = $name.'_thb.jpg created';
      }
    break;
  case 2:
    $success = imagejpeg($thumb, THUMBS_DIR.$name.'_thb.jpg', 100);
    $thumb_name = $name.'_thb.jpg created';
    break;
  case 3:
    $success = imagepng($thumb, THUMBS_DIR.$name.'_thb.png');
    $thumb_name = $name.'_thb.png created';
  }
if ($success) {
  $result = "$thumb_name created";
  }
else {
  $result = 'Problem creating thumbnail';
  }
```

As with the earlier switch statement, you need to check whether the server supports GIF. Even if the server can read GIF files, it might not be able to create them, so case 1 begins by using function_exists() to establish if it's safe to use imagegif(). If it is, imagegif() is used to save the thumbnail to file. If GIF creation isn't supported, the else clause uses imagejpeg() to save it as a JPEG file with a quality of 50.

> Note that function_exists() *takes the name of the function as a string without the final parentheses like this:*
>
> ```
> if (function_exists('imagegif'))    // RIGHT
> if (function_exists(imagegif()))    // WRONG
> ```

The functions that save the image to file return a Boolean true or false, which is stored in $success. A message reporting the outcome is stored in $result.

7. All that remains is to remove from memory the two image resources that you've been working with. Place this code under the final comment:

```
// remove the image resources from memory
imagedestroy($source);
imagedestroy($thumb);
```

In spite of its destructive name, imagedestroy() has no effect on the original image, nor on the thumbnail that's just been saved to file. The function simply frees up the server memory by destroying the image resources required during processing.

8. Before testing the page, you need to add some code just after the opening <body> tag to display the message reporting the outcome like this:

```
<body>
<?php
if (isset($result)) {
  echo "<p>$result</p>";
  }
?>
<form id="form1" name="form1" method="post" action="">
```

9. Save create_thumb.php and load it in a browser. Select an image from the drop-down menu and click Create thumbnail. If all goes well, there should be a scaled-down version of the image you chose in the thumbs subfolder of upload_test. Check your code, if necessary, with create_thumb03.php in the download files.

Resizing an image automatically on upload

Now that you have a script that creates a thumbnail from a larger image, it takes only a few minor changes to merge it with the file upload script from Chapter 6. Rather than build the entire script in a single page, this is a good opportunity to use a PHP include (includes were covered in Chapter 4).

PHP Solution 8-3: Merging the image upload and resizing scripts

The starting point for this PHP Solution is create_thumb.php from the preceding section, together with upload.php from Chapter 6. Alternatively, use create_thumb03.php and upload_thumb01.php from the download files for this chapter. The finished scripts are in create_thumb.inc.php and upload_thumb02.php.

1. In create_thumb.php, select the entire PHP block above the DOCTYPE declaration. Copy the selected code to your computer clipboard, and paste it inside a blank PHP page. The new page should contain PHP script only; you don't need a DOCTYPE or XHTML skeleton. Save the page in the includes folder as create_thumb.inc.php.

2. Remove the comment on line 2 together with the conditional statement that surrounds the script (don't forget the closing curly brace just before the closing PHP tag). You should be left with the following:

```
<?php
  // define constants
  define('SOURCE_DIR', 'C:/htdocs/phpsolutions/images/');
  define('THUMBS_DIR', 'C:/upload_test/thumbs/');
  define('MAX_WIDTH', 120);
  define('MAX_HEIGHT', 90);
```

```php
// get image name and build full pathname
if (!empty($_POST['pix'])) {
  $original = SOURCE_DIR.$_POST['pix'];
}
else {
  $original = NULL;
}
// abandon processing if no image selected
if (!$original) {
  $result = 'No image selected';
}
// otherwise resize the image
else {
// begin by getting the details of the original
list($width, $height, $type) = getimagesize($original);
// calculate the scaling ratio
if ($width <= MAX_WIDTH && $height <= MAX_HEIGHT) {
  $ratio = 1;
  }
elseif ($width > $height) {
  $ratio = MAX_WIDTH/$width;
  }
else {
  $ratio = MAX_HEIGHT/$height;
  }
// strip the extension off the image filename
$imagetypes = array('/\.gif$/', '/\.jpg$/', '/\.jpeg$/', '/\.png$/');
$name = preg_replace($imagetypes, '', basename($original));

// create an image resource for the original
switch($type) {
  case 1:
    $source = @ imagecreatefromgif($original);
    if (!$source) {
      $result = 'Cannot process GIF files. Please use JPEG or PNG.';
      }
    break;
  case 2:
    $source = imagecreatefromjpeg($original);
    break;
  case 3:
    $source = imagecreatefrompng($original);
    break;
  default:
    $source = NULL;
    $result = 'Cannot identify file type.';
  }
// make sure the image resource is OK
if (!$source) {
```

```
        $result = 'Problem copying original';
        }
    else {
        // calculate the dimensions of the thumbnail
        $thumb_width = round($width * $ratio);
        $thumb_height = round($height * $ratio);
        // create an image resource for the thumbnail
        $thumb = imagecreatetruecolor($thumb_width, $thumb_height);
        // create the resized copy
        imagecopyresampled($thumb, $source, 0, 0, 0, 0, $thumb_width, ➥
$thumb_height, $width, $height);
        // save the resized copy
        switch($type) {
          case 1:
            if (function_exists('imagegif')) {
              $success = imagegif($thumb, THUMBS_DIR.$name.'_thb.gif');
              $thumb_name = $name.'_thb.gif';
              }
            else {
              $success = imagejpeg($thumb, THUMBS_DIR.$name.'_thb.jpg',50);
              $thumb_name = $name.'_thb.jpg';
              }
            break;
          case 2:
            $success = imagejpeg($thumb, THUMBS_DIR.$name.'_thb.jpg', 100);
            $thumb_name = $name.'_thb.jpg';
            break;
          case 3:
            $success = imagepng($thumb, THUMBS_DIR.$name.'_thb.png');
            $thumb_name = $name.'_thb.png';
          }
        if ($success) {
          $result = "$thumb_name created";
          }
        else {
          $result = 'Problem creating thumbnail';
          }
        // remove the image resources from memory
        imagedestroy($source);
        imagedestroy($thumb);
        }
    }
?>
```

As the script now stands, it looks for the name of an image submitted from a form as $_POST['pix'], and located on the server in whatever you have defined as SOURCE_DIR. To create a thumbnail from an uploaded image, you need to adapt the script so that it processes the temporary upload file.

If you cast your mind back to Chapter 6, PHP stores an upload file in a temporary location until you move it to its target location. This temporary file is accessed using the tmp_name element of the $_FILES superglobal array and is discarded when the script ends. Instead of moving the temporary file to the upload folder, you can adapt the script in create_thumb.inc.php to resize the image, and save the scaled-down version instead.

3. The form in upload.php uses image as the name attribute of the file upload field, so the original image (referred to as $original) is now in $_FILES['image']['tmp_name']. Change the opening section of the code like this (new code is in bold):

```
// define constants
define('THUMBS_DIR', 'C:/upload_test/thumbs/');
define('MAX_WIDTH', 120);
define('MAX_HEIGHT', 90);

// process the uploaded image
if (is_uploaded_file($_FILES['image']['tmp_name'])) {
  $original = $_FILES['image']['tmp_name'];
  // begin by getting the details of the original
  list($width, $height, $type) = getimagesize($original);
```

This removes the definition of SOURCE_DIR, which is no longer needed, and simplifies the original if... else statements at the beginning of the script. The code in upload.php takes care of checking that a file has been selected, so all that's needed here is to use is_uploaded_file() to check that the temporary file is a genuine upload and to assign it to $original.

If you ever had any doubts, this should convince you just how useful variables are. From this point on, the script treats the temporary upload file in exactly the same way as a file already on the server. The remaining steps also demonstrate the value of recycling code.

4. Save create_thumb.inc.php. The rest of the changes are made in the upload file.

5. Open upload.php from Chapter 6 and save it as upload_thumb.php.

6. Locate the following section of code in upload_thumb.php (it should be around lines 32 through 60):

```
if ($sizeOK && $typeOK) {
  switch($_FILES['image']['error']) {
    case 0:
      // $username would normally come from a session variable
      $username = 'davidp';
      // if the user's subfolder doesn't exist yet, create it
      if (!is_dir(UPLOAD_DIR.$username)) {
        mkdir(UPLOAD_DIR.$username);
        }
      // check if a file of the same name has been uploaded
      if (!file_exists(UPLOAD_DIR.$username.'/'.$file)) {
```

```
        // move the file to the upload folder and rename it
        $success = move_uploaded_file($_FILES['image']['tmp_name'], ➥
UPLOAD_DIR.$username.'/'.$file);
        }
      else {
        // get the date and time
        ini_set('date.timezone', 'Europe/London');
        $now = date('Y-m-d-His');
        $success = move_uploaded_file($_FILES['image']['tmp_name'], ➥
UPLOAD_DIR.$username.'/'.$now.$file);
        }
      if ($success) {
        $result = "$file uploaded successfully";
        }
      else {
        $result = "Error uploading $file. Please try again.";
        }
      break;
```

7. Change it to this:

```
if ($sizeOK && $typeOK) {
  switch($_FILES['image']['error']) {
    case 0:
      include('../includes/create_thumb.inc.php');
      break;
```

That's it! Save upload_thumb.php and test it by selecting an image from your local file system: a scaled-down copy will be created in the thumbs subfolder of upload_test (see Figure 8-2).

Check your code, if necessary, with create_thumb.inc.php and upload_test02.php in the download files.

Figure 8-2. A 400 × 300 pixel image has been automatically resized and renamed on upload.

To understand what has happened, cast your mind back to Chapter 6. The switch statement checks the value of $_FILES['image']['error']. If it's 0, it means that the upload succeeded. The original script moved the temporary upload file to its target destination. The include command simply replaces that part of the script with the code that creates the thumbnail.

Further improvements

You now have a powerful mini-application that automatically resizes images on upload, but what if you want to preserve the original image as well? Nothing could be simpler. The page containing the upload form already defines the upload folder as UPLOAD_DIR, so you simply need to move the temporary upload file (currently referred to as $original) with move_uploaded_file().

> **PHP Solution 8-4: Saving the uploaded original and scaled-down version**

Continue working with the same files. Alternatively, use create_thumb.inc.php and upload_thumb02.php from the download files. The finished scripts are in create_both.inc.php and upload_both.php.

1. Open upload_thumb.php and save a copy as upload_both.php.

2. In upload_both.php, locate the line that includes the script that creates the scaled-down image. It should be around line 35, and looks like this:

   ```
   include('../includes/create_thumb.inc.php');
   ```

   Change it like this and save the page:

   ```
   include('../includes/create_both.inc.php');
   ```

3. Open create_thumb.inc.php and save a copy in the includes folder as create_both.inc.php.

4. In create_both.inc.php, locate the section of code that strips the extension from the filename (around line 22), and insert the new code highlighted in bold:

   ```
   // strip the extension off the image filename
   $imagetypes = array('/\.gif$/', '/\.jpg$/', '/\.jpeg$/', '/\.png$/');
   $name = preg_replace($imagetypes, '', ➥
   basename($_FILES['image']['name']));

   // move the temporary file to the upload folder
   $moved = @ move_uploaded_file($original, ➥
   UPLOAD_DIR.$_FILES['image']['name']);
   if ($moved) {
     $result = $_FILES['image']['name'].' successfully uploaded; ';
     $original = UPLOAD_DIR.$_FILES['image']['name'];
     }
   else {
   ```

```
    $result = 'Problem uploading '.$_FILES['image']['name'].'; ';
    }
```

```
// create an image resource for the original
```

The new code moves the temporary upload file to the upload folder and saves it with its original name. The move_uploaded_file() function returns a Boolean true or false, so by assigning the result to $moved, you can tell whether the operation is successful. If it is, a suitable message is created, and the pathname of the uploaded file is reassigned to $original. *This is very important*, because move_uploaded_file() immediately discards the temporary uploaded file. So, from this point onward, the original file is now the one that has just been saved on the server.

If $moved is false, there's no point in reassigning the value of $original, which still points to the temporary upload file. This means you still have a chance of creating the thumbnail, even if the main upload fails. I've inserted the error control operator (@) in front of move_uploaded_file() to prevent the display of PHP error messages, so it's important to create a custom error message indicating what the problem is.

5. The outcome of the upload operation uses the same variable, $result, as the section of the script that creates the resized image, so you need to make sure that the second outcome is added to the first. Do this with the combined concatenation operator (.=) toward the end of the script, by inserting a period in front of the equal sign like this:

```
if ($success) {
    $result .= "$thumb_name created";
    }
else {
    $result .= 'Problem creating thumbnail';
    }
```

> As it stands, the script gives you the chance to salvage at least part of the operation if the main upload fails. If you don't want a thumbnail without the main image, move the last four lines of new code in step 4 immediately below the code in step 5. This brings the thumbnail creation script inside the first half of the conditional statement, so it runs only if $moved is true.

6. Save create_both.inc.php, and load upload_both.php into a browser. Test it by selecting an image on your local computer and clicking Upload. The original image should be copied to the upload_test folder and a scaled-down version to the thumbs subfolder.

You may be wondering why I inserted the new code in step 4 in that particular location, because it doesn't really matter when you move the uploaded file, as long as the script can create an image resource from it. The answer is because the script currently overwrites existing images of the same name. For a really robust solution, you need to assign a unique name to each file as it's uploaded. By placing move_uploaded_file() at this point, you can use the value of $name to generate a unique name for the uploaded file and its thumbnail.

Rather than show you how to do it step by step, I'll just give you a few hints. The getNextFilename() function from the previous chapter automatically generates a new filename. It takes three arguments: the target folder (directory), the filename's prefix, and the file type. The target directory is UPLOAD_DIR, the filename's prefix is stored in $name, and the file type is stored in $type. However, $type is currently a number, so you need to convert it to a string. If you store the new name in $newName, you can use it in combination with basename() to build the name for the thumbnail so that the original image and thumbnail have the same number. Refer back to PHP Solution 4-3 for an explanation of how to use basename().

The changes involved are quite simple and involve fewer than 20 lines of code. The solution is in upload_both_new.php and create_both_new.inc.php in the download files. The new code is clearly marked and commented.

Transferring your test files to a remote server

If you have been testing these files locally, the only changes that you need to make when deploying them on a remote server are to the definitions of UPLOAD_DIR and THUMBS_DIR. Use a fully qualified path to each folder (directory). Don't forget that the necessary read, write, and execute permissions need to be set on the upload folders. Also make sure that the path to any include files reflects your site structure.

Change the values of MAX_HEIGHT and MAX_WIDTH if you want the resized images to be larger or smaller than 120×90 pixels.

Summary

Although this is a relatively short chapter, it covers a lot of ground and brings together techniques from Chapters 4, 6, and 7, in combination with the PHP image manipulation functions. To get the most out of working with PHP, it's important to understand the flow of a script so that you can incorporate solutions from other scripts. It would be a major project to attempt to build from scratch a form that uploads an image, makes a scaled-down copy, and gives both of them new names. However, breaking the task down into discrete sections, as done here, makes it a lot easier. It also gives you the opportunity to reuse code from one project in another, saving time and effort.

There are many other things you can do with the GD extension, including adding dynamic text to images and generating bar charts. For more details, take a look at Chapter 8 of *PHP 5 Recipes: A Problem-Solution Approach* by Lee Babin and others (Apress, ISBN: 1-59059-509-2).

9 PAGES THAT REMEMBER: SIMPLE LOGIN AND MULTIPAGE FORMS

What this chapter covers:

- Understanding sessions
- Creating a file-based login system
- Setting a time limit for sessions
- Using sessions to keep track of information

The Web is a brilliant illusion. When you visit a well-designed website, you get a great feeling of continuity, as though flipping through the pages of a book or a magazine. Everything fits together as a coherent entity. The reality is quite different. Each part of an individual page is stored and handled separately by the web server. Apart from needing to know where to send the relevant files, the server has no interest in who you are. Each time a PHP script runs, the variables exist only in the server's memory and are normally discarded as soon as the script finishes. Even variables in the $_POST and $_GET arrays have only a brief life span. Their value is passed once to the next script and then removed from memory unless you do something with it, such as store the information in a hidden form field. Even then, it persists only if the form is submitted.

To get around these problems, PHP uses **sessions**. After briefly describing how sessions work, I'll show you how you can use session variables to create a simple file-based login system and pass information from one page to another without the need to use hidden form fields.

What sessions are and how they work

A session ensures continuity by storing a random identifier on the web server and on the visitor's computer (as a cookie). The web server uses the cookie to recognize that it's communicating with the same person (or, to be more precise, with the same computer). Figures 9-1 and 9-2 show the details of a simple session created in my local testing environment. As you can see from the left screenshot in Figure 9-1, the cookie stored in the browser is called PHPSESSID, and the content is a jumble of letters and numbers (it's actually a 32-digit hexadecimal number). A matching file, which contains the same jumble of letters and numbers as part of its filename, is created on the web server (shown on the right).

Figure 9-1. PHP sessions store a unique identifier as a cookie in the browser (left) and on the server (right).

When a session is initiated, the server stores information in session variables that can be accessed by other pages as long as the session remains active (normally until the browser is closed). Because the identifier is unique to each visitor, the information stored in session variables cannot be seen by anyone else. This means sessions are ideal for user authentication, although they can be used for any situation where you want to preserve information for the same user when passing from one page to the next, such as with a multipage form or a shopping cart.

The only information stored on the user's computer is the cookie that contains the identifier, which is meaningless by itself. This means there is no danger of private information being exposed through someone examining the contents of a cookie on a shared computer.

The session variables and their values are stored on the web server. Figure 9-2 shows the contents of a simple session file. As you can see, it's in plain text, and the content isn't difficult to decipher. The session shown in the figure has two variables: name and location. The variable names are followed by a vertical pipe, then the letter "s", a colon, a number, another colon, and the variable's value in quotes. The "s" stands for string, and the number indicates how many characters the string contains.

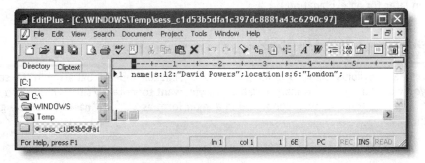

Figure 9-2. The details of the session are stored on the server in plain text.

This setup has several implications. The cookie containing the identifier normally remains active until the browser is closed. So, if several people share the same computer, they all have access to each other's sessions unless they always close the browser before handing over to the next person, something over which you have no control. So, it's important to provide a logout mechanism to delete both the cookie and the session variables, keeping your site secure. You can also create a timeout mechanism, which automatically prevents anyone regaining access after a certain period of inactivity.

The fact that session variables are stored in plain text on the web server is not, in itself, a cause for concern. As long as the server is correctly configured, the session files cannot be accessed through a browser. Inactive files are also routinely deleted by PHP (in theory, the lifetime is 24 minutes, but this cannot be relied upon). Nevertheless, it should be obvious that, if an attacker manages to compromise the server or hijack a session, the information could be exposed. So, although sessions are generally secure enough for password protecting parts of a website or working with multipage forms, you should never use session variables to store sensitive information, such as passwords or credit card details. As you'll see in "Using sessions to restrict access" later in the chapter, although a password is used to gain access to a protected site, the password itself is stored (preferably encrypted) in a separate location, and not as a session variable.

Sessions are supported by default, so you don't need any special configuration. However, since they rely on a cookie, sessions won't work if cookies are disabled in the user's browser. It is possible to configure PHP to send the identifier through a query string, but this is not considered safe.

Creating PHP sessions

Just put the following command in every PHP page that you want to use in a session:

```
session_start();
```

This command should be called only once in each page, and it must be called before the PHP script generates any output, so the ideal position is immediately after the opening PHP tag. If any output is generated before the call to session_start(), the command fails and the session won't be activated for that page. (See "The 'Headers already sent' error" section later for an explanation.)

Creating and destroying session variables

You create a session variable by adding it to the $_SESSION superglobal array in the same way you would assign an ordinary variable. Say you want to store a visitor's name and display a greeting. If the name is submitted in a login form as $_POST['name'], you assign it like this:

```
$_SESSION['name'] = $_POST['name'];
```

$_SESSION['name'] can now be used in any page that begins with session_start(). Because session variables are stored on the server, you should get rid of them as soon as they are no longer required by your script or application. Unset a session variable like this:

```
unset($_SESSION['name']);
```

To unset *all* session variables—for instance, when you're logging someone out—set the $_SESSION superglobal array to an empty array, like this:

```
$_SESSION = array();
```

> Do not be tempted to try unset($_SESSION). *It works all right—but it's a little too effective. It not only clears the current session, but also prevents any further sessions from being stored.*

Destroying a session

By itself, unsetting all the session variables effectively prevents any of the information from being reused, but you should also invalidate the session cookie like this:

```
if (isset($_COOKIE[session_name()])) {
  setcookie(session_name(), '', time()-86400, '/');
  }
```

This uses the function session_name() to get the name of the session dynamically, and resets the session cookie to an empty string and to expire 24 hours ago (86400 is the number of seconds in a day). The final argument ('/') applies the cookie to the whole domain.

Finally, destroy the session with the following command:

```
session_destroy();
```

By destroying a session like this, there is no risk of an unauthorized person gaining access either to a restricted part of the site or to any information exchanged during the session. However, a visitor may forget to log out, so it's not always possible to guarantee that the session_destroy() command will be triggered, which is why it's so important not to store sensitive information in a session variable.

> *You may find* session_register() *and* session_unregister() *in old scripts. These functions are deprecated. Use* $_SESSION['*variable_name*'] *and* unset($_SESSION['*variable_name*']) *instead.*

9

The "Headers already sent" error

Although using PHP sessions is very easy, there's one problem that causes beginners a great deal of head banging. Instead of everything working the way you expect, you see the following message:

Warning: Cannot add header information - headers already sent

I've mentioned this problem several times before in conjunction with the header() function. It affects session_start() and setcookie() as well. In the case of session_start(), the solution is simple: make sure that you put it immediately after the opening PHP tag (or very soon thereafter), and check that there's no whitespace before the opening tag. Some Mac users say they get the problem even if there is no whitespace ahead of the PHP tag. This is usually caused by editing software inserting an invisible control character at the beginning of the script. If this happens to you, try a different script editor.

When using setcookie() to destroy the session cookie, though, it's quite likely that you may need to send output to the browser before calling the function. In this case, PHP lets you save the output in a buffer using ob_start(). You then flush the buffer with ob_end_flush() after setcookie() has done its job. I'll show you how to do this in PHP Solution 9-2.

Using sessions to restrict access

The first words that probably come to mind when thinking about restricting access to a website are username and password. Although these generally unlock entry to a site, neither is essential to a session. You can store any value as a session variable and use it to determine whether to grant access to a page. For instance, you could create a variable called $_SESSION['status'] and give visitors access to different parts of the site depending on its value, or no access at all if it hasn't been set.

A little demonstration should make everything clear, and show you how sessions work in practice.

PHP Solution 9-1: A simple session example

This should take only a few minutes to build, but you can also find the complete code in session01.php, session02.php, and session03.php, in the download files for this chapter.

1. Create a page called session01.php in a new folder called sessions in the phpsolutions site root. Insert a form with a text field called name and a submit button. Set the method to post and action to session02.php. The form should look like this:

```
<form id="form1" name="form1" method="post" action="session02.php">
  <p>
    <label for="name">Name:</label>
    <input type="text" name="name" id="name" />
  </p>
  <p>
    <input type="submit" name="Submit" value="Submit" />
  </p>
</form>
```

2. In another page called session02.php, insert this above the DOCTYPE declaration:

```
<?php
// initiate session
session_start();
// check that form has been submitted and that name is not empty
if ($_POST && !empty($_POST['name'])) {
  // set session variable
  $_SESSION['name'] = $_POST['name'];
  }
?>
```

The inline comments explain what's going on. The session is started, and as long as $_POST['name'] isn't empty, its value is assigned to $_SESSION['name'].

3. Insert the following code between the <body> tags in session02.php:

```
<?php
// check session variable is set
```

```php
if (isset($_SESSION['name'])) {
    // if set, greet by name
    echo 'Hi, '.$_SESSION['name'].'. <a href="session03.php">Next</a>';
    }
else {
    // if not set, send back to login
    echo 'Who are you? <a href="session01.php">Login</a>';
    }
?>
```

If $_SESSION['name'] has been set, a welcome message is displayed along with a link to session03.php. Otherwise, the page tells the visitor that it doesn't recognize who's trying to gain access, and provides a link back to the first page.

> *Take care when typing the following line:*
>
> ```php
> echo 'Hi, '.$_SESSION['name'].'. <a href="session03.php">Next</a>';
> ```
>
> *The first two periods (surrounding $_SESSION['name']) are the PHP concatenation operator. The third period (immediately after a single quote) is an ordinary period that will be displayed as part of the string.*

4. Create session03.php. Type the following above the DOCTYPE to initiate the session:

```php
<?php session_start(); ?>
```

5. Insert the following code between the <body> tags of session03.php:

```php
<?php
// check whether session variable is set
if (isset($_SESSION['name'])) {
    // if set, greet by name
    echo 'Hi, '.$_SESSION['name'].'. See, I remembered your name!<br />';
    // unset session variable
    unset($_SESSION['name']);
    // invalidate the session cookie
    if (isset($_COOKIE[session_name()])) {
        setcookie(session_name(), '', time()-86400, '/');
    }
    // end session
    session_destroy();
    echo '<a href="session02.php">Page 2</a>';
    }
else {
    // display if not recognized
    echo 'Sorry, I don\'t know you.<br />';
    echo '<a href="session01.php">Login</a>';
    }
?>
```

If $_SESSION['name'] has been set, the page displays it, then unsets it and invalidates the current session cookie. By placing session_destroy() at the end of the first code block, the session and its associated variables will cease to be available.

6. Load session01.php into a browser, and type your name in the text field. Click Submit.

7. You should see something like the following screenshot. At this stage there is no apparent difference between what happens here and in an ordinary form.

8. When you click Next, the power of sessions begins to show. The page remembers your name, even though the $_POST array is no longer available to it. There's a problem, though, with that headers already sent error message. We'll fix that later.

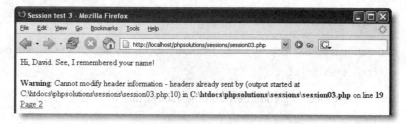

9. Click the link to Page 2 (just below the error message). The session has been destroyed, so this time session02.php has no idea who you are.

10. Type the address of session03.php in the browser address bar and load it. It, too, has no recollection of the session, and displays an appropriate message.

You need to get rid of the warning message in step 8, not only because it looks bad, but also because it means setcookie() can't invalidate the session cookie. Even though session_start() comes immediately after the opening PHP tag in session03.php, the warning message is triggered by the DOCTYPE declaration, the <head>, and other XHTML being output before setcookie(). Although you could put setcookie() in the PHP block above the DOCTYPE declaration, you would also need to assign the value of $_SESSION['name'] to an ordinary variable, because it ceases to exist after the session is destroyed. Rather than pull the whole script apart, the answer is to buffer the output with ob_start().

PHP Solution 9-2: Buffering the output with ob_start()

Continue working with session03.php from the previous section.

1. Amend the PHP block above the DOCTYPE declaration like this:

```php
<?php
session_start();
ob_start();
?>
```

This turns on output buffering and prevents output being sent to the browser until the end of the script, or until you specifically flush the output with ob_end_flush().

2. Flush the output immediately after invalidating the session cookie like this:

```php
// invalidate the session cookie
if (isset($_COOKIE[session_name()])) {
  setcookie(session_name(), '', time()-86400, '/');
  }
ob_end_flush();
```

3. Save session03.php and test the sequence again. This time, there should be no warning. More importantly, the session cookie will no longer be valid.

As you have just seen, the combination of session variables and conditional statements lets you present completely different pages to a visitor depending on whether a session variable has been set. All you need to do is add a password checking system, and you have a basic user authentication system.

Using file-based authentication

In PHP Solution 7-2, I showed you how to use the file() function to read each line of a text file into an array. You can now adapt that script to create a simple login system using sessions. Each person's username and password is separated by a comma and recorded on a new line of a text file like this:

```
david, codeslave
chris, bigboss
```

I'll use the same text file as before: filetest03.txt, which is in the private folder that was set up in Chapter 7. Refer back to Chapter 7 if you haven't already set up a folder for PHP to read and write files.

PHP Solution 9-3: Building the login page

The finished code for this page is in login.php in the download files for this chapter.

1. Create a file called login.php in the sessions folder, and build a form with a text input field each for username and password, plus a submit button named login, like this:

```
<form id="form1" name="form1" method="post" action="">
  <p>
    <label for="username">Username:</label>
    <input type="text" name="username" id="username" />
  </p>
  <p>
    <label for="textfield">Password</label>
    <input type="password" name="pwd" id="pwd" />
  </p>
  <p>
    <input name="login" type="submit" id="login" value="Log in" />
  </p>
</form>
```

2. Now add the PHP code above the DOCTYPE declaration to process the login form. It's adapted from the main PHP code block in file.php in Chapter 7, so you can copy and paste most of it from the earlier file. All the changes are highlighted in bold.

```
<?php
// process the script only if the form has been submitted
if (array_key_exists('login', $_POST)) {
  // start the session
  session_start();
  // include nukeMagicQuotes and clean the $_POST array
  include('../includes/corefuncs.php');
  nukeMagicQuotes();
  $textfile = 'C:/private/filetest03.txt';
  if (file_exists($textfile) && is_readable($textfile)) {
    // read the file into an array called $users
    $users = file($textfile);

    // loop through the array to process each line
    for ($i = 0; $i < count($users); $i++) {
      // separate each element and store in a temporary array
      $tmp = explode(', ', $users[$i]);
      // assign each element of the temp array to a named array key
      $users[$i] = array('name' => $tmp[0], 'password' => ➥
rtrim($tmp[1]));
      // check for a matching record
      if ($users[$i]['name'] == $_POST['username'] && ➥
$users[$i]['password'] == $_POST['pwd']) {
```

```
                // if there's a match, set a session variable
                $_SESSION['authenticated'] = 'Jethro Tull';
                break;
                }
        }
    // if the session variable has been set, redirect
    if (isset($_SESSION['authenticated'])) {
        header('Location: http://localhost/phpsolutions/sessions/ ➥
menu.php');
        exit;
        }
    // if the session variable hasn't been set, refuse entry
    else {
        $error = 'Invalid username or password.';
        }
    }
  // error message to display if text file not readable
  else {
    $error = 'Login facility unavailable. Please try later.';
    }
  }
?>
```

PHP Solution 7-2 explains how the original script reads the external text file, so I'll concentrate on the new code. First, the entire script has been moved above the DOCTYPE declaration and is enveloped in a conditional statement. The name attribute of the submit button is login, so array_key_exists() checks whether it's in the $_POST array to ensure that the script runs only when the form is submitted. You need to initiate a session only if the form has been submitted, so the first command inside the conditional statement is session_start(). Although the user input is unlikely to contain quotes, it's wise to strip any backslashes from the $_POST array, so corefuncs.php is included and a call made to nukeMagicQuotes() (see Chapter 3).

The next section of new code is inside the loop that extracts the name and password from each line. If the record matches username and pwd in the $_POST array, the script creates a variable called $_SESSION['authenticated'] and assigns it the name of one of the great folk-rock bands of the 70s. There's nothing magic about either of these (apart from Jethro Tull's music); I've chosen the name and value of the variable arbitrarily. All that matters is a session variable is created. Since you're looking for only one record, you can use break to exit the loop as soon as a match is found.

The rest of the script checks whether the session variable has been created. If it has, the user is redirected to menu.php by the header() function (adjust the URL to match your setup, if necessary), and exit prevents the script from running any further.

If the session variable hasn't been set, the username and/or password weren't found, and a suitable error message is prepared. The final else clause prepares a different error message in the event that the external file couldn't be read.

9

3. Add the following short code block just after the opening `<body>` tag to display any error messages, and save `login.php`:

```
<body>
<?php
if (isset($error)) {
  echo "<p>$error</p>";
  }
?>
<form id="form1" name="form1" method="post" action="">
```

Sharp-eyed readers will probably have noticed that the code in the loop in step 2 could be simplified like this:

```
for ($i = 0; $i < count($users); $i++) {
  // separate each element and store in a temporary array
  $tmp = explode(', ', $users[$i]);
  // check for a matching record
  if ($tmp[0] == $_POST['username'] && rtrim($tmp[1]) == ➡
$_POST['pwd']) {
    // if there's a match, set a session variable
    $_SESSION['authenticated'] = 'Jethro Tull';
    break;
    }
  }
```

There is no need to assign the name and password to named array elements, because you don't need the values after you've found a match. The reason I left in the line that assigns each element of the temporary array to a named key is because it makes the script easier to understand. When developing scripts, I often find it's better to use explicit steps like this, rather than attempt to use the shortest possible code. Short code can be very satisfying, but it's often more difficult to read and troubleshoot.

Now, before you can test `login.php`, you need to create `menu.php` and restrict access with a session.

PHP Solution 9-4: Restricting access to a page with a session

The code for this section is in `menu01.php` and `secretpage01.php` in the download files for this chapter.

1. Create two pages in the sessions folder called `menu.php` and `secretpage.php`. It doesn't matter what they contain, as long as they link to each other.

2. Protect access to each page by inserting the following above the DOCTYPE declaration:

```
<?php
session_start();
```

```
// if session variable not set, redirect to login page
if (!isset($_SESSION['authenticated'])) {
  header('Location: http://localhost/phpsolutions/sessions/login.php');
  exit;
  }
?>
```

After starting the session, the script checks whether $_SESSION['authenticated'] has been set. If it hasn't, it redirects the user to login.php and exits. That's all there is to it! The script doesn't need to know the value of $_SESSION['authenticated'], although you could make doubly sure by amending line 4 like this:

if (!isset($_SESSION['authenticated']) || $_SESSION['authenticated'] ➥ != 'Jethro Tull') {

This now also rejects a visitor if $_SESSION['authenticated'] has the wrong value.

3. Save menu.php and secretpage.php, and try to load either of them into a browser. You should always be redirected to login.php.

4. Enter a valid username and password in login.php, and click Log in. You should be redirected immediately to menu.php, and the link to secretpage.php should also work.

All you need to do to protect any page on your site is add the eight lines of code in step 2 above the DOCTYPE declaration. As well as logging into a site, users should be able to log out.

PHP Solution 9-5: Creating a reusable logout button

Continue working with the files from the preceding section. The finished files are in menu03.php, logout.inc.php, and secretpage02.php in the download files for this chapter.

1. Create a logout button in the `<body>` of menu.php by inserting the following form:

```
<form id="logoutForm" name="logoutForm" method="post" action="">
  <input name="logout" type="submit" id="logout" value="Log out" />
</form>
```

The page should look similar to the following screenshot:

2. You now need to add the script that runs when the logout button is clicked. Amend the code above the DOCTYPE declaration like this (the code is in menu02.php):

```php
<?php
session_start();
// if session variable not set, redirect to login page
if (!isset($_SESSION['authenticated'])) {
  header('Location: http://localhost/phpsolutions/sessions/login.php');
  exit;
  }
// run this script only if the logout button has been clicked
if (array_key_exists('logout', $_POST)) {
  // empty the $_SESSION array
  $_SESSION = array();
  // invalidate the session cookie
  if (isset($_COOKIE[session_name()])) {
    setcookie(session_name(), '', time()-86400, '/');
  }
  // end session and redirect
  session_destroy();
  header('Location: http://localhost/phpsolutions/sessions/login.php');
  exit;
  }
?>
```

This is the same code as in "Destroying a session" earlier in the chapter. The only differences are that it's enclosed in a conditional statement so that it runs only when the logout button is clicked, and it uses header() to redirect the user to login.php.

3. Save menu.php and test it by clicking Log out. You should be redirected to login.php. Any attempt to return to menu.php or secretpage.php will bring you back to login.php.

4. You can put the same code in every restricted page; but PHP is all about saving work, not making it. It makes sense to turn this into an include file. Create a new file called logout.inc.php in the includes folder. Cut and paste the new code from steps 1 and 2 into the new file like this (it's in logout.inc.php in the download files):

```php
<?php
// run this script only if the logout button has been clicked
if (array_key_exists('logout', $_POST)) {
  // empty the $_SESSION array
  $_SESSION = array();
  // invalidate the session cookie
  if (isset($_COOKIE[session_name()])) {
    setcookie(session_name(), '', time()-86400, '/');
  }
  // end session and redirect
  session_destroy();
```

```
    header('Location: http://localhost/phpsolutions/sessions/login.php');
    exit;
    }
?>
<form id="logoutForm" name="logoutForm" method="post" action="">
    <input name="logout" type="submit" id="logout" value="Log out" />
</form>
```

5. At the same point in menu.php from which you cut the code for the form, include the new file like this:

```
<?php include('../includes/logout.inc.php'); ?>
```

Including the code from an external file like this means that there will be output to the browser before the calls to setcookie() and header(). So you need to buffer the output, as shown in PHP Solution 9-2.

6. Add ob_start(); immediately after the call to session_start() at the top of menu.php.

> There's no need to add ob_end_flush() to logout.inc.php. *You don't want to flush the buffer when logging out a user. You could add it to* menu.php *after the* include *command, but it's not necessary, as PHP automatically flushes the buffer at the end of the script if you haven't already done so explicitly.*

7. Save menu.php and test the page. It should look and work exactly the same as before.

8. Repeat steps 5 and 6 with secretpage.php. You now have a simple, reusable logout button that can be incorporated in any restricted page.

Although this file-based user authentication setup is adequate for restricting access to web pages, all the passwords are stored in plain text. For greater security, it's advisable to encrypt passwords.

Encrypting passwords

PHP provides a simple and effective way to encrypt passwords, using the SHA-1 (US Secure Hash Algorithm 1; for more info, see www.faqs.org/rfcs/rfc3174), which produces a 40-digit hexadecimal number. When encrypted with SHA-1, codeslave turns into this:

```
fe228bd899980a7e23fd08082afddb74a467e467
```

SHA-1 is considered secure because it's said to be computationally infeasible to work out the original text or to find two sets of text that produce the same number. This means that even if your password file is exposed, no one will be able to work out what the passwords are. It also means that you have no way of converting fe228bd899980a7e23fd08082afddb74a467e467 back to codeslave. In one respect, this is unimportant: when a user logs in, you encrypt the password again and compare the two encrypted versions. The disadvantage is that there is

9

no way that you can send users password reminders if they forget them; you must generate a new password. Nevertheless, good security demands encryption.

Another precaution that's worth taking is adding a **salt** to the password before encrypting it. This is a random value that's added to make decryption even harder. Even if two people choose the same password, adding a unique value to the password before encryption ensures that the encrypted values are different. Sounds difficult? Not really, as you'll see over the next few pages.

You need to create a user registration form that checks the following:

- The password and username contain a minimum number of characters.
- The password matches a second entry in a confirmation field.
- The username isn't already in use.

PHP Solution 9-6: Creating a file-based user registration form

This PHP Solution assumes that you have set up a private folder that PHP has write access to, as described in Chapter 7. It also assumes that you are familiar with "Appending content with fopen()" in the same chapter. The finished code for this section is in register02.php in the download files.

1. Create a page called register.php in the sessions folder, and insert a form with three text input fields and a submit button. Lay out the form, and name the input elements as shown in the following screen. If you want to save time, use register01.php in the download files.

2. When building a script to process the input from a form, it's a good idea to map out the flow of the script as comments, and then fill in the details. As always, you want the processing script to run only if the form has been submitted, so everything needs to be enclosed in a conditional statement that checks whether the name attribute of the submit button is in the $_POST array. Then you need to

remove any backslashes from the $_POST array and check that the input meets your minimum requirements.

You can't check whether the username is unique until you open the file that contains the registered usernames and passwords, but you know there's no point in going any further if the input is too short or the passwords don't match. So let's build the basic code skeleton. Insert the following code above the DOCTYPE declaration:

```php
<?php
// execute script only if form has been submitted
if (array_key_exists('register', $_POST)) {
  // remove backslashes from the $_POST array
  include('../includes/corefuncs.php');
  nukeMagicQuotes();
  // check length of username and password
  // check that the passwords match
  // continue if OK
  }
?>
```

All this does at the moment is remove backslashes from the $_POST array with the nukeMagicQuotes() function from Chapter 3. Let's check the user input.

3. When checking the length of user input, begin by stripping any whitespace from both ends with trim() and saving the result to a shorter variable. Saving to a shorter variable avoids the need to type out the full $_POST variable name every time. It also makes it easier to incorporate user input in a string because you don't need to worry about the quotes in the $_POST variable name.

Then pass the new variable to strlen(), which returns the length of a string. If either the username or password is too short, you need an error message to display. Add this code immediately after the appropriate comment:

```php
// check length of username and password
$username = trim($_POST['username']);
$pwd = trim($_POST['pwd']);
if (strlen($username) < 6 || strlen($pwd) < 6) {
  $result = 'Username and password must contain at least 6 characters';
  }
```

You could check that strlen() is greater than 5. However, you still need to make sure that both passwords match. Consequently, it's more efficient to turn the logic around and test for things that you *don't* want. In pseudo-code, the logic works like this:

```
if (username or password has less than the minimum) {
  input is not OK
  }
elseif (the passwords do not match) {
  input is not OK
  }
else {
  input is OK to process
  }
```

9

4. Add the second test after the appropriate comment like this:

```
// check that the passwords match
elseif ($pwd != $_POST['conf_pwd']) {
$result = 'Your passwords don\'t match';
}
```

5. You can now add the `else` clause that runs only if the first two tests fail, indicating that the input is OK. This is where the main action takes place.

```
// continue if OK
  else {
  // main processing code goes here
  }
```

Let's pause to consider what the main script needs to do. First, you need to encrypt the password by combining it with the username as a salt. Then, before writing the details to a text file, you must check whether the username is unique. This presents a problem of which mode to use with fopen().

> *The various* fopen() *modes are described in Chapter 7.*

Ideally, you want the internal pointer at the beginning of the file so that you can loop through existing records. The r+ mode does this, but the operation fails unless the file already exists. You can't use w+, because it deletes existing content. You can't use x+ either, because it fails if a file of the same name already exists. That leaves a+ as the only option with the flexibility you need: it creates the file if necessary, and lets you read and write. The file is empty the first time you run the script (you can tell because the filesize() function returns 0), so you can go ahead and write the details. If filesize() doesn't return 0, you need to reset the internal pointer and loop through the records to see if the username is already registered. If there's a match, you break out of the loop and prepare an error message. If there isn't a match by the end of the loop, you not only know it's a new username, you also know you're at the end of the file. So, you write a new line followed by the new record. Now that you understand the flow of the script, you can insert it into register.php.

6. Replace the placeholder comment in the `else` clause from the preceding step with the following code:

```
// continue if OK
else {
  // encrypt password, using username as salt
  $pwd = sha1($username.$pwd);
  // define filename and open in read-write append mode
  $filename = 'C:/private/encrypted.txt';
  $file = fopen($filename, 'a+');
  // if filesize is zero, no names yet registered
  // so just write the username and password to file
  if (filesize($filename) === 0) {
```

```php
    fwrite($file, "$username, $pwd");
    }
  // if filesize is greater than zero, check username first
  else {
    // move internal pointer to beginning of file
    rewind($file);
    // loop through file one line at a time
    while (!feof($file)) {
      $line = fgets($file);
      // split line at comma, and check first element against username
      $tmp = explode(', ', $line);
      if ($tmp[0] == $username) {
        $result = 'Username taken - choose another';
        break;
        }
      }
    // if $result not set, username is OK
    if (!isset($result)) {
      // insert line break followed by username, comma, and password
      fwrite($file, "\r\n$username, $pwd");
      $result = "$username registered";
      }
    // close the file
    fclose($file);
    }
  }
```

The preceding explanation and inline comments should help you follow the script. The only line that you need to alter is this:

```php
$filename = 'C:/private/encrypted.txt';
```

Change it to the pathname of the file where you want to store usernames and passwords. If you're on a Mac or plan to deploy this script on a Linux server, you also need to change the following line:

```php
fwrite($file, "\r\n$username, $pwd");
```

Remove the \r at the beginning of the second argument. Mac and Linux don't need a carriage return to create a new line.

7. The final piece of coding displays the value of $result after the script has run. It goes just before the form like this:

```php
<h1>Register user</h1>
<?php
if (isset($result)) {
  echo "<p>$result</p>";
  }
?>
<form id="form1" name="form1" method="post" action="">
```

8. Save register.php and test it. Try it with a username or password with fewer than six characters and with passwords that don't match. Also try using the same password for two different usernames. I registered two users, both with the password codeslave. As Figure 9-3 shows, it's impossible to tell from the encrypted versions that both users have the same password.

Figure 9-3. Using a salt produces completely different encryptions of the same password.

Now that you have encrypted passwords, you need to change the login form to handle the new setup.

PHP Solution 9-7: Using an encrypted login

All that's necessary is to select the text file that contains the encrypted passwords and to encrypt the password before comparing it with the one stored in the file.

1. Open login.php from PHP Solution 9-3 or use login.php from the download files. Near the top of the script (around line 9), change the name of the text file, and add the following two lines shown in bold:

```
$textfile = 'C:/private/encrypted.txt';
$username = trim($_POST['username']);
$pwd = sha1($username.trim($_POST['pwd']));
if (file_exists($textfile) && is_readable($textfile)) {
```

This removes any whitespace from the username and assigns it to a shorter variable. The next line also removes whitespace from the submitted password and adds the username to the front before passing it to sha1() for encryption.

2. Now use the shorter variables in the line of code that compares the username and password in the text file. Find the following line:

```
if ($users[$i]['name'] == $_POST['username'] && ➥
$users[$i]['password'] == $_POST['pwd']) {
```

Change it like this:

```
if ($users[$i]['name'] == $username && $users[$i]['password'] == ➥
$pwd) {
```

If you used the shorter version in PHP Solution 9-3, change this line:

```
if ($tmp[0] == $_POST['username'] && rtrim($tmp[1]) == $_POST['pwd']) {
```

Amend it as follows:

```
if ($tmp[0] == $username && rtrim($tmp[1]) == $pwd) {
```

3. Save `login.php` and test it. It should work the same as before, but be more secure. Check your code if necessary with `login_encrypted.php` in the download files.

PHP Solutions 9-3 to 9-7 show you how to create a simple, yet effective user authentication system that doesn't require a database back end. However, it does have its limitations. Above all, it's essential that the text file containing the usernames and passwords be outside the server root. Even though the passwords are encrypted, knowing the usernames reduces the effort that an attacker needs to try to break through your security. Another weakness is that the salt is the username. Ideally, you should create a random salt for each password, but you need to store it somewhere. If it's in the same file as the usernames, they would both be exposed at the same time.

Using a database for user authentication gets around many of these problems. It involves more coding, but is likely to be more secure. Also, once you get more than a few records, querying a database is usually much faster than looping through a text file line by line. Of course, the weakest link in most security systems lies in easily guessed passwords, or users revealing their login details (intentionally or otherwise) to unauthorized users. Chapter 15 covers user authentication with a database.

Setting a time limit on sessions

Setting a time limit on a PHP session is easy. When the session first starts, typically when the user logs in, store the current time in a session variable. Then compare it with the latest time whenever the user does anything that triggers a page to load. If the difference is greater than a predetermined limit, destroy the session and its variables. Otherwise, update the variable to the latest time.

9

PHP Solution 9-8: Ending a session after a period of inactivity

This assumes that you have set up a login system as described in PHP Solutions 9-3 to 9-7. The completed scripts are in `login_timeout.php`, `menu_timeout.php`, and `secretpage_timeout.php` in the download files for this chapter.

1. You need to store the current time after the user's credentials have been authenticated, but before the script redirects the user to the restricted part of the site. Locate the redirect code in `login.php` (around line 31), and insert the new code highlighted in bold as follows:

```
// if the session variable has been set, redirect
if (isset($_SESSION['authenticated'])) {
  // get the time the session started
  $_SESSION['start'] = time();
  header('Location: http://localhost/phpsolutions/sessions/menu.php');
  exit;
}
```

The `time()` function returns a current timestamp. By storing it in `$_SESSION['start']`, it becomes available to every page that begins with `session_start()`.

2. When a session times out, just dumping a user unceremoniously back at the login screen isn't very friendly, so it's a good idea to explain what's happened. Scroll down to the main body of the page, and add the code highlighted in bold:

```php
<?php
if (isset($error)) {
  echo "<p>$error</p>";
  }
elseif (isset($_GET['expired'])) {
?>
  <p>Your session has expired. Please log in again.</p>
<?php } ?>
```

The message is shown if the URL contains a variable called expired in a query string.

3. Open menu.php, and amend the PHP code above the DOCTYPE declaration like this:

```php
<?php
session_start();
ob_start();
// set a time limit in seconds
$timelimit = 15;
// get the current time
$now = time();
// where to redirect if rejected
$redirect = 'http://localhost/phpsolutions/sessions/login.php';
// if session variable not set, redirect to login page
if (!isset($_SESSION['authenticated'])) {
  header("Location: $redirect");
  exit;
  }
// if timelimit has expired, destroy session and redirect
elseif ($now > $_SESSION['start'] + $timelimit) {
  // empty the $_SESSION array
  $_SESSION = array();
  // invalidate the session cookie
  if (isset($_COOKIE[session_name()])) {
    setcookie(session_name(), '', time()-86400, '/');
  }
  // end session and redirect with query string
  session_destroy();
  header("Location: {$redirect}?expired=yes");
  exit;
  }
// if it's got this far, it's OK, so update start time
else {
  $_SESSION['start'] = time();
  }
?>
```

The inline comments explain what is going on; and you should recognize most of the elseif clause from PHP Solution 9-5. PHP measures time in seconds, and I've set $timelimit (in line 5) to a ridiculously short 15 seconds purely for demonstration purposes. To set a more reasonable limit of, say, 15 minutes, change this later like this:

$timelimit = 15 * 60; // 15 minutes

You could, of course, set $timelimit to 900, but why bother when PHP can do the hard work for you?

If the sum of $_SESSION['start'] plus $timelimit is less than the current time (stored as $now), you end the session and redirect the user to the login page. The line that performs the redirect adds a query string to the end of the URL like this:

http://localhost/phpsolutions/sessions/login.php?expired=yes

The code in step 2 takes no notice of the value of expired; adding yes as the value just makes it look user-friendlier in the browser address bar.

If the script gets as far as the final else, it means that $_SESSION['authenticated'] has been set, and that the time limit hasn't been reached, so $_SESSION['start'] is updated to the current time, and the page displays as normal.

4. Copy the code in the preceding step, and use it to replace the code above the DOCTYPE declaration in secretpage.php.

5. Save all three pages, and load either menu.php or secretpage.php into a browser. If the page displays, click Log out. Then log back in, and navigate back and forth between menu.php and secretpage.php. Once you have verified that the links work, wait 15 seconds or more, and try to navigate back to the other page. You should be automatically logged out and presented with the following screen:

9

The code in step 2 is quite long, and is identical for every page that requires it, so it's an ideal candidate for turning into an include. That way, you need update only one script if you decide to change the time limit or the redirect page. The start_session() command can also go in the include file as long as it comes before the use of any session variables.

Passing information through multipage forms

Variables passed through the $_POST and $_GET arrays have only a fleeting existence. Once they have been passed to a page, they're gone, unless you save their values in some way. The usual method of preserving information that's passed from one form to another is to extract its value from the $_POST array and store it in a hidden field in XHTML like this:

```
<input type="hidden" name="address" id="address" ➡
value="<?php echo $_POST['address']; ?>" />
```

As their name suggests, hidden fields are part of a form's code, but nothing is displayed onscreen. Hidden fields are fine for one or two items, but say you have a survey that's spread over four pages. If you have 10 items on a page, you need a total of 60 hidden fields (10 on the second page, 20 on the third, and 30 on the fourth). Session variables can save you all that coding. They can also make sure that visitors always start on the right page of a multipage form.

PHP Solution 9-9: Using sessions for a multipage form

In the download files for this chapter, you'll find four pages called multiple01.php, multiple02.php, multiple03.php, and multiple04.php. The first three contain just a single field for the user to enter name, age, and address. The final page displays the contents of the $_SESSION array after each page has been submitted. The forms are simple so that you can concentrate on how the PHP works.

1. Copy the four files from the download folder for this chapter, and save them in the sessions folder. If you are using Windows, and have set up your testing environment as suggested in Chapter 2, the pages should work without any changes. If you are on a Mac, are using a remote server, or have a different testing environment, open each page and change the URLs in the header() functions to match your setup. For instance, on a Mac, I need to change the code in multiple01.php from this:

   ```
   header('Location: http://localhost/phpsolutions/sessions/ ➡
   multiple02.php');
   ```

   to this:

   ```
   header('Location: http://localhost/~davidpowers/phpsolutions/ ➡
   sessions/multiple02.php');
   ```

   The header() function is used once each in multiple01.php and multiple04.php, and twice each in the other two pages.

2. Once you have made any necessary changes, attempt to load any of the final three pages into a browser. You should be taken directly to multiple01.php. The pages use the same technique as PHP Solution 9-4. The only difference is that the session variable is called $_SESSION['formStarted'] instead of $_SESSION['authenticated']. For the purposes of this demonstration, multiple01.php begins by clearing existing session variables. In a real application, this may not be appropriate. The code in multiple04.php shows how to exclude any session variables that you don't want to pass on with the final form submission.

3. Try clicking the Next button in multiple01.php. The form tells you that the name field is missing. Enter anything, and click Next again. The second form asks for Age. Click Next, and the form takes you without complaint to the third page, which asks for Address. This page won't let you get away with entering nothing. Enter anything, and click Send details. You should see something like the following screenshot:

Rather than go through the code in detail, I'll leave you to read the inline comments of the four pages. The first three pages use techniques from the rest of this chapter, combined with the form processing techniques from Chapter 5. The main code in the final page looks like this:

```php
<p>The details submitted were as follows:</p>
<ul>
<?php
// unset the formStarted variable
unset($_SESSION['formStarted']);
foreach ($_SESSION as $key => $value) {
  // skip the submit buttons
  // use identity operator with strpos to prevent false negatives
  if (strpos($key, 'Submit') === 0) {
    continue;
    }
  echo "<li>$key: $value</li>";
  }
  // clear the $_SESSION array and destroy session
  $_SESSION = array();
  session_destroy();
?>
</ul>
```

It cleans up the $_SESSION array by removing $_SESSION['formStarted'] and session variables created by each of the submit buttons. The name and value of the submit button is always part of the $_POST array, so each submit button is added to $_SESSION array as you progress through the forms. You can skip them in the foreach loop by using strpos() to test for the string Submit. Use the same technique for any other session variables that you want to exclude.

The strpos() function takes two arguments: a string that you want to search, and a character or substring that you want to find in it. If it finds the substring that you're looking for, strpos() returns the position of the first character. Since the position of characters in strings is always counted from 0, it's essential to use the identical operator (three equal signs) to make sure that the result of strpos($key, 'Submit') is genuinely 0, and not a false negative. To see what I mean, alter the following line:

```
if (strpos($key, 'Submit') === 0) {  // CORRECT
```

Change it to this:

```
if (strpos($key, 'Submit') == 0) {  // WRONG
```

If you test the sequence again, you'll see that no results are displayed. This is because strpos() returns false if it can't find the substring; and PHP interprets 0 as false. What you're looking for is not false, but Submit at the beginning of the string—in other words, *position* 0. The identical operator guarantees that the items you're comparing not only have the same value, but are also of the same data type.

> Don't worry if that last part went over your head. Just remember that when using strpos() *to find a character or substring at the start of a string, use the identical operator (===) and not the equality operator (==).*

The foreach loop on the final page of this example displays the contents of the $_SESSION array onscreen. In a real application, you would use the session variables to build the content of an email message or to prepare a SQL query to insert the information in a database.

Coming up . . .

If you started this book with little or no knowledge of PHP, you're no longer in the beginners' league, but are leveraging the power PHP in a lot of useful ways. Hopefully, by now, you'll have begun to appreciate that the same or similar techniques crop up again and again. Instead of just copying code, you should start to recognize techniques that you can adapt to your needs and experiment on your own.

The rest of this book continues to build on your knowledge, but brings a new factor into play: the MySQL relational database, which will take your PHP skills to a higher level. The next chapter shows you how to install MySQL and get it ready for use. Then you'll learn the basics of working with MySQL and a PHP-driven graphical interface called phpMyAdmin before bringing PHP back into the picture.

10 SETTING UP MYSQL AND PHPMYADMIN

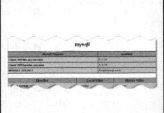

What this chapter covers:

- Installing the MySQL database on Windows and Mac OS X
- Securing the database
- Setting up the phpMyAdmin graphical interface
- Backing up and transferring data to another server

Dynamic websites take on a whole new meaning in combination with a database. Drawing content from a database allows you to present material in ways that would be impractical—if not impossible—with a static website. Examples that spring to mind are online stores, such as Amazon.com; news sites, such as the International Herald Tribune (www.iht.com); and the big search engines, including Google and Yahoo! Database technology allows these websites to present thousands, sometimes millions, of unique pages with remarkably little underlying code. Even if your ambitions are nowhere near as grandiose, a database can increase your website's richness of content with relatively little effort. First of all, though, you need to choose and install a database system.

Why MySQL?

Of all the available databases, why choose MySQL? The following reasons should convince you:

- **Cost:** The MySQL Community Edition is free under the open source GPL license (www.gnu.org/copyleft/gpl.html).
- **Powerful:** The same basic database system as the Community Edition is used by leading organizations such as NASA, Yahoo!, and Alcatel. It's feature-rich and fast.
- **Widespread availability:** MySQL is the most popular open source database. Most hosting companies automatically offer MySQL in combination with PHP.
- **Cross-platform compatibility:** MySQL runs on Windows, Mac OS X, and Linux. A database created on one system requires no conversion when transferred to another.
- **Open source:** Although there is a commercial version, the code and features in the Community Edition are identical. New features are being added constantly.
- **Security:** Bugs, when found, are dealt with quickly.

So, are there any drawbacks to MySQL? I'd love to be able to say it's perfect, but MySQL is not as fully featured as its main commercial rivals, Microsoft SQL Server and Oracle, or its main open source rival, PostgreSQL (www.postgresql.org). However, the missing features are primarily of interest to advanced users, and most are expected to be implemented by MySQL 5.2 (currently, MySQL 5.1 is in an advanced beta stage).

Perhaps the biggest drawback for people who don't come from a programming background is the fact that MySQL doesn't come with a glossy interface. That's because MySQL is a database workhorse. It's fast and efficient, and is particularly suited to web-based applications. There are several graphical interfaces available, the most popular being phpMyAdmin, which is free and the default method many hosting companies provide for accessing MySQL. This chapter shows you how to install both of them.

Which version?

MySQL and phpMyAdmin release new versions at a fast-and-furious pace. While this means that new features become available as soon as they're developed, and bugs get squashed quickly, hosting companies rarely keep pace. In fact, many hosting companies are still running the MySQL 3.23 series—an excellent database, even though it is two major versions behind the current release.

Rather than attempting to find old versions to match the setup on your hosting company, I recommend that you install the latest stable version of both MySQL and phpMyAdmin. That way, you will find it easier to get help if you run into difficulties. Wherever possible, I have designed the code in this book to be backward compatible with MySQL 3.23, and I point out anything that isn't.

You can get MySQL from the downloads page at http://dev.mysql.com/downloads. Select the link for the Current Release (Recommended) of MySQL Community Edition— Database Server and Client.

The installation instructions for MySQL are different for Windows and Mac OS X, so Mac users should skip ahead to the relevant section of the chapter.

> *Because new versions are coming out all the time, I recommend that you check my website at* http://foundationphp.com/phpsolutions/updates.php *before going ahead. Any major updates to the instructions will be listed there.*

Installing MySQL on Windows

MySQL comes in a range of versions, but the one you should choose is **Windows Essentials**. It contains all the important stuff, and certainly everything you need for this book. If you have a version older than MySQL 4.1.5 already installed on your computer, you *must* uninstall the old version first.

These instructions are based on the 5.0 series of MySQL, which is installed in `C:\Program Files\MySQL\MySQL Server 5.0`. *I expect MySQL 5.1 to become the recommended release shortly after publication of this book. On past experience, the default location changes for each series of Windows Essentials, so 5.1 is likely to be installed in* `C:\Program Files\MySQL\MySQL Server 5.1`, *and Windows treats different series as completely separate programs. If you upgrade from one series to another, any existing databases need to be transferred to the new version as if it were a different server (see the section titled "Backup and data transfer" near the end of this chapter).*

Installing the Windows Essentials version of MySQL

1. Go to the MySQL download site and select the link for the current release.

2. In the page that opens, scroll down to find the section marked Windows downloads. There is a separate Windows x64 downloads section for 64-bit versions of Windows. Choose Windows Essentials from the appropriate section, and click the download link. (You may be invited to Pick a mirror instead. This directs you to a mirror site closer to your location, and usually offers a faster download.)

3. Download the MySQL file to your hard disk. It will have a name like `mysql-essential-x.x.x-win32.msi`, where *x.x.x* represents the version number. The 64-bit version is called `mysql-essential-x.x.x-win64.msi`. Make sure you have the correct version.

4. Exit all other Windows programs, and double-click the icon of the file you have just downloaded. This is a self-extracting Windows Installer package.

5. Windows Installer will begin the installation process and open a welcome dialog box. If you are upgrading an existing version of the *same series* of Windows Essentials to a more recent one, the dialog box will inform you that it has detected your current installation and will remove it before installing the new one. However, all your databases will remain intact. Click Next to continue.

6. Another dialog box may give you the opportunity to change the installation destination. Accept the default and click Next.

7. In the next dialog box, accept the default setup (Typical) and click Next.

8. If you're happy to go ahead with installation, click Install in the next dialog box.

9. Before launching into the actual installation, MySQL invites you to sign up for a free MySQL.com account. I suggest that you select Skip Sign-Up and click Next. After you finish setting everything up, visit `www.mysql.com/register.php` to see if you're interested in the benefits offered. The main advantage is that you get automatic notification of new versions and links to helpful articles about new features of MySQL.

10. The actual installation now takes place and is normally very quick. When everything's finished, you're presented with a final dialog box.

- If this is a new installation or if you are upgrading from one series to another, click Finish to launch the Configuration Wizard, which is described in the next section.

- If you are upgrading to a later version of the same series (such as from 5.0.10 to 5.0.24), deselect the check box labeled Configure the MySQL Server now before clicking Finish. MySQL should be ready to use, but needs to be restarted manually (see "Starting and stopping MySQL manually on Windows" later in the chapter). If you have a software firewall, you might also be prompted to allow connections to and from MySQL.

Configuring MySQL Windows Essentials

There are a lot of dialog boxes to go through, although all you usually need to do is accept the default setting. These instructions are based on version 1.0.8 of the Configuration Wizard.

1. The Configuration Wizard opens with a welcome screen. Click Next to proceed.

2. The first dialog box asks whether you want a detailed or standard configuration. Choose the default Detailed Configuration option and click Next.

3. The three options on the next screen affect the amount of computer resources devoted to MySQL. Accept the default Developer Machine and click Next. If you choose either of the other options, all other programs will slow down to a crawl.

4. The next dialog box asks you to select from the following three types of database:

- Multifunctional Database: Allows you to use both InnoDB and MyISAM tables.

- Transactional Database Only: InnoDB tables only. MyISAM is disabled.

- Non-Transactional Database Only: MyISAM tables only. InnoDB is disabled.

Most hosting companies support only MyISAM tables, so choose Non-Transactional Database Only. Unless you plan to learn MySQL in depth, there is little advantage in choosing Multifunctional Database, which requires an extra 30MB of disk space.

> *If you choose* Multifunctional Database, *you need to edit the MySQL configuration file later, as described in "Changing the default table type on Windows Essentials."*

5. What you see next may vary. If you chose Non-Transactional Database Only in the preceding step, you should be taken directly to step 6. However, you may see a dialog box inviting you to select a drive for the InnoDB data file. Unless you chose Multifunctional Database, just click Next and move on to step 6.

10

If you plan to use InnoDB, you need to tell MySQL where to store the data. The InnoDB engine uses a single **tablespace** that acts as a sort of virtual file system. InnoDB files, once created, cannot be made smaller. The default location for the tablespace is C:\Program Files\MySQL\MySQL Server 5.0\data. If you want to locate the tablespace elsewhere, the drop-down menu offers some suggested alternatives. When you have made your choice, click Next.

6. Leave the next dialog box at the default Decision Support (DSS)/OLAP and click Next.

7. The next dialog box sets the networking options and SQL mode. The important settings are in the top half. Make sure Enable TCP/IP Networking is checked, and leave Port Number on the default setting of 3306. The lower half of the dialog box lets you choose whether to run MySQL in strict mode. In an ideal world, you should accept this default setting, but it may cause problems with some PHP applications written before strict mode was introduced. Deselect the Strict mode check box and click Next.

8. MySQL has impressive support for most of the world's languages. The next dialog box invites you to choose a default character set. In spite of what you might think, this has no bearing on the range of languages supported—all are supported by default. The character set mainly determines the order in which data is sorted. Unless you have a specific reason for choosing anything other than the default Standard Character Set, I suggest that you accept it without making any changes, as shown. Click Next.

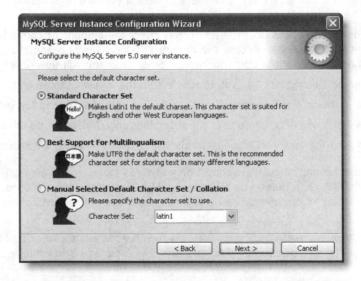

9. The recommended way of running MySQL is as a Windows service. If you accept the defaults as shown in the top half of the next dialog box, MySQL will always start automatically when you boot your computer and run silently in the background. (If MySQL has already been installed as a Windows service, this section will be grayed out.) If for any reason you don't want MySQL to start automatically, uncheck the Launch the MySQL Server automatically option. You can easily change this option later (see the section "Starting and stopping MySQL manually on Windows" later in this chapter).

The lower half of the dialog box gives you the option to include the bin directory in your Windows PATH. This option enables you to interact directly with MySQL and its related utilities at the command line without the need to change directory every time. You won't need to do this very often—if at all—but selecting this option makes life a little more convenient if the occasion ever arises. Click Next.

If you get a warning message that a Windows service with the name MySQL already exists, you will be asked if you want to use this name. You must click No and choose a different name from the dropdown menu in the Service Name field.

10. A fresh installation of MySQL has no security settings, so anyone can tamper with your data. MySQL uses the name **root** to signify the main database administrator with unrestricted control over all aspects of the database. Choose a password that you can remember, and enter it in both boxes.

Unless you access your development server from a different computer over a network, leave the Enable root access from remote machines check box unchecked.

Do *not* check Create An Anonymous Account. It will make your database insecure.

If you are upgrading an existing version of Windows Essentials and want to keep your current root password, deselect the Modify Security Settings check box. If this is a first-time installation, you probably won't have this check box.

Click Next when you have finished.

11. At long last, everything is ready. Click Execute. If you have installed a software firewall, it will probably warn you that MySQL is trying to connect to a DNS server. You must allow the connection; otherwise, MySQL will never work.

12. Assuming that all was okay, you should see a screen confirming that the configuration process is complete. MySQL should now be running—even if you selected the option not to start automatically (the option applies only to automatic start on bootup).

13. If you want to change the configuration at a later date, launch the Configuration Wizard from the Windows Start menu by choosing Programs ➤ MySQL ➤ MySQL Server 5.0 ➤ MySQL Server Instance Config Wizard. The dialog box that opens offers the following two options:

- Reconfigure Instance: This takes you through all the dialog boxes again.
- Remove Instance: This does not remove MySQL from your system, but removes the Windows service that automatically starts MySQL when you boot your computer. Unfortunately, it also removes the MySQL configuration file. See "Starting and stopping MySQL manually on Windows" for a less radical solution.

Changing the default table type on Windows Essentials

The instructions in this section are required only if you selected Multifunctional Database in step 4 of "Configuring MySQL Windows Essentials."

The Windows Configuration Wizard sets InnoDB as the default table storage engine for a multifunctional database. Since most hosting companies don't support InnoDB, you should reset the default to MyISAM. All it requires is a simple change to the MySQL configuration file: my.ini.

1. Use Windows Explorer to navigate to the folder in which MySQL was installed. The default is C:\Program Files\MySQL\MySQL Server 5.0.

2. Locate the file called my.ini, and double-click it. The file will open in Notepad.

3. Approximately 80 lines from the top you should find a line that reads as follows:

default-storage-engine=INNODB

Change it to the following:

default-storage-engine=**MyISAM**

4. Save the file and close it. To make the change effective, restart MySQL. MySQL will now create all new tables in the default MyISAM format. To use the InnoDB format for a database, you can change the table type in phpMyAdmin, the graphical interface for MySQL that you will install later in the chapter.

Starting and stopping MySQL manually on Windows

Most of the time, MySQL will be configured to start up automatically, and you can forget about it entirely. There are times, however, when you need to know how to start or stop MySQL manually—whether for maintenance, to conserve resources, or because you're paranoid about security (a physical firewall is probably a much better solution).

1. Select Control Panel from the Windows Start menu. Double-click the Administrative Tools icon and then double-click the Services icon in the window that opens.

2. In the Services panel, scroll down to find MySQL and highlight it by clicking once. You can now use the video recorder–type icons at the top of the panel to stop or start the server. The text links on the left of the panel do the same.

3. To change the automatic startup option, highlight MySQL in the Services panel, right-click to reveal a context menu, and choose Properties.

4. In the dialog box that opens, activate the Startup type drop-down menu and choose Automatic, Manual, or Disabled. Click OK. That's all there is to it.

Using the MySQL monitor on Windows

Although most of your interaction with MySQL will be through phpMyAdmin or your own PHP scripts, it's useful to know how to access MySQL through the MySQL monitor (or the Command Line Client, as it's called in Windows Essentials). It's also a good way to test that your installation went without problems.

To start a session From the Windows Start menu, select Programs ➤ MySQL ➤ MySQL Server 5.0 ➤ MySQL Command Line Client. This will open the Command Line Client, which will ask you for your password. Type in the root password that you chose in step 10 of the section "Configuring MySQL Windows Essentials" and press Enter. As long as the server is running—and you typed your password correctly—you will see a welcome message similar to the one shown here.

If you get your password wrong, your computer will beep and close the window. If you find this happening repeatedly, even though you're sure you typed in your password correctly, there are two likely explanations. The first is that your Caps Lock key is on—MySQL passwords are case-sensitive. The other is that the MySQL server isn't running. Refer to the previous section on how to control MySQL manually before doing too much damage by banging your forehead on the keyboard.

> *Being unable to connect to MySQL because the server isn't running is probably the most common beginner's mistake. The MySQL server runs in the background, waiting for requests. Opening the Command Line Client does not start MySQL; it opens the MySQL monitor, which is a channel for you to send instructions to the server. Equally, closing the Command Line Client does not stop MySQL. The server continues running in the background until the computer is closed down or until you stop it manually.*

Ending your session After you finish working with the MySQL monitor, type exit or quit at the mysql> prompt, followed by Enter. The MySQL Command Line Client window closes automatically.

Updating the PHP connector files

Since the release of PHP 5.0.0, the code libraries that control connection between PHP and MySQL are no longer integrated into the PHP core. MySQL recommends that you replace the following three files with versions created by MySQL:

- `php_mysql.dll`
- `php_mysqli.dll`
- `libmysql.dll`

The versions created by MySQL are compiled against the most recent MySQL Client libraries, so they contain fixes for bugs that may not have filtered through to the PHP versions. It takes about a week after the release of a new version of either MySQL or PHP for the updated connector files to become available. Using the previous version of connector files should not make any difference.

1. Go to http://dev.mysql.com/downloads/connector/php.

2. Download the ZIP files for both the mysqli extension and mysql extension for the latest version of MySQL.

3. Unzip both files to a temporary folder. When you unzip the second one, you will be warned that `libmysql.dll` already exists. Accept the option to overwrite it. You should now have the three files as shown here in your temporary folder (the version numbers may, of course, be different).

4. Stop Apache or IIS (refer back to Chapter 2, if necessary).

5. Cut `libmysql.dll` to your clipboard and paste it in the main PHP folder (C:\php, if you followed the recommended setup in Chapter 2). When prompted, confirm that you want to overwrite the existing file.

6. Cut `php_mysql.dll` and `php_mysqli.dll` to your clipboard and paste them in the PHP extension folder (C:\php\ext). Confirm that you want to overwrite the existing files.

7. Restart Apache or IIS.

8. Load a page containing the script `<?php phpinfo(); ?>` into a browser, and check that you have entries for mysql and mysqli as shown in the following screenshots. The Client API version should be the same as the number indicated on the MySQL download site in step 2.

mysql	
MySQL Support	enabled
Active Persistent Links	0
Active Links	0
Client API version	5.0.24
Directive	Local Value	Master Value
allow_pe...	On	

mysqli	
Mysqli Support	**enabled**
Client API library version	5.0.24
Client API header version	5.0.24
MYSQLI_SOCKET	/tmp/mysql.sock

Directive	Local Value	Master Value
"default,"	value	ue

Assuming everything went well, skip ahead to the section "Using MySQL with a graphical interface." If you cannot find mysql and mysqli in the PHP configuration, read on.

Troubleshooting

You must be able to see the mysql and mysqli entries in the PHP configuration page before attempting to go any further. Without them, you can't connect to MySQL. The most common cause for them failing to appear lies in Windows not reading the correct version of php.ini, or not being able to find php.ini at all. This usually happens if you had a previous installation of PHP and didn't remove it from the Windows system folders. After running phpinfo(), check the value for Configuration File (php.ini) Path (it's the sixth item from the top). If it's pointing to C:\WINDOWS\php.ini or C:\WINNT\php.ini, you should return to Chapter 2 and follow the advice on removing an old version of PHP.

Unfortunately, this doesn't always work, as there may be other programs preventing Windows from reading the correct version of php.ini. If this happens to you, the most practical solution is to copy php.ini to C:\WINDOWS or C:\WINNT (depending on your system). You will probably also need to copy libmysql.dll to C:\WINDOWS\system32 or C:\WINNT\system32.

Setting up MySQL on Mac OS X

MySQL is available as a Mac PKG file, so everything is taken care of for you, apart from some minor configuration.

10

> *When upgrading an existing installation of MySQL, the Mac installer will not move your data files. You must first create a backup, as described at the end of this chapter, and reload them after upgrading. You must also shut down the MySQL server. If you have never installed MySQL before, you don't need any special preparations; just follow these instructions.*

Downloading and installing MySQL

1. Go to www.mysql.com/downloads, and select the link for the Current Release (Recommended) of MySQL Community Edition—Database Server and Client.

> *MySQL 5 is not supported on Jaguar (OS X 10.2). Download the most recent version of MySQL 4.1 instead. It should be listed among Older Releases or Archives.*

2. Scroll down to the Mac OS X downloads section and choose the Standard version for your processor and version of OS X—there are separate packages for PowerPC, 64-bit PowerPC, and Intel Macs. The Intel Mac version is labeled x86. As you can see from the screenshot in the next step, the PKG filename includes not only the MySQL version number, but also the version of OS X and processor for which it has been compiled (osx10.4-powerpc). The size of the download file is approximately 27MB.

> *The Mac files are listed close to the bottom of the downloads page. Make sure you don't scroll too far down. There is a separate section at the bottom for TAR files, which require manual installation. When the download starts, check that the file has a* .dmg *filename extension. If the file has a* .tar.gz *extension, cancel the download and find the Mac section higher up the page.*

3. Double-click the DMG icon to mount the disk image on your desktop.

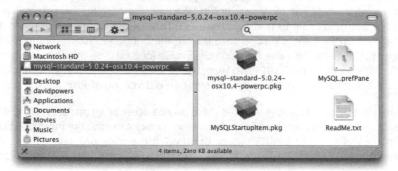

4. Double-click the mysql-standard-*x.x.x*.pkg icon to start the installation process. The Mac OS X installer opens. Follow the instructions onscreen.

5. Double-click the MySQLStartupItem.pkg icon, and follow the instructions onscreen.

6. Open a Finder window and drag the MySQL.prefPane icon onto Applications ➤ System Preferences. This installs a MySQL control panel. A dialog box asks whether you want it to be available to yourself or all users. Make your choice, and click Install.

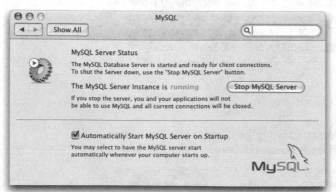

The MySQL preference pane should open. Click Start MySQL Server and enter your Mac administrator password when prompted. It may take a few seconds before the preference pane reports that the server is running, as shown here.

To start or stop the MySQL server in the future, open the preference pane by clicking the MySQL icon in the Other section of System Preferences.

Adding MySQL to your PATH

You normally access MySQL through phpMyAdmin (introduced later in this chapter) or your own PHP scripts, but sometimes you need to access it directly in Terminal. To avoid having to type out the full path every time, add it to the PATH in your environmental variables. If you have a new installation of Mac OS X 10.3 or later, Terminal uses what is known as the "bash shell." If you upgraded from Jaguar using Archive and Install, you will probably be using the "tcsh shell." The only way to make sure is to open Terminal (in Applications ➤ Utilities) and check the title bar. It will either say Terminal — bash, as shown in the following screenshot, or Terminal — tcsh. Use the appropriate set of instructions.

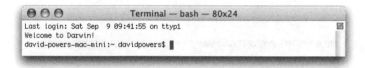

Amending PATH in the bash shell in OS X 10.4 or later

1. Open BBEdit or TextWrangler.

2. From the File menu, choose Open Hidden and browse to your home folder. If there is a file called .profile (with a period as the first character), as shown in the screenshot, highlight it, and click Open.

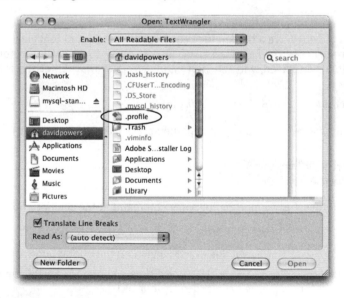

3. The file exists only if you have already made changes to the way Terminal operates. If .profile doesn't exist, click Cancel, and open a blank file.

10

4. If you have opened an existing version of .profile, add the following code on a separate line at the end. Otherwise, enter it in the blank page.

```
export PATH="$PATH:/usr/local/mysql/bin"
```

5. Select File ➤ Save, and save the file as .profile in your own home folder. The period at the beginning of the filename should provoke the following warning:

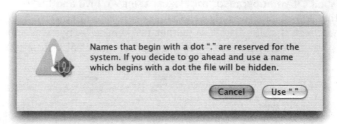

6. Select Use "." and close your text editor.

Amending PATH in the bash shell in OS X 10.3

You can't edit hidden files in TextWrangler or BBEdit in OS X 10.3 (Panther), so you need to use one of Terminal's text editors.

1. Open Terminal and type the following command followed by Return:

```
pico ~/.profile
```

2. If you already have a hidden file called .profile, the contents will be displayed in Terminal. Use the keyboard arrow keys to move to a new line before typing. If nothing is displayed, you can start typing straight away. Enter the following line of code:

```
export PATH="$PATH:/usr/local/mysql/bin"
```

3. Save the file by pressing Ctrl+X, and then press Y and Return. Close Terminal.

Amending PATH in the tcsh shell

1. Open Terminal and enter the following command at the shell prompt:

```
echo 'setenv PATH /usr/local/mysql/bin:$PATH' >> ~/.tcshrc
```

Make sure you copy everything exactly, including the quotes and spacing as shown.

2. Press Return and close Terminal. The next time you open Terminal, the MySQL program directory will have been added to your PATH.

Securing MySQL on Mac OS X

Although you have a fully functioning installation of MySQL, by default it has no security. Even if you're the only person working on your computer, you need to set up a similar system of passwords and user accounts as on your hosting company's server. There's one important account that exists by default on all MySQL servers. It's called root, and it is the main database administrator with unlimited powers over database files. When you first install MySQL, access to the root account isn't password-protected, so you need to block this security gap. The MySQL root user, by the way, is totally unrelated to the Mac OS X root user, which is disabled by default. Enabling root for MySQL has *no* effect on the OS X root user.

> *If you have just added MySQL to your* PATH, *you must close and reopen Terminal before embarking on this section. Otherwise, Terminal won't be able to find MySQL.*

Setting the MySQL root password

1. Open Terminal and type the following command:

   ```
   mysql -u root
   ```

   The command contains three elements:

   - mysql: The name of the program
   - -u: Tells the program that you want to log in as a specified user
   - root: The name of the user

2. You should see a welcome message like this:

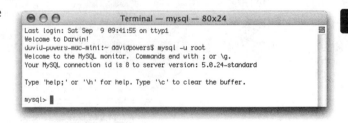

10

3. The most common problem is getting an error message like this instead:

   It means that mysqld, the MySQL server, is not running. Use the MySQL control panel in System Preferences to start the server.

   Another common problem is for Terminal to report command not found. That means you have either mistyped the command or that you haven't added the MySQL program files directory to your PATH, as described in the previous section.

4. Assuming that you have logged in successfully, as described in step 2, type the following command at the mysql> prompt:

```
use mysql
```

This command tells MySQL that you want to use the database called mysql, which contains all the details of authorized users and the privileges they have to work on database files. You should see the message Database changed, which means MySQL is ready for you to work on the files controlling administrative privileges.

5. Now enter the command to set a password for the root user. Substitute *myPassword* with the actual password you want to use. Also make sure you use quotes where indicated and finish the command with a semicolon.

```
UPDATE user SET password = PASSWORD('myPassword') WHERE user = 'root';
```

6. Next, remove anonymous access to MySQL:

```
DELETE FROM user WHERE user = '';
```

The quotes before the semicolon are two single quotes with no space in between.

7. Tell MySQL to update the privileges table:

```
FLUSH PRIVILEGES;
```

The sequence of commands should produce a series of results like this:

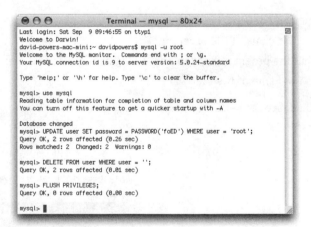

8. To exit the MySQL monitor, type exit, followed by Return. This simply ends your session with the MySQL monitor. *It does not shut down the MySQL server.*

9. Now try to log back in by using the same command as in step 2. MySQL won't let you in. Anonymous access and password-free access have been removed. To get in this time, you need to tell MySQL that you want to use a password:

```
mysql -u root -p
```

10. When you press Return, you will be prompted for your password. Nothing will appear onscreen as you type, but as long as you enter the correct password, MySQL will let you back in. Congratulations, you now have a secure installation of MySQL.

Using MySQL with a graphical interface

Although you can do everything using MySQL monitor, it's a lot easier to use a graphic interface. There are several to choose from, both commercial and free. Among the free offerings are two from MySQL itself: MySQL Administrator and MySQL Query Browser (www.mysql.com/products/tools). Two other popular graphical front ends for MySQL are the commercial product, Navicat (www.navicat.com), and SQLyog (www.webyog.com), which is available in both commercial and free versions.

However, the most popular graphical interface for MySQL is phpMyAdmin (www.phpmyadmin. net). It's a PHP-based administrative system for MySQL that has been around since 1998, and it constantly evolves to keep pace with MySQL developments. It works on Windows, Mac OS X, and Linux and currently supports all versions of MySQL from 3.23.32 to 5.0. What's more, many hosting companies provide it as the standard interface to MySQL.

Because phpMyAdmin has a very intuitive interface, I suggest that you try it first. If you work with databases on a regular basis, you may want to explore the other graphical interfaces later. However, since phpMyAdmin is free, you have nothing to lose—and you may find it does everything you want.

Setting up phpMyAdmin on Windows and Mac

Since phpMyAdmin is PHP-based, all that's needed to install it is download the files, unzip them to a website in your local testing environment, and create a simple configuration file.

Downloading and installing phpMyAdmin

1. Go to www.phpmyadmin.net and download the latest stable version. The files can be downloaded in three types of compressed file: BZIP2, GZIP, and ZIP. Choose whichever format you have the decompression software for.

2. Unzip the downloaded file. It will extract the contents to a folder called phpMyAdmin-x.x.x, where x represents the version number.

3. Highlight the folder icon and cut it to your clipboard. On Windows, paste it inside the folder designated as your web server root (C:\htdocs, if you followed my example). If you're on a Mac and want phpMyAdmin to be available to all users, put the folder in Macintosh HD:Library:WebServer:Documents, rather than in your own Sites folder.

4. Rename the folder you have just moved to this: phpMyAdmin.

5. Like Apache and PHP, phpMyAdmin uses a text file to store all the configuration details. Since version 2.7.0, you no longer edit the phpMyAdmin configuration file, but store your personal details in a new file, which should be named config.inc.php. There are two ways of doing this: using a built-in script called setup.php or manually. I prefer the manual method, but instructions for both methods follow.

10

Configuring phpMyAdmin with setup.php

1. Create a new subfolder called config within the phpMyAdmin folder. Windows users skip to step 3. Mac users continue with step 2.

2. On Mac OS X, use Finder to locate the config folder that you have just created. Ctrl-click and select Get Info. In Ownership & Permissions, expand Details, and click the lock icon so that you can make changes to the settings. Change the setting for Others to Read & Write. Close the config Info panel.

3. Open a browser, and type the following into the address bar:

   http://localhost/phpmyadmin/scripts/setup.php

   If you created the phpMyAdmin folder inside your Sites folder on a Mac, use the following address, replacing *username* with your Mac username:

   http://localhost/~*username*/phpmyadmin/scripts/setup.php

4. You should see the page shown in Figure 10-1.

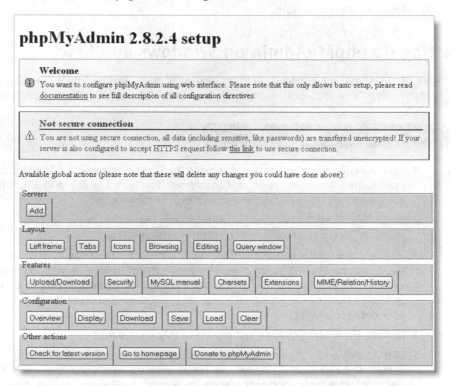

Figure 10-1. A built-in script automates the configuration of phpMyAdmin.

Ignore any warning about the connection not being secure. This is intended for server administrators installing phpMyAdmin on a live Internet server. If, on the other hand, you see the following warning, it means that you have not set up the config folder correctly, and should go back to step 1.

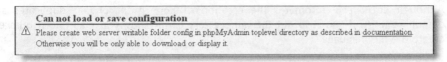

Can not load or save configuration

⚠ Please create web server writable folder config in phpMyAdmin toplevel directory as described in <u>documentation</u>. Otherwise you will be only able to download or display it.

5. Click the Add button in the Servers section. This loads a form with most of the necessary information already filled in. Check the following settings:

- Server hostname: localhost
- Server port: **Leave blank unless** your web server is running on a nonstandard port, such as 8080
- Server socket: **Leave blank**
- Connection type: tcp
- PHP extension to use: mysqli

6. The default setting for Authentication type is config. **If you don't need to password protect access to phpMyAdmin, check that** User for config auth **is set to** root, **and enter your MySQL root password in the next field,** Password for config auth.

If you want to restrict access to phpMyAdmin by prompting users for a password, **change** Authentication type **to** http, **and delete** root **from the** User for config auth **field.**

7. Scroll down to the Actions field and click Add. As shown here, there are two Add buttons close to each other. Click the one circled in the screenshot.

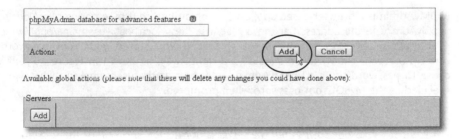

8. The next screen will probably warn you that you didn't set up a phpMyAdmin database, so won't be able to use all the phpMyAdmin features. This is not important. You can set one up later if you decide to use the advanced features of phpMyAdmin.

9. Scroll down to the Configuration section near the bottom of the page and click Save.

10. Open the config folder in Explorer or Finder. You should see a new file called config.inc.php. Move it to the main phpMyAdmin folder. The official instructions tell you to delete the config folder, but this isn't necessary in a local testing environment.

10

Configuring phpMyAdmin manually

Although `setup.php` automates the creation of `config.inc.php`, it duplicates some default settings. If you strip out the unnecessary commands, you may find it quicker to create the file manually.

1. If you don't need to password protect access to phpMyAdmin, type the following code into a blank document:

```php
<?php
$i = 1;
$cfg['Servers'][$i]['extension'] = 'mysqli';
$cfg['Servers'][$i]['password']  = 'mysqlRootPassword';
?>
```

Use your own MySQL root password in place of *mysqlRootPassword*.

If you need password protection for phpMyAdmin, use the following code instead:

```php
<?php
$i = 1;
$cfg['Servers'][$i]['extension'] = 'mysqli';
$cfg['Servers'][$i]['auth_type'] = 'http';
?>
```

2. Save the file as `config.inc.php` in the main phpMyAdmin folder. Erm . . . that's it.

Launching phpMyAdmin

phpMyAdmin is a browser-based application, so you launch it by entering http://localhost/ phpMyAdmin/ in the address bar (on a Mac, use http://localhost/~username/phpMyAdmin/ if you put phpMyAdmin in your Sites folder). If you stored your root password in `config.inc.php`, phpMyAdmin should load right away, as shown in Figure 10-2. If you chose to password protect phpMyAdmin, enter root as the username and whatever you specified as the MySQL root password when prompted.

> If you get a message saying that the server is not responding or that the socket is not correctly configured, make sure that the MySQL server is running.

The phpMyAdmin front page has a drop-down menu labeled Theme/Style. Currently, there are two options: Original and Darkblue/orange. Figure 10-2 shows the default Original style. However, all subsequent screenshots are taken using the Darkblue/orange style, because the tabbed interface fits better on the printed page. Choose whichever style you prefer.

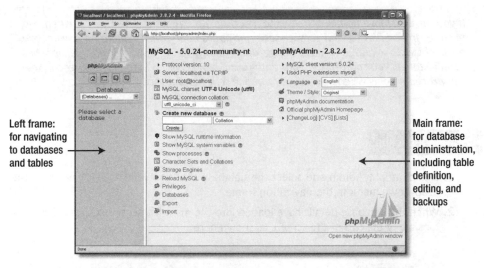

Left frame:
for navigating
to databases
and tables

Main frame:
for database
administration,
including table
definition,
editing, and
backups

Figure 10-2. phpMyAdmin is a very user-friendly and stable graphical interface to MySQL.

Logging out of phpMyAdmin

If you opted to password protect phpMyAdmin, the Log out link is at the bottom left of the front page, just beneath Import (as shown in the screenshot). When you click the link, you are immediately prompted for your username and password. Click Cancel, and you will be presented with a screen informing you that you supplied the wrong username/password—in other words, you have been logged out. Odd, but that's the way it works.

> *You cannot log back in to phpMyAdmin from the wrong username/password screen. You must enter the original URL into the browser address bar first.*

Backup and data transfer

MySQL doesn't store your database in a single file that you can simply upload to your website. Even if you find the right files (on Windows, they're located in C:\Program Files\MySQL\MySQL Server 5.0\data), you're likely to damage them unless the MySQL server is turned off. Anyway, most hosting companies won't permit you to upload the raw files because it would also involve shutting down their server, causing a great deal of inconvenience for everyone.

Nevertheless, moving a database from one server to another is very easy. All it involves is creating a backup **dump** of the data and loading it into the other database with phpMyAdmin. The dump is a text file that contains all the necessary Structured Query Language (SQL) commands to populate an individual table or even an entire database elsewhere. phpMyAdmin can create backups of your entire MySQL server, individual databases, selected tables, or individual tables. To make things simple, the following instructions show you how to back up only a single database.

If you have just installed MySQL for the first time, bookmark this section for when you need to upload files to your remote server or upgrade MySQL. If you're on a Mac, you must always back up your data before upgrading MySQL. Once the new version has been installed, you can transfer your data to the new server. Windows users need follow this procedure only when upgrading from one series to another, such as 5.0 to 5.1.

Creating a backup

1. Launch phpMyAdmin and select the database that you want to back up from the drop-down menu in the navigation frame.

2. When the database details have loaded into the main frame, select Export from the tabs along the top of the screen, as shown here:

3. The rather fearsome looking screen shown in Figure 10-3 opens. In spite of all the options, you need to concern yourself with only a few.

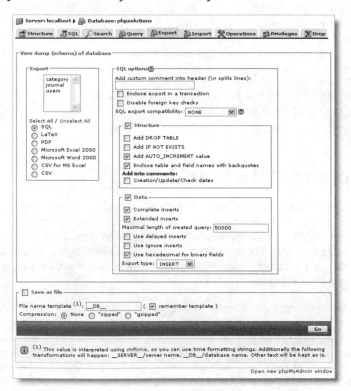

Figure 10-3. phpMyAdmin offers a wide range of choices when exporting data from MySQL.

4. The Export section on the left of the screen lists all the tables in your database. Click Select All and leave the radio buttons on the default SQL.

5. If the database has *never* been transferred to the other server before, the only option that you need to set on the right side of the screen is the drop-down menu labeled SQL export compatibility. The setting depends on the version of MySQL on the other server (only the first two numbers, such as 3.23, 4.0, 4.1, or 5.0, are important):

   ■ If the other server is running the same version of MySQL, choose NONE.

   ■ If transferring between MySQL 4.1 and MySQL 5.0 (in either direction), choose NONE.

   ■ If the other server is running MySQL 3.23, choose MYSQL323.

   ■ If the other server is running MySQL 4.0, choose MYSQL40.

6. If the database has *already* been transferred on a previous occasion, select Add DROP TABLE in the Structure section. The existing contents of each table are dropped and are replaced with the data in the backup file.

7. Put a check mark in the box alongside Save as file at the bottom of the screen. The default setting in File name template is __DB__, which automatically gives the backup file the same name as your database. So, in this case, it will become phpsolutions.sql. If you add anything after the final double underscore, phpMyAdmin will add this to the name. For instance, you might want to indicate the date of the backup, so you could add 20070228 for a backup made on February 28, 2007. The file would then be named phpsolutions20070228.sql.

Loading data from a backup file

1. Upload the SQL file to your remote server. (This isn't necessary if you are transferring data to a new installation of MySQL on your local computer.)

2. If a database of the same name doesn't already exist on the target server, create the database, but don't create any tables.

3. Launch the version of phpMyAdmin that is used by the target server and select the database that you plan to transfer the data to. Click the Import tab in the main frame. (On versions of phpMyAdmin earlier than 2.7.0, click the SQL tab instead.)

4. Use the Browse button to locate the SQL file and click Go. That's it!

10

Looking ahead . . .

Now that you have MySQL and phpMyAdmin installed, you're no doubt straining at the leash to get to work with your first database. Before you can do so, you need to set up at least one user account in MySQL and learn a little about how a database table is structured. That's what the next chapter is all about, but it won't be page after page of dull theory. By the end of the chapter, you will have built a simple database ready to start using with PHP and display dynamic data in your web pages.

11 GETTING STARTED WITH A DATABASE

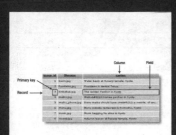

What this chapter covers:

- Creating MySQL user accounts
- Creating a new database
- Defining a database table
- Choosing the right column type
- Using MySQL, MySQLI, and PDO to query a database

When I first started working with databases, one of the greatest frustrations was that all the books and online tutorials I consulted assumed that you already knew the basics of database design and construction, or—if you didn't—that you planned to use Microsoft Access. MySQL is very different from Access, which is intended for use in small office environments. MySQL is not only fast and multiplatform; it's capable of handling a high number of simultaneous connections without any perceptible loss of performance. The differences between MySQL and Access also affect the way that you construct and interact with the database. After describing the basics of a database, I'll show you how to set up MySQL user accounts, create your first database, and connect to it with PHP. I'll also show you how to choose the correct data type to store each piece of information.

How a database stores information

MySQL is a relational database system. All the data is stored in tables, very much in the same way as in a spreadsheet, with information organized into rows and columns. Figure 11-1 shows the database table that you will build later in this chapter, as displayed in phpMyAdmin.

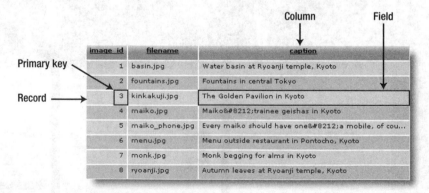

Figure 11-1. Information in a database table is stored in rows and columns, just like in a spreadsheet.

Each **column** has a name (image_id, filename, and caption) indicating what it stores.

The rows aren't labeled, but the first column (image_id) contains a unique identifier known as a **primary key**, which can be used to identify the data associated with a particular row.

Each row contains an individual **record** of related data. The significance of primary keys is explained in the next section.

The intersection of a row and a column, where the data is stored, is called a **field**. So, for instance, the caption field for the third record in Figure 11-1 contains the value "The Golden Pavilion in Kyoto" and the primary key for that record is 3.

> *The terms "field" and "column" are often used interchangeably, particularly by phpMyAdmin. A field holds one piece of information for a single record, whereas a column contains the same field for all records.*

How primary keys work

Although Figure 11-1 shows image_id as a consecutive sequence from 1 to 8, they're not row numbers. Figure 11-2 shows the same table with the captions sorted in alphabetical order. The field highlighted in Figure 11-1 has moved to the seventh row, but it still has the same image_id and filename.

image_id	filename	caption ▲
8	ryoanji.jpg	Autumn leaves at Ryoanji temple, Kyoto
5	maiko_phone.jpg	Every maiko should have one—a mobile, of cou...
2	fountains.jpg	Fountains in central Tokyo
4	maiko.jpg	Maiko—trainee geishas in Kyoto
6	menu.jpg	Menu outside restaurant in Pontocho, Kyoto
7	monk.jpg	Monk begging for alms in Kyoto
3	kinkakuji.jpg	The Golden Pavilion in Kyoto
1	basin.jpg	Water basin at Ryoanji temple, Kyoto

Now in the seventh row, but image_id remains unchanged

Figure 11-2. Even when the table is sorted in a different order, each record can be identified by its primary key.

11

Although the primary key is rarely displayed, it identifies the record and all the data stored in it. Once you know the primary key of a record, you can update it, delete it, or use it to display data in a separate page. Don't worry about how you find the primary key. You'll see in the next chapter that it's easily done using Structured Query Language (SQL), the standard means of communicating with all major databases. The important thing to remember is that you should assign a primary key to every record.

- A primary key doesn't need to be a number, but *it must be unique*.
- Social security, staff ID, or product numbers make good primary keys. They may consist of a mixture of numbers, letters, and other characters, but are always different.
- MySQL will generate a primary key for you automatically.
- Once a primary key has been assigned, it should never—repeat, never—be changed.

Because a primary key must be unique, MySQL doesn't normally reuse the number when a record is deleted. This leaves holes in the sequence. *Don't even think about renumbering.* Gaps in the sequence are of no importance whatsoever. The purpose of the primary key is to identify the record, and by changing the numbers to close the gaps, you put the integrity of your database at serious risk.

> *Some people want to remove gaps in the sequence to keep track of the number of records in a table. It's not necessary, as you'll discover later in the chapter.*

Linking tables with primary and foreign keys

A major difference between a spreadsheet and a relational database like MySQL is that most databases store data in lots of smaller tables, rather than in one huge table. The main reason for doing this is to prevent duplication and inconsistency. Let's say you're building a database of your favorite quotations. Instead of typing out the name of the author each time, it's more efficient to put the authors' names in a separate table, and store a reference to an author's primary key with each quotation.

Storing a primary key from one table in another table is known as creating a **foreign key**. As you can see in Figure 11-3, every record in the left-hand table identified by author_id 32 is a quotation from William Shakespeare. Because the name is stored in only one place, it guarantees that it's always spelled correctly. And if you do make a spelling mistake, just a single correction is all that's needed to ensure that the change is reflected throughout the database.

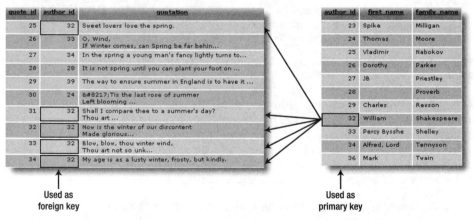

Figure 11-3. Foreign keys are used to link information stored in separate tables.

Using foreign keys to link information in different tables is one of the most powerful aspects of a relational database. It can also be difficult to grasp in the early stages, so we'll work with single tables until Chapter 14, which covers foreign keys in detail. In the meantime, bear the following points in mind:

- When used as the primary key of a table, the identifier must be unique. So each author_id in the table on the right is used only once.
- When used as a foreign key, there can be multiple references to the same identifier. So 32 appears several times in the author_id column in the table on the left.

> As long as author_id *remains unique in the table where it's the primary key, you know that it always refers to the same person.*

Breaking down information into small chunks

You may have noticed that the table on the right in Figure 11-3 has separate columns for each author's first name and family name. This is an important principle of a relational database: *break down complex information into its component parts, and store each part separately.*

It's not always easy to decide how far to go with this process. In addition to first and last name, you might want separate columns for title (Mr., Mrs., Ms., Dr., and so on) and for middle names or initials. Addresses are best broken down into street, town, county, state, zip code, and so on. Although it may be a nuisance to break down information into small chunks, you can always use SQL and/or PHP to join them together again. However, once you have more than a handful of records, it's a major undertaking to try to separate complex information stored in a single field.

Checkpoints for good database design

There is no *right* way to design a database—each one is different. However, the following guidelines should point you in the right direction:

- Give each record in a table a unique identifier (primary key).
- Put each group of associated data in a table of its own.
- Cross-reference related information by using the primary key from one table as the foreign key in other tables.
- Store only one item of information in each field.
- Stay DRY (don't repeat yourself).

In the early stages, you are likely to make design mistakes that you later come to regret. Try to anticipate future needs, and make your table structure flexible. You can add new tables at any time to respond to new requirements.

That's enough theory for the moment. Let's get on with something more practical by building a database for the Japan Solutions website from Chapters 4 and 5.

11

Setting up the phpsolutions database

MySQL is a relational database management system (RDMS), which can support a large number of databases. In a local testing environment, there's no limit to the number of databases that you can create, and you can call them whatever you like. I am going to assume that you are working in a local testing environment and will show you how to set up a database called phpsolutions, together with two user accounts called psquery and psadmin.

> On shared hosting, you may be limited to just one database set up by the hosting company. If you don't have the freedom to set up a new database and user accounts, substitute the name and username allocated by your hosting company for phpsolutions and psadmin respectively throughout the rest of this book.

MySQL naming rules

The basic MySQL naming rules for databases, tables, and columns are as follows:

- Names can be up to 64 characters long.
- Legal characters are numbers, letters, the underscore, and $.
- Names can begin with a number, but cannot consist exclusively of numbers.

Some hosting companies seem blissfully ignorant of these rules and assign clients databases that contain one or more hyphens (an illegal character) in their name. If a database, table, or column name contains spaces or illegal characters, you must always surround it by backticks (`) in SQL queries. Note that this is not a single quote ('), but a separate character.

When choosing names, you might accidentally choose one of MySQL's many reserved words (http://dev.mysql.com/doc/refman/5.0/en/reserved-words.html), such as date or time. One technique to avoid this is to use compound words, such as arrival_date, arrival_time, and so on. Alternatively, surround all names with backticks. phpMyAdmin does this automatically, but you need to do this manually when writing your own SQL in a PHP script.

Case sensitivity of names

Windows and Mac OS X treat MySQL names as case-insensitive. However, Linux and Unix servers respect case sensitivity. To avoid problems when transferring databases and PHP code from your local computer to a remote server, I strongly recommend that you use lowercase exclusively in database, table, and column names. When building names from more than one word, join them with an underscore.

Using phpMyAdmin to create a new database

Creating a new database in phpMyAdmin is easy.

1. Launch phpMyAdmin in a browser, as described in the previous chapter.

2. Type the name of the new database (phpsolutions) into the field labeled Create new database. Leave the Collation drop-down menu at its default setting, and click Create, as shown in the following screenshot:

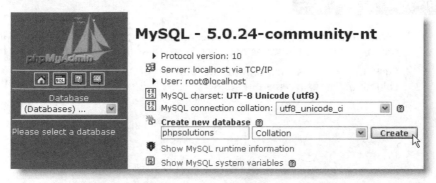

> Collation determines the sort order of records. Unless you are using a language other than English, Swedish, or Finnish, you never need to change its value. Even if you use a different language, you should use the Collation option only if your remote server uses MySQL 4.1 or higher.

3. The next screen should confirm that the database has been created and offer you the opportunity to create your first table. Before creating any tables in a new database, it's a good idea to create user accounts for it. Leave phpMyAdmin open, as you'll continue using it in the next section.

Creating database-specific user accounts

At the moment, your installation of MySQL has only one registered user—the superuser account called "root," which has complete control over everything. The root user should *never* be used for anything other than top-level administration, such as the creation and removal of databases, creating user accounts, and exporting and importing data. Each individual database should have at least one—preferably two—dedicated user accounts with limited privileges.

When you put a database online, you should grant users the least privileges they need, and no more. There are four important privileges—all named after the equivalent SQL commands:

- **SELECT**: Retrieves records from database tables
- **INSERT**: Inserts records into a database

11

- **UPDATE**: Changes existing records
- **DELETE**: Deletes records, but not tables or databases (the command for that is DROP)

Most of the time, visitors need only to retrieve information, so the psquery user account will have the SELECT privilege only. However, for user registration or site administration, you need all four privileges. These will be made available to the psadmin account.

Granting user privileges

1. Return to the main phpMyAdmin screen by clicking either the little house icon at the top left of the left frame or Server: localhost at the top left of the main frame.

2. Click the Privileges link toward the bottom of the left column of the main screen.

Most links and tabs in phpMyAdmin are context-sensitive. It's important to go back to the main screen and click the Privileges *link rather than the* Privileges *tab at the top of the previous screen. The link on the phpMyAdmin main screen lets you set up new user accounts. The* Privileges *tab at the top of a page only provides information about existing accounts.*

3. This opens the User overview screen. If you have just installed MySQL, there should be only one user: root. Click the Add a new User link halfway down the page.

4. In the page that opens, enter psadmin (or the name of the user account that you want to create) in the User name field. Select Local from the Host drop-down menu. This automatically enters localhost in the field alongside. Selecting this option allows the psadmin user to connect to MySQL only from the same computer. Then enter a password in the Password field, and type it again for confirmation in the Re-type field.

In the download files for this book, I've used a simple password (kyoto), but for a database on the Internet, you should choose a password that's hard to guess. MySQL passwords are case-sensitive.

5. Beneath the Login Information table is one labeled Global privileges. These give a user privileges on all databases, including the mysql one, which contains sensitive information. Granting such extensive privileges is insecure, so leave the Global privileges table unchecked, and click the Go button right at the bottom of the page.

6. The next page confirms that the psadmin user has been created and displays many options, beginning with the Global privileges table again. Scroll down below this to the section labeled Database-specific privileges. Activate the drop-down menu, as shown here, to display a list of all databases on your system. Select phpsolutions.

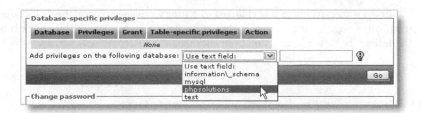

A new installation of MySQL 5 contains three databases: information_schema *(phpMyAdmin escapes the underscore by preceding it with a backslash),* mysql, *and* test. *The first,* information_schema, *is a virtual database that contains details of all other databases on the same server. You can view the contents in phpMyAdmin, but you can't edit them. The* mysql *database contains details of all user accounts and privileges. You should never edit it directly unless you're sure what you're doing. Always use the* Privileges *link on the main phpMyAdmin page to manage user accounts, privileges, and passwords. The* test *database is empty.*

7. The next screen allows you to set the privileges for this user on just the phpsolutions database. You want psadmin to have all four privileges listed earlier, so click the check boxes next to SELECT, INSERT, UPDATE, and DELETE. (If you hover your mouse pointer over each option, phpMyAdmin displays a tooltip describing what the option is for, as shown.) After selecting the four privileges, click the top Go button. (Always click the Go button at the foot of or alongside the section with the options you want to set.)

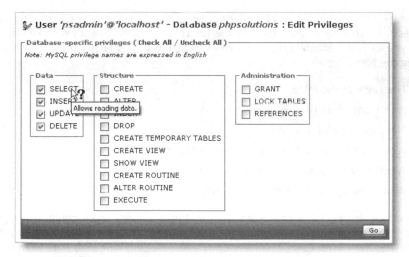

8. phpMyAdmin presents you with confirmation that the privileges have been updated for the psadmin user account: the page displays the Database-specific privileges table again, in case you need to change anything. Click the Privileges tab at the top of the page. You should now see psadmin listed with root in the User overview.

11

If you ever need to make any changes to a user's privileges, click the Edit Privileges icon to the right of the listing, as shown. To delete a user, select the check box to the left of the User column, and then click Go in the Remove selected users section.

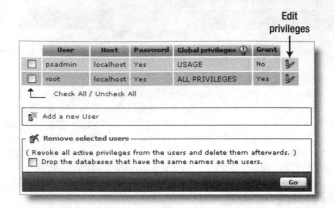

9. Click Add a new User, and repeat steps 4 through 8 to create a second user account called psquery. This user will have much more restricted privileges, so when you get to step 7, check only the SELECT option. The password I used for psquery is fuji. Again, for an online database, you should choose something more robust.

Creating a database table

Now that you have a database and dedicated user accounts, you can begin creating tables. Let's begin by creating a table to hold the details of images, as shown in Figure 11-1. Before you can start entering data, you need to define the table structure. This involves deciding the following:

- The name of the table
- How many columns it will have
- The name of each column
- What type of data will be stored in each column
- Whether the column must always have data in each field
- Which column contains the table's primary key

If you look at Figure 11-1, you can see that the table contains three columns: image_id (primary key), filename, and caption. Because it contains details of images, that's a good name to use. There's not much point in storing a filename without a caption, so every column must contain data. Great! Apart from the data type, all the decisions have been made. I'll explain the data types as we go along.

Defining the images table

1. Launch phpMyAdmin in a browser, if it's not already open, and select phpsolutions from the Database drop-down menu in the left frame. Type the name of the new table (images) in the field labeled Create new table on database phpsolutions, and enter 3 as the Number of fields. (As mentioned before, phpMyAdmin refers to columns as fields. What it means is how many fields each record has.) Then click the Go button.

2. The next screen is where you define the table. Unless you have a large monitor, you will probably need to scroll horizontally to see all of it. The following screenshot shows all the fields filled in, but the values may be difficult to read, so they are also listed in Table 11-1 (Collation and Default are omitted, as they are both left blank).

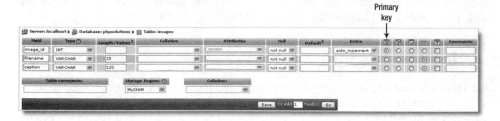

Table 11-1. Settings for the images table

Field	Type	Length/Values	Attributes	Null	Extra	Primary key
image_id	INT		UNSIGNED	not null	auto_increment	Selected
filename	VARCHAR	25		not null		
caption	VARCHAR	120		not null		

The first column, image_id, is defined as type INT, which stands for integer. Its attribute is set to UNSIGNED, which means that only positive numbers are allowed. It's also set to auto_increment, and is the table's primary key, so MySQL automatically inserts in this column the next available number (starting at 1) whenever a new record is inserted.

The next column, filename, is defined as type VARCHAR with a length of 25. This means it accepts up to 25 characters of text.

The final column, caption, is also VARCHAR with a length of 120, so it accepts up to 120 characters of text.

All columns are defined as not null, so they must always contain something. However, that "something" can be as little as an empty string. I'll describe the column types in more detail in "Choosing the right column type in MySQL" later in the chapter.

When you have finished, click the Save button at the bottom-center of the screen.

3. The next screen displays the SQL query that phpMyAdmin used to define the images table. Beneath that, you'll see the structure of the table displayed like this:

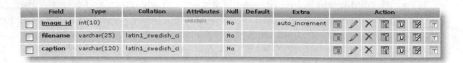

	Field	Type	Collation	Attributes	Null	Default	Extra	Action
☐	image_id	int(10)		UNSIGNED	No		auto_increment	
☐	filename	varchar(25)	latin1_swedish_ci		No			
☐	caption	varchar(120)	latin1_swedish_ci		No			

Don't be alarmed by the fact that Collation displays latin1_swedish_ci. MySQL is based in Sweden, and Swedish uses the same sort order as English (and Finnish). The underlining of image_id indicates that it's the table's primary key. To change any settings, click the pencil-like icon in the appropriate row. This opens a version of the previous screen and allows you to change the values. If you made a complete mess and want to start again, click the Drop tab at the top right of the screen, and confirm that you want to drop the table. (In SQL, *delete* refers only to records. You *drop* a table or a database.)

Inserting records into a table

Now that you have a table, you need to put some data into it. Eventually, you'll need to build your own content management system using XHTML forms, PHP, and SQL; but the quick and easy way to do it is with phpMyAdmin. First, I'll show you how to enter a couple of records manually; and then I'll show you how to cheat by loading the entire table from a SQL file.

Using phpMyAdmin to insert records manually

1. If phpMyAdmin is still displaying the structure of the images table as at the end of the previous section, skip to step 2. Otherwise, launch phpMyAdmin, and select the phpsolutions database from the drop-down menu in the left frame. Then click the Structure icon alongside images, as shown in the following screenshot:

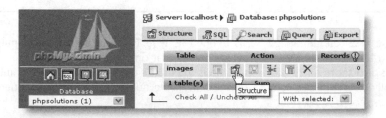

The breadcrumb trail at the top of the main frame provides the context for the tabs across the head of the page. The Structure *tab at the top left of the preceding screenshot refers to the structure of the phpsolutions database. At the moment, it contains only one table,* images. *To access the structure of an individual table, click the* Structure *icon alongside its name. Use your mouse pointer to reveal tooltips for each icon. Some, such as* Browse, *are grayed out because there are no records in the table.*

2. Click the Insert tab in the center top of the page. This displays the following screen, ready for you to insert up to two records:

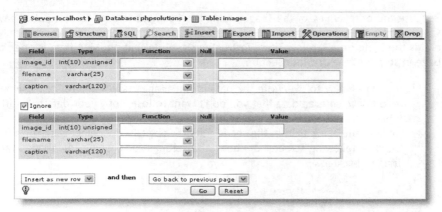

3. The forms display the names and details of each column. You can ignore the Function fields. MySQL has a large number of functions that you can apply to the values being stored in your table. You'll learn more about them in the following chapters. The Value field is where you enter the data you want to insert in the table.

Because you have defined image_id as auto_increment, MySQL inserts the next available number automatically. So you *must* leave the first Value field blank. Fill in the next two Value fields as follows:

- filename: basin.jpg

- caption: Water basin at Ryoanji temple, Kyoto

4. Deselect the check box labeled Ignore. If you forget to do this, anything entered in the second form won't be inserted into the table.

5. Again, leave the Value field for image_id blank, and fill in the next two fields like this:

- filename: fountains.jpg

- caption: Fountains in central Tokyo

6. Click Go. You should be taken back to the table structure page, but the SQL used to insert the records is displayed at the top of the page. I'll explain the basic SQL commands in the remaining chapters, but studying the SQL that phpMyAdmin displays is a good way to learn how to build your own queries. SQL is closely based on human language, so it isn't all that difficult to learn.

7. Click the Browse tab at the top left of the page. You should now see the first two entries in the images table, as shown here:

As you can see, MySQL has automatically inserted 1 and 2 in the image_id fields.

You could continue typing out the details of the remaining six images, but let's speed things up a bit by using a SQL file that contains all the necessary data.

Loading the images records from a SQL file

Because the primary key of the images table has been set to auto_increment, it's necessary to drop the original table and all its data. The SQL file does this automatically and builds the table from scratch. These instructions assume that phpMyAdmin is open at the page in step 7 of the previous section.

1. If you're happy to overwrite the data in the images table, skip to step 2. However, if you have entered data that you don't want to lose, copy your data to a different table. Click the Operations tab at the top of the page, type the name of the new table in the blank field in the section titled Copy table to (database.table), and click Go. The following screenshot shows the settings for copying the images table to images_backup:

After clicking Go, you should see confirmation that the table has been copied. The breadcrumb trail at the top of the page indicates that phpMyAdmin is still in the images table, so you can proceed to step 2, even though you have a different page onscreen.

2. Click the Import tab at the top right of the page. In the next screen, click the Browse (or Choose File) button in File to import, and navigate to images.sql in the download files. Leave all options at their default setting, and click Go at the foot of the page.

Import

┌─ File to import ───┐
│ Location of the text file [vnloads\ch11\images.sql] [Browse...] (Max: 2,048KB) │
│ Character set of the file: [utf8 ▾] │
│ Imported file compression will be automatically detected from: None, gzip, zip │
└──┘

┌─ Partial import ───┐
│ [✓] Allow interrupt of import in case script detects it is close to time limit. This might be good way to │
│ import large files, however it can break transactions. │
│ Number of records(queries) to skip from start [0] │
└──┘

┌─ Format of imported file ──┐
│ ○ CSV │
│   ┌─ SQL options ─────────────────────┐ │
│ ○ CSV using LOAD DATA │ This format has no options │ │
│   └───────────────────────────────────┘ │
│ ⦿ SQL │
│   [Go] │
└──┘

> *Use* images323.sql *for MySQL 3.23 or* images40.sql *for MySQL 4.0. Older versions of phpMyAdmin don't have an* Import *tab. Click the* SQL *tab instead. The* File *to import form is at the bottom of the page. It looks slightly different, but works the same way.*

3. phpMyAdmin drops the original table, creates a new version, and inserts all the records. When you see confirmation that the file has been imported, click the Browse button at the top left of the page. You should now see the same data as shown in Figure 11-1 at the beginning of the chapter.

Now that you've got some useful data in your database table, it's time to bring it together with PHP, but first, a quick overview of the main column types in MySQL.

Choosing the right column type in MySQL

You may have received a bit of a shock when selecting Type for the image_id column. phpMyAdmin lists all available column types—there are 28 in MySQL 5.0. Rather than confuse you with unnecessary details, I'll explain just the most commonly used. You can find full details of all column types in the MySQL documentation at http://dev.mysql.com/doc/refman/5.0/en/data-types.html.

Storing text

The difference between the main text column types boils down to the maximum number of characters that can be stored in an individual field, and whether you can set a default value.

- **CHAR**: A fixed-length character string. You must specify the required length in the Length/Values field. The maximum permitted value in all versions of MySQL is 255. You can define a default value.

- **VARCHAR**: A variable-length character string. You must specify the maximum number of characters you plan to use in the Length/Values field in phpMyAdmin. Prior to MySQL 5.0, the limit is 255. This has been increased to 65,535 in MySQL 5.0. Accepts a default value.

- **TEXT**: Stores text up to a maximum of 65,535 characters (slightly longer than this chapter). Cannot define a default value.

TEXT is convenient because you don't need to specify a maximum size (in fact, you can't). Although the maximum length of VARCHAR is the same as TEXT in MySQL 5.0, other factors may limit the actual amount that can be stored. Keep it simple: use VARCHAR for short text items and TEXT for longer ones.

> *The term "characters" here refers only to characters in the Latin1 (ISO-8859-1) character set—the default encoding for most Western European languages. If you store your data in UTF-8 (Unicode), the limit is calculated in bytes. Accented characters in Spanish, French, and other Western languages require only one byte in Latin1, but occupy two bytes in UTF-8.*

11

Storing numbers

The most frequently used numeric column types are as follows:

- **INT**: Any whole number (integer) between –2,147,483,648 and 2,147,483,647. If the column is declared as UNSIGNED, the range is from 0 to 4,294,967,295.
- **FLOAT**: A floating-point number. You can optionally specify two comma-separated numbers in the Length/Values field. The first number specifies the number of digits before the decimal point, and the second specifies the precision to which the decimal portion should be rounded. Since PHP will format numbers after calculation, I recommend that you use FLOAT without the optional parameters.
- **DECIMAL**: A floating-point number *stored as a string. This column type is best avoided.*

DECIMAL is intended for currencies, but you can't perform calculations with strings inside a database, so it's more practical to use INT. For dollars or euros, store currencies as cents; for pounds, use pence. Then use PHP to divide the result by 100, and format the currency as desired.

> *Don't use commas or spaces as the thousands-separator. Apart from numerals, the only characters permitted in numbers are the negative operator (-) and the decimal point (.).*

Storing dates and times

MySQL stores dates in the format YYYY-MM-DD. This comes as a shock to many people, but it's the standard approved by the ISO (International Organization for Standardization), and avoids the ambiguity inherent in different national conventions. I'll return to the subject of dates in Chapter 14. The most important column types for dates and times are as follows:

- **DATE**: A date stored as YYYY-MM-DD. The supported range is 1000-01-01 to 9999-12-31.
- **DATETIME**: A combined date and time displayed in the format YYYY-MM-DD HH:MM:SS.
- **TIMESTAMP**: A timestamp (normally generated automatically by the computer). Legal values range from the beginning of 1970 to partway through 2037.

> *MySQL timestamps are based on a human-readable date and, since MySQL 4.1, use the same format as DATETIME. As a result, they are incompatible with Unix and PHP timestamps, which are based on the number of seconds elapsed since January 1, 1970. Don't mix them.*

Storing predefined lists

MySQL lets you store two types of predefined list that could be regarded as the database equivalents of radio button and check box states:

- **ENUM**: This column type stores a single choice from a predefined list, such as "yes, no, don't know" or "male, female." The maximum number of items that can be stored in the predefined list is a mind-boggling 65,535—some radio-button group!

- **SET**: This column type stores zero or more choices from a predefined list. The list can hold a maximum of 64 choices.

While ENUM is quite useful, SET tends to be less so, mainly because it violates the principle of storing only one piece of information in a field. The type of situation where it can be useful is when recording optional extras on a car or multiple choices in a survey.

Storing binary data

Storing binary data, such as images, isn't a good idea. It bloats your database, and you can't display images directly from a database. However, the following column types are designed for binary data:

- **TINYBLOB**: Up to 255 bytes
- **BLOB**: Up to 64KB
- **MEDIUMBLOB**: Up to 16MB
- **LONGBLOB**: Up to 4GB

With such whimsical names, it's a bit of a letdown to discover that BLOB stands for **binary large object**.

Connecting to MySQL with PHP

11

One of the great features of PHP is that it supports all the major database systems—and some not so major ones, too. It's also a weakness, because PHP uses dedicated functions for each type of database. This isn't a problem if you use the same database all the time, but it makes code less portable. Consequently, PHP Data Objects (PDO) were introduced in PHP 5.1. The idea is that you write just one set of code, and it will work with any database. Strictly speaking, this isn't 100% true, because there are variations in the way you write SQL for some databases. Nevertheless, it's a major change; and the plan is to move PHP database connection entirely to PDO.

Unfortunately, there's a rather large fly in the ointment . . . Even two years after the release of PHP 5, a large number of hosting companies still offered only PHP 4, and seemed to be in no hurry to upgrade. As a result, if your remote server runs on PHP 4, you still need to use the original MySQL extension. Just to make things more complicated, PHP 5 also offers the MySQL Improved (MySQLI) extension, which is intended for use with MySQL 4.1 and above. So, before you can work with PHP and MySQL on your website, you need to check which versions are running. You have the following options:

- If your remote server runs PHP 4, you must use the MySQL extension.
- If your remote server runs PHP 5 *and* MySQL 4.1 or above, use the MySQL Improved extension or—if it's available—PDO.

Checking your remote server setup

As always, run the following one-line script to find out the PHP configuration of your remote server:

```php
<?php phpinfo(); ?>
```

Scroll down the configuration page, and look for the following sections.

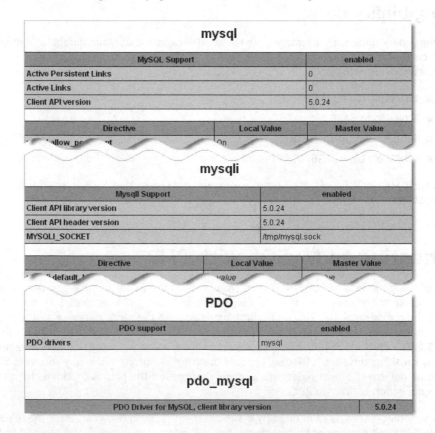

mysql	
MySQL Support	enabled
Active Persistent Links	0
Active Links	0
Client API version	5.0.24

Directive	Local Value	Master Value
allow_p...	On	

mysqli	
Mysqli Support	enabled
Client API library version	5.0.24
Client API header version	5.0.24
MYSQLI_SOCKET	/tmp/mysql.sock

Directive	Local Value	Master Value
default_...	value	...ue

PDO	
PDO support	enabled
PDO drivers	mysql

pdo_mysql	
PDO Driver for MySQL, client library version	5.0.24

All websites should have the first section (mysql), but the mysqli and PDO sections will depend on the server and the version of PHP installed. If you have PDO, you must also make sure that mysql is listed among the PDO drivers.

If your host provides phpMyAdmin, the easiest way to check MySQL is to look at the top left of the main phpMyAdmin screen: the MySQL version number is displayed there. If you don't have phpMyAdmin on your remote server, use `mysql_version.php` in the download files for this chapter. Insert the hostname, username, and password that your hosting company has given you for connecting to MySQL. Save the file, upload it to your site, and view it in a browser. It will display the version running on your server.

After you have checked your remote server settings, remove `mysql_version.php` and the `phpinfo()` script. Although the information may seem harmless, it could be of use to a potential attacker.

How PHP communicates with MySQL

Regardless of whether you use PHP's MySQL functions, the MySQL Improved functions, or PDO, the process always follows this sequence:

1. Connect to MySQL using the hostname, username, and password.
2. Select the database you want to work with (combined with 1 in MySQLI and PDO).
3. Prepare a SQL query.
4. Execute the query and save the result.
5. Extract the data from the result (usually with a loop).

Username and password are straightforward: they're the username and password of the accounts you have just created or the account given to you by your hosting company. But what about hostname? In a local testing environment it's `localhost`. What comes as a surprise is that MySQL normally uses `localhost` even on a remote server. This is because the database server is normally located on the same server as your website. In other words, the web server and MySQL are local to each other. However, if your hosting company has installed MySQL on a separate machine, it will tell you the address to use. The important thing to realize is that the MySQL hostname is not the same as your website domain name.

Let's take a quick look at how you connect to a MySQL server with each of the methods.

11

> When using the original MySQL extension or MySQLI, some commands are followed by the rather foreboding or die(). This stops the script from going any further if the command fails, and displays any error message that you have inserted between the parentheses. PDO requires a different approach because of the way it handles connection errors.

Connecting with the original MySQL extension

You connect to the MySQL server with the `mysql_connect()` function, which takes three arguments: hostname, username, and password, like this:

```
$conn = mysql_connect($hostname, $username, $password) ➡
or die ('Cannot connect to MySQL server');
```

It doesn't matter whether you pass the arguments as variables or as literal strings. If the connection is successful, the function returns a reference to the connection, which can be stored as a variable.

After connecting, you need to select the individual database using mysql_select_db() like this:

```
mysql_select_db('phpsolutions') or die ('Cannot open database');
```

Connecting with the MySQL Improved extension

The MySQL Improved extension has two interfaces: procedural and object-oriented. The procedural interface is designed to ease the transition from the original MySQL functions. Since the object-oriented version is more compact, that's the version adopted here.

To connect to a MySQL server, you create a mysqli object by passing four arguments to new mysqli(): the hostname, username, password, and the name of the database. The new keyword tells PHP that you want to create an object. Don't worry if you're not familiar with object-oriented programming (OOP). For the most part, objects act like ordinary variables. The main difference is that objects have methods (functions) and properties (values), which are accessed using the -> operator.

So this is how you would connect to the phpsolutions database:

```
$conn = new mysqli($hostname, $username, $password, 'phpsolutions') ➡
or die ('Cannot open database');
```

This stores the connection object as $conn.

Connecting with PDO

PHP Data Objects are similar to the MySQLI object-oriented interface, but require a slightly different approach. The most important difference is that, if you're not careful, a PDO displays your database username and password onscreen when it can't connect to the database. This is because a PDO uses a type of error handling called **exceptions**, which are new to PHP 5. Unless you **catch the exception**, PHP displays debugging information onscreen. This is great for testing purposes, but a disaster in an online situation. Fortunately, the way you catch an exception is very easy.

To create a connection to the MySQL server, you create a data object by passing the following three arguments to new PDO():

- A string specifying the database type, the hostname, and the name of the database. The string must be presented in the following format:

  'mysql:host=*hostname*;dbname=*databaseName*'

- The username.
- The user's password.

When creating a PDO—or using any other code that might trigger an exception (the technical term is **throw** an exception)—you need to wrap it in a try/catch block. This works in the same way as if... else. PHP attempts to execute the code in the try block. If it works, fine. If it doesn't, it throws an exception for the catch block to ... well, catch. The code looks like this:

```
try {
  $conn = new PDO("mysql:host=$hostname;dbname=phpsolutions", ➥
  $username, $password);
  }
catch (PDOException $e) {
  echo 'Error: '.$e->getMessage();
  exit;
  }
```

The catch keyword is followed by a pair of parentheses, which take two arguments: the type of exception (in this case, PDOException) and a variable to catch the exception. The variable can be anything, but the convention is to use $e.

> *In PHP 5.1.6,* PDOException *is case-insensitive. However, there is a move to make PHP more case-sensitive, so it's a good idea to adhere to this mixture of uppercase and lowercase.*

The catch block uses the -> operator, which tells PHP that you want to use a method (function) or property (variable) with a particular object. The getMessage() method (function) gets the error message generated by the exception. Because there's no point going any further, exit on the next line terminates the script. It's not obligatory to display the error message generated by the exception. You can put anything you like in the catch block. It may be more user-friendly to send the visitor to an error page using header(), as described in "Redirecting to another page" in Chapter 5.

> *Exceptions are an advanced subject that I wouldn't normally cover. However, failure to connect to the database with PDO throws an* automatic *exception, so you* must *handle it in this way to prevent the exposure of your username and password. Other PDO errors don't throw exceptions, so this is the only place I'll use a* try/catch *block.*

11

Building a database connection function

Connecting to a database is a routine chore that needs to be performed in every page from now on; and routine tasks are often best left to functions and/or include files. If any of the details change, you need change them in one place only.

PHP Solution 11-1: Making a reusable database connector

The finished script is in the download files for this chapter. There are three versions—one each for the original MySQL extension (conn_mysql.inc.php), MySQL Improved (conn_mysqli.inc.php), and PDO (conn_pdo.inc.php).

1. In a blank file, insert the following code:

```php
<?php
function dbConnect($type) {
  if ($type  == 'query') {
    $user = 'psquery';
    $pwd = 'fuji';
    }
  elseif ($type == 'admin') {
    $user = 'psadmin';
    $pwd = 'kyoto';
    }
  else {
    exit('Unrecognized connection type');
    }
  // Connection code goes here
  }
?>
```

This is the basic skeleton for all versions of a function called dbConnect(), which takes a single argument: the type of connection you want. The if... elseif conditional statement checks the value of the argument and switches between the psquery and psadmin username and password as appropriate.

If your remote server allows you only one username and password, you can omit the argument and the conditional statement, and just use the following code:

```php
<?php
function dbConnect() {
  // Connection code goes here
  }
?>
```

2. Replace the Connection code goes here comment. The code differs according to which connection method you need to use, as described earlier.

If you are using the original MySQL extension (PHP 4 and/or MySQL prior to version 4.1), use this:

```php
$conn = mysql_connect('localhost', $user, $pwd) ➥
or die ('Cannot connect to MySQL server');
mysql_select_db('phpsolutions') or die ('Cannot open database');
return $conn;
```

If you are using MySQL Improved (PHP 5 and MySQL 4.1 or later), use this:

```
$conn = new mysqli('localhost', $user, $pwd, 'phpsolutions') ➡
or die ('Cannot open database');
return $conn;
```

If you are using PDO (PHP 5.1 and MySQL 4.1 or later), use this:

```
try {
  $conn = new PDO('mysql:host=localhost;dbname=phpsolutions', ➡
$user, $pwd);
  return $conn;
  }
catch (PDOException $e) {
  echo 'Cannot connect to database';
  exit;
  }
```

The script for each version simply encapsulates the connection code described in the preceding section and returns $conn, which is a reference to the database connection (MySQL) or the connection object (MySQLI and PDO).

3. Because this is an include file, make sure there are no new lines or whitespace before or after the PHP tags. Save the page in the includes folder. You can either use the same name as for the download file for your particular version or call it connection.inc.php.

> *Throughout the rest of the book, in scripts that are not specific to one particular connection method, I use the generic filename* connection.inc.php *to refer to the file that contains the* dbConnect() *function. Make sure that you use the correct version for the database connection functions you're using.*

To use this function, include connection.inc.php, and call the function like this for the psquery user:

```
$conn = dbConnect('query');
```

For the psadmin user, call it like this:

```
$conn = dbConnect('admin');
```

Regardless of whether you are using the original MySQL extension, MySQLI, or PDO, $conn contains the correct type of connection to the phpsolutions database. To adapt this for any other database, change the username, password, and database name in connection.inc.php.

11

Finding the number of results from a query

Counting the number of results from a database query is useful in several ways. It's necessary for creating a navigation system to page through a long set of results (you'll learn how to do that in the next chapter). It's also important for user authentication (covered in Chapter 15). If you get no results from matching a username and password, you know that the login procedure should fail.

The original MySQL extension and MySQL Improved both have a convenient method of finding out the number of results returned by a query. However, this isn't available with PDO, so you need to take a different approach. If you're using PDO, skip ahead to PHP Solution 11-3.

PHP Solution 11-2: Counting records in a result set (MySQL and MySQLI)

As you work through this PHP Solution, you'll see just how similar the code is for the original MySQL extension and MySQL Improved. This makes transferring from one to the other very easy, but you also need to be careful not to mix the two styles. I have indicated the differences clearly in steps 4 and 5.

1. Create a new folder called `mysql` in the phpsolutions site root, and create a new file called `mysql.php` inside the folder. The page will eventually be used to display a table, so it should have a DOCTYPE declaration and an XHTML skeleton.

2. Include the appropriate connection file for MySQL or MySQLI above the DOCTYPE declaration, and create a connection to MySQL like this:

```php
<?php
include('../includes/connection.inc.php');
// connect to MySQL
$conn = dbConnect('query');
?>
```

You don't need administrative privileges for this exercise, so I have used the account that has only SELECT privileges.

3. Next, prepare the SQL query. Add this code immediately after the previous step (but before the closing PHP tag):

```php
// prepare the SQL query
$sql = 'SELECT * FROM images';
```

This means "select everything from the images table." The asterisk (*) is shorthand for "all columns."

4. Now execute the query.

The original MySQL extension uses a function called `mysql_query()`, which takes the SQL query as an argument. The code looks like this (it goes immediately after step 3):

```php
// submit the query and capture the result
$result = mysql_query($sql) or die(mysql_error());
```

The code for MySQL Improved is very similar. You apply the query() method to the connection object ($conn) using the -> operator, and pass the SQL query as an argument like this:

```
// submit the query and capture the result
$result = $conn->query($sql) or die(mysqli_error());
```

Note that both methods store the result in a variable, which I have imaginatively named $result. If there is a problem, the database server returns an error message, which can be retrieved using mysql_error() or mysqli_error(), depending on your method of connection. By placing this function between the parentheses of or die(), the script comes to a halt if there's a problem and displays the error message.

5. Assuming there's no problem, the variable $result now holds a reference to the number of records found by the SQL query.

If you're using the original MySQL extension, pass the variable holding the result to mysql_num_rows() like this (put the code immediately after the preceding step):

```
// find out how many records were retrieved
$numRows = mysql_num_rows($result);
```

In MySQL Improved, the number of results is held in the num_rows property of the result object ($result). You access it with the -> operator like this:

```
// find out how many records were retrieved
$numRows = $result->num_rows;
```

> *There are no parentheses following* num_rows *in the MySQLI version. This is because it's a property (or value) of the result object. Functions and methods are followed by parentheses, but variables and properties are not.*

6. You can now display the value of $numRows in the body of the page like this:

```
<p>A total of <?php echo $numRows; ?> records were found.</p>
```

7. Save the page and load it into a browser. You should see the following result:

Check your code, if necessary, with mysql01.php or mysqli01.php in the download files.

11

PHP Solution 11-3: Counting records in a result set (PDO)

Because PDO doesn't have an equivalent of the MySQLI num_rows property or the MySQL function mysql_num_rows(), you need to use a SQL function called COUNT().

1. Create a new folder called mysql in the phpsolutions site root, and create a new file called pdo.php inside the folder. The page will eventually be used to display a table, so it should have a DOCTYPE declaration and an XHTML skeleton.

2. Include the PDO connection file above the DOCTYPE declaration, and create a connection to MySQL like this:

```php
<?php
include('../includes/conn_pdo.inc.php');
// connect to MySQL
$conn = dbConnect('query');
?>
```

You don't need administrative privileges for this exercise, so I have used the account that has only SELECT privileges.

3. Next, prepare the SQL query. Add this code immediately after the previous step (but before the closing PHP tag):

```php
// prepare the SQL query
$sql = 'SELECT COUNT(*) FROM images';
```

This means "count every record in the images table." The asterisk (*) is shorthand for "all columns." The COUNT() function gets the total number of records. Make sure you don't leave a space between COUNT and the opening parenthesis, as this generates a SQL error.

4. Now execute the query and store the result in a variable like this (the code goes immediately after the code in step 3):

```php
// submit the query and capture the result
$result = $conn->query($sql);
$error = $conn->errorInfo();
if (isset($error[2])) die($error[2]);
```

$conn is the variable that you used to create the connection, so $conn->query() means "run this query with my connection." The result is stored in a variable, which I've named, rather predictably, $result.

PDO uses errorInfo() to build an array of error messages from the database. The third element of the array is created only if something goes wrong. I've stored the result of $conn->errorInfo() as $error, so you can tell if anything went wrong by using isset() to check whether $error[2] has been defined. If it has, die() brings the script to a halt and displays the error message.

5. The SQL query in step 3 returns only one piece of information: the number of records found, so you can use the fetchColumn() method with $result to retrieve

it, and store the number of rows found like this (put the code immediately after the preceding step):

```
// find out how many records were retrieved
$numRows = $result->fetchColumn();
```

6. You can now display the value of $numRows in the body of the page like this:

```
<p>A total of <?php echo $numRows; ?> records were found.</p>
```

7. Save the page and load it into a browser. You should see the same result as shown in step 8 of PHP Solution 11-2. Check your code, if necessary, with pdo01.php.

Displaying the results of a query

In spite of the different ways that MySQL, MySQLI, and PDO communicate with a database, they all produce a result that contains all the information sent back from the database (and stored as $result). In PHP Solution 11-2, $result contains every field in every record. In PHP Solution 11-3, a different query was used because PDO handles the counting of records differently; but if you run the same query with PDO, $result also contains every field in every record.

It's tempting to think of this result as an array. In one sense, it is; but you can't use it in the same way as arrays that you have encountered so far. To extract the information, you need to deal with one record at a time. The most common way is to use a loop in combination with a function (or method) to extract the current record into a temporary array, which you can then use to display the information it holds.

With the MySQL extension, you do it like this:

```
while ($row = mysql_fetch_assoc($result)) {
    // do something with the current record
}
```

With MySQLI, instead of passing $result to a function, you use the -> operator like this:

```
while ($row = $result->fetch_assoc()) {
    // do something with the current record
}
```

PDO handles it slightly differently. You can use the query() method directly inside a foreach loop to create an array for each record like this:

```
foreach ($conn->query($sql) as $row) {
    // do something with the current record
}
```

In each case, $row is an associative array containing every field in the current record. So, in the case of the images table, $row contains these three elements: $row['image_id'], $row['filename'], and $row['caption']. In other words, each element is named after the corresponding column in the table.

11

PHP Solution 11-4: Displaying the images table using MySQL

Continue using the file from PHP Solution 11-2. The finished code is in `mysql02.php`.

1. Add the following code to the main body of the page (new code is in bold):

```
<p>A total of <?php echo $numRows; ?> records were found.</p>
<table>
  <tr>
    <th>image_id</th>
    <th>filename</th>
    <th>caption</th>
  </tr>
<?php
while ($row = mysql_fetch_assoc($result)) {
?>
  <tr>
    <td><?php echo $row['image_id']; ?></td>
    <td><?php echo $row['filename']; ?></td>
    <td><?php echo $row['caption']; ?></td>
  </tr>
<?php } ?>
</table>
</body>
```

The `while` loop iterates through the database result, using `mysql_fetch_assoc()` to extract each record into `$row`. Each element of `$row` is displayed in a table cell. The loop continues until `mysql_fetch_assoc($result)` comes to the end of the result set.

2. Save `mysql.php` and view it in a browser. You should see the contents of the images table displayed as shown in the following screenshot:

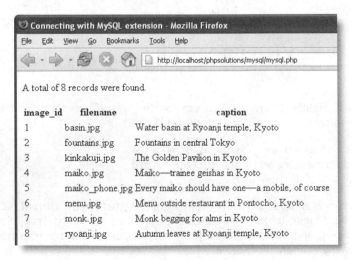

PHP Solution 11-5: Displaying the images table using MySQLI

Continue using the file from PHP Solution 11-2. The finished code is in `mysqli02.php`.

1. Insert the same code into the body of the page as in step 1 of PHP Solution 11-4. However, replace this line:

```
while ($row = mysql_fetch_assoc($result)) {
```

with this:

```
while ($row = $result->fetch_assoc()) {
```

2. Save the page and view it in a browser. It should look like the preceding screenshot.

PHP Solution 11-6: Displaying the images table using PDO

Because PDO doesn't have a convenient way of finding the number of records in a result set, you need to submit a second query to the database. It's also necessary to release the database resources associated with the first query.

Continue working with the same file as in PHP Solution 11-3. The finished script is in `pdo02.php`.

1. Amend the last section of code above the DOCTYPE declaration to release the database resource after the first query, and store the second query in a variable like this:

```
// find out how many records were retrieved
$numRows = $result->fetchColumn();
// free the database resources
$result->closeCursor();
// prepare second SQL query
$getDetails = 'SELECT * FROM images';
?>
```

The `closeCursor()` method frees the connection to the database so that further queries can be executed. You apply it to the current result; not to the connection. The second query, stored in `$getDetails`, retrieves all the records in the images table.

2. Insert the same code into the body of the page as in step 1 of PHP Solution 11-4. However, replace this line:

```
while ($row = mysql_fetch_assoc($result)) {
```

with this:

```
foreach ($conn->query($getDetails) as $row) {
```

3. Save the page and view it in a browser. It should look like the screenshot in PHP Solution 11-4.

11

MySQL connection crib sheet

Tables 11-2 to 11-4 summarize the basic details of connection and database query for MySQL, MySQLI, and PDO. Some commands will be used in later chapters, but are included here for ease of reference.

Table 11-2. Connection to MySQL with the original MySQL extension

Action	Usage	Comments
Connect	`$conn = mysql_connect($h,$u,$p);`	All arguments optional; first three always needed in practice: hostname, username, password.
Choose DB	`mysql_select_db('dbName');`	Server connection can be second, optional argument.
Submit query	`$result = mysql_query($sql);`	Requires one argument: string containing SQL query. Server connection can be second, optional argument. Returns result set.
Count results	`$numRows = mysql_num_rows($result);`	Takes result set as sole argument.
Extract record	`$row = mysql_fetch_assoc($result);`	Takes result set as sole argument. Extracts current record as associative array.
Extract record	`$row = mysql_fetch_row($result);`	Takes result set as sole argument. Extracts current record as indexed (numbered) array.

As noted in Table 11-2, you can use a reference to the database connection as an optional argument with `mysql_select_db()` and `mysql_query()`. There is no need to do this unless you are using more than one connection (say, with different usernames), because PHP automatically uses the most recent link opened by `mysql_connect()`.

Table 11-3. Connection to MySQL with the MySQL Improved object-oriented interface

Action	Usage	Comments
Connect	`$conn = new mysqli($h,$u,$p,$d);`	All arguments optional; first four always needed in practice: hostname, username, password, database name. Creates connection object.
Choose DB	`$conn->select_db('dbName');`	Use to select different database.
Submit query	`$result = $conn->query($sql);`	Returns result object.
Count results	`$numRows = $result->num_rows;`	Returns number of rows in result object.

Action	Usage	Comments
Release DB resources	$result->free_result();	Frees up connection to allow new query.
Extract record	$row = $result->fetch_assoc();	Extracts current row from result object as associative array.
Extract record	$row = $result->fetch_row();	Extracts current row from result object as indexed (numbered) array.

Table 11-4. Connection to MySQL with PDO

Action	Usage	Comments
Connect	$conn = new PDO(DSN,$u,$p);	In practice, requires three arguments: data source name (DSN), username, password. Must be wrapped in try/catch block.
Choose DB	See comments	Choice of database is integral part of DSN.
Submit query	$result = $conn->query($sql);	Can also be used inside foreach loop to extract each record.
Count results	See comments	Use SELECT COUNT(*) in SQL query.
Get single result	$item = $result->fetchColumn();	Gets first record in first column of result. To get result from other columns, use column number (from 0) as argument.
Get next record	$row = $result->fetch();	Gets next row from result set as associative array.
Release DB resources	$result->closeCursor();	Frees up connection to allow new query.
Extract records	foreach($conn->query($sql) as $row) {	Extracts current row from result set as associative array.

When using PDO with MySQL, the data source name (DSN) is a string that takes the following format:

```
'mysql:host=hostname;dbname=databaseName'
```

11

If you need to specify a different port from the MySQL default (3306), use the following format, substituting the actual port number:

```
'mysql:host=hostname;port=3307;dbname=databaseName'
```

MySQL Improved and PDO also use prepared statements, which offer greater security when incorporating user input into SQL queries. Prepared statement commands are covered in Chapter 13.

Summary

It's unfortunate that connection to MySQL is in such a transitional phase. Because PDO is so new, it may undergo further changes, but along with MySQLI, it has significant advantages over the original MySQL extension, particularly in improved protection against malicious attacks. However, I suspect that a high proportion of readers will have no option other than to use the traditional method of connecting to MySQL. The good news is that, for the foreseeable future at least, PHP plans to continue support for all three options. This means that even when you move to a server that supports PDO, your MySQL or MySQLI scripts will still work.

In the next chapter, we'll turn those boring lists of filenames and captions into something a lot more attractive—an online mini photo gallery. See you there.

What this chapter covers:

- Why storing images in a database is a bad idea, and what you should do instead
- Planning the layout of a dynamic gallery
- Displaying a fixed number of results in a row
- Limiting the number of records retrieved at a time
- Paging through a long set of results

In the last chapter, I showed you how to display the contents of the images table in a web page. It didn't look very attractive—text in an unadorned table. However, I hope you will have realized by now that all you need to do to display the images themselves is add `<img>` tags to the underlying XHTML, and you'll end up with something far more impressive. In fact, by the end of this chapter, you will have created the mini photo gallery shown in Figure 12-1.

Figure 12-1. The mini photo gallery is driven entirely by drawing information from a database.

Although it uses images, the gallery demonstrates some cool features that you will want to incorporate into text-driven pages, too. For instance, the grid of thumbnail images on the left displays two images per row. Just by changing two numbers, you can make the grid as many columns wide and as many rows deep as you like. Clicking one of the thumbnails replaces the main image and caption. It's the same page that reloads, but exactly the same technique is used to create online catalogs that take you to another page with more details about a product. The Next link at the foot of the thumbnails grid shows you the next set of photographs, using exactly the same technique as you use to page through a long set of search results. This gallery isn't just a pretty face or two . . .

First of all, a word about images and databases.

Why not store images in a database?

The `images` table contains only filenames and captions, but not the images themselves. Even though I said in the last chapter that you can always add new columns or tables to a database when new requirements arise, I'm not going to add anything to the `images` table. Instead, I intend to leave the images in their original location within the website—for the simple reason that storing images in a database is usually more trouble than it's worth. The main problems are as follows:

- Images cannot be indexed or searched without storing textual information separately.
- Images are usually large, bloating the size of tables.
- Table fragmentation affects performance if images are deleted frequently.
- Retrieving images from a database involves passing the image to a separate script, slowing down display in a web page.

Storing images in a database is messy, and involves more scripting. It's much more efficient to store images in an ordinary folder on your website and use the database for information about the images. You need just two pieces of information in the database—the filename and a caption that can also be used as `alt` text. You could also store the image's height and width, but it's not absolutely necessary. As you saw in Chapter 4, you can generate that information dynamically.

Planning the gallery

Unless you're good at visualizing how a page will look simply by reading its source code, I find that the best way to design a database-driven site is to start with a static page and fill it with placeholder text and images. I then create my CSS style rules to get the page looking the way I want, and finally replace each placeholder element with PHP code. Each time I replace something, I check the page in a browser to make sure that everything is still holding together.

Figure 12-2 shows the static mockup that I made of the gallery and points out the elements that need to be converted to dynamic code. The images are the same as those used for the random image generator in Chapter 4 and are all different sizes. I experimented by scaling the images to create the thumbnails, but decided that the result looked too untidy, so I made the thumbnails a standard size (80 × 54 pixels). Also, to make life easy, I gave each thumbnail the same name as the larger version and stored them in a separate folder called thumbs.

As you saw in the previous chapter, displaying the contents of the entire `images` table was easy. You created a single table row, with the contents of each field in a separate table cell. By looping through the result set, each record displayed on a row of its own, simulating the column structure of the database table. This time, the two-column structure of the thumbnail grid no longer matches the database structure. This means that you need to count how many thumbnails have been inserted in each row before triggering the creation of the next row.

12

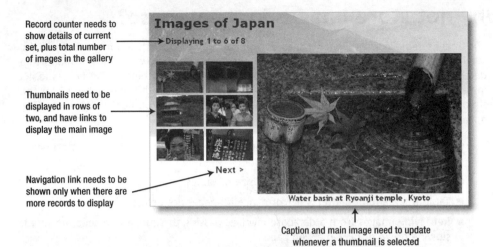

Record counter needs to show details of current set, plus total number of images in the gallery

Thumbnails need to be displayed in rows of two, and have links to display the main image

Navigation link needs to be shown only when there are more records to display

Caption and main image need to update whenever a thumbnail is selected

Figure 12-2. Working out what needs to be done to convert a static gallery to a dynamic one

Figure 12-3 shows the framework I created to hold the gallery together. The table of thumbnails and the main_image <div> are floated left and right respectively in a fixed-width wrapper <div> called gallery. I don't intend to go into the details of the CSS, but you may study that at your leisure.

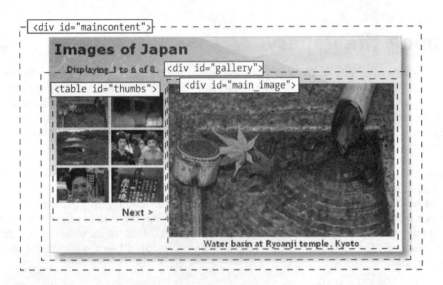

Figure 12-3. The underlying structure of the image gallery

Once I had worked out what needed to be done, I stripped out the code for thumbnails 2 to 6, and for the navigation link (which is nested in the final row of the thumbs table). The following listing shows what was left in the maincontent <div> of gallery.php, with the elements that need to be converted to PHP code highlighted in bold (you can find the code in gallery01.php in the download files for this chapter):

```
<div id="maincontent">
  <h1>Images of Japan</h1>
  <p id="picCount">Displaying 1 to 6 of 8</p>
  <div id="gallery">
    <table id="thumbs">
      <tr>
        <!-- This row needs to be repeated -->
        <td><a href="gallery.php"><img src="images/thumbs/basin.jpg" ➥
alt="" width="80" height="54" /></a></td>
      </tr>
      <!-- Navigation link needs to go here -->
    </table>
    <div id="main_image">
      <p><img src="images/basin.jpg" alt="" width="350" height="237" ➥
/></p>
      <p>Water basin at Ryoanji temple, Kyoto</p>
    </div>
  </div>
</div>
```

Converting the gallery elements to PHP

Before you can display the contents of the gallery, you need to connect to the phpsolutions database and retrieve all the records stored in the images table. The procedure for doing so is the same as in the previous chapter, using the following simple SQL query:

```
SELECT * FROM images
```

You can then use the first record to display the first image and its associated caption and thumbnail.

PHP Solution 12-1: Displaying the first image

If you set up the Japan Journey website in Chapter 4, you can work directly with the original gallery.php. Alternatively, use gallery01.php from the download files for this chapter. You also need to copy title.inc.php, menu.inc.php, and footer.inc.php to the includes folder of the phpsolutions site.

1. Load gallery.php into a browser to make sure that it displays correctly. The maincontent part of the page should look like Figure 12-4, with one thumbnail image and a larger version of the same image.

Figure 12-4. The stripped-down version of the static gallery ready for conversion

2. The gallery depends entirely on a successful connection to the database, so the first thing you need to do is include connection.inc.php. Add the following code just before the closing PHP tag above the DOCTYPE declaration in gallery.php (new code is highlighted in bold):

```
<?php
include('includes/title.inc.php');
// include MySQL connector function
if (! @include('includes/connection.inc.php'))
  echo 'Sorry, database unavailable';
  exit;
  }
?>
```

Remember, connection.inc.php needs to be the correct version for the way you plan to connect to MySQL—using the original MySQL extension, the MySQL Improved object-oriented interface, or PDO. The include command for the connection script is used as the condition for an if statement. The condition also uses the negative operator (an exclamation mark) and the error control operator (@). If the connection script is included successfully, the code inside the if statement is ignored; but if the file can't be found, a custom error message is displayed, and the rest of the script is abandoned. In a live application, you would probably redirect visitors to a custom error page.

3. Connect to the database by calling the dbConnect() function in the include file, and prepare the SQL query ready to submit it. The gallery needs only SELECT privileges for the database, so pass query as the argument to dbConnect() like this (the code for steps 3 to 5 goes immediately before the closing PHP tag):

```
// create a connection to MySQL
$conn = dbConnect('query');
// prepare SQL to retrieve image details
$sql = 'SELECT * FROM images';
```

4. The code for submitting the query and extracting the first record from the result depends on which method of connection you are using. For the original MySQL functions, use this:

```
// submit the query
$result = mysql_query($sql) or die(mysql_error());
// extract the first record as an array
$row = mysql_fetch_assoc($result);
```

For MySQL Improved, use this:

```
// submit the query
$result = $conn->query($sql) or die(mysqli_error());
// extract the first record as an array
$row = $result->fetch_assoc();
```

For PDO, use this:

```
// submit the query
$result = $conn->query($sql);
// get any error messages
$error = $conn->errorInfo();
if (isset($error[2])) die($error[2]);
// extract the first record as an array
$row = $result->fetch();
```

The code for the original MySQL extension and MySQL Improved is exactly the same as you used in the previous chapter.

The PDO code, however, introduces a new method, fetch(), which gets the next record from the result set. You can't use a foreach loop like in the previous chapter, because you need to get the first result on its own.

5. All three methods now have the first record from the result set stored as an array in $row. This means that $row['image_id'] contains the primary key of the first record, $row['filename'] contains its filename, and $row['caption'] contains its caption. You need the filename, caption, and the dimensions of the large version so that you can display the images in the main body of the page. Add the following code:

```
// get the name and caption for the main image
$mainImage = $row['filename'];
$caption = $row['caption'];
// get the dimensions of the main image
$imageSize = getimagesize('images/'.$mainImage);
```

The getimagesize() function was described in Chapters 4 and 8.

6. You can now use this information to display the thumbnail, main image, and its caption dynamically. The main image and thumbnail have the same name, but you eventually want to display all thumbnails by looping through the full result set, so the dynamic code that needs to go in the table cell needs to refer to the current record—in other words, $row['filename'] and $row['caption'], rather than to

12

$mainImage and $caption. You'll see later why I've assigned the values from the first record to separate variables. Amend the code in the table like this:

```
<td><a href="gallery.php"> ➟
<img src="images/thumbs/<?php echo $row['filename']; ?>" ➟
alt="<?php echo $row['caption']; ?>" width="80" height="54" /> ➟
</a></td>
```

7. Save gallery.php and view it in a browser. It should look the same as Figure 12-4. The only difference is that the thumbnail and its alt text are dynamically generated. You can verify this by looking at the source code. The original static version had an empty alt attribute, but as the following screenshot shows, it now contains the caption from the first record:

```
<table id="thumbs">
    <tr>
                            <!--This row needs to be repeated-->
        <td><a href="gallery.php"><img src="images/thumbs/basin.jpg"
alt="Water basin at Ryoanji temple, Kyoto" width="80" height="54" /></a></td>
    </tr>
                    <!-- Navigation link needs to go here -->
</table>
```

If things go wrong, make sure there's no gap between the static and dynamically generated text in the image's src attribute. Also check that you're using the right code for the type of connection you have created with MySQL. You can check your code against gallery_mysql02.php, gallery_mysqli02.php, or gallery_pdo02.php.

8. Once you have confirmed that you're picking up the details from the database, you can convert the code for the main image. Amend it like this (new code is in bold):

```
<div id="main_image">
    <p><img src="images/<?php echo $mainImage; ?>" ➟
alt="<?php echo $caption; ?>" <?php echo $imageSize[3]; ?> /></p>
    <p><?php echo $caption; ?></p>
</div>
```

As explained in Chapter 4, getimagesize() returns an array, the fourth element of which contains a string with the width and height of an image ready for insertion into an <img> tag. So $imageSize[3] inserts the correct dimensions for the main image.

9. Test the page again. It should still look the same as Figure 12-4, but the images and caption are being drawn dynamically from the database. You can check your code against gallery_mysql03.php, gallery_mysqli03.php, or gallery_pdo03.php.

Building the dynamic elements

The first thing that you need to do after converting the static page is to display all the thumbnails and build dynamic links that will enable you to display the large version of any thumbnail that has been clicked. Displaying all the thumbnails is easy—just loop through them (we'll work out how to display them in rows of two later). Activating the link for each thumbnail requires a little more thought. You need a way of telling the page which large image to display.

Passing information through a query string

In the last section, you used $mainImage to identify the large image, so you need a way of changing its value whenever a thumbnail is clicked. The answer is to add the image's filename to a query string at the end of the URL in the link like this:

```
<a href="gallery.php?image=filename">
```

You can then check whether the $_GET array contains an element called image. If it does, change the value of $mainImage. If it doesn't, leave $mainImage as the filename from the first record in the result set.

Time to dive back into the code . . .

> **PHP Solution 12-2: Activating the thumbnails**

Continue working with the same file as in the previous section. Alternatively, use gallery_mysql03.php, gallery_mysqli03.php, or gallery_pdo03.php from the download files.

1. Locate the <a> tag surrounding the thumbnail. It looks like this:

```
<a href="gallery.php">
```

Change it like this:

```
<a href="<?php echo $_SERVER['PHP_SELF']; ?>?image=<?php echo ➥
$row['filename']; ?>">
```

Be careful when typing the code. It's easy to mix up the question marks in the PHP tags with the question mark at the beginning of the query string. It's also important there are no spaces surrounding ?image=.

So, what's all this about? $_SERVER['PHP_SELF'] is a handy predefined variable that refers to the name of the current page. You could just leave gallery.php hard-coded in the URL, but I suspect that many of you will use the download files, which have a variety of names. Using $_SERVER['PHP_SELF'] ensures that the URL is pointing to the correct page. The rest of the code builds the query string with the current filename.

2. Save the page, and load it into a browser. Hover your mouse pointer over the thumbnail, and check the URL displayed in the status bar. It should look like this:

```
http://localhost/phpsolutions/gallery.php?image=basin.jpg
```

If nothing is shown in the status bar, click the thumbnail. The page shouldn't change, but the URL in the address bar should now include the query string. Check that there are no gaps in the URL or query string.

12

327

3. To show all the thumbnails, you need to wrap the table cell in a loop. Insert a new line after the XHTML comment about repeating the row, and create the first half of a do... while loop like this (see Chapter 3 for details of the different types of loops):

```
<!-- This row needs to be repeated -->
<?php do { ?>
```

4. You already have the details of the first record in the result set, so the code to get subsequent records needs to go after the closing </td> tag. Create some space between the closing </td> and </tr> tags, and insert the following code. It's slightly different for each method of database connection.

For the MySQL original extensions, use this:

```
    </td>
<?php
$row = mysql_fetch_assoc($result);
} while ($row);
?>
</tr>
```

For the MySQL Improved object-oriented interface, use this:

```
    </td>
<?php
$row = $result->fetch_assoc();
} while ($row);
?>
</tr>
```

For PDO, use this:

```
    </td>
<?php
$row = $result->fetch();
} while ($row);
?>
</tr>
```

This fetches the next row in the result set and sends the loop back to the top. Because $row['filename'] and $row['caption'] have different values, the next thumbnail and its associated alt text are inserted into a new table cell. The query string is also updated with the new filename.

5. Save the page, and test it in a browser. You should now see all eight thumbnails in a single row across the top of the gallery, as shown at the top of the next page.

Hover your mouse pointer over each thumbnail, and you should see the query string display the name of the file. You can check your code against gallery_mysql04.php, gallery_mysqli04.php, or gallery_pdo04.php.

Water basin at Ryoanji temple, Kyoto

6. Clicking the thumbnails still doesn't do anything, so you need to create the logic that changes the main image and its associated caption. Locate this section of code in the block above the DOCTYPE declaration:

```
// get the name and caption for the main image
$mainImage = $row['filename'];
$caption = $row['caption'];
```

Highlight the line that defines $caption, and cut it to your clipboard. Wrap the other line in a conditional statement like this:

```
// get the name for the main image
if (isset($_GET['image'])) {
  $mainImage = $_GET['image'];
  }
else {
  $mainImage = $row['filename'];
  }
```

The $_GET array contains values passed through a query string, so if $_GET['image'] has been set (defined), it takes the filename from the query string and stores it as $mainImage. If $_GET['image'] doesn't exist, the value is taken from the first record in the result set as before.

7. You finally need to get the caption for the main image. It's no longer going to be the same every time, so you need to move it to the loop that displays the thumbnails. It goes right after the opening curly brace of the loop. Position your cursor after the brace and insert a couple of lines, and then paste the caption definition that you cut in the previous step. You want the caption to match the main image, so if the current record's filename is the same as $mainImage, that's the one you're after. Wrap the code that you have just pasted in a conditional statement like this:

```
<?php
do {
  // set caption if thumbnail is same as main image
  if ($row['filename'] == $mainImage) {
    $caption = $row['caption']; // this is the line you pasted
    }
?>
```

12

329

8. Save the page and reload it in your browser. This time, when you click a thumbnail, the main image and caption will change. Check your code, if necessary, against gallery_mysql05.php, gallery_mysqli05.php, or gallery_pdo05.php.

Passing information through a query string like this is an important aspect of working with PHP and database results. Although form information is normally passed through the $_POST array, the $_GET array is frequently used to pass details of a record that you want to display, update, or delete. Like the $_POST array, the $_GET array automatically inserts backslashes if magic quotes are turned on in php.ini. Since only the filename is being passed through the query string, there's no need to use the nukeMagicQuotes() function from Chapter 3 because quotes are illegal in filenames. That's one reason I didn't pass the caption through the query string. Getting it directly from the database avoids the problem of handling backslashes.

Creating a multicolumn table

With only eight images, the single row of thumbnails across the top of the gallery doesn't look too bad. However, it's useful to be able to build a table dynamically with a loop that inserts a specific number of table cells in a row before moving to the next row. You do this by keeping count of how many cells have been inserted. When you get to the limit for the row, check whether any more rows are needed. If so, insert a closing tag for the current row and an opening tag for the next one. What makes it easy to implement is the modulo operator, %, which returns the remainder of a division.

This is how it works. Let's say you want two cells in each row. When the first cell is inserted, the counter is set to 1. If you divide 1 by 2 with the modulo operator (1%2), the result is 1. When the next cell is inserted, the counter is increased to 2. The result of 2%2 is 0. The next cell produces this calculation: 3%2, which results in 1; but the fourth cell produces 4%2, which is again 0. So, every time that the calculation results in 0, you know—or to be more exact, PHP knows—you're at the end of a row.

So how do you know if there are any more rows left? Each time you iterate through the loop, you extract the next record into an array called $row. By using is_array(), you can check whether $row contains the next result. If it does, you add the tags for the next row. If is_array($row) is false, you've run out of records in the result set. Phew . . . let's try it.

PHP Solution 12-3: Looping horizontally and vertically

Continue working with the files from the preceding section. Alternatively, use gallery_mysql05.php, gallery_mysqli05.php, or gallery_pdo05.php.

1. You may decide at a later stage that you want to change the number of columns in the table, so it's a good idea to create a constant at the top of the script, where it's easy to find, rather than burying the figures deep in your code. Insert the following code just before the database connection:

```
// define number of columns in table
define('COLS', 2);
```

2. You need to initialize the cell counter outside the loop, so amend the beginning of the loop like this:

```
<?php
// initialize cell counter outside loop
$pos = 0;
do {
  // set caption if thumbnail is same as main image
  if ($row['filename'] == $mainImage) {
```

3. The remainder of the code goes after the table cell. It should be easy to follow with the inline comments and the description at the beginning of this section. Amend the code as follows (the first line of code inside the block is part of the existing code, and will look slightly different if you're using MySQLI or PDO):

```
    </td>
    <?php
    $row = mysql_fetch_assoc($result);
    // increment counter after next row extracted
    $pos++;
    // if at end of row and records remain, insert tags
    if ($pos%COLS === 0 && is_array($row)) {
      echo '</tr><tr>';
      }
    } while($row);  // end of existing loop
    // new loop to fill in final row
    while ($pos%COLS) {
      echo '<td> </td>';
      $pos++;
      }
    ?>
    </tr>
</table>
```

A new loop is added at the end of the existing loop. If there are no more records, and $pos%COLS doesn't equal 0, it means you have an incomplete row at the bottom of the table, so the second loop continues incrementing $pos while $pos%COLS produces a remainder (which is interpreted as true) and inserting an empty cell. Note that this second loop is *not* nested inside the first. It runs only after the first loop has ended.

4. Save the page and reload it in a browser. The single row of thumbnails across the top of the gallery should now be neatly lined up two by two, as shown to the right.

Water basin at Ryoanji temple, Kyoto

Try changing the value of COLS and reloading the page. See how easy it is to control the number of cells in each row by changing just one number. You can check your code against gallery_mysql06.php, gallery_mysqli06.php, or gallery_pdo06.php.

12

Paging through a long set of records

The grid of eight thumbnails fits quite comfortably in the gallery, but what if you have 28 or 48? The answer is to limit the number of results displayed on each page, and build a navigation system that lets you page back and forth through the results. You've seen this technique countless times when using a search engine; now you're going to learn how to build it yourself.

The task can be broken down into the following two stages:

1. Selecting a subset of records to display

2. Creating the navigation links to page through the subsets

Both stages are relatively easy to implement, although it involves applying a little conditional logic. Keep a cool head, and you'll breeze through it.

Selecting a subset of records

Limiting the number of results on a page is simple. Add the LIMIT keyword to the SQL query like this:

```
SELECT * FROM images LIMIT startPosition, maximum
```

The LIMIT keyword can be followed by one or two numbers. If you use just one number, it sets the maximum number of records to be retrieved. That's useful, but it's not what we need to build a paging system. For that, you need to use two numbers: the first indicates which record to start from, and the second stipulates the maximum number of records to be retrieved. MySQL counts records from 0, so to display the first six images, you need the following SQL:

```
SELECT * FROM images LIMIT 0, 6
```

To show the next set, the SQL needs to change to this:

```
SELECT * FROM images LIMIT 6, 6
```

There are only eight records in the images table, but the second number is only a maximum, so this retrieves records 7 and 8.

To build the navigation system, you need a way of generating these numbers. The second number never changes, so let's define a constant called SHOWMAX. Generating the first number (call it $startRecord) is pretty easy, too. Start numbering the pages from 0, and multiply the second number by the current page number. So, if you call the current page $curPage, the formula looks like this:

```
$startRecord = $curPage * SHOWMAX;
```

And for the SQL, it becomes this:

```
SELECT * FROM images LIMIT $startRecord, SHOWMAX
```

If $curPage is 0, $startRecord is also 0 (0 × 6), but when $curPage increases to 1, $startRecord changes to 6 (1 × 6), and so on.

Since there are only eight records in the images table, you need a way of finding out the total number of records to prevent the navigation system from retrieving empty result sets. In the last chapter, you used $numRows to get this information. However, the technique that was used for the original MySQL extension and the MySQL Improved object-oriented interface won't work, because mysql_num_rows() and the num_rows property report the number of records in the *current* result set. Since you're limiting the number of records retrieved at any one time to a maximum of six, you need a different way to get the total. If you're using PDO, you already know the answer is this:

```
SELECT COUNT(*) FROM images
```

COUNT() is a SQL function that calculates the total number of results in a query. When used like this in combination with an asterisk, it gets the total number of records in the table. So, to build a navigation system, you need to run both SQL queries: one to find the total number of records, and the other to retrieve the required subset. MySQL is fast, so the result is almost instantaneous.

I'll deal with the navigation links later. Let's begin by limiting the number of thumbnails on the first page.

PHP Solution 12-4: Displaying a subset of records

Continue working with the same file. Alternatively, use gallery_mysql06.php, gallery_mysqli06.php, or gallery_pdo06.php.

1. Define SHOWMAX and the SQL query to find the total number of records in the table. Amend the code toward the top of the page like this (new code is shown in bold):

```
// define number of columns in table
define('COLS', 2);
// set maximum number of records per page
define('SHOWMAX', 6);
// create a connection to MySQL
$conn = dbConnect('query');
// prepare SQL to get total records
$getTotal = 'SELECT COUNT(*) FROM images';
```

> *Although* COLS *and* SHOWMAX *are defined as constants, it doesn't prevent you from offering visitors a choice of how many columns and items to display on a page. You could use variables as the second arguments to* define()*, and draw their values from user input.*

12

2. You now need to run the new SQL query. The code goes immediately after the code in the preceding step, but differs according to the type of MySQL connection.

If you're using the original MySQL extension, add this:

```
// submit query and store result as $totalPix
$total = mysql_query($getTotal);
$row = mysql_fetch_row($total);
$totalPix = $row[0];
```

This introduces a new function, mysql_fetch_row(), which gets a single record from a result set as an indexed array (one that refers to elements by numbers). The result of SELECT COUNT(*) contains just one field, so you access it as $row[0].

For MySQL Improved, use this:

```
// submit query and store result as $totalPix
$total = $conn->query($getTotal);
$row = $total->fetch_row();
$totalPix = $row[0];
```

This uses the MySQLI equivalent of mysql_fetch_row() just described. The result set for the query has been saved as $total, so $total->fetch_row() gets the record as an indexed array.

For PDO, use this:

```
// submit query and store result as $totalPix
$total = $conn->query($getTotal);
$row = $total->fetchColumn();
$totalPix = $row[0];
$total->closeCursor();
```

This is the same as in the previous chapter, using fetchColumn() to get a single result, and closeCursor() to free the database connection for the next query.

3. Next, set the value of $curPage. The navigation links that you will create later pass the value of the required page through a query string, so you need to check whether curPage has been set in the $_GET array. If it has, use that value. Otherwise, set the current page to 0. Insert the following code immediately after the code in the previous step:

```
// set the current page
$curPage = isset($_GET['curPage']) ? $_GET['curPage'] : 0;
```

This uses the conditional operator (see Chapter 3). If you find the conditional operator hard to understand, use the following code instead. It has exactly the same meaning.

```
if (isset($_GET['curPage'])) {
  $curPage = $_GET['curPage'];
  }
else {
  $curPage = 0;
  }
```

4. You now have all the information that you need to calculate the start row, and to build the SQL query to retrieve a subset of records. Add the following code immediately after the code in the preceding step:

```
// calculate the start row of the subset
$startRow = $curPage * SHOWMAX;
```

The original SQL query should now be on the next line. Amend it like this:

```
// prepare SQL to retrieve subset of image details
$sql = "SELECT * FROM images LIMIT $startRow,".SHOWMAX;
```

> *Notice that I've used double quotes this time, because I want PHP to process $startRow. Unlike variables, constants aren't processed inside double-quoted strings. So SHOWMAX is added to the end of the SQL query with the concatenation operator (a period). The comma inside the closing quotes is part of the SQL, separating the two arguments of the LIMIT clause.*

5. Save the page and reload it into a browser. Instead of eight thumbnails, you should see just six, as shown here:

Water basin at Ryoanji temple, Kyoto

Change the value of SHOWMAX to see a different number of thumbnails. The text above the thumbnail grid doesn't update because it's still hard-coded, so let's fix that.

6. Locate the following line of code in the main body of the page:

```
<p id="picCount">Displaying 1 to 6 of 8</p>
```

12

Replace it with this:

```
<p id="picCount">Displaying <?php echo $startRow+1;
if ($startRow+1 < $totalPix) {
  echo ' to ';
  if ($startRow+SHOWMAX < $totalPix) {
    echo $startRow+SHOWMAX;
    }
  else {
    echo $totalPix;
    }
  }
echo " of $totalPix";
?></p>
```

Let's take this line by line. The value of $startRow is zero-based, so you need to add 1 to get a more user-friendly number. So, $startRow+1 displays 1 on the first page and 7 on the second page.

In the second line, $startRow+1 is compared with the total number of records. If it's less, that means the current page is displaying a range of records, so the third line displays the text "to" with a space on either side.

You then need to work out the top number of the range, so a nested if... else conditional statement adds the value of the start row to the maximum number of records to be shown on a page. If the result is less than the total number of records, $startRow+SHOWMAX gives you the number of the last record on the page. However, if it's equal to or greater than the total, you display $totalPix instead.

Finally, you come out of both conditional statements and display "of" followed by the total number of records.

7. Save the page and reload it in a browser. You still get only the first subset of thumbnails, but you should see the second number change dynamically whenever you alter the value of SHOWMAX. Check your code, if necessary, against gallery_mysql07.php, gallery_mysqli07.php, or gallery_pdo07.php.

Navigating through subsets of records

As I mentioned in step 3 of the preceding section, the value of the required page is passed to the PHP script through a query string. When the page first loads, there is no query string, so the value of $curPage is set to 0. Although a query string is generated when you click a thumbnail to display a different image, it includes only the filename of the main image, so the original subset of thumbnails remains unchanged. To display the next subset, you need to create a link that increases the value of $curPage by 1. It follows, therefore, that to return to the previous subset, you need another link that reduces the value of $curPage by 1.

That's simple enough, but you also need to make sure that these links are displayed only when there is a valid subset to navigate to. For instance, there's no point in displaying a back link on the first page, because there isn't a previous subset. Similarly, you shouldn't display a forward link on the page that displays the last subset, because there's nothing to navigate to.

Both issues are easily solved by using conditional statements. There's one final thing that you need to take care of. You must also include the value of the current page in the query string generated when you click a thumbnail. If you fail to do so, $curPage is automatically set back to 0, and the first set of thumbnails is displayed instead of the current subset.

PHP Solution 12-5: Creating the navigation links

Continue working with the same file. Alternatively, use gallery_mysql07.php, gallery_mysqli07.php, or gallery_pdo07.php.

1. I have placed the navigation links in an extra row at the bottom of the thumbnail table. Insert this code between the placeholder comment and the closing </table> tag:

```
<!-- Navigation link needs to go here -->
<tr><td>
<?php
// create a back link if current page greater than 0
if ($curPage > 0) {
    echo '<a href="'.$_SERVER['PHP_SELF'].'?curPage='.($curPage-1).'"> ➥
&lt; Prev</a>';
    }
// otherwise leave the cell empty
else {
    echo ' ';
    }
?>
</td>
<?php
// pad the final row with empty cells if more than 2 columns
if (COLS-2 > 0) {
    for ($i = 0; $i < COLS-2; $i++) {
        echo '<td> </td>';
        }
    }
?>
<td>
<?php
// create a forward link if more records exist
if ($startRow+SHOWMAX < $totalPix) {
    echo '<a href="'.$_SERVER['PHP_SELF'].'?curPage='.($curPage+1).'"> ➥
Next &gt;</a>';
    }
```

12

```
      // otherwise leave the cell empty
      else {
        echo ' ';
        }
      ?>
      </td></tr>
      </table>
```

It looks like a lot, but the code breaks down into three sections: the first creates a back link if $curPage is greater than 0; the second pads the final table row with empty cells if there are more than two columns; and the third uses the same formula as before ($startRow+SHOWMAX < $totalPix) to determine whether to display a forward link.

When typing this code, make sure that you get the combination of quotes right in the links. The other point to note is that the $curPage-1 and $curPage+1 calculations are enclosed in parentheses to avoid the period after the number being misinterpreted as a decimal point. It's used here as the concatenation operator to join the various parts of the query string.

2. You now need to add the value of the current page to the query string in the link surrounding the thumbnail. Locate this section of code:

```
<a href="<?php echo $_SERVER['PHP_SELF']; ?>?image=<?php echo ➥
$row['filename']; ?>">
```

Change it like this:

```
<a href="<?php echo $_SERVER['PHP_SELF']; ?>?image=<?php echo ➥
$row['filename']; ?>&amp;curPage=<?php echo $curPage; ?>">
```

You want the same subset to be displayed when clicking a thumbnail, so you just pass the current value of $curPage through the query string.

> Notice that I have used the HTML entity & to add a second name/value pair to the query string. This is displayed in the browser status bar or address bar simply as an ampersand. Although using an ampersand on its own also works, & is required for valid XHTML.

3. Save the page and test it. Click the Next link, and you should see the remaining subset of thumbnails, as shown in Figure 12-5. There are no more images to be displayed, so the Next link disappears, but there's a Prev link at the bottom left of the thumbnail grid. The record counter at the top of the gallery now reflects the range of thumbnails being displayed, and if you click the right thumbnail, the same subset remains onscreen while displaying the appropriate large image. You're done!

Figure 12-5. The page navigation system is now complete.

Check your code, if necessary, against gallery_mysql08.php, gallery_mysqli08.php, or gallery_pdo08.php.

Summary

Wow! In a few pages, you have turned a boring list of filenames into a dynamic online gallery, complete with a page navigation system. All that's necessary is to create a thumbnail for each major image, upload both images to the appropriate folder, and add the file name and a caption to the images table in the database. As long as the database is kept up to date with the contents of the images and thumbs folders, you have a dynamic gallery. Not only that, you've learned how to select subsets of records, link to related information through a query string, and build a page navigation system.

The more you use PHP, the more you realize that the skill doesn't lie so much in remembering how to use lots of obscure functions, but in working out the logic needed to get PHP to do what you want. It's a question of if this, do that; if something else, do something different. Once you can anticipate the likely eventualities of a situation, you can normally build the code to handle it.

So far, you've concentrated on extracting records from a simple database table. In the next chapter, I'll show you how to insert, update, and delete material.

12

13 MANAGING CONTENT

What this chapter covers:

- Preventing SQL injection attacks
- Inserting, updating, and deleting database records
- Using prepared statements with MySQLI and PDO

Although you can use phpMyAdmin for a lot of database administration, there are some things for which it's out of the question. The last thing you want is to give outsiders the freedom to poke around your database, adding and deleting vital records at will. You need to build your own forms and create customized content management systems.

At the heart of every content management system lie just four SQL commands: SELECT, INSERT, UPDATE, and DELETE. All four commands either rely on or can accept user input. So you need to make sure that any input doesn't expose your data to attack or accidental corruption. The MySQL Improved extension and PDO offer new, more robust ways of handling user input; but the original MySQL functions are just as safe if handled properly. To demonstrate the basic SQL commands, this chapter shows you how to build a simple content management system for a blog-style table called journal.

Even if you don't want to build your own content management system, the four commands covered in this chapter are essential for just about any database-driven page: user login, user registration, search form, search results, etc.

Keeping your data safe

All too often, security issues get brushed aside when learning to communicate with a database. You're not only learning the mechanics of connecting to a database and extracting the results, but there's a whole new language to come to grips with—Structured Query Language (SQL). There *is* a lot to absorb, but security should be among your highest priorities for these reasons:

- There's no point in spending a lot of effort building a database, if it's all going to be blown away by an attacker or careless input.
- Handling security properly is probably the least difficult aspect of communicating with a database through PHP. All that's needed are a couple of simple precautions.

Understanding the danger of SQL injection

SQL injection is very similar to the email header injection I warned you about in Chapter 5. An injection attack tries to insert spurious conditions into a SQL query in an attempt to expose or corrupt your data. Although you haven't studied WHERE clauses with SELECT queries yet, the meaning of the following query should be easy to understand:

```
SELECT * FROM users WHERE username = 'xyz' AND pwd = 'abc'
```

It's the basic pattern for a login application. If the query finds a record where username is xyz and pwd is abc, you know that a correct combination of username and password have been submitted, so the login succeeds. All an attacker needs to do is inject an extra condition like this:

```
SELECT * FROM users WHERE username = 'xyz' AND pwd = 'abc' OR 1 = 1
```

The OR means only one of the conditions needs to be true, so the login succeeds even without a correct username and password. SQL injection relies on quotes and other control characters not being properly escaped when part of the query is derived from a variable or user input. This sort of attack was one of the main reasons behind the introduction of magic quotes (see Chapter 3), which automatically insert a backslash in front of quotation marks passed through the $_POST, $_GET, and $_COOKIES arrays. Although the backslashes prevent SQL injection, they cause problems in variables intended for display onscreen. So beginners find their heads whirling in confusion over when to remove backslashes and when to leave them in. To make the situation even more confusing, not all servers use magic quotes.

Relying on magic quotes or—if they are turned off—inserting backslashes with the addslashes() function is no longer considered sufficient protection from SQL injection. Users of the original MySQL extension should use the rather clumsily named mysql_real_escape_string() function. The MySQL Improved extension and PDO offer a more sophisticated approach known as **prepared statements**, which I'll describe shortly. Both methods guarantee your code against SQL injection. Whichever method you use, you should remove magic quotes by using the nukeMagicQuotes() function from Chapter 3. First, though, let's take a look at how you write SQL queries.

Basic rules for writing SQL

SQL syntax doesn't have many rules, and all of them are quite simple.

SQL is case-insensitive

You've probably noticed that the SQL queries in the previous chapter and the preceding examples use a combination of uppercase and lowercase. All words in uppercase are SQL keywords; everything else is in lowercase. However, this is purely a convention. The following are all equally correct:

```
SELECT * FROM images
select * from images
SeLEcT * fRoM images
```

Although SQL keywords are case-insensitive, the same *doesn't* apply to database column names. The advantage of using uppercase for keywords is that it makes SQL queries easier to identify within your code. You're free to choose whichever style suits you best, but the ransom-note style of the last example is probably best avoided.

Whitespace is ignored

This allows you to spread SQL queries over several lines for increased readability. The one place where whitespace is *not* allowed is between a function name and the opening parenthesis: COUNT (*) generates an error; it must be COUNT(*).

13

Strings must be quoted

All strings must be quoted in a SQL query. It doesn't matter whether you use single or double quotes, as long as they are in matching pairs. Quotes inside strings should be handled either by passing the string to `mysql_real_escape_string()` (when using the original MySQL extension) or by using a prepared statement (with MySQL Improved or PDO).

Handling numbers

As a general rule, numbers should not be quoted, as anything in quotes is a string. However, MySQL accepts numbers enclosed in quotes and treats them as their numeric equivalent. Be careful to distinguish between a real number and any other data type made up of numbers. For instance, a date is made up of numbers, but should be enclosed in quotes and stored in a date-related column type. Similarly, telephone numbers should be enclosed in quotes and stored in a text-related column type.

Incorporating variables into SQL queries

There are two ways of incorporating variables into SQL queries: direct incorporation and using prepared statements (MySQL Improved and PDO only).

Direct incorporation

When using the original MySQL extension, you have no option but to build SQL queries in the same way as you did with the page navigation system in PHP Solution 12-4 in the previous chapter. In other words, you must incorporate variables directly in the SQL query like this:

```
$sql = "SELECT * FROM images LIMIT $startRow,".SHOWMAX;
```

Both $startRow and SHOWMAX are numbers, so they don't need to be quoted. As explained in the previous chapter, constants cannot be used in a double-quoted string, so SHOWMAX is appended to the rest of the query without any quotes. However, a query that incorporates string variables needs quotes around the strings like this:

```
$sql = "SELECT * FROM users WHERE username = '$name' AND pwd = '$pwd'";
```

Before incorporating variables that come from an external source into a SQL query like this, you must always pass the variable first to `mysql_real_escape_string()` to ensure that it's safe. The reason it was safe to embed $startRow and SHOWMAX directly in the query without using `mysql_real_escape_string()` is because both variables are defined within your own script. Although $startRow usually derives its value from an external source ($curPage), multiplying $curPage by SHOWMAX always produces a number (0 if $curPage can't be converted to a number). This neutralizes any threat.

> *You can use* `mysql_real_escape_string()` *only with a database connection created using the original MySQL extension—in other words,* `mysql_connect()`. *It does* **not** *work with MySQL Improved or PDO. Although there are equivalent functions for MySQL Improved (www.php.net/manual/en/function.mysqli-real-escape-string.php) and PDO (www.php.net/manual/en/function.pdo-quote.php), it is strongly recommended that you use prepared statements instead of embedding variables that contain data from an external source.*

MySQLI prepared statements

Instead of embedding variables in the SQL query, you replace them with question marks like this:

```
$sql = 'SELECT * FROM users WHERE username = ? AND pwd = ?';
```

Getting the values of the variables into the placeholders is a four- or five-stage process, as follows:

1. Initialize the statement.

2. Pass the SQL query to the statement to make sure it's valid.

3. Bind the variables to the query.

4. Bind any results to variables (optional).

5. Execute the statement.

Let's say you have established a MySQLI connection called $conn; this is how it looks in PHP code:

```
// initialize statement
$stmt = $conn->stmt_init();
if ($stmt->prepare($sql)) {
  // bind the query parameters
  $stmt->bind_param('ss', $_POST['name'], $_POST['pwd']);
  // execute the query
  $stmt->execute();
}
```

To initialize the prepared statement, apply the stmt_init() method to the database connection ($conn), and store it in a variable. You can use any variable you like, but $stmt makes it clear what it's for.

You then pass the SQL query to $stmt->prepare(). This checks that you haven't used question mark placeholders in the wrong place, and that when everything is put together, the query is valid SQL. If there are any mistakes, $stmt->prepare() returns false, so you need to enclose the next steps in a conditional statement to ensure they run only if everything is still OK.

Binding the parameters means replacing the question marks with the actual values held in the variables. This is what protects your database from SQL injection. You pass the variables to $stmt->bind_param() in the same order as you want them inserted into the SQL query, together with a first argument specifying the data type of each variable, again in the same order as the variables. The data type must be specified by one of the following four characters:

- **b**: Binary (such as an image, Word document, or PDF file)
- **d**: Double (floating point number)
- **i**: Integer (whole number)
- **s**: String (text)

13

The number of variables passed to $stmt->bind_param() must be exactly the same as the number of question mark placeholders. Once the statement has been prepared, you call $stmt->execute(), and the result is stored in $stmt.

This example doesn't show the binding of result parameters. That's explained in PHP Solution 13-6.

Error messages can be accessed by using $stmt->error.

PDO prepared statements

Whereas MySQLI always uses question marks as placeholders in prepared statements, PDO offers several options. I'll describe the two most useful: question marks and named place-holders.

Question mark placeholders Instead of embedding variables in the SQL query, you replace them with question marks like this:

```
$sql = 'SELECT * FROM users WHERE username = ? AND pwd = ? ';
```

This is identical to MySQLI. However, the way that you bind the values of the variables to the placeholders is completely different. It involves just two steps, as follows:

1. Prepare the statement to make sure the SQL is valid.

2. Execute the statement by passing the variables to it as an array.

Assuming you have created a PDO database connection called $conn, the PHP code looks like this:

```
// prepare statement
$stmt = $conn->prepare($sql);
// execute query by passing array of variables
$stmt->execute(array($_POST['name'], $_POST['pwd']));
```

The first line of code prepares the statement and stores it as $stmt. The second line binds the values of the variables and executes the statement all in one go. The variables must be in the same order as the placeholders. Even if there is only one placeholder, the variable must be passed to execute() as an array. You'll see this later in PHP Solution 13-7. The result of the query is stored in $stmt.

Named placeholders Instead of embedding variables in the SQL query, you replace them with named placeholders beginning with a colon like this:

```
$sql = 'SELECT * FROM users WHERE username = :name AND pwd = :pwd';
```

With named placeholders, you can either bind the values individually or pass an associative array to execute(). When binding the values individually, the PHP code looks like this:

```
$stmt = $conn->prepare($sql);
// bind the parameters and execute the statement
$stmt->bindParam(':name', $_GET['name'], PDO::PARAM_STR);
$stmt->bindParam(':pwd', $_POST['pwd'], PDO::PARAM_STR);
$stmt->execute();
```

You pass three arguments to $stmt->bindParam(): the name of the placeholder, the variable that you want to use as its value, and a constant specifying the data type. The main constants are as follows:

- **PDO::PARAM_INT**: Integer (whole number)
- **PDO::PARAM_LOB**: Binary (such as an image, Word document, or PDF file)
- **PDO::PARAM_STR**: String (text)

There doesn't appear to be a constant for floating point numbers, but the third argument is optional, so you can just leave it out.

If you pass the variables as an associative array, you can't specify the data type. The PHP code for the same example using an associative array looks like this:

```
// prepare statement
$stmt = $conn->prepare($sql);
// execute query by passing array of variables
$stmt->execute(array(':name' => $_POST['name'], ':pwd' => ➥
$_POST['pwd']));
```

In both cases, the result of the query is stored in $stmt.

Error messages can be accessed in the same way as with a PDO connection. However, instead of applying the errorInfo() method to the connection variable, apply it to the PDO statement like this:

```
$error = $stmt->errorInfo();
if (isset($error[2])) {
  echo $error[2];
  }
```

Setting up a content management system

Now that we've got the theory out of the way, let's get on with something a bit more practical by building a content management system for a table called journal. Managing the content in a database table involves four stages, which I normally assign to four separate but interlinked pages, as follows:

- A page to insert new records
- A page to list all existing records
- A page to update existing records
- A page that asks for confirmation before deleting a record

The list of records serves two purposes: first, to identify what's stored in the database; and more importantly, to link to the update and delete scripts by passing the record's primary key through a query string. As Figure 13-1 shows, you can put the details of the record into a form ready for editing or display sufficient details to confirm that the correct entry is being deleted.

13

347

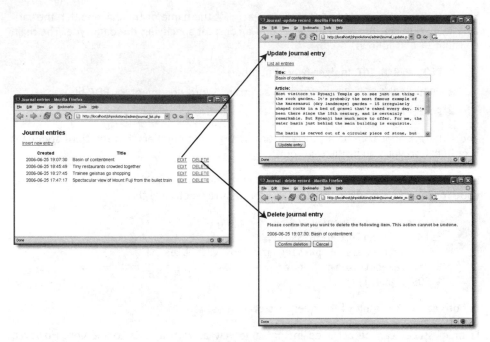

Figure 13-1. The list of records passes the primary key of the selected record to the update and delete pages.

The journal table contains a series of titles and text articles to be displayed in the Japan Journey site as shown in Figure 13-2. In the interests of keeping things simple, the table contains just five columns: article_id (primary key), title, article, updated, and created.

Figure 13-2. The contents of the journal table displayed in the Japan Journey website

The final two columns hold the date and time when the article was last updated, and when it was originally created. Although it may seem illogical to put the updated column first, this is to take advantage of the way MySQL automatically updates the first TIMESTAMP column in a table. The created column gets its value from a MySQL function called NOW(), neatly sidestepping the problem of preparing the date in the correct format for MySQL. The thorny issue of dates will be tackled in the next chapter.

Creating the journal database table

If you just want to get on with studying the content management pages, use journal.sql in the download files for this chapter. Open phpMyAdmin, select the phpsolutions database, and import the table in the same way as in the previous chapter. The SQL file creates the table and populates it with four short articles. Use journal40.sql for MySQL 4.0 or journal323.sql for MySQL 3.23.

If you would prefer to create everything yourself from scratch, open phpMyAdmin, select the phpsolutions database, and create a new table called journal with five fields (columns). Use the settings shown in the following screenshot and Table 13-1.

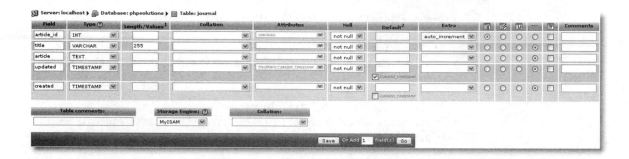

Table 13-1. Column definitions for the journal table

Field	Type	Length/Values	Attributes	Null	Default	Extra	Primary key
article_id	INT		UNSIGNED	not null		auto_ increment	Selected
title	VARCHAR	255		not null			
article	TEXT			not null			
updated	TIMESTAMP		ON UPDATE CURRENT_ TIMESTAMP	not null	CURRENT_ TIMESTAMP		
created	TIMESTAMP			not null			

13

The ON UPDATE CURRENT_TIMESTAMP and CURRENT_TIMESTAMP options aren't available on older versions of phpMyAdmin and/or MySQL. This doesn't matter, because the default is for the first TIMESTAMP column in a table to update automatically whenever a record is updated. You don't want the second TIMESTAMP column to update, in order to keep track of when a record was originally created.

Creating the basic insert and update form

SQL makes an important distinction between inserting and updating records by providing separate commands. INSERT is used only for creating a brand new record. Once a record has been inserted, any changes must be made with UPDATE. Since this involves working with identical fields, you can use the same page for both operations. However, this makes the PHP more complex, so I prefer to create the insert page first, save a copy as the update page, and then code them separately.

The form in the insert page needs just two input fields: for the title and the article. The contents of the remaining three columns (the primary key and the two timestamps) are handled automatically either by MySQL or by the SQL query that you will build shortly. The code for the insert form looks like this:

```
<form id="form1" name="form1" method="post" action="">
  <p>
    <label for="title">Title:</label>
    <input name="title" type="text" class="widebox" id="title" />
  </p>
  <p>
    <label for="article">Article:</label>
    <textarea name="article" cols="60" rows="8" class="widebox" ➡
id="article"></textarea>
  </p>
  <p>
    <input type="submit" name="insert" value="Insert new entry" />
  </p>
</form>
```

You can find the full code in journal_insert01.php in the download files for this chapter. The content management forms have been given some basic styling with admin.css, which should be placed in the assets folder. When viewed in a browser, the form looks like this:

350

The update form is identical except for the submit button, which looks like this (the full code is in journal_update01.php):

```
<input type="submit" name="update" value="Update entry" />
```

I've given the input fields the same names as the columns in the journal table. This makes it easier to keep track of variables when coding the PHP and SQL later.

> As a security measure, some developers recommend using different names from the database columns because anyone can see the names of input fields just by looking at the form's source code. Using different names makes it more difficult to break into the database. This shouldn't be a concern in a password-protected part of a site. However, you may want to consider the idea for publicly accessible forms, such as those used for user registration or login.

Inserting new records

The basic SQL for inserting new records into a table looks like this:

```
INSERT [INTO] table_name (column_names)
VALUES (values)
```

The INTO is in square brackets, which means that it's optional. It's purely there to make the SQL read a little more like human language. The column names can be in any order you like, but the values in the second set of parentheses must be in the same order.

Although the code is very similar for the original MySQL extension, MySQL Improved, and PDO, I'll deal with each one separately to avoid confusion.

> Many of the scripts in this chapter use a technique known as setting a flag. A **flag** is a Boolean variable that is initialized to either true or false, and used to check whether something has happened. For instance, if $OK is initially set to false, and reset to true only when a database query executes successfully, it can be used as the condition controlling another code block.

PHP Solution 13-1: Inserting a new record with the original MySQL extension

13

Use journal_insert01.php from the download files. The finished code is in journal_insert_mysql.php.

1. The code that inserts a new record should be run only if the form has been submitted, so it's enclosed in a conditional statement that checks for the name

attribute of the submit button (insert) in the $_POST array. Put the following above the DOCTYPE declaration:

```php
<?php
if (array_key_exists('insert', $_POST)) {
  include('../includes/conn_mysql.inc.php');
  include('../includes/corefuncs.php');
  // remove backslashes
  nukeMagicQuotes();
  // prepare an array of expected items
  // create database connection
  // make $_POST data safe for insertion into database
  // prepare the SQL query
  // process the query
  // if successful, redirect to list of existing records
  }
?>
```

After including the MySQL connection function and the file that contains nukeMagicQuotes(), the code removes backslashes from the $_POST array. The rest of the code consists of six comments that map out the remaining steps.

2. First, you need to ensure that you handle only expected data, and that it's safe to insert in the database. Add the code in bold at the points indicated by the comments:

```php
// prepare an array of expected items
$expected = array('title', 'article');
// create database connection
$conn = dbConnect('admin');
// make $_POST data safe for insertion into database
foreach ($_POST as $key => $value) {
  if (in_array($key, $expected)) {
    ${$key} = mysql_real_escape_string($value);
    }
  }
```

This stores the names of the fields that you expect from the form, and then connects to the database as the administrative user (psadmin). The connection must be established before using mysql_real_escape_string(). The conditional statement in the loop checks that the current $_POST array element is in the $expected array before passing it to mysql_real_escape_string() and saving the result with a shorter variable name. So $_POST['title'] becomes $title, and $_POST['article'] becomes $article. The data is now safe to incorporate into a SQL query.

3. Because the $_POST variables have been assigned to shorter variables, it's easy to build the SQL query using a combination of single and double quotes like this:

```php
// prepare the SQL query
$sql = "INSERT INTO journal (title, article, created)
        VALUES('$title', '$article', NOW())";
```

Although there are five columns in the journal table, the INSERT command needs values for only three; the primary key and the updated columns are filled automatically by MySQL. As explained earlier, text values must be in quotes in SQL queries, so $title and $article are enclosed in single quotes. The whole query is enclosed in double quotes to ensure that the variables are processed.

The value for the created column is generated by a MySQL function, NOW(), which generates a current timestamp. In the update query later, this column remains untouched, preserving the original date and time.

4. Finally, you submit the query, using mysql_query(). If the query is processed successfully, you redirect the page to a list of existing records. Add the following code:

```
// process the query
$result = mysql_query($sql) or die(mysql_error());
// if successful, redirect to list of existing records
if ($result) {
  header('Location: http://localhost/phpsolutions/admin/ ➥
journal_list.php');
  exit;
  }
}
?>
```

There's nothing new about this last section of code. Before testing the page, you need to build journal_list.php, which is described in PHP Solution 13-4.

PHP Solution 13-2: Inserting a new record with MySQL Improved

Use journal_insert01.php in the download files. The finished code is in journal_insert_mysqli.php.

1. The code that inserts a new record should be run only if the form has been submitted, so it's enclosed in a conditional statement that checks for the name attribute of the submit button (insert) in the $_POST array. Put the following above the DOCTYPE declaration:

```
<?php
if (array_key_exists('insert', $_POST)) {
  include('../includes/conn_mysqli.inc.php');
  include('../includes/corefuncs.php');
  // remove backslashes
  nukeMagicQuotes();
  // initialize flag
  $OK = false;
  // create database connection
  // create SQL
  // initialize prepared statement
  // redirect if successful or display error
  }
?>
```

13

After including the MySQLI connection function and the file that contains nukeMagicQuotes(), the code removes backslashes from the $_POST array and sets $OK to false. The four comments at the end map out the remaining steps.

2. The first stage in creating a prepared statement is to build a SQL query with place-holders for the data that will be derived from variables. Create a connection to the database as the administrative user (psadmin), and build the SQL like this:

```
// create database connection
$conn = dbConnect('admin');
// create SQL
$sql = 'INSERT INTO journal (title, article, created)
        VALUES(?, ?, NOW())';
```

The values that will be derived from $_POST['title'] and $_POST['article'] are represented by question mark placeholders. The value for the created column is a MySQL function, NOW(), which generates a current timestamp. In the update query later, this column remains untouched, preserving the original date and time.

3. The next stage is to initialize the prepared statement and replace the question marks with the values held in the variables—a process called **binding the parameters**. Insert the code the following code:

```
// initialize prepared statement
$stmt = $conn->stmt_init();
if ($stmt->prepare($sql)) {
  // bind parameters and execute statment
  $stmt->bind_param('ss', $_POST['title'], $_POST['article']);
  $OK = $stmt->execute();
  }
```

This is the vital section that protects your database from SQL injection. You pass the variables to $stmt->bind_param() in the same order as you want them inserted into the SQL query, together with a first argument specifying the data type of each variable, again in the same order as the variables. Both are strings, so this argument is 'ss'. Once the statement has been prepared, you call $stmt->execute() and capture the success or failure of the operation in $OK.

4. Finally, redirect the page to a list of existing records or display any error message. Add this code after the previous step:

```
  // redirect if successful or display error
  if ($OK) {
    header('Location: http://localhost/phpsolutions/admin/ ➥
journal_list.php');
    exit;
    }
  else {
    echo $stmt->error;
    }
  }
?>
```

That completes the insert page, but before testing it, create journal_list.php, which is described in PHP Solution 13-4.

PHP Solution 13-3: Inserting a new record with PDO

Use journal_insert01.php from the download files. The finished code is in journal_insert_pdo.php.

1. The code that inserts a new record should be run only if the form has been submitted, so it's enclosed in a conditional statement that checks for the name attribute of the submit button (insert) in the $_POST array. Put the following above the DOCTYPE declaration:

```php
<?php
if (array_key_exists('insert', $_POST)) {
    include('../includes/conn_pdo.inc.php');
    include('../includes/corefuncs.php');
    // remove backslashes
    nukeMagicQuotes();
    // initialize flag
    $OK = false;
    // create database connection
    // create SQL
    // prepare the statement
    // bind the parameters and execute the statement
    // redirect if successful or display error
}
?>
```

After including the PDO connection function and the file that contains nukeMagicQuotes(), the code removes backslashes from the $_POST array and sets $OK to false. The five comments at the end map out the remaining steps.

2. The first stage in creating a prepared statement is to build a SQL query with placeholders for the data that will be derived from variables. Create a connection to the database as the administrative user (psadmin), and build the SQL like this:

```php
// create database connection
$conn = dbConnect('admin');
// create SQL
$sql = 'INSERT INTO journal (title, article, created)
        VALUES(:title, :article, NOW())';
```

The values that will be derived from variables are represented by named placeholders consisting of the column name preceded by a colon (:title and :article). The value for the created column is a MySQL function, NOW(), which generates a current timestamp. In the update query later, this column remains untouched, preserving the original date and time.

13

3. The next stage is to initialize the prepared statement and bind the values from the variables to the placeholders—a process known as **binding the parameters**. Add the following code:

```
// prepare the statement
$stmt = $conn->prepare($sql);
// bind the parameters and execute the statement
$stmt->bindParam(':title', $_POST['title'], PDO::PARAM_STR);
$stmt->bindParam(':article', $_POST['article'], PDO::PARAM_STR);
$OK = $stmt->execute();
```

This begins by passing the SQL query to the prepare() method of the database connection ($conn), and storing a reference to the statement as a variable ($stmt).

Next, the values in the variables are bound to the placeholders in the SQL query. Because the previous step uses explicit names for the placeholders, you need to do this separately for each variable. The execute() method runs the query, and the success or failure of the operation is stored in $OK.

4. Finally, redirect the page to a list of existing records or display any error message. Add this code after the previous step:

```
  // redirect if successful or display error
  if ($OK) {
    header('Location: http://localhost/phpsolutions/admin/ ➥
journal_list.php');
    exit;
    }
  else {
    $error = $stmt->errorInfo();
    echo $error[2];
    }
  }
?>
```

Since the prepared statement has been stored as $stmt, you can access an array of error messages using $stmt->errorInfo(). The most useful information is stored in the third element of the array.

That completes the insert page, but before testing it, create journal_list.php, which is described next.

Linking to the update and delete pages

Before you can update or delete a record, you need to find its primary key. A practical way of doing this is to display a list of all records. The following SQL query retrieves everything from the journal table:

```
SELECT * FROM journal
```

356

To sort the results, add an ORDER BY clause. This sorts the records in alphabetical order by title:

```
SELECT * FROM journal ORDER BY title
```

It's often convenient to display the most recent entry at the top of the list, so you can sort the results by the created column. To sort them in reverse (descending) order, add the DESC keyword like this:

```
SELECT * FROM journal ORDER BY created DESC
```

You can use the results of this query to display a list of all records, complete with links to the update and delete pages. By adding the value of article_id to a query string in each link, you automatically identify the record to be updated or deleted. As you can see in Figure 13-3, the URL displayed in the browser status bar (bottom left) identifies the article_id of the article Trainee geishas go shopping as 2. This is used by journal_update.php to display the correct record ready for updating. The same information is conveyed in the DELETE link to journal_delete.php.

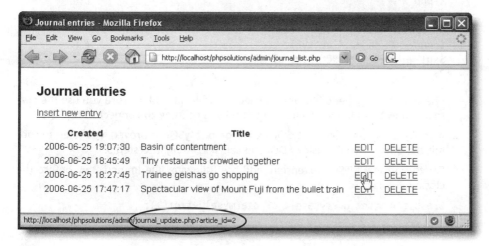

Figure 13-3. The EDIT and DELETE links contain the record's primary key in a query string.

To create a list like this, you need to start with a table that contains two rows and as many columns as you want to display, plus two extra columns for the EDIT and DELETE links. The first row is used for column headings. The second row is wrapped in a PHP loop to display all the results. The table in journal_list.php starts off like this (it's in journal_list01.php in the download files):

```
<table>
  <tr>
    <th scope="col">Created</th>
    <th scope="col">Title</th>
    <th> </th>
    <th> </th>
  </tr>
```

13

```
<tr>
  <td></td>
  <td></td>
  <td><a href="journal_update.php">EDIT</a></td>
  <td><a href="journal_delete.php">DELETE</a></td>
</tr>
</table>
```

> **PHP Solution 13-4: Creating the links to the update and delete pages**

Use journal_list01.php in the download files. Depending on the method used to connect to MySQL, the finished code is in journal_list_mysql.php, journal_list_mysqli.php, or journal_list_pdo.php.

1. You need to connect to MySQL and create the SQL query. Add the following code above the DOCTYPE declaration:

```php
<?php
include('../includes/connection.inc.php');
// create database connection
$conn = dbConnect('query');
$sql = 'SELECT * FROM journal ORDER BY created DESC';
?>
```

I have used the generic filename connection.inc.php. Make sure you use the correct connection file for whichever method you're using to connect to MySQL.

2. If you're using the original MySQL extension or MySQL Improved, you need to submit the query. If you're using PDO, you can skip straight to step 3.

For the original MySQL extension, add the following line immediately before the closing PHP tag:

```php
$result = mysql_query($sql) or die(mysql_error());
```

For MySQL Improved, use this line instead:

```php
$result = $conn->query($sql) or die(mysqli_error());
```

3. You now need to enclose the second table row in a loop and retrieve each record from the result set. The following code goes between the closing </tr> tag of the first row and the opening <tr> tag of the second row.

For the original MySQL extension, use this:

```php
</tr>
<?php while($row = mysql_fetch_assoc($result)) { ?>
<tr>
```

For MySQL Improved, use this:

```php
</tr>
<?php while($row = $result->fetch_assoc()) { ?>
<tr>
```

For PDO, use this:

```
</tr>
<?php foreach ($conn->query($sql) as $row) { ?>
<tr>
```

This is the same as in the previous chapter, so it should need no explanation.

4. Display the created and title fields for the current record in the first two cells of the second row like this:

```
<td><?php echo $row['created']; ?></td>
<td><?php echo $row['title']; ?></td>
```

5. Add the query string and value of the article_id field for the current record to both URLs in the next two cells like this:

```
<td><a href="journal_update.php?article_id=<?php echo ➥
$row['article_id']; ?>">EDIT</a></td>
<td><a href="journal_delete.php?article_id=<?php echo ➥
$row['article_id']; ?>">DELETE</a></td>
```

What you're doing here is adding ?article_id= to the URL, and then using PHP to display the value of $row['article_id']. It's important that you don't leave any spaces that might break the URL or the query string. A common mistake is to leave spaces around the equal sign. After the PHP has been processed, the opening <a> tag should look like this (although the number will vary according to the record):

```
<a href="journal_update.php?article_id=2">
```

6. Finally, close the loop surrounding the second table row with a curly brace like this:

```
  </tr>
  <?php } ?>
</table>
```

7. Save journal_list.php and load the page into a browser. Assuming that you loaded the contents of journal.sql into the phpsolutions database earlier, you should see a list of four items, as shown in Figure 13-3. You can now test journal_insert.php. After inserting an item, you should be returned to journal_list.php, and the date and time of creation, together with the title of the new item, should be displayed at the top of the list. Check your code against the download files if you encounter any problems.

> *The code in* journal_list.php *assumes that there will always be some records in the table. As an exercise, use the technique in PHP Solution 11-2 (MySQL original and MySQLI), or 11-3 (PDO) to count the number of results, and use a conditional statement to display a suitable message if no records are found. The solution is in* journal_list_norec_mysql.php, journal_list_norec_mysqli.php, *and* journal_list_norec_pdo.php.

13

Updating records

An update page needs to perform two separate processes, as follows:

1. Retrieve the selected record and display it ready for editing

2. Update the edited record in the database

The first stage uses the primary key passed in the URL query string. So far, you have used SELECT to retrieve all records or a range of records (using LIMIT). To retrieve a specific record identified by its primary key, you add a WHERE clause to the end of the SELECT query like this:

```
SELECT * FROM table_name WHERE primary_key_column = primary_key
```

> *Whereas PHP uses two equal signs (==) to test for equality, MySQL uses only one (=). Don't get the two mixed up.*

After you have edited the record in the update page, you submit the form and pass all the details to an UPDATE command. The basic syntax of the SQL UPDATE command looks like this:

```
UPDATE table_name SET column_name = value, column_name = value
WHERE condition
```

The condition when updating a specific record is the primary key. So, when updating article_id 2 in the journal table, the basic UPDATE query looks like this:

```
UPDATE journal SET title = value, article = value
WHERE article_id = 2
```

Although the basic principle is the same for each method of connecting to MySQL, the code differs sufficiently to warrant separate instructions.

PHP Solution 13-5: Updating a record with the original MySQL extension

Use journal_update01.php from the download files. The code for the first stage of the update process is in journal_update_mysql01php, and the final code is in journal_update_mysql02.php.

1. The first stage involves retrieving the details of the record that you want to update. Since the primary key is passed through the query string, you need to extract it from the $_GET array and make sure that it's safe to use before incorporating it into your SQL query. Put the following code above the DOCTYPE declaration:

```php
<?php
include('../includes/conn_mysql.inc.php');
include('../includes/corefuncs.php');
```

```
// remove backslashes
nukeMagicQuotes();
// initialize flag
$done = false;
// prepare an array of expected items
$expected = array('title', 'article', 'article_id');
// create database connection
$conn = dbConnect('admin');
// get details of selected record
if ($_GET && !$_POST) {
  if (isset($_GET['article_id']) && is_numeric($_GET['article_id'])) {
    $article_id = $_GET['article_id'];
    }
  else {
    $article_id = NULL;
    }
  if ($article_id) {
    $sql = "SELECT * FROM journal
            WHERE article_id = $article_id";
    $result = mysql_query($sql) or die (mysql_error());
    $row = mysql_fetch_assoc($result);
    }
  }
// redirect page if $article_id is invalid
if (!isset($article_id)) {
  header('Location: http://localhost/phpsolutions/admin/ ➥
journal_list.php');
  exit;
  }
?>
```

Although this is very similar to the code used for the insert page, the first few lines are *outside* the conditional statement. Both stages of the update process require the include files, the removal of backslashes, and the database connection, so this avoids the need to duplicate code. The $done flag is initialized as false and will be used later to test whether the update succeeded.

There's an important addition to the $expected array. When a record is first inserted, the primary key is generated automatically by MySQL. However, when you update a record, you need its article_id to identify it.

The first conditional statement checks that the $_GET array contains at least one value and that the $_POST array is empty. This makes sure that the code inside is executed only when the query string is set, but the form hasn't been submitted. Before building the SQL query, you need to check that $_GET['article_id'] has been defined and pass it to is_numeric() to make sure that it contains only a number. If someone comes directly to this page or an attacker tries to pass anything else to your query, $article_id is set to NULL.

If everything is OK, the SQL query is submitted. The result should contain only one record, so its contents are extracted straight away and stored in $row.

13

The final conditional statement redirects the page to journal_list.php if $article_id was set to NULL earlier. A variable that has been set to NULL is considered unset, so !isset($article_id) returns true if $article_id is NULL.

2. Now that you have retrieved the contents of the record, you need to display them in the update form by using PHP to populate the value attribute of each input field. Before doing so, it's a good idea to check that you actually have something to display. If someone changes the value of article_id in the query string, you may get an empty result set, so there is no point in going any further. Add the following conditional statement immediately before the opening <form> tag:

```
<p><a href="journal_list.php">List all entries</a> </p>
<?php if (empty($row)) { ?>
<p class="warning">Invalid request: record does not exist.</p>
<?php } else { ?>
<form id="form1" name="form1" method="post" action="">
```

If $row contains no values, empty($row) returns true and displays the warning message. The form is wrapped in the else clause and is displayed only if the query finds a valid record to be updated. Add the closing curly brace of the else clause immediately after the closing </form> tag like this:

```
</form>
<?php } ?>
</body>
```

3. If $row isn't empty, you can display the results of the query without further testing. However, you need to pass text values to htmlentities() to avoid any problems with the display of quotes. Change the code in the title input field like this:

```
<input name="title" type="text" class="widebox" id="title" ➥
value="<?php echo htmlentities($row['title']); ?>" />
```

4. Do the same for the article text area. Because text areas don't have a value attribute, the code goes between the opening and closing <textarea> tags like this:

```
<textarea name="article" cols="60" rows="8" class="widebox" ➥
id="article"><?php echo htmlentities($row['article']); ?></textarea>
```

Make sure there is no space between the opening and closing PHP and <textarea> tags. Otherwise, you will get unwanted spaces in your updated record.

5. The UPDATE command needs to know the primary key of the record you want to change. Store the primary key in a hidden field so that it is submitted in the $_POST array with the other details. Because hidden fields are not displayed onscreen, the following code can go anywhere inside the form:

```
<input name="article_id" type="hidden" value="<?php ➥
echo $row['article_id']; ?>" />
```

6. Save the update page, and test it by loading journal_list.php into a browser and selecting the EDIT link for one of the records. The contents of the record should be displayed in the form fields as shown in Figure 13-4.

The Update entry button doesn't do anything yet. Just make sure that everything is displayed correctly, and confirm that the primary key is registered in the hidden field. You can check your code, if necessary, against journal_update_mysql01.php.

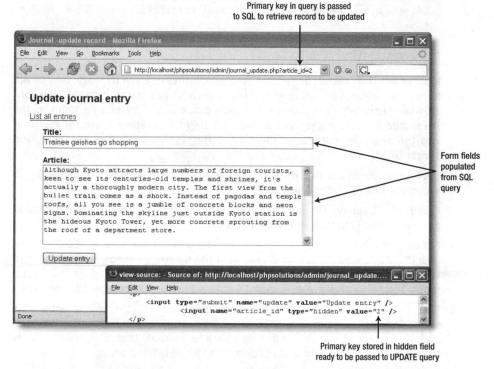

Figure 13-4. An update form uses the primary key to retrieve and display a record ready for editing.

7. The name attribute of the submit button is update, so all the update processing code needs to go in a conditional statement that checks for the presence of update in the $_POST array. Place the code highlighted in bold just before the page redirect script:

```
  $row = mysql_fetch_assoc($result);
  }
// if form has been submitted, update record
if (array_key_exists('update', $_POST)) {
  // prepare expected items for insertion into database
  foreach ($_POST as $key => $value) {
    if (in_array($key, $expected)) {
      ${$key} = mysql_real_escape_string($value);
      }
    }
  // abandon the process if primary key invalid
  if (!is_numeric($article_id)) {
    die('Invalid request');
    }
```

13

```
        // prepare the SQL query
        $sql = "UPDATE journal SET title = '$title', article = '$article'
        WHERE article_id = $article_id";
        // submit the query
        $done = mysql_query($sql) or die(mysql_error());
        }
// redirect page on success or $article_id is invalid
if ($done || !isset($article_id)) {
```

Most of this code should be familiar. Any backslashes inserted by magic quotes will have been removed by nukeMagicQuotes() because you placed it outside the conditional statements in step 1, so this code block begins by passing items in the $expected array to mysql_real_escape_string() to prepare them for insertion into the database, and storing them in shorter variables ($title, $article, and $article_id).

Because it's possible to tamper with a hidden field, you make sure that $article_id is numeric before carrying on.

In the UPDATE query, strings need to be quoted, so the entire query is enclosed in double quotes, with $title and $article in single quotes.

Although the mysql_query() function returns a result set from a SELECT query, with UPDATE, it returns true or false. So, if the update succeeds, $done is reset to true. You need to add $done || to the condition that controls the page redirection script. This redirects the page either if $done is true or if $article_id is invalid.

8. Save journal_update.php and test it by loading journal_list.php, selecting one of the EDIT links, and making changes to the record that is displayed. When you click Update record, you should be taken back to journal_list.php. You can verify that your changes were made by clicking the same EDIT link again.

   Check your code, if necessary, with journal_update_mysql02.php.

PHP Solution 13-6: Updating a record with MySQL Improved

Use journal_update01.php from the download files. The code for the first stage of the update process is in journal_update_mysqli01php, and the final code is in journal_update_mysqli02.php.

1. The first stage involves retrieving the details of the record that you want to update. Put the following code above the DOCTYPE declaration:

```
<?php
include('../includes/conn_mysqli.inc.php');
include('../includes/corefuncs.php');
// remove backslashes
nukeMagicQuotes();
// initialize flags
$OK = false;
$done = false;
```

```
    // create database connection
    $conn = dbConnect('admin');
    // get details of selected record
    if (isset($_GET['article_id']) && !$_POST) {
      // prepare SQL query
      $sql = 'SELECT article_id, title, article
              FROM journal WHERE article_id = ?';
      // initialize statement
      $stmt = $conn->stmt_init();
      if ($stmt->prepare($sql)) {
        // bind the query parameters
        $stmt->bind_param('i', $_GET['article_id']);
        // bind the results to variables
        $stmt->bind_result($article_id, $title, $article);
        // execute the query, and fetch the result
        $OK = $stmt->execute();
        $stmt->fetch();
        }
      }
    // redirect if $_GET['article_id'] not defined
    if (!isset($_GET['article_id'])) {
      header('Location: http://localhost/phpsolutions/admin/ ➡
    journal_list.php');
      exit;
      }
    // display error message if query fails
    if (isset($stmt) && !$OK && !$done) {
      echo $stmt->error;
      }
    ?>
```

Although this is very similar to the code used for the insert page, the first few lines are *outside* the conditional statements. Both stages of the update process require the include files, the removal of backslashes, and the database connection, so this avoids the need to duplicate the same code later. Two flags are initialized: $OK to check the success of retrieving the record, and $done to check whether the update succeeds.

The first conditional statement makes sure that $_GET['article_id'] exists and that the $_POST array is empty. So the code inside the braces is executed only when the query string is set, but the form hasn't been submitted.

You prepare the SELECT query in the same way as for an INSERT command, using a question mark as a placeholder for the variable. However, note that instead of using an asterisk to retrieve all columns, the query specifies three columns by name like this:

```
$sql = 'SELECT article_id, title, article
        FROM journal WHERE article_id = ?';
```

13

This is because a MySQLI prepared statement lets you bind the result of a SELECT query to variables; and to be able to do this, you must specify the column names and the order you want them to be in.

First, you need to initialize the prepared statement and bind $_GET['article_id'] to the query with $stmt->bind_param(). Because the value of article_id must be an integer, you pass 'i' as the first argument.

The next line binds the result to variables in the same order as the columns specified in the SELECT query.

```
$stmt->bind_result($article_id, $title, $article);
```

You can call the variables whatever you like, but it makes sense to use the same names as the columns. Binding the result like this avoids the necessity to use array names, such as $row['article_id'], later on.

Then the code executes the query and fetches the result.

The next conditional statement redirects the page to journal_list.php if $_GET['article_id'] hasn't been defined. This prevents anyone from trying to load the update page directly in a browser.

The final conditional statement displays an error message if the prepared statement has been created, but both $OK and $done remain false. You haven't added the update script yet, but if the record is retrieved or updated successfully, one of them will be switched to true. So if both remain false, you know there was something wrong with one of the SQL queries.

2. Now that you have retrieved the contents of the record, you need to display them in the update form by using PHP to populate the value attribute of each input field. If the prepared statement succeeded, $article_id should contain the primary key of the record to be updated, because it's one of the variables you bound to the result set with $stmt->bind_result().

However, if someone alters the query string to an invalid number, $article_id will be set to 0, so there is no point in displaying the update form. Add the following conditional statement immediately before the opening <form> tag:

```
<p><a href="journal_list.php">List all entries </a></p>
<?php if($article_id == 0) { ?>
<p class="warning">Invalid request: record does not exist.</p>
<?php } else { ?>
<form id="form1" name="form1" method="post" action="">
```

3. Add the closing curly brace of the else clause immediately after the closing </form> tag like this:

```
</form>
<?php } ?>
</body>
```

This wraps the update form in the else clause, preventing it from being displayed if no valid record is found.

4. If $article_id is not 0, you know that $title and $article also contain valid values and can be displayed in the update form without further testing. However, you

need to pass text values to htmlentities() to avoid problems with displaying quotes. Display $title in the value attribute of the title input field like this:

```
<input name="title" type="text" class="widebox" id="title" ➥
value="<?php echo htmlentities($title); ?>" />
```

5. Do the same for the article text area. Because text areas don't have a value attribute, the code goes between the opening and closing <textarea> tags like this:

```
<textarea name="article" cols="60" rows="8" class="widebox" ➥
id="article"><?php echo htmlentities($article); ?></textarea>
```

Make sure there is no space between the opening and closing PHP and <textarea> tags. Otherwise, you will get unwanted spaces in your updated record.

6. The UPDATE command needs to know the primary key of the record you want to change. You need to store the primary key in a hidden field so that it is submitted in the $_POST array with the other details. Because hidden fields are not displayed onscreen, the following code can go anywhere inside the form:

```
<input name="article_id" type="hidden" value="<?php ➥
echo $article_id; ?>" />
```

7. Save the update page, and test it by loading journal_list.php into a browser and selecting the EDIT link for one of the records. The contents of the record should be displayed in the form fields as shown in Figure 13-4.

The Update entry button doesn't do anything yet. Just make sure that everything is displayed correctly, and confirm that the primary key is registered in the hidden field. You can check your code, if necessary, against journal_update_mysqli01.php.

8. The name attribute of the submit button is update, so all the update processing code needs to go in a conditional statement that checks for the presence of update in the $_POST array. Place the following code highlighted in bold immediately above the code in step 1 that redirects the page:

```
      $stmt->fetch();
      }
    }
// if form has been submitted, update record
if (array_key_exists('update', $_POST)) {
  // prepare update query
  $sql = 'UPDATE journal SET title = ?, article = ?
          WHERE article_id = ?';
  // initialize statement
  $stmt = $conn->stmt_init();
  if ($stmt->prepare($sql)) {
    $stmt->bind_param('ssi', $_POST['title'], $_POST['article'], ➥
$_POST['article_id']);
    $done = $stmt->execute();
    }
  }
```

13

```
// redirect page on success or if $_GET['article_id']) not defined
if ($done || !isset($_GET['article_id'])) {
```

This is very similar to the INSERT query. The UPDATE query is prepared with question mark placeholders where values are to be supplied from variables. You then initialize the statement and bind the variables with $stmt->bind_param(). The first two variables are strings, and the third is an integer, so the first argument is 'ssi'.

If the UPDATE query succeeds, $done is set to true. You need to add $done || to the condition in the redirect script. This ensures that the page is redirected either if the update succeeds or if someone tries to access the page directly.

9. Save journal_update.php and test it by loading journal_list.php, selecting one of the EDIT links, and making changes to the record that is displayed. When you click Update record, you should be taken back to journal_list.php. You can verify that your changes were made by clicking the same EDIT link again. Check your code, if necessary, with journal_update_mysqli02.php.

PHP Solution 13-7: Updating a record with PDO

Use journal_update01.php from the download files. The code for the first stage of the update process is in journal_update_pdo01php, and the final code is in journal_update_pdo02.php.

1. The first stage involves retrieving the details of the record that you want to update. Put the following code above the DOCTYPE declaration:

```php
<?php
include('../includes/conn_pdo.inc.php');
include('../includes/corefuncs.php');
// remove backslashes
nukeMagicQuotes();
// initialize flags
$OK = false;
$done = false;
// create database connection
$conn = dbConnect('admin');
// get details of selected record
if (isset($_GET['article_id']) && !$_POST) {
  // prepare SQL query
  $sql = 'SELECT * FROM journal WHERE article_id = ?';
  $stmt = $conn->prepare($sql);
  // execute query by passing array of variables
  $OK = $stmt->execute(array($_GET['article_id']));
  // fetch the result
  $row = $stmt->fetch();
  // assign result array to variables
  if (is_array($row)) {
    extract($row);
  }
}
```

```
// redirect if $_GET['article_id'] not defined
if (!isset($_GET['article_id'])) {
  header('Location: http://localhost/phpsolutions/admin/ ➥
journal_list.php');
  exit;
  }
// display error message if query fails
if (isset($stmt) && !$OK && !$done) {
  $error = $stmt->errorInfo();
  if (isset($error[2])) {
    echo $error[2];
    }
  }
?>
```

Although this is very similar to the code used for the insert page, the first few lines are *outside* the first conditional statement. Both stages of the update process require the include files, the removal of backslashes, and the database connection, so this avoids the need to duplicate the same code later. Two flags are initialized: $OK to check the success of retrieving the record and $done to check whether the update succeeds.

The first conditional statement checks that $_GET ['article_id'] exists and that the $_POST array is empty. This makes sure that the code inside is executed only when the query string is set, but the form hasn't been submitted.

When preparing the SQL query for the insert form, you used named placeholders for the variables. This time, let's use a question mark like this:

```
$sql = 'SELECT * FROM journal WHERE article_id = ?';
```

When using question marks as placeholders, you pass the variables directly as an array to $stmt->execute() like this:

```
$OK = $stmt->execute(array($_GET['article_id']));
```

Even though there is only one variable this time, it must still be presented as an array.

There's only one record to fetch in the result, so it's stored immediately in $row, and the extract() function is used to assign the values to simple variables. (See "A quick warning about extract()" later in this chapter for a description of how it works.) If someone alters the query string and searches for a nonexistent record, $row will be empty, so it's necessary to test it with is_array() before passing it to extract().

The next conditional statement redirects the page to journal_list.php if $_GET['article_id'] hasn't been defined. This prevents anyone from trying to load the update page directly in a browser.

The final conditional statement displays an error message if the prepared statement has been created, but both $OK and $done remain false. You haven't added the update script yet, but if the record is retrieved or updated successfully, one of them will be switched to true. So if both remain false, you know there was something wrong with one of the SQL queries.

13

369

2. Now that you have retrieved the contents of the record, you need to display them in the update form by using PHP to populate the value attribute of each input field. Before doing so, it's a good idea to check that you actually have something to display. Add the following conditional statement immediately before the opening `<form>` tag:

```
<p><a href="journal_list.php">List all entries</a> </p>
<?php if (!isset($article_id)) { ?>
<p class="warning">Invalid request: record does not exist.</p>
<?php } else { ?>
<form id="form1" name="form1" method="post" action="">
```

If someone changes the value of article_id in the query string, you may get an empty result set, so extract() cannot create $article_id. In that event, there's no point in going any further, and a warning message is displayed. The form is wrapped in the else clause and displayed only if the query finds a valid record. Add the closing curly brace of the else clause immediately after the closing `</form>` tag like this:

```
</form>
<?php } ?>
</body>
```

3. If $article_id has been defined, you know that $title and $article also exist and can be displayed in the update form without further testing. However, you need to pass text values to htmlentities() to avoid problems with displaying quotes. Display $title in the value attribute of the title input field like this:

```
<input name="title" type="text" class="widebox" id="title" ➥
value="<?php echo htmlentities($title); ?>" />
```

4. Do the same for the article text area. Because text areas don't have a value attribute, the code goes between the opening and closing `<textarea>` tags like this:

```
<textarea name="article" cols="60" rows="8" class="widebox" ➥
id="article"><?php echo htmlentities($article); ?></textarea>
```

Make sure there is no space between the opening and closing PHP and `<textarea>` tags. Otherwise, you will get unwanted spaces in your updated record.

5. The UPDATE command needs to know the primary key of the record you want to change. You need to store the primary key in a hidden field so that it is submitted in the $_POST array with the other details. Because hidden fields are not displayed onscreen, the following code can go anywhere inside the form:

```
<input name="article_id" type="hidden" value="<?php ➥
echo $article_id; ?>" />
```

6. Save the update page, and test it by loading journal_list.php into a browser and selecting the EDIT link for one of the records. The contents of the record should be displayed in the form fields as shown in Figure 13-4.

The Update entry button doesn't do anything yet. Just make sure that everything is displayed correctly, and confirm that the primary key is registered in the hidden field. You can check your code, if necessary, against journal_update_pdo01.php.

7. The name attribute of the submit button is update, so all the update processing code needs to go in a conditional statement that checks for the presence of update in the $_POST array. Place the following code highlighted in bold immediately above the code in step 1 that redirects the page:

```
    extract($row);
    }
// if form has been submitted, update record
if (array_key_exists('update', $_POST)) {
    // prepare update query
    $sql = 'UPDATE journal SET title = ?, article = ?
            WHERE article_id = ?';
    $stmt = $conn->prepare($sql);
    // execute query by passing array of variables
    $done = $stmt->execute(array($_POST['title'], $_POST['article'], ➥
$_POST['article_id']));
    }
// redirect page on success or $_GET['article_id'] not defined
if ($done || !isset($_GET['article_id'])) {
```

Again, the SQL query is prepared using question marks as placeholders for values to be derived from variables. This time there are three placeholders, so the corresponding variables need to be passed as an array to $stmt->execute(). Needless to say, the array must be in the same order as the placeholders.

If the UPDATE query succeeds, $done is set to true. You need to add $done || to the condition in the redirect script. This ensures that the page is redirected either if the update succeeds or if someone tries to access the page directly.

8. Save journal_update.php and test it by loading journal_list.php, selecting one of the EDIT links, and making changes to the record that is displayed. When you click Update record, you should be taken back to journal_list.php. You can verify that your changes were made by clicking the same EDIT link again. Check your code, if necessary, with journal_update_pdo02.php.

Deleting records

Deleting a record in a database is similar to updating one. The basic DELETE command looks like this:

```
DELETE FROM table_name WHERE condition
```

What makes the DELETE command potentially dangerous is that it is final. Once you have deleted a record, there's no going back—it's gone forever. There's no Recycle Bin or Trash to fish it out from. Even worse, the WHERE clause is optional. If you omit it, every single record in the table is irrevocably sent into cyber-oblivion. Consequently, it's a good idea to use PHP logic to display details of the record to be deleted, and ask the user to confirm or cancel the process (see Figure 13-5).

13

Figure 13-5. Deleting a record is irreversible, so it's a good idea to get confirmation before going ahead.

Building and scripting the delete page is almost identical to the update page, so I won't give step-by-step instructions. However, here are the main points:

- Retrieve the details of the selected record.
- Display sufficient details, such as the title, for the user to confirm that the correct record has been selected.
- Give the Confirm deletion and Cancel buttons different name attributes, and use each name attribute in array_key_exists() to control the action taken.
- Instead of wrapping the entire form in the else clause, use conditional statements to hide the Confirm deletion button and the hidden field.

The code that performs the deletion for each method follows.

For the original MySQL extension:

```
if (array_key_exists('delete', $_POST)) {
  if (!is_numeric($_POST['article_id'])) {
    die('Invalid request');
    }
  $sql = "DELETE FROM journal
          WHERE article_id = {$_POST['article_id']}";
  $deleted = mysql_query($sql) or die(mysql_error());
  }
```

> *The curly braces around* $_POST['article_id'] *are needed even though the variable uses single quotes. This is a quirk of PHP. Elements of associative arrays (ones that use a string as the array key) need special treatment inside double-quoted strings.*

For MySQL Improved:

```
if (array_key_exists('delete', $_POST)) {
  $sql = 'DELETE FROM journal WHERE article_id = ?';
  $stmt = $conn->stmt_init();
```

```
    if ($stmt->prepare($sql)) {
      $stmt->bind_param('i', $_POST['article_id']);
      $deleted = $stmt->execute();
      }
    }
```

For PDO:

```
    if (array_key_exists('delete', $_POST)) {
      $sql = 'DELETE FROM journal WHERE article_id = ?';
      $stmt = $conn->prepare($sql);
      $deleted = $stmt->execute(array($_POST['article_id']));
      }
```

You can find the finished code in journal_delete_mysql.php, journal_delete_mysqli.php, and journal_delete_pdo.php.

A quick warning about extract()

PHP Solution 13-7 employs a function called extract() to create shorter variables from the results of a database query. It's a very useful function, but since it appears in a section that you might not read unless you're using PDO, it deserves to be described separately. Take the following associative array:

```
    $book = array('author' => 'David Powers', 'title' =>'PHP Solutions');
```

Pass the array to extract() like this:

```
    extract($book);
```

This creates a variable from each array key with the same value as the equivalent array element. In other words, you get $author with the value David Powers, and $title with the value PHP Solutions.

This is so convenient that it's tempting to use extract() to convert the contents of the $_POST and $_GET arrays into the equivalent variables. It works, but is fraught with danger, because the default behavior is to overwrite existing variables of the same name. It's far safer to process $_POST and $_GET variables individually or by testing for them in an array of expected items, as shown earlier in this chapter.

You can influence the behavior of extract() by using a constant as the second argument. For instance, EXTR_PREFIX_ALL prefixes all variables with a string supplied as the third argument like this:

```
    extract($book, EXTR_PREFIX_ALL, 'php');
```

This produces two variables called $php_author and $php_title.

13

The extract() function generates a PHP warning if you pass it anything other than an array, so it's always a good idea to test any argument with is_array() first like this:

```
if (is_array($myVariable)) {
  extract($myVariable);
  }
```

You should also test for the existence of any variables you expect to be created by extract(). Alternatively, set a Boolean flag to true or false depending on the outcome of the is_array() test.

To find out more about extract() and the other constants you can use with it, see www.php.net/manual/en/function.extract.php.

Reviewing the four essential SQL commands

Now that you have seen SELECT, INSERT, UPDATE, and DELETE in action, let's review the basic syntax. This is not an exhaustive listing, but it concentrates on the most important options, including some that have not yet been covered. I have used the same typographic conventions as the MySQL online manual at http://dev.mysql.com/doc/refman/5.0/en (which you may also want to consult):

- Anything in uppercase is a SQL command.
- Expressions in square brackets are optional.
- Lowercase italics represent variable input.
- A vertical pipe (|) separates alternatives.

Although some expressions are optional, they must appear in the order listed. For example, in a SELECT query, WHERE, ORDER BY, and LIMIT are all optional; but LIMIT can never come before WHERE or ORDER BY.

SELECT

SELECT is used for retrieving records from one or more tables. Its basic syntax is as follows:

```
SELECT [DISTINCT] select_list
FROM table_list
[WHERE where_expression]
[ORDER BY col_name | formula] [ASC | DESC]
[LIMIT [skip_count,] show_count]
```

The DISTINCT option tells the database you want to eliminate duplicate rows from the results.

The *select_list* is a comma-separated list of columns that you want included in the result. To retrieve all columns, use an asterisk (*). The asterix shorthand must always be used on its own; it cannot be combined with other column names. For example, you cannot use it with an alias (see "Extracting a fixed number of characters" in the next chapter) to mean "all other columns." If the same column name is used in more than one table, you must use unambiguous references by using the syntax *table_name*.*column_name*.

The *table_list* is a comma-separated list of tables from which the results are to be drawn. All tables that you want to be included in the results *must* be listed.

The WHERE clause specifies search criteria. For example:

```
WHERE quotations.family_name = authors.family_name
WHERE quotations.author_id = 32
```

WHERE expressions can use comparison, arithmetic, logical, and pattern-matching operators. The most important ones are listed in Table 13-2.

Table 13-2. The main operators used in MySQL WHERE expressions

Comparison		Arithmetic	
<	Less than	+	Addition
<=	Less than or equal to	-	Subtraction
=	Equal to	*	Multiplication
!=	Not equal to	/	Division
>	Greater than	DIV	Integer division
>=	Greater than or equal to	%	Modulo
IN()	Included in list		
BETWEEN *min* AND *max*	Between (and including) two values		
Logical		**Pattern matching**	
AND	Logical and	LIKE	Case-insensitive match
&&	Logical and	NOT LIKE	Case-insensitive nonmatch
OR	Logical or	LIKE BINARY	Case-sensitive match
||	Logical or (best avoided)	NOT LIKE BINARY	Case-sensitive nonmatch

13

DIV is the counterpart of the modulo operator. It produces the result of division as an integer with no fractional part, whereas modulo produces only the remainder.

```
5 / 2     /* result 2.5 */
5 DIV 2   /* result 2  */
5 % 2     /* result 1  */
```

I suggest you avoid using || because it has a completely different meaning in standard SQL. By not using it with MySQL, you avoid confusion if you ever work with a different relational database.

IN() evaluates a comma-separated list of values inside the parentheses and returns true if one or more of the values is found. Although BETWEEN is normally used with numbers, it also applies to strings. For instance, BETWEEN 'a' AND 'd' returns true for *a*, *b*, *c*, and *d* (but not their uppercase equivalents). Both IN() and BETWEEN can be preceded by NOT to perform the opposite comparison.

LIKE, NOT LIKE, and the related BINARY operators are used for text searches in combination with the following two wildcard characters:

■ %: matches any sequence of characters or none.

■ _ (an underscore): matches exactly one character.

So, the following WHERE clause matches Dennis, Denise, and so on, but not Aiden:

```
WHERE first_name LIKE 'den%'
```

To match Aiden, put % at the front of the search pattern. Because % matches any sequence of characters or none, '%den%' still matches Dennis and Denise. To search for a literal percentage sign or underscore, precede it with a backslash (\% or _).

Conditions are evaluated from left to right, but can be grouped in parentheses if you want a particular set of conditions to be considered together.

ORDER BY specifies the sort order of the results. This can be specified as a single column, a comma-separated list of columns, or an expression such as RAND(), which randomizes the order. The default sort order is ascending (a–z, 0–9), but you can specify DESC (descending) to reverse the order.

LIMIT followed by one number stipulates the maximum number of records to return. If two numbers are given separated by a comma, the first tells the database how many rows to skip (see "Selecting a subset of records" in Chapter 12).

For more details on SELECT, see http://dev.mysql.com/doc/refman/5.0/en/select.html.

INSERT

The INSERT command is used to add new records to a database. The general syntax is as follows:

```
INSERT [INTO] table_name (column_names)
VALUES (values)
```

The word INTO is optional; it simply makes the command read a little more like human language. The column names and values are comma-delimited lists, and both must be in the same order. So, to insert the forecast for New York (blizzard), Detroit (smog), and Honolulu (sunny) into a weather database, this is how you would do it:

```
INSERT INTO forecast (new_york, detroit, honolulu)
VALUES ('blizzard', 'smog', 'sunny')
```

The reason for this rather strange syntax is to allow you to insert more than one record at a time. Each subsequent record is in a separate set of parentheses, with each set separated by a comma:

```
INSERT numbers (x,y)
VALUES (10,20),(20,30),(30,40),(40,50)
```

You'll use this multiple insert syntax in the next chapter. Any columns omitted from an INSERT query are set to their default value. *Never set an explicit value for the primary key where the column is set to* auto_increment; leave the column name out of the INSERT statement. For more details, see http://dev.mysql.com/doc/refman/5.0/en/insert.html.

UPDATE

This command is used to change existing records. The basic syntax looks like this:

```
UPDATE table_name
SET col_name = value [, col_name = value]
[WHERE where_expression]
```

The WHERE expression tells MySQL which record or records you want to update (or perhaps in the case of the following example, dream about):

```
UPDATE sales SET q1_2007 = 25000
WHERE title = 'PHP Solutions'
```

For more details on UPDATE, see http://dev.mysql.com/doc/refman/5.0/en/update.html.

13

DELETE

DELETE can be used to delete single records, multiple records, or the entire contents of a table. The general syntax for deleting from a single table is as follows:

```
DELETE FROM table_name [WHERE where_expression]
```

Although phpMyAdmin prompts you for confirmation before deleting a record, MySQL itself takes you at your word, and performs the deletion immediately. DELETE is totally unforgiving—once the data is deleted, it is gone *forever*. The following query will delete all records from a table called subscribers where the date in expiry_date has already passed:

```
DELETE FROM subscribers WHERE expiry_date < NOW()
```

For more details, see http://dev.mysql.com/doc/refman/5.0/en/delete.html.

> *Although the* WHERE *clause is optional in both* UPDATE *and* DELETE, *you should be aware that if you leave* WHERE *out, the entire table is affected. This means that a careless slip with either of these commands could result in every single record being identical—or wiped out.*

Security and error messages

When developing a website with PHP and MySQL, it's essential to display error messages so that you can debug your code if anything goes wrong. However, raw error messages look unprofessional in a live website. They can also reveal clues about your database structure to potential attackers. Therefore, before deploying your scripts live on the Internet, you should go through them, removing all instances of mysql_error() (MySQL), mysqli_error() (MySQLI), or echo $error[2] (PDO).

The simplest way to handle this is to replace the MySQL error messages with a neutral message of your own, such as "Sorry, the database is unavailable." A more professional way is to replace or die() routines with an if... else conditional statement, and to use the error control operator (see "Preventing errors when an include file is missing" in Chapter 4) to suppress the display of error messages. For example, you may have the following line in a current script:

```
$result = mysql_query($sql) or die(mysql_error());
```

You can rewrite it like this:

```
$result = @ mysql_query($sql);
if (!$result) {
  // redirect to custom error page
  }
```

Summary

The availability of three different methods of connecting to MySQL with PHP is both a good thing and a bad thing. The downside is that you can't learn just one way of doing things. Even if you have a remote server that supports PDO, the most up-to-date method, most books and tutorials will continue to be based on the original MySQL extension. What's more, you can't mix the different techniques in the same script. This makes life difficult for beginners and experts alike.

The upside is that neither PHP nor MySQL is standing still. Prepared statements make database queries more secure by removing the need to ensure that quotes and control characters are properly escaped. They also speed up your application if the same query needs to be repeated during a script using different variables. Instead of validating the SQL every time, the script needs do it only once with the placeholders.

Although this chapter has concentrated on content management, the same basic techniques apply to most interaction with a database. Of course, there's a lot more to SQL—and to PHP. In the next chapter, I'll address some of the most common problems, such as displaying only the first sentence or so of a long text field, handling dates, and working with more than one table in a database.

13

14 SOLUTIONS TO COMMON
PHP/MYSQL PROBLEMS

What this chapter covers:

- Extracting the first section of a longer text item
- Using an alias in a SQL query
- Formatting dates with PHP and MySQL
- Working with multiple tables in MySQL

We have some unfinished business left over from the last chapter. Figure 13-2 shows content from the journal table with just the first two sentences of each article displayed and a link to the rest of the article. However, I didn't show you how it was done. The full list of articles in journal_list.php also displays the MySQL timestamp in its raw state, which isn't very elegant, particularly if you're using MySQL 3.23 or 4.0. In addition to tidying up those two things, this chapter addresses some of the most common questions about working with PHP and MySQL, such as inserting dates into a database, formatting text retrieved from a database, and working with multiple-table databases. I hope that, by this stage, you have built up sufficient confidence to start adapting scripts without the need for detailed instructions every step of the way, so I'll concentrate on the main new features.

Let's start by extracting the first few lines from the beginning of a longer piece of text.

Displaying a text extract

There are many ways to extract the first few lines or characters from a longer piece of text. Sometimes, you need just the first 20 or 30 characters to identify an item. At other times, it's preferable to show complete sentences or paragraphs.

> *To view the example files for this section, copy them from the download files for this chapter to the site root of your* phpsolutions *site. Each file requires the following files in the* includes *folder:* footer.inc.php, menu.inc.php, title.inc.php, *and the correct connection file for the method you are using with MySQL.*

Extracting a fixed number of characters

You can extract a fixed number of characters from the beginning of a text item either with the PHP substr() function or with the LEFT() function in a SQL query.

Using PHP

The PHP substr() function extracts a substring from a longer string. It takes three arguments: the string you want to extract the substring from, the starting point (counted from 0), and the number of characters to be extracted. So, the following code displays the first 100 characters of $row['article']:

```
echo substr($row['article'], 0, 100);
```

The substr() function leaves the original string intact. If you omit the third argument, substr() extracts everything to the end of the string. This makes sense only if you choose a starting point other than 0.

Using MySQL

The MySQL LEFT() function extracts a specified number of characters from the beginning of a column. It takes two arguments: the column name and the number of characters to be extracted. So, the following retrieves article_id, title, and the first 100 characters from the article column of the journal table:

```
SELECT article_id, title, LEFT(article, 100)
FROM journal ORDER BY created DESC
```

Whenever you use a function in a SQL query like this, the column name no longer appears in the result set as article, but as LEFT(article, 100) instead. So it's a good idea to assign an **alias** to the affected column using the AS keyword. You can either reassign the column's original name as the alias or use a descriptive name as in the following example (the code is in journal_left_mysql.php, journal_left_mysqli.php, and journal_left_pdo.php in the download files):

```
SELECT article_id, title, LEFT(article, 100) AS first100
FROM journal ORDER BY created DESC
```

If you process each record as $row, the extract is in $row['first100']. To retrieve both the first 100 characters and the full article, simply include both in the query like this:

```
SELECT article_id, title, LEFT(article, 100) AS first100, article
FROM journal ORDER BY created DESC
```

However, taking a fixed number of characters from the beginning of an article produces a very crude result, as Figure 14-1 shows. For a public web page, you need a more subtle approach.

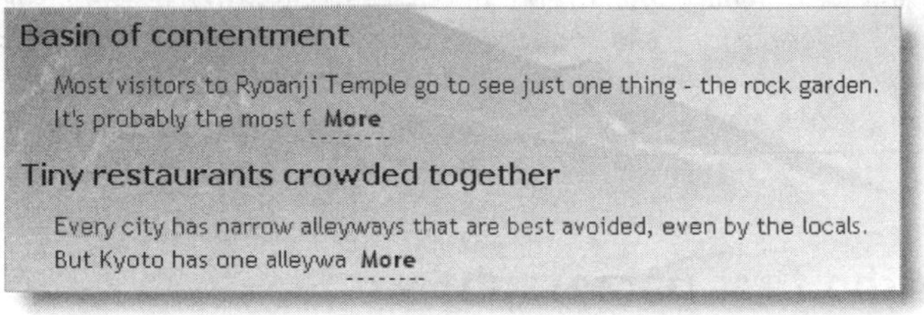

Figure 14-1. Selecting the first 100 characters from an article chops words in half and looks very unprofessional.

14

Ending an extract on a complete word

To end an extract on a complete word, you need to find the final space, and use that to determine the length of the substring. So, if you want the extract to be a maximum of

100 characters, use either of the preceding methods to start with, and store the result in $extract. Then you can use the PHP string functions strrpos() and substr() to find the last space and end the extract like this (the code is in journal_word_mysql.php, journal_word_mysqli.php, and journal_word_pdo.php):

```
$extract = $row['first100'];
// find position of last space in extract
$lastSpace = strrpos($extract, ' ');
// use $lastSpace to set length of new extract and add ...
echo substr($extract, 0, $lastSpace).'... ';
```

This produces the more elegant result shown in Figure 14-2. It uses strrpos(), which finds the last position of a character within another string. Since you're looking for a space, the second argument is a pair of quotes with a single space between them. The result is stored in $lastSpace, which is passed as the third argument to substr(), finishing the extract on a complete word. Finally, add a string containing three dots and a space, and join the two with the concatenation operator (a period or dot).

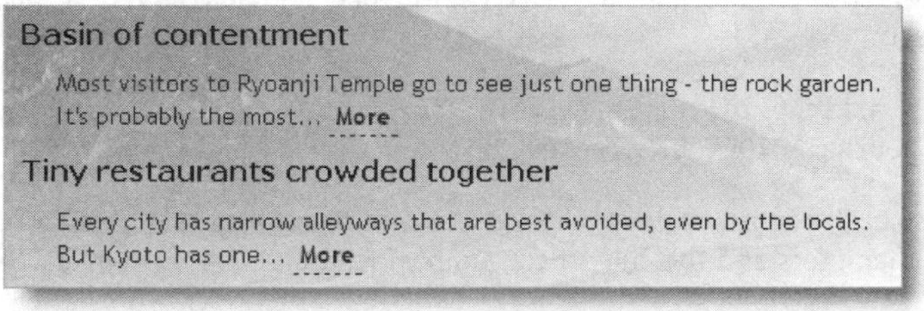

Figure 14-2. Two lines of PHP code produce a more elegant result by ending the extract on a complete word.

> Don't confuse strrpos(), which finds the last instance of a character within a string, with its counterpart strpos(), which finds the first instance. You can use strpos() to search not only for a single character, but also for a string within a string. The ability to use strrpos() to search for a substring is available only in PHP 5 and above. Both functions also have case-insensitive versions. To find out more, visit www.php.net/manual/en/function.strpos.php.

Extracting the first paragraph

Assuming that you have entered your text in the database using the Enter or Return key to indicate new paragraphs, this is very easy. Simply retrieve the full text, use strpos() to find the first new line character, and use substr() to extract the first section of text up to that point.

The download files journal_para_mysql.php, journal_para_mysqli.php, and journal_para_pdo.php use the following SQL query:

```
SELECT article_id, title, article
FROM journal ORDER BY created DESC
```

The following code is used to display the first paragraph of article:

```
echo substr($row['article'], 0, strpos($row['article'], "\n"));
```

If that makes your head spin, take a look at the third argument on its own:

```
strpos($row['article'], "\n")
```

This locates the first new line character in $row['article']. You could rewrite the code like this:

```
$newLine = strpos($row['article'], "\n");
echo substr($row['article'], 0, $newLine);
```

Both sets of code do exactly the same thing, but PHP lets you nest a function as an argument passed to another function. As long as the nested function returns a valid result, you can frequently use shortcuts like this.

Displaying paragraphs

Since we're on the subject of paragraphs, many beginners are confused by the fact that all the text retrieved from a database is displayed as a continuous block, with no separation between paragraphs. XHTML ignores whitespace, including new lines. To get text stored in a database displayed as paragraphs, you have two main options: convert new lines to <br /> tags, or store your text as XHTML.

The first of these options is simpler. Pass your text to the nl2br() function before displaying it like this:

```
echo nl2br($row['article']);
```

Voilà!—paragraphs. Yes, I know that they aren't properly marked up as paragraphs. Databases can store XHTML, but they cannot create it for you.

Extracting complete sentences

PHP has no concept of what constitutes a sentence. Counting periods means you ignore all sentences that end with an exclamation point or question mark. You also run the risk of breaking a sentence on a decimal point or cutting off a closing quote after a period. To overcome these problems, I have devised a PHP function called getFirst() that identifies the punctuation at the end of a normal sentence:

- A period, question mark, or exclamation point
- Optionally followed by a single or double quote
- Followed by one or more spaces

14

The getFirst() function takes two arguments: the text from which you want to extract the first section and the number of sentences you want to extract. The second argument is optional; if it's not supplied, the function extracts the first two sentences. The code looks like this (it's in getFirst.inc.php):

```
function getFirst($text, $number=2) {
    // regular expression to find typical sentence endings
    $pattern = '/([.?!]["\']?)\s/';
    // use regex to insert break indicator
    $text = preg_replace($pattern, '$1bRE@kH3re', $text);
    // use break indicator to create array of sentences
    $sentences = explode('bRE@kH3re', $text);
    // check relative length of array and requested number
    $howMany = count($sentences);
    $number = $howMany >= $number ? $number : $howMany;
    // rebuild extract and return as single string
    $remainder = array_splice($sentences, $number);
    $result = array();
    $result[0] = implode(' ', $sentences);
    $result[1] = empty($remainder) ? false : true;
    return $result;
}
```

You don't need to understand the fine details, but the line highlighted in bold uses preg_replace() to insert a combination of characters so unlikely to occur in normal text that it can be used to identify the end of each sentence. The function returns an array containing two elements: the extracted sentences and a Boolean variable indicating whether there's anything more following the extract. You can use the second element to create a link to a page containing the full text.

PHP Solution 14-1: Displaying the first two sentences of an article

If you created the Japan Journey site earlier in the book, use journal.php. Alternatively, use journal01.php from the download files for this chapter, and copy it to the phpsolutions site root. You also need footer.inc.php, menu.inc.php, title.inc.php, and the correct MySQL connection file in the includes folder. The finished code is in journal_mysql.php, journal_mysqli.php, and journal_pdo.php.

> For the sake of brevity, in this chapter I am not going to wrap the include commands in conditional statements. An include file should always be accessible as long as it's located within the same domain and the filepath is correct. Remember, though, that the accidental deletion or corruption of an include file will result in your site being disfigured with warning messages if your server has display_errors turned on. Also, calls to functions in external files will generate a fatal error unless you first use function_exists() as described in Chapter 4.

1. Copy getFirst.inc.php from the download files to the includes folder, and include it in the PHP code block above the DOCTYPE declaration. Also include the correct connection file for the method you're using to connect to MySQL, and create a connection to the database. This page shouldn't be given any administrative privileges, so use query as the argument passed to dbConnect() like this:

```
include('includes/getFirst.inc.php');
include('includes/connection.inc.php');
// create database connection
$conn = dbConnect('query');
```

2. Prepare a SQL query to retrieve all records from the journal table like this:

```
$sql = 'SELECT * FROM journal ORDER BY created DESC';
```

3. If you're using the original MySQL extension, submit the query like this:

```
$result = mysql_query($sql);
```

For MySQL Improved, use this:

```
$result = $conn->query($sql);
```

There's no need to submit the query at this stage for PDO.

4. Create a loop inside the maincontent <div> to display the results.

For the MySQL original extension, use this:

```
<div id="maincontent">
<?php
while ($row = mysql_fetch_assoc($result)) {
?>
<h2><?php echo $row['title']; ?></h2>
  <p><?php $extract = getFirst($row['article']);
  echo $extract[0];
  if ($extract[1]) {
    echo '<a href="details.php?article_id='.$row['article_id'].'"> ➥
More</a>';
    } ?></p>
<?php } ?>
</div>
```

The code is the same for MySQL Improved and PDO, except for this line:

```
while ($row = mysql_fetch_assoc($result)) {
```

For MySQL Improved, replace it with this:

```
while ($row = $result->fetch_assoc()) {
```

For PDO, use this instead:

```
foreach ($conn->query($sql) as $row) {
```

14

The main part of the code is inside the <p> tags. The getFirst() function processes $row['article'] and stores the result in $extract. The first two sentences of article in $extract[0] are immediately displayed. If $extract[1] contains anything, it means there is more to display. So the code inside the if statement displays a link to details.php with the article's primary key in a query string.

5. Save the page and test it in a browser. You should see the first two sentences of each article displayed as shown in Figure 13-2 in the previous chapter. Test the function by adding a number as a second argument to getFirst() like this:

```
$extract = getFirst($row['article'], 3);
```

This displays the first three sentences. If you increase the number so that it equals or exceeds the number of sentences in an article, the More link won't be displayed.

We'll look at detail.php later in the chapter after linking the journal and images tables with a foreign key. Before that, let's tackle the minefield presented by using dates with a database.

Let's make a date

Dates and time are so fundamental to modern life that we rarely pause to think how complex they are. There are 60 seconds to a minute and 60 minutes to an hour, but 24 hours to a day. Months range between 28 and 31 days, and a year can be either 365 or 366 days. The confusion doesn't stop there, because 7/4 means July 4 to an American or Japanese, but 7 April to a European. As if all that weren't confusing enough, PHP and MySQL handle dates differently. Time to bring order to chaos . . .

How MySQL handles dates

In MySQL, dates and time always follow the same order: largest unit first, followed by the next largest, down to the smallest. In other words: year, month, date, hour, minutes, seconds. Hours are always measured using the 24-hour clock with midnight expressed as 00:00:00. Even if this seems unfamiliar to you, it's the recommendation laid down by the International Organization for Standardization (ISO).

If you attempt to store a date in any other format than year, month, date, MySQL stores it as 0000-00-00. MySQL allows considerable flexibility about the separator between the units (any punctuation symbol is OK), but there is no argument about the order—it's fixed.

I'll come back later to the way you insert dates into MySQL, because it's best to validate them and format them with PHP. First, let's take a look at some of the things you can do with dates once they're stored in MySQL. MySQL has a wide range of date and time functions, all of which are listed together with examples at http://dev.mysql.com/doc/refman/5.0/en/date-and-time-functions.html.

One of the most useful functions is DATE_FORMAT(), which does exactly what its name suggests.

Formatting dates in a SELECT query

The syntax for DATE_FORMAT() is as follows:

    DATE_FORMAT(*date*, *format*)

Normally, *date* is the table column to be formatted, and *format* is a string composed of formatting specifiers and any other text you want to include. Table 14-1 lists the most common specifiers.

Table 14-1. Frequently used MySQL date format specifiers

Period	Specifier	Description	Example
Year	%Y	Four-digit format	2006
	%y	Two-digit format	06
Month	%M	Full name	January, September
	%b	Abbreviated name, three letters	Jan, Sep
	%m	Number with leading zero	01, 09
	%c	Number without leading zero	1, 9
Day of month	%d	With leading zero	01, 25
	%e	Without leading zero	1, 25
	%D	With English text suffix	1st, 25th
Weekday name	%W	Full text	Monday, Thursday
	%a	Abbreviated name, three letters	Mon, Thu
Hour	%H	24-hour clock with leading zero	01, 23
	%k	24-hour clock without leading zero	1, 23
	%h	12-hour clock with leading zero	01, 11
	%l (lowercase "L")	12-hour clock without leading zero	1, 11
Minutes	%i	With leading zero	05, 25
Seconds	%S	With leading zero	08, 45
AM/PM	%p		

14

As explained earlier, when using a function in a SQL query, assign the result to an alias using the AS keyword. Referring to Table 14-1, you can now format the date in the created column of the journal table. To present it in a common U.S. style and retain the name of the original column, use the following:

```
DATE_FORMAT(created, '%c/%e/%Y') AS created
```

To format the same date in European style, reverse the first two specifiers like this:

```
DATE_FORMAT(created, '%e/%c/%Y') AS created
```

PHP Solution 14-2: Formatting a MySQL date or timestamp

Use admin/journal_list.php from Chapter 13. The completed code is in journal_list_fmt_mysql.php, journal_list_fmt_mysqli.php, and journal_list_fmt_pdo.php in the download files for this chapter.

1. Locate the SQL query in journal_list.php. It looks like this:

   ```
   $sql = 'SELECT * FROM journal ORDER BY created DESC';
   ```

2. Change it like this:

   ```
   $sql = 'SELECT article_id, title,
               DATE_FORMAT(created, "%a, %b %D, %Y") AS created
               FROM journal ORDER BY created DESC';
   ```

   I used single quotes around the whole SQL query, so the format string inside DATE_FORMAT() needs to be in double quotes. Make sure there is no gap before the opening parenthesis of DATE_FORMAT().

3. Save the page and load it into a browser. The dates should now be formatted as shown in Figure 14-3. Experiment with other specifiers to suit your preferences.

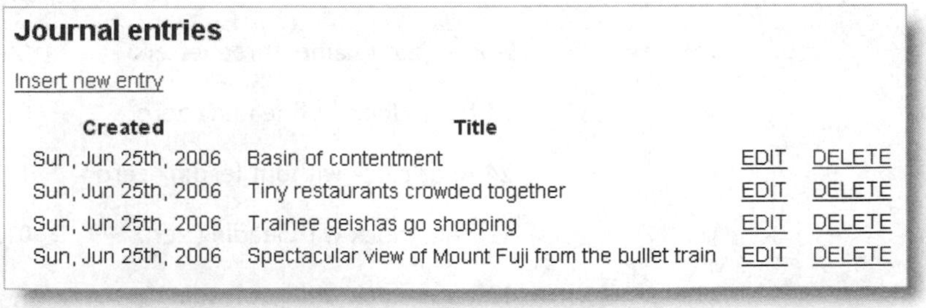

Journal entries

Insert new entry

Created	Title		
Sun, Jun 25th, 2006	Basin of contentment	EDIT	DELETE
Sun, Jun 25th, 2006	Tiny restaurants crowded together	EDIT	DELETE
Sun, Jun 25th, 2006	Trainee geishas go shopping	EDIT	DELETE
Sun, Jun 25th, 2006	Spectacular view of Mount Fuji from the bullet train	EDIT	DELETE

Figure 14-3. The MySQL timestamps are now nicely formatted.

Adding to and subtracting from dates

When working with dates, it's often useful to add or subtract a specific time period. For instance, you may want to display items that have been added to the database within the past seven days, or stop displaying articles that haven't been updated for three months.

MySQL makes this easy with DATE_ADD() and DATE_SUB(). Both functions have synonyms called ADDDATE() and SUBDATE(), respectively.

The basic syntax is the same for all of them and looks like this:

```
DATE_ADD(date, INTERVAL value interval_type)
```

When using these functions, *date* can be the column containing the date you want to alter, a string containing a particular date (in YYYY-MM-DD format), or a MySQL function, such as NOW(). INTERVAL is a keyword followed by a *value* and an interval type, the most common of which are listed in Table 14-2.

Table 14-2. Most frequently used interval types with DATE_ADD() and DATE_SUB()

Interval type	Meaning	Value format
DAY	Days	Number
DAY_HOUR	Days and hours	String presented as 'DD hh'
WEEK	Weeks	Number
MONTH	Months	Number
QUARTER	Quarters	Number
YEAR	Years	Number
YEAR_MONTH	Years and months	String presented as 'YY-MM'

The interval types are constants, so don't add "S" to the end of DAY, WEEK, and so on to make them plural.

One of the most useful applications of these functions is to display only the most recent items in a table.

PHP Solution 14-3: Displaying items updated within the past week

Use journal.php from PHP Solution 14-1. The finished code is in journal_week_mysql.php, journal_week_mysqli.php, and journal_week_pdo.php.

1. Locate the SQL query in journal.php. It looks like this:

```
$sql = 'SELECT * FROM journal ORDER BY created DESC';
```

2. Change it like this:

```
$sql = 'SELECT * FROM journal
        WHERE updated > DATE_SUB(NOW(), INTERVAL 1 WEEK)
        ORDER BY created DESC';
```

This tells MySQL that you want only items that have been updated in the past week.

14

3. Save and reload the page in your browser. Depending on when you last updated an item in the journal table, you should see nothing or a limited range of items. If necessary, change the interval type to DAY or HOUR to test that the time limit is working.

4. Open journal_list.php, select an item that isn't displayed in journal.php, and edit it. Reload journal.php. The item that you have just updated should now be displayed.

Working with dates in PHP

PHP handles dates in a very different way from MySQL that's not as easy to visualize in everyday terms. MySQL timestamps are based on the human calendar and look like this:

```
2006-07-05 10:32:19   // MySQL 4.1 and above
20060705103219        // Prior to MySQL 4.1
```

The format prior to MySQL 4.1 is more difficult to read because it doesn't have any punctuation, but once you know that the units are year, month, and so on, the meaning is easy to work out.

The same moment in time is represented like this in PHP:

```
1152091939   // Unix timestamp for 10:32:19 BST on July 5, 2006
```

This seemingly arbitrary figure is the number of seconds since midnight UTC (Coordinated Universal Time)[1] on January 1, 1970—a point in time commonly referred to as the **Unix epoch** and used as the basis for date and time calculations in many computing languages. Except when referring to the current time, all dates in PHP need to be converted to a Unix timestamp. After performing any calculations, you format the result in a more human-readable way by using the date() or strftime() function, which I'll describe shortly. But first, let's take a look at time zones and Unix timestamps.

Setting the correct time zone

The internal workings of the PHP date and time functions were revised in PHP 5.1 and require a time zone to be defined. Normally, this should be done by setting the value of date.timezone in php.ini; but if your hosting company forgets to do so, or you want to use a different time zone, you need to set it yourself. You can do this three different ways.

The simplest way is to add the following at the beginning of any script that uses date or time functions:

```
ini_set('date.timezone', 'timezone');
```

---

1. According to Wikipedia (http://en.wikipedia.org), the abbreviation "UTC" for "Coordinated Universal Time" is a compromise, as the International Telecommunication Union wanted the term to have a single abbreviation for all languages, and English and French speakers each wanted the term presented in their respective language. A variation of the English term "coordinated universal time" was agreed upon, with the verbal adjective trailing as in French, so that the abbreviation UTC can also be read as "universal time, coordinated."

You can find a full list of valid time zones at www.php.net/manual/en/timezones.php. The correct setting for where I live is this:

```
ini_set('date.timezone', 'Europe/London');
```

ini_set() fails silently if your server doesn't support the date.timezone setting. As long as you use a valid PHP time zone, your scripts will automatically use this setting whenever your server is upgraded.

A slightly longer way is to add this (with the appropriate time zone) before using date and time functions:

```
if (function_exists('date_default_timezone_set')) {
  date_default_timezone_set('Europe/London');
  }
```

If your remote server runs Apache, you may be able to set a default time zone for your entire site by putting the following in an .htaccess file in the site root (use the correct time zone for your location):

```
php_value date.timezone 'Europe/London'
```

This works only if Apache has been set up to allow .htaccess to override default settings.

Creating a Unix timestamp

PHP offers two main ways of creating a Unix timestamp. The first uses mktime() and is based on the actual date and time; the other attempts to parse any English date or time expression with strtotime().

The mktime() function takes six arguments as follows:

```
mktime(hour, minutes, seconds, month, date, year)
```

All arguments are optional. If a value is omitted, it is set to the current date and time. However, you can't skip arguments; as soon as you leave one out, all remaining ones must also be omitted. Consequently, if you are interested only in the date, you need to set the first three arguments to 0 (midnight) like this:

```
$Xmas2006 = mktime(0, 0, 0, 12, 25, 2006);
```

The strtotime() function attempts to parse dates from American English, but holds some unpleasant surprises. The following expressions produce the correct timestamp for Christmas Day 2006:

```
$Xmas2006 = strtotime('12/25/2006');
$Xmas2006 = strtotime('2006-12-25');
```

However, replacing the slashes with hyphens in the first example, as follows, produces a false result:

```
$notXmas = strtotime('12-25-2006'); // produces Dec 31, 1969 timestamp
```

14

To avoid such problems, it's best to use the name of the month, either spelled out in full or just the first three letters, and to place the year at the end of the string.

The real value of strtotime(), however, lies in its ability to add or subtract from dates by parsing simple time-related expressions. For instance, strtotime() understands all these expressions:

```
strtotime('tomorrow');
strtotime('yesterday');
strtotime('last Monday');
strtotime('next Thursday');
strtotime('-3 weeks');
strtotime('+1 week 2 days');
```

> *Be careful when using "next" in a* strtotime() *expression. In versions prior to PHP 4.4, it is incorrectly interpreted as +2, instead of +1.*

The previous examples calculate the timestamp based on the current date and time. However, you can supply a specific timestamp as a second, optional argument to strtotime(). This means you can add or subtract from a particular date. The following example calculates the timestamp for January 6, 2007:

```
$Xmas2006 = mktime(0, 0, 0, 12, 25, 2006);
strtotime('+12 days', $Xmas2006);
```

If you ever need to generate a Unix timestamp from a date-type column in MySQL, you can use the UNIX_TIMESTAMP() function in a SELECT statement like this:

```
SELECT UNIX_TIMESTAMP(created) AS PHPtimestamp FROM journal
```

Formatting dates in PHP

PHP offers two functions that format dates: date(), which displays the names of weekdays and months in English only, and strftime(), which uses the server's locale. So, if the server's locale is set to Spanish, date() displays Saturday, but strftime() displays sábado. Both functions take as their first, required argument a string that indicates the format in which you want to display the date. A second, optional argument specifies the timestamp, but if it's omitted, the current date and time are assumed.

There are a lot of format characters. Some are easy to remember, but many seem to have no obvious reasoning behind them. You can find a full list at www.php.net/manual/en/function.date.php and www.php.net/manual/en/function.strftime.php. Table 14-3 lists the most useful.

Table 14-3. The main format characters used in the date() and strftime() functions

Unit	date()	strftime()	Description	Example
Day	d	%d	Day of the month with leading zero	01 through 31
	j	%e*	Day of the month without leading zero	1 through 31
	S		English ordinal suffix for day of the month	st, nd, rd, or th
	D	%a	First three letters of day name	Sun, Tue
	%1 (lowercase "L")	%A	Full name of day	Sunday, Tuesday
Month	m	%m	Number of month with leading zero	01 through 12
	n		Number of month without leading zero	1 through 12
	M	%b	First three letters of month name	Jan, Jul
	F	%B	Full name of month	January, July
Year	Y	%Y	Year displayed as four digits	2006
	y	%y	Year displayed as two digits	06
Hour	g		Hour in 12-hour format without leading zero	1 through 12
	h	%I	Hour in 12-hour format with leading zero	01 through 12
	G		Hour in 24-hour format without leading zero	0 through 23
	H	%H	Hour in 24-hour format with leading zero	01 through 23
Minutes	i	%M	Minutes with leading zero if necessary	00 through 59
Seconds	s	%S	Seconds with leading zero if necessary	00 through 59
AM/PM	a	%p	Lowercase	am
AM/PM	A		Uppercase	PM

* Note: %e is not supported on Windows.

14

You can combine these format characters with punctuation to display the current date in your web pages according to your own preferences. For instance, the following code (also in dates.php in the download files for this chapter) produces output similar to that shown in the following screenshot:

```
<p>American style: <?php echo date('l, F jS, Y'); ?></p>
<p>European style: <?php echo date('l, jS F Y'); ?></p>
```

Inserting dates into MySQL

MySQL's requirement for dates to be formatted as YYYY-MM-DD presents a headache for online forms that allow users to input dates. As you have seen, the current date and time can be inserted automatically by using a TIMESTAMP column or the MySQL NOW() function. It's when you need any other date that the problems arise.

If you can trust users to follow a set pattern for inputting dates, such as MM/DD/YYYY, you can use the PHP explode() function to split the date parts into an array and rearrange them like this:

```
if (isset($_POST['theDate'])) {
  $date = explode('/', $_POST['theDate']);
  $mysqlFormat = "$date[2]-$date[0]-$date[1]";
  }
```

To perform the same conversion from DD/MM/YYYY, just reorder the date parts like this:

```
$mysqlFormat = "$date[2]-$date[1]-$date[0]";
```

This works, but as soon as someone deviates from the format, you end up with invalid dates in your database. It's better to ensure that dates are both valid and in the correct format.

PHP Solution 14-4: Validating and formatting dates for MySQL input

This PHP Solution concentrates on checking the validity of a date and converting it to MySQL format. It's designed to be incorporated in an insert or update form of your own. The finished code is in date_converter02.php in the download files for this chapter.

1. Create a page called date_converter.php, and insert a form containing the following code (or use date_converter01.php in the download files):

```
<form id="form1" name="form1" method="post" action="">
<p>
  <label for="select">Month:</label>
  <select name="month" id="month">
    <option value=""></option>
  </select>
  <label for="day">Date:</label>
  <input name="day" type="text" id="day" size="2" maxlength="2" />
  <label for="year">Year:</label>
  <input name="year" type="text" id="year" size="4" maxlength="4" />
</p>
<p>
  <input type="submit" name="convert" id="convert" value="Convert" />
</p>
</form>
```

This code creates a drop-down menu called month and two text input fields called day and year. The drop-down menu doesn't have any values at the moment, but it will be populated by a PHP loop. The day and year fields both have maxlength attributes that limit the number of characters accepted. The submit button is called convert, but the name in a real application should be whatever you use for your insert or update form.

2. Amend the section that builds the drop-down menu like this:

```
<select name="month" id="month">
  <?php
  $months = array('Jan','Feb','Mar','Apr','May','Jun','Jul','Aug', ➥
'Sep','Oct','Nov','Dec');
  ini_set('date.timezone', 'Europe/London');
  $thisMonth = date('n');
  for ($i = 1; $i <= 12; $i++) { ?>
    <option value="<?php echo $i < 10 ? '0'.$i : $i; ?>"
    <?php if ($i == $thisMonth) { echo ' selected="selected"'; } ?>>
    <?php echo $months[$i-1]; ?>
    </option>
  <?php } ?>
</select>
```

This creates an array of month names and uses the date() function to find the number of the current month (set the correct time zone for your location). A for loop then populates the menu's <option> tags. I have set the initial value of $i to 1, because I want to use it for the value of the month. The following code tests whether $i is less than 10. If it is, a leading zero is added to the number:

```
echo $i < 10 ? '0'.$i : $i;
```

If the values of $i and $thisMonth are the same, the if statement inserts selected="selected" into the <option> tag. The final part of the script displays the

14

name of the month by drawing it from the $months array. Because indexed arrays begin at 0, you need to subtract 1 from the value of $i to get the right month.

3. Save the page and test it in a browser. It should look like the following screenshot, and the current month should be automatically displayed in the drop-down menu.

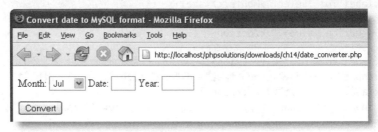

If you test the text input fields, the Date field should accept no more than two characters, and the Year field a maximum of four. Even though this reduces the possibility of mistakes, you still need to validate the input and format the date correctly.

4. The code that performs all the checks goes above the DOCTYPE declaration. It's a straightforward chain of if... else statements, which looks like this:

```php
if (array_key_exists('convert', $_POST)) {
  $m = $_POST['month'];
  $d = trim($_POST['day']);
  $y = trim($_POST['year']);
  if (empty($d) || empty($y)) {
    $error = 'Please fill in all fields';
    }
  elseif (!is_numeric($d) || !is_numeric($y)) {
    $error = 'Please use numbers only';
    }
  elseif (($d < 1 || $d > 31) || ($y < 1000 || $y > 9999)) {
    $error = 'Please use numbers within the correct range';
    }
  elseif (!checkdate($m,$d,$y)) {
    $error = 'You have used an invalid date';
    }
  else {
    $d = $d < 10 ? '0'.$d : $d;
    $mysqlFormat = "$y-$m-$d";
    }
}
```

You don't need to perform any checks on the value of the month, because the drop-down menu has generated it. So, after you trim any whitespace from around the day and year, these values are checked to see if they are empty or not numeric. The third test looks for numbers within acceptable ranges. The range for years is dictated by the legal range for MySQL. In the unlikely event that you need a year out of that range, you must choose a different column type to store the data.

By using a series of elseif clauses, this code stops testing as soon as it meets the first mistake. If the input has survived the first three tests, it's then subjected to the PHP function checkdate(), which is smart enough to know when it's a leap year and prevents mistakes such as September 31.

Finally, if the input has passed all these tests, it's rebuilt in the correct format for insertion into MySQL. The first line of the final else clause uses the ternary operator, as described in step 2, to add a leading zero to the day of the month if necessary.

5. For testing purposes, add this code just above the form in the main body of the page:

```
if ($_POST) {
  echo '<p>';
  if (isset($error)) {
    echo $error;
    }
  elseif (isset($mysqlFormat)) {
    echo $mysqlFormat;
    }
  echo '</p>';
  }
```

6. Save the page and test it by entering a date and clicking Convert. If the date is valid, you should see it converted to MySQL format at the top of the page, as shown in the following screenshot:

If you enter an invalid date, you should see an appropriate message instead.

Although date_converter.php just displays the result, when adapting the code for an insert form, for example, use the tests like this:

```
if (isset($error)) {
  // abandon insertion of data and display error messages
  }
elseif (isset($mysqlFormat)) {
  // go ahead with insertion of data
  }
```

14

Working with multiple database tables

As I explained in Chapter 11, one of the major strengths of a relational database is the ability to link data in different tables by using the primary key from one table as a foreign key in another table. The phpsolutions database has two tables: images and journal. It's time to join them. The first step is to decide what sort of relationship you want to establish between the tables.

Understanding table relationships

The simplest type of relationship is **one-to-one** (often represented as **1:1**). In the context of the phpsolutions database, you might associate a single photo in the images table with an article in the journal table, as shown in Figure 14-4.

Figure 14-4. A one-to-one relationship links one record directly with another.

Since there are only a handful of records in each table, this is the only relationship; as more articles are added, it's likely to change. The photo associated with the first article in Figure 14-4 shows maple leaves floating on the water, so it might be suitable to illustrate an article about the changing seasons or autumn hues. The crystal-clear water, bamboo water scoop, and bamboo pipe also suggest other themes that the photo could be used to illustrate. So you could easily end up with the same photo being used for several articles, or a **one-to-many** (or **1:n**) relationship, as represented by Figure 14-5.

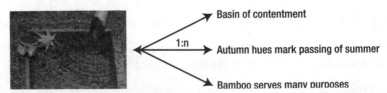

Figure 14-5. A one-to-many relationship links one record with several others.

SQL normally links records in separate tables with a WHERE clause that matches the foreign key in one table with the primary key in another like this:

```
SELECT title, article, filename, caption
FROM journal, images
```

```
WHERE article_id = 2
AND journal.image_id = images.image_id
```

The WHERE clause begins by identifying the article you want and then matching the primary and foreign keys of the image associated with the article. So, when linking tables, you need to establish a 1:1 relationship. Reading Figure 14-5 from left to right, the image has a 1:n relationship with several articles. Read it from right to left, and each article has a 1:1 relationship with the image. What this means is that you need to store the image_id as a foreign key in the journal table, and not the other way around. The journal table thus becomes a secondary or child table in relation to images. As you'll see later, this has important implications when you come to delete records from either table.

> When using more than one table in a SQL query, ambiguous column references, such as image_id in the previous example, need to be qualified in the form table_name.column_name. You don't need to qualify columns that have unique names, although it's valid to do so. See "Reviewing the four essential SQL commands" at the end of the previous chapter.

What happens if you want to associate more than one image to each article? You could create several columns to hold the foreign keys, but this rapidly becomes unwieldy. You might start off with image1, image2, and image3, but if most articles have only one image, two columns are redundant for much of the time. And are you going add an extra column for that extra-special article that requires four images?

When faced with the need to accommodate **many-to-many** (or **n:m**) relationships, you need a different approach. The images and journal tables don't contain sufficient records to demonstrate n:m relationships, but we could easily add a categories table (see Figure 14-6). All images in the figure belong to the Kyoto category, but the image of the monk is the only one that also fits into People. The middle two images belong to Autumn and the bottom one to Eating.

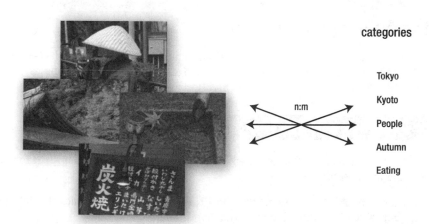

categories

Tokyo

Kyoto

People

Autumn

Eating

n:m

Figure 14-6. Databases often require many-to-many relationships between tables.

14

401

The way to resolve complex relationships to 1:1 is to create a **lookup table**. This is a special table containing just two columns, both of which are declared a joint primary key. Figure 14-7 shows how this works. Although each image is related to several categories and vice versa, relationships in the lookup table (image_cat_lookup) are always one-to-one. So, to find all images that belong to the People category, you create a SQL query that matches cat_id in the categories table with cat_id in the lookup table *and* image_id in the lookup table with image_id in the images table. You then narrow down the search to results where category equals People. The SQL required for the search looks like this:

```
SELECT filename, caption
FROM images, image_cat_lookup, categories
WHERE categories.cat_id = image_cat_lookup.cat_id
AND image_cat_lookup.image_id = images.image_id
AND category = 'People'
```

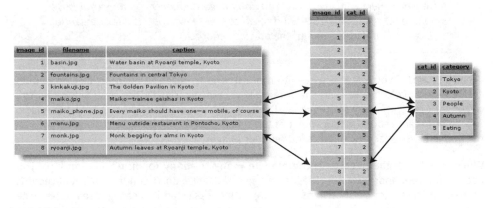

Figure 14-7. A lookup table resolves many-to-many relationships as 1:1.

Now that you know the theory behind working with multiple tables, let's put it into practice.

Linking an image to an article

Let's begin with the straightforward scenario outlined in Figures 14-4 and 14-5, and add an extra column to the journal table to store image_id as a foreign key and associate an image with individual articles.

> **PHP Solution 14-5: Adding an extra column to a table**

This PHP Solution assumes that you created the journal table in the phpsolutions database in the last chapter.

1. Launch phpMyAdmin, select the phpsolutions database, and click the link for the journal table in the left-hand navigation frame.

2. Below the journal table structure in the main frame is a form that allows you to add extra columns. You want to add only one column, so the default value in the Add field(s) text box is fine. It's normal practice to put foreign keys immediately after the table's primary key, so select the After radio button and make sure the drop-down menu is set to article_id, as shown in the following screenshot. Then click Go.

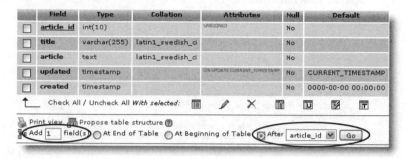

3. This opens the screen for you to define column attributes. Use the following settings:

- Field: image_id
- Type: INT
- Attributes: UNSIGNED
- Null: null

Do *not* select auto_increment or primary key. The Null column has been set to null because not all articles will necessarily be associated with an image. Click Save.

4. You will be returned to the journal table structure, which should now look like this:

Field	Type	Collation	Attributes	Null	Default	Extra
article_id	int(10)		UNSIGNED	No		auto_increment
image_id	int(10)		UNSIGNED	Yes	NULL	
title	varchar(255)	latin1_swedish_ci		No		
article	text	latin1_swedish_ci		No		
updated	timestamp		ON UPDATE CURRENT_TIMESTAMP	No	CURRENT_TIMESTAMP	
created	timestamp			No	0000-00-00 00:00:00	

5. If you click the Browse tab at the top left of the screen, you will see that the value of image_id is NULL in each record. The challenge now is to insert the correct foreign keys without the need to look up the numbers manually. We'll tackle that next.

Inserting a foreign key in a database record basically consists of the following two steps:

1. Use a SELECT query to find the primary key that you want to use as a foreign key.

2. Use an INSERT or UPDATE query to add the foreign key to the target record.

14

The results of the SELECT query are used to build a drop-down menu in the insert and update forms (see Figure 14-8), and store each item's primary key in the value attribute of the <option> tag. When the form is submitted, the selected value is incorporated into the INSERT or UPDATE query as the foreign key.

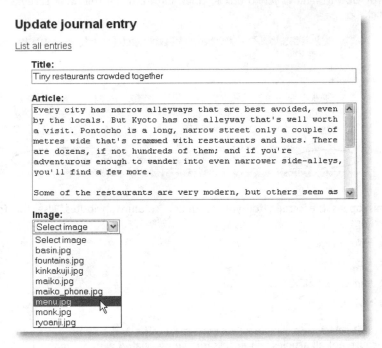

Figure 14-8. A dynamically generated drop-down menu is used to insert the appropriate foreign key.

The principle is the same for both forms, but I'll focus on the update form, as you need to ensure that the drop-down menu displays the correct value for an existing foreign key. The steps involved are the same for the original MySQL extension, MySQL Improved, and PDO, but the SQL is different, so I'll explain each one separately.

PHP Solution 14-6: Adding the image foreign key (MySQL)

This PHP Solution builds on admin/journal_update.php from the previous chapter. The final code is in journal_update_fk_mysql.php in the download files for this chapter.

1. The foreign key is going to be added to the UPDATE query, so you need to add image_id to the array of expected elements in the $_POST array. Change the definition of $expected (around line 9) like this (new code is in bold):

   ```
   $expected = array('title', 'article', 'article_id', 'image_id');
   ```

2. You need to display the contents of the images table in the update form by running a second SELECT statement. Add the following code after the article text area (all the code is new, but the PHP sections are highlighted in bold for ease of reference):

```
<p>
  <label for="image_id">Image:</label>
  <select name="image_id" id="image_id">
    <option value="">Select image</option>
    <?php
    // get details of images
    $getImages = 'SELECT * FROM images ORDER BY filename';
    $imageList = mysql_query($getImages) or die (mysql_error());
    while ($image = mysql_fetch_assoc($imageList)) {
    ?>
    <option value="<?php echo $image['image_id']; ?>"
    <?php
    if ($image['image_id'] == $row['image_id']) {
      echo ' selected="selected"';
      }
    ?>><?php echo $image['filename']; ?>
    </option>
    <?php } ?>
  </select>
</p>
```

The first <option> tag is hard-coded with the label Select image, and its value is
set to an empty string. The remaining <option> tags are populated dynamically
by a while loop that extracts each record to a variable called $image. You can't
use $row, because that's already being used to store the details of the record
from the articles table. A conditional statement checks whether the current
image_id is the same as the one already stored in the articles table. If it is,
selected="selected" is inserted into the <option> tag so that it displays the
correct value in the drop-down menu.

Make sure you don't omit the third character in the following line:

```
?>><?php echo $image['filename']; ?>
```

It's the closing angle bracket of the <option> tag, sandwiched between two PHP tags.

3. Save the page and load it into a browser. You should be automatically redirected to
   journal_list.php. Select one of the EDIT links, and make sure that your page
   looks like Figure 14-8. Check the browser source code view to verify that the value
   attributes of the <option> tags contain the primary key of each image.

4. The final stage is to add the image_id to the UPDATE query after first checking that
   it contains a valid value. Amend the update code like this:

```
// abandon the process if primary key invalid
if (!is_numeric($article_id)) {
  die('Invalid request');
  }
// check the value of image_id
if (empty($image_id) || !is_numeric($image_id)) {
  $image_id = NULL;
  }
```

14

```
// prepare the SQL query
$sql = "UPDATE journal SET image_id = $image_id,
        title = '$title', article = '$article'
        WHERE article_id = $article_id";
```

If $image_id contains no value or if it's not a number, its value is set to NULL. This is a keyword, so it's not enclosed in quotes. Equally, $image_id isn't enclosed in quotes in the SQL query because it's either a number or NULL.

5. Test the page again, select a filename from the drop-down menu, and click Update entry. You can verify whether the foreign key has been inserted into the articles table by refreshing Browse in phpMyAdmin or by selecting the same article for updating. This time, the correct filename should be displayed in the drop-down menu.

Check your code against journal_update_fk_mysql.php, if necessary.

PHP Solution 14-7: Adding the image foreign key (MySQL Improved)

This PHP Solution builds on admin/journal_update.php from the previous chapter. The final code is in journal_update_fk_mysqli.php in the download files for this chapter.

1. The existing SELECT query that retrieves details of the article to be updated needs to be amended so that it includes the foreign key, image_id, and the result needs to be bound to a new result variable, $image_id. You then need to run a second SELECT query to get the details of the images table, but before you can do so, you need to free the database resources by applying the free_result() method on the prepared statement ($stmt). Add the following code highlighted in bold to the existing script:

```
if ($_GET && !$_POST) {
  // prepare SQL query
  $sql = 'SELECT article_id, image_id, title, article
          FROM journal WHERE article_id = ?';
  // initialize statement
  $stmt = $conn->stmt_init();
  if ($stmt->prepare($sql)) {
    // bind the query parameters
    $stmt->bind_param('i', $_GET['article_id']);
    // bind the results to variables
    $stmt->bind_result($article_id, $image_id, $title, $article);
    // execute the query, and fetch the result
    $OK = $stmt->execute();
    $stmt->fetch();
    // free the database resources for the second query
    $stmt->free_result();
  }
}
```

2. You need to display the contents of the images table inside the form. Since the second SELECT statement doesn't rely on external data, it's simpler to use the query() method instead of a prepared statement. Add the following code after the article text area (it's all new code, but the PHP sections are highlighted in bold for ease of reference):

```
<p>
  <label for="image_id">Image:</label>
  <select name="image_id" id="image_id">
    <option value="">Select image</option>
    <?php
    // get details of the images
    $getImages = 'SELECT * FROM images ORDER BY filename';
    $imageList = $conn->query($getImages) or die(mysqli_error($conn));
    while ($image = $imageList->fetch_assoc()) {
    ?>
    <option value="<?php echo $image['image_id']; ?>"
    <?php
    if ($image['image_id'] == $image_id) {
      echo ' selected="selected"';
      }
    ?>><?php echo $image['filename']; ?>
    </option>
    <?php } ?>
  </select>
</p>
```

The first <option> tag is hard-coded with the label Select image, and its value is set to an empty string. The remaining <option> tags are populated by a while loop that extracts each record to an array called $image. I have used this instead of $row for ease of comparison with the MySQL script, which still needs $row for the first SELECT query. It also serves as a reminder that $row is a convention, not a requirement.

A conditional statement checks whether the current image_id is the same as the one already stored in the articles table. If it is, selected="selected" is inserted into the <option> tag so that it displays the correct value in the drop-down menu.

Make sure you don't omit the third character in the following line:

```
?>><?php echo $image['filename']; ?>
```

It's the closing angle bracket of the <option> tag, sandwiched between two PHP tags.

3. Save the page and load it into a browser. You should be automatically redirected to journal_list.php. Select one of the EDIT links, and make sure that your page looks like Figure 14-8. Check the browser source code view to verify that the value attributes of the <option> tags contain the primary key of each image.

4. The final stage is to add the image_id to the UPDATE query like this:

```
$sql = 'UPDATE journal SET image_id = ?, title = ?, article = ?
        WHERE article_id = ?';
```

14

and bind it to the prepared statement like this:

```
$stmt->bind_param('issi', $_POST['image_id'], $_POST['title'], ➡
$_POST['article'], $_POST['article_id']);
```

Since $_POST['image_id'] is the first parameter and must be an integer, you add i to the beginning of the first argument.

5. Test the page again, select a filename from the drop-down menu, and click Update entry. You can verify whether the foreign key has been inserted into the articles table by refreshing Browse in phpMyAdmin or by selecting the same article for updating. This time, the correct filename should be displayed in the drop-down menu.

Check your code against journal_update_fk_mysqli.php, if necessary.

PHP Solution 14-8: Adding the image foreign key (PDO)

This PHP Solution builds on admin/journal_update.php from the previous chapter. The final code is in journal_update_fk_pdo.php in the download files for this chapter.

1. The existing code retrieves the details of the record to be updated, but you also need to run a second query to display the contents of the images table. This means you must use closeCursor() to free the database resources like this:

```
// assign result array to variables
extract($row);
// free the database resources for the second query
$stmt->closeCursor();
}
// if form has been submitted, update record
```

2. Run the second query and display the contents of the images table in the form by inserting the following code after the article text area (it's all new code, but the PHP sections are highlighted in bold for ease of reference):

```
<p>
  <label for="image_id">Image:</label>
  <select name="image_id" id="image_id">
    <option value="">Select image</option>
    <?php
    // get details of the images
    $getImages = 'SELECT * FROM images ORDER BY filename';
    foreach ($conn->query($getImages) as $image) {
    ?>
    <option value="<?php echo $image['image_id']; ?>"
    <?php
    if ($image['image_id'] == $image_id) {
      echo ' selected="selected"';
      }
    ?>><?php echo $image['filename']; ?>
```

```
    </option>
    <?php } ?>
  </select>
</p>
```

The first <option> tag is hard-coded with the label Select image, and its value is set to an empty string. The remaining <option> tags are populated by a foreach loop that extracts each record to an array called $image. I have used this instead of $row for ease of comparison with the MySQL script, which still needs $row for the first SELECT query. It also serves as a reminder that $row is a convention, not a requirement.

A conditional statement checks whether the current image_id is the same as the one already stored in the articles table. If it is, selected="selected" is inserted into the <option> tag so that it displays the correct value in the drop-down menu.

Make sure you don't omit the third character in the following line:

```
?>><?php echo $image['filename']; ?>
```

It's the closing angle bracket of the <option> tag, sandwiched between two PHP tags.

3. Save the page and load it into a browser. You should be automatically redirected to journal_list.php. Select one of the EDIT links, and make sure that your page looks like Figure 14-8. Check the browser source code view to verify that the value attributes of the <option> tags contain the primary key of each image.

4. The final stage is to add the image_id to the UPDATE query like this:

```
$sql = 'UPDATE journal SET image_id = ?, title = ?, article = ?
       WHERE article_id = ?';
```

and then add it to the array of values to be bound to the prepared statement like this:

```
$done = $stmt->execute(array($_POST['image_id'], $_POST['title'], ➥
$_POST['article'], $_POST['article_id']));
```

5. Test the page again, select a filename from the drop-down menu, and click Update entry. You can verify whether the foreign key has been inserted into the articles table by refreshing Browse in phpMyAdmin or by selecting the same article for updating. This time, the correct filename should be displayed in the drop-down menu.

Check your code against journal_update_fk_pdo.php, if necessary.

Since the code for the insert forms is very similar, I haven't included separate instructions, but you can study the code in journal_insert_fk_mysql.php, journal_insert_fk_mysqli.php, *and* journal_insert_fk_pdo *in the download files for this chapter.*

14

Selecting records from multiple tables

Now that you can store a reference to an image as a foreign key in the journal table, you can build a page to show the full article together with its associated image. This involves writing a SELECT query that uses the foreign key to link the images and journal tables.

PHP Solution 14-9: Building the details page

This PHP Solution builds on the preceding discussion of foreign keys, and assumes that you have added a column for image_id in the journal table and amended journal_update.php to add the image_id foreign key to individual records. The starting point is in details01.php in the download files for this chapter. The finished script is in details_mysql.php, details_mysqli.php, and details_pdo.php.

1. Copy details01.php to the phpsolutions site root, and rename it details.php. Make sure that footer.inc.php, menu.inc.php, and title.inc.php are in the includes folder, and load the page in a browser. It should look like the following screenshot:

2. Load journal_list.php into a browser, and update the following three articles by assigning the image filename as indicated:

   - Basin of contentment: basin.jpg
   - Tiny restaurants crowded together: menu.jpg
   - Trainee geishas go shopping: maiko.jpg

   Check that the foreign keys have been registered by navigating to the journal table in phpMyAdmin and clicking the Browse tab. At least one article should have NULL as the value for image_id, as shown in Figure 14-9.

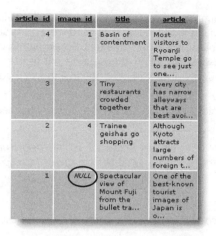

article_id	image_id	title	article
4	1	Basin of contentment	Most visitors to Ryoanji Temple go to see just one...
3	6	Tiny restaurants crowded together	Every city has narrow alleyways that are best avoi...
2	4	Trainee geishas go shopping	Although Kyoto attracts large numbers of foreign t...
1	NULL	Spectacular view of Mount Fuji from the bullet tra...	One of the best-known tourist images of Japan is o...

Figure 14-9. One of the articles is not associated with an image, so the foreign key is set to NULL.

3. In details.php, include the appropriate MySQL connection function and prepare the SQL query inside the PHP code block above the DOCTYPE declaration like this:

```php
<?php
include('includes/title.inc.php');
// include the connector function for MySQL, MySQLI, or PDO
if (! @include('includes/connection.inc.php')) {
  echo 'Sorry page unavailable';
  exit;
  }
// connect to the database
$conn = dbConnect('query');
// check for article_id in query string
if (isset($_GET['article_id']) && is_numeric($_GET['article_id'])) {
  $article_id = $_GET['article_id'];
  }
else {
  $article_id = 0;
  }
// prepare SQL query
$sql = "SELECT title, article, filename, caption
        FROM journal, images
        WHERE journal.article_id = $article_id
        AND journal.image_id = images.image_id";
// process the query and results
?>
```

I have used the generic connection.inc.php. Replace it with the correct version for MySQL, MySQLI, or PDO. This is a public page, so you should connect to the database

14

using the account that doesn't have administrative privileges. The code then checks for article_id in the URL query string and stores it as $article_id if it exists and is numeric. Otherwise, it sets the value to 0. By setting this value to 0, the SQL query will produce no results. You could choose a default article instead, but leave it at 0 for the moment because I want to illustrate an important point shortly.

The SQL query is the same as described earlier in the section titled "Understanding table relationships," except that the article number has been replaced by $article_id.

> *Since the data type of $article_id has been checked, it's safe to use directly in the SQL query, so there's no need to use a prepared statement for MySQL Improved or PDO.*

4. Now add the code to process the query and results just before the closing PHP tag.

   For the original MySQL extension, use this:

   ```
   $result = mysql_query($sql) or die (mysql_error());
   $row = mysql_fetch_assoc($result);
   ```

   For MySQL Improved, use this:

   ```
   $result = $conn->query($sql) or die (mysqli_error());
   $row = $result->fetch_assoc();
   ```

   For PDO, use this:

   ```
   $result = $conn->query($sql);
   $row = $result->fetch();
   ```

5. The rest of the code displays the results of the SQL query in the main body of the page. Replace the placeholder text in the <h2> tags like this:

   ```
   <h2><?php if ($row) {
       echo $row['title'];
       }
   else {
       echo 'No record found';
       }
   ?>
   </h2>
   ```

   If the SELECT query finds no results, $row will be empty, which PHP interprets as false. So this displays the title, or No record found if the result set is empty.

6. Even if the result set isn't empty, not all articles are associated with an image, so the pictureWrapper <div> needs to be wrapped in a conditional statement that also checks that $row['filename'] contains a value. Amend the <div> like this:

   ```
   <?php
   if ($row && !empty($row['filename'])) {
       $filename = "images/{$row['filename']}";
       $imageSize = getimagesize($filename);
   ?>
   <div id="pictureWrapper">
   ```

```
<img src="<?php echo $filename; ?>" alt="<?php echo $row['caption']; ?>"
<?php echo $imageSize[3];?> />
</div>
<?php } ?>
```

This uses code that was described in Chapter 12, so I won't go into it again.

7. Finally, you need to display the article. Amend the rest of the code like this:

```
<p>
<?php
if ($row) {
  echo nl2br($row['article']);
  }
else {
?>
<p> </p>
<p> </p>
<p> </p>
<?php }?>
</p>
```

By passing the article to nl2br(), all the new line characters are converted to XHTML line breaks (<br />). If the result set is empty, three empty paragraphs are displayed instead. This prevents the footer from ending up behind the navigation menu.

8. Save the page and load journal.php into a browser. Click the More link for an article that has an image assigned through a foreign key. You should see details.php with the full article and image laid out as shown in Figure 14-10. Check your code, if necessary, with details_mysql.php, details_mysqli.php, or details_pdo.php.

Figure 14-10. The details page draws the article from one table and the image from another.

9. Click the link back to journal.php and test the other items. Each article that has an image associated with it should display correctly. But what happens when you click the More link for the article that doesn't have an image? This time you should see the result shown in Figure 14-11.

Figure 14-11. The lack of an associated image causes the SELECT query to produce an empty result set.

You know that the article is in the database because the first two sentences wouldn't be displayed in journal.php otherwise. To understand this sudden "disappearance," you need to look at the SELECT query more closely. If you take the values shown in Figure 14-9, the article with no image is article_id 1, and the value of journal.image_id for that record is NULL. So the WHERE clause becomes this:

```
WHERE journal.article_id = 1
AND NULL = images.image_id
```

When you use AND as part of a condition in a WHERE clause, *both* conditions must be true. Since every record in the images table has a primary key, it's impossible ever to match NULL with images.image_id. As a result, this SELECT query can never work if the foreign key is missing.

How about replacing AND with OR? Yes, that works, but it doesn't produce the result that you want. Since article_id = 1 is true, the second condition is never considered. Try changing the query, and you'll see that the same image is displayed for every article, even for the one that doesn't have an image associated with it. The solution is to join the tables using what's called a **left join**.

Finding records that don't have a matching foreign key

Take the SELECT query, and remove the condition that searches for a specific article, which leaves this:

```
SELECT title, article, filename, caption
FROM journal, images
WHERE journal.image_id = images.image_id
```

If you run this query in the SQL tab of phpMyAdmin, it produces the following result:

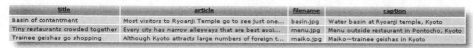

title	article	filename	caption
Basin of contentment	Most visitors to Ryoanji Temple go to see just one...	basin.jpg	Water basin at Ryoanji temple, Kyoto
Tiny restaurants crowded together	Every city has narrow alleyways that are best avoi...	menu.jpg	Menu outside restaurant in Pontocho, Kyoto
Trainee geishas go shopping	Although Kyoto attracts large numbers of foreign t...	maiko.jpg	Maiko—trainee geishas in Kyoto

When you list the tables as a comma-separated list in the FROM clause, MySQL performs a full join between the tables, and the SELECT query succeeds only if there is a full match. However, when you perform a left join, MySQL includes records that have a match in the left table, but not in the right one. Left and right refer to the order in which you perform the join. So, rewrite the SELECT query like this:

```
SELECT title, article, filename, caption
FROM journal LEFT JOIN images
ON journal.image_id = images.image_id
```

When you run it in phpMyAdmin, you get all four articles like this:

title	article	filename	caption
Basin of contentment	Most visitors to Ryoanji Temple go to see just one...	basin.jpg	Water basin at Ryoanji temple, Kyoto
Tiny restaurants crowded together	Every city has narrow alleyways that are best avoi...	menu.jpg	Menu outside restaurant in Pontocho, Kyoto
Trainee geishas go shopping	Although Kyoto attracts large numbers of foreign t...	maiko.jpg	Maiko—trainee geishas in Kyoto
Spectacular view of Mount Fuji from the bullet tra...	One of the best-known tourist images of Japan is o...	NULL	NULL

As you can see, MySQL populates the empty fields from the right table (images) with NULL.

The LEFT JOIN syntax is as follows:

```
FROM column_name LEFT JOIN column_name ON matching_condition
```

When the column names of the matching condition are the same in both tables, you can use this alternative syntax:

```
FROM column_name LEFT JOIN column_name USING (column_name)
```

Any WHERE clause comes after the LEFT JOIN. So, to find the details for article_id 1 regardless of whether it has a match in image_id, you rewrite the original SELECT query like this:

```
SELECT title, article, filename, caption
FROM journal LEFT JOIN images USING (image_id)
WHERE article_id = 1
```

So, now you can rewrite the SQL query in details.php like this:

```
$sql = "SELECT title, article, filename, caption
        FROM journal LEFT JOIN images USING (image_id)
        WHERE journal.article_id = $article_id";
```

14

If you click the More link to view the article that doesn't have an associated image, you should now see the article correctly displayed as shown in Figure 14-12. The other articles should still display correctly, too. The finished code is in details_lj_mysql.php, details_lj_mysqli.php, and details_lj_pdo.php.

Figure 14-12. Using a left join also retrieves articles that don't have a matching image_id as a foreign key.

Creating an intelligent link

The link at the bottom of details.php goes straight back to journal.php. That's fine with only four items in the journal table, but once you start getting more records in a database, you need to build a paging mechanism as I showed you in Chapter 12. The problem with a paging mechanism is that you need a way to return visitors to the same point in the result set that they came from.

> **PHP Solution 14-10: Creating a link that returns to the same point in a paging mechanism**

This PHP Solution checks whether the visitor arrived from an internal or external link. If the referring page was within the same site, the link returns the visitor to the same place. If the referring page was an external site, or if the server doesn't support the necessary superglobal variables, the script substitutes a standard link. It is shown here in the context of details.php, but it can be used on any page.

1. Locate the back link in the main body of details.php. It looks like this:

```
<p><a href="journal.php">Back to the journal</a></p>
```

2. Place your cursor immediately to the right of the first quotation mark, and insert the following code highlighted in bold:

```
<p><a href="
<?php
// check that browser supports $_SERVER variables
if (isset($_SERVER['HTTP_REFERER']) && isset($_SERVER['HTTP_HOST'])) {
  $url = parse_url($_SERVER['HTTP_REFERER']);
  // find if visitor was referred from a different domain
  if ($url['host'] == $_SERVER['HTTP_HOST']) {
    // if same domain, use referring URL
    echo $_SERVER['HTTP_REFERER'];
    }
  }
else {
  // otherwise, send to main page
  echo 'journal.php';
  } ?>">Back to the journal</a></p>
```

$_SERVER['HTTP_REFERER'] and $_SERVER['HTTP_HOST'] are superglobal variables that contain the URL of the referring page and the current hostname. You need to check their existence with isset() because some Windows servers don't support them. The parse_url() function creates an array containing each part of a URL, so $url['host'] contains the hostname. If it matches $_SERVER['HTTP_HOST'], you know that the visitor was referred by an internal link, so the full URL of the internal link is inserted in the href attribute. This includes any query string, so the link sends the visitor back to the same position in a paging mechanism. Otherwise, an ordinary link is created to the target page.

The finished code is in details_link_mysql.php, details_link_mysqli.php, and details_link_pdo.php.

Creating a lookup table

When dealing with many-to-many relationships in a database, you need to build a lookup table like the one in Figure 14-7. What's unusual about a lookup table is that it consists of just two columns, which are jointly declared as the table's primary key (known as a **composite primary key**). If you look at Figure 14-13 on the next page, you'll see that the image_id and cat_id columns both contain the same number several times—something that's unacceptable in a primary key, which must be unique. However, in a composite primary key, it's the combination of both values that is unique. The first two combinations, 1,2 and 1,4, are not repeated anywhere else in the table, nor are any of the others. If you refer back to Figure 14-7, you'll see that image_id 1 refers to basin.jpg, while cat_id 2 and 4 refer to the Kyoto and Autumn categories. Although this sort of relationship is easy to understand, creating and maintaining a lookup table is a little more complex. However, it's not difficult, as long as you follow a logical sequence.

14

Figure 14-13. In a lookup table, both columns together form a composite primary key.

The first thing to decide is the priority of the relationship between the tables. In the case of assigning photos to certain categories, it makes little sense to list all the images each time you add a new category. You're far more likely to want to assign the appropriate categories to an image when it's first inserted in the database. This means that you can create the categories independently, and put all the lookup table logic in the image insert form.

Setting up the categories and lookup tables

In the download files, you'll find `categories.sql`, `categories40.sql`, and `categories323.sql`, which contain the SQL to create the categories table and the lookup table, `image_cat_lookup`, together with some sample data. Alternatively, you can build the tables yourself easily in phpMyAdmin using the settings in Tables 14-4 and 14-5. Both database tables have just two columns (fields).

Table 14-4. Settings for the `categories` table

Field	Type	Length/Values	Attributes	Null	Extra	Primary key
cat_id	INT		UNSIGNED	not null	auto_increment	Selected
category	VARCHAR	20		not null		

Table 14-5. Settings for the `image_cat_lookup` table

Field	Type	Length/Values	Attributes	Null	Extra	Primary key
image_id	INT		UNSIGNED	not null		Selected
cat_id	INT		UNSIGNED	not null		Selected

The important thing about the definition for a lookup table is that *both* columns are set as primary key, and that auto_increment is *not selected* for either column. You must declare both columns as primary key at the same time. This is because each table can have only one primary key. Declaring them together ensures that the table recognizes them as a composite primary key.

Inserting new records with a lookup table

Figure 14-14 shows how you might implement an image insert form (you can find the code in `image_insert_mysql.php`, `image_insert_mysqli.php`, and `image_insert_pdo.php` in the download files).

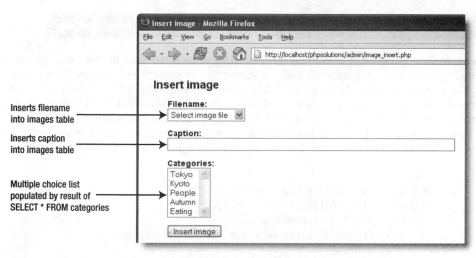

Inserts filename into images table

Inserts caption into images table

Multiple choice list populated by result of SELECT * FROM categories

Figure 14-14. The image insert form queries the categories table ready for selection.

I have used the buildFileList5() function from Chapter 7 to populate a drop-down menu with the names of available images. The key feature to notice is that the multiple-choice list is populated dynamically with the cat_id and category values. Consequently, when the Insert image button is clicked, the $_POST array contains values for filename, caption, and—if any categories have been selected—an array called categories. This triggers the following sequence:

1. The user input is validated. If there are any problems, an error message is prepared and the script goes straight to step 9.

2. The images table is checked to see if the filename has already been registered.

3. If the filename is registered, the script creates an error message and skips to step 9.

4. The image details are inserted into the images table.

5. The $_POST array is checked to see if any categories were selected. If not, the script skips to step 9.

6. A SELECT query gets the primary key (image_id) of the newly inserted record.

7. A loop builds image_id, cat_id pairs.

8. A second INSERT query stores the image_id, cat_id pairs in the lookup table.

9. If there are no errors, the page is redirected to a list of images in the database; otherwise, an error message is displayed.

Incidentally, mapping out the sequence of events like this is a good way to design PHP scripts. It gives you a clear idea of where you're going and breaks down your coding task into manageable chunks. Although my steps give details of how I plan to achieve something, such as by using a loop, start out simply by defining your objectives. You can also use your steps as comments within the page.

14

PHP Solution 14-11: Inserting a new image with categories in a lookup table

Rather than go through everything step by step, I have reproduced the code for the MySQL version of the page in its entirety, indicating the point at which each stage of the process begins. For the most part, the inline comments should be sufficient for you follow the flow of the script, but I've highlighted in bold several sections that merit further explanation. The only difference in the MySQL Improved and PDO versions is in the commands used to submit the queries to the database. If deploying this on a PHP 4 server, include buildFileList4.php and use the buildFileList4() function instead of buildFileList5().

```php
<?php
include('../includes/buildFileList5.php');
include('../includes/corefuncs.php');
include('../includes/conn_mysql.inc.php');
// connect to the database with administrative privileges
$conn = dbConnect('admin');
// process the form when submitted
if (array_key_exists('insert', $_POST)) {
  // STEP 1
  // remove magic quotes and validate input
  nukeMagicQuotes();
  $filename = $_POST['filename'];
  $caption = trim($_POST['caption']);
  if (empty($filename) || empty($caption)) {
    $error = 'You must select a filename and enter a caption.';
    }
  // carry only if input OK
  else {
    // prepare text for database query
    $filename = mysql_real_escape_string($filename);
    $caption = mysql_real_escape_string($caption);
    // STEP 2
    // check whether the filename is already registered in the database
    $checkUnique = "SELECT filename FROM images
                    WHERE filename = '$filename'";
    $result = mysql_query($checkUnique);
    $numRows = mysql_num_rows($result);
    // STEP 3
    // if $numRows is greater than 0, the image is a duplicate
    if ($numRows > 0) {
      $error = "$filename is already registered in the database.";
      }
    // STEP 4
    // if not a duplicate, proceed with insertion
    else {
      // insert the image details into the images table
      $insert = "INSERT INTO images (filename, caption)
                 VALUES ('$filename', '$caption')";
    mysql_query($insert);
```

```php
    // STEP 5
    // initialize an array for the categories
    $categories = array();
    // check whether any categories have been selected
    if (isset($_POST['categories'])) {
      // STEP 6
      // get the primary key of the image just inserted
      $getImageId = "SELECT image_id FROM images
                     WHERE filename = '$filename'
                     AND caption = '$caption'";
      $result = mysql_query($getImageId);
      $row = mysql_fetch_assoc($result);
      $image_id = $row['image_id'];
      // STEP 7
      // loop through the selected categories and build value pairs
      // ready for insertion into the lookup table
      foreach ($_POST['categories'] as $cat_id) {
        if (is_numeric($cat_id)) {
          $categories[] = "($image_id, $cat_id)";
          }
        }
      }
    // join the value pairs as a comma-separated string
    if (!empty($categories)) {
      $categories = implode(',', $categories);
      $noCats = false;
      }
    else {
      $noCats = true;
      }
    // STEP 8
    // insert the categories into the lookup table
    if (!$noCats) {
      $insertCats = "INSERT INTO image_cat_lookup (image_id, cat_id)
                     VALUES $categories";
      mysql_query($insertCats);
      }
    // STEP 9
    // redirect the page after insertion
    // this is inside the else clause initiated in step 4
    // it is ignored if there were errors in steps 1 or 3
    header('Location: http://localhost/phpsolutions/admin/ ➥
image_list.php');
    exit;
    }
  }
}
?>
<!DOCTYPE html PUBLIC "-//W3C//DTD XHTML 1.0 Transitional//EN" ➥
"http://www.w3.org/TR/xhtml1/DTD/xhtml1-transitional.dtd">
```

14

```html
<html xmlns="http://www.w3.org/1999/xhtml">
<head>
<meta http-equiv="Content-Type" content="text/html;
charset=iso-8859-1" />
<title>Insert image</title>
<link href="../assets/admin.css" rel="stylesheet" type="text/css" />
</head>

<body>
<h1>Insert image </h1>
<?php if (isset($error)) { ?>
<p class="warning"><?php echo $error; ?></p>
<?php } ?>
<form id="form1" name="form1" method="post" action="">
  <p>
    <label for="filename">Filename:</label>
    <select name="filename" id="filename">
      <option value="">Select image file</option>
      <?php buildFileList5('../images/'); ?>
            </select>
  </p>
  <p>
    <label for="textfield">Caption:</label>
    <input name="caption" type="text" class="widebox" id="caption" />
  </p>
  <p>
    <label for="categories">Categories:</label>
    <select name="categories[]" size="5" multiple="multiple"
id="categories">
    <?php
    // build multiple choice list with contents of categories table
    $allCats = 'SELECT * FROM categories';
    $catList = mysql_query($allCats);
    while ($row = mysql_fetch_assoc($catList)) {
    ?>
    <option value="<?php echo $row['cat_id']; ?>">
    <?php echo $row['category']; ?>
    </option>
    <?php } ?>
    </select>
  </p>
  <p>
    <input name="insert" type="submit" id="insert"
value="Insert image" />
  </p>
</form>
</body>
</html>
```

The validation in step 1 checks only that filename and caption are not empty. In a real application you would probably want to conduct further checks, such as making sure that the caption is a minimum length and doesn't exceed the maximum number of characters in your database column. (Use the strlen() function, as described in PHP Solution 9-6.) Devising validation checks is not just about keeping out intruders, but also making sure that data inserted into your database meets the criteria that you expect. The quality of information in your database is only as good as what you put in.

The filename is checked against existing records in the images table. If the result set contains any records, it means the file is already registered, so an error message is prepared. The rest of the script is enveloped in an else clause, so the insertion goes ahead only if the filename isn't a duplicate.

The SELECT query highlighted in step 6 uses the filename and caption of the record just entered as search criteria. This is a more accurate way of finding the primary key than a technique that you often see recommended. By calling the mysql_insert_id() function, you can get the primary key of the most recently inserted record (as long as it uses auto_increment). MySQL Improved and PDO both offer equivalents with the insert_id and lastInsertId properties. respectively. Most of the time, this will give you the information that you want, but on a busy server, someone else might insert another record at the same time. To be sure that you get the correct primary key, it's best to be specific in your request.

The foreach loop in step 7 checks that the values in $_POST['categories'] are numeric. The following line then combines each one with the primary key of the image and adds it to the $categories array:

```
$categories[] = "($image_id, $cat_id)";
```

Let's say that $image_id is 9, and $cat_id is 5. The next array element in $categories is this:

```
(9, 5)
```

After the loop has completed, the following line converts $categories into a comma-separated string:

```
$categories = implode(',', $categories);
```

So, if categories 2, 4, and 5 were selected in the insert form, $categories ends up like this:

```
(9, 2),(9, 4),(9, 5)
```

Finally, this is incorporated into the following SQL query:

```
$insertCats = "INSERT INTO image_cat_lookup (image_id, cat_id)
                VALUES $categories";
```

The result is the following INSERT query:

```
INSERT INTO image_cat_lookup (image_id, cat_id)
VALUES (9, 2),(9, 4),(9, 5)
```

14

As explained in "Reviewing the four essential SQL commands" in the previous chapter, this is the way you insert multiple records with a single INSERT query.

The code that builds the multiple-choice list in the main body of the page is a straightforward SELECT query that uses a loop to display the <option> tags. The thing to note here is that the name attribute of the <select> tag must be followed by a pair of square brackets to store all selections as an array. As you might recall from Chapter 5, a multiple-choice list is omitted from the $_POST array if no items are selected. That's why step 5 needs to check if $_POST['categories'] has been defined. Failure to do so produces nasty error messages that prevent the page from working properly.

Adding a new category

A question that may be going through your mind is, "How can I add a new category at the same time as adding a new image?" The simple answer is that you can't. Inserting records into a database follows a linear sequence. The new category must be added to the categories table before you can register its primary key into the lookup table.

There are several approaches you can take to resolve this problem. I'll use the images and categories tables as an example, but the following points apply equally to any situation involving a lookup table:

- Always create a new category before inserting a new image.
- If you realize you need a new category when inserting an image, insert the image first, and then create the new category. Finally, update the image record to associate the new category with it.
- Redesign the image insert form with a check box and text field for a new category. If the check box is selected, insert the new category into the categories table, retrieve its primary key, and then build the INSERT query for the lookup table.

Although you can combine both insert operations in the same form, both records must exist in their respective tables before you can link them through a lookup table.

Updating records with a lookup table

Updating records that have references in a lookup table is very similar to inserting new records with a lookup table, except that you don't need to query the database to find out the primary key of the record being updated—you wouldn't be able to update it if you didn't already know its primary key. However, the lookup table needs special treatment because each record consists of nothing more than a composite primary key. Trying to work out which combinations to retain and which to delete will tie you in knots. The simple answer is to delete all references in the lookup table to the record that is being updated, and insert them anew.

So, in the previous example, if the image_id of the record being updated is 9, you issue this command:

```
DELETE FROM image_cat_lookup WHERE image_id = 9
```

If there is no change to the categories associated with the image, you just insert the same ones again. However, if the categories have been changed to 3 and 5, the INSERT query changes to this:

```
INSERT INTO image_cat_lookup (image_id, cat_id)
VALUES (9, 3),(9, 5)
```

Inserting the same values again may seem like a waste of effort, but MySQL handles it in a split second.

PHP Solution 14-12: Updating an image and its categories in the lookup table

The chain of events for updating a record from the images table and its related categories goes like this:

1. Display a list of existing records in the images table.

2. Select the record to be updated, and send its primary key to the update form in the URL query string.

3. Display the details of the record in the update form, and store the primary key in a hidden field. Display the filename in a read-only field, to prevent corruption of data.

4. Display the contents of the categories table in the update form, and use the lookup table to select the currently associated categories.

5. When the update form is submitted, validate the user input. If any required fields are missing, reassign the values from the $_POST array to the same variables used in step 4, and prepare an error message. This enables you to redisplay the update form again with all values preserved. If there are any problems, go straight to step 10.

6. If the user input is OK, update the fields in the images table.

7. Delete all references in the lookup table to the image_id of the record that has just been updated.

8. Check the $_POST array to see if any categories were selected.

9. If any categories were selected, build an INSERT query to store the image_id, cat_id pairs in the lookup table. Then execute the query.

10. Redirect the page to the list of records, or redisplay the update form for corrections.

The fully commented code for each method of connecting to MySQL is in the download files for this chapter in image_update_mysql.php, image_update_mysqli.php, and image_update_pdo.php.

Deleting records that have dependent foreign keys

Once you have added a foreign key, it's important to make sure dependencies between tables aren't broken when records are deleted. This is known as maintaining **referential**

integrity. SQL enforces referential integrity through foreign key constraints. Unfortunately, the default MyISAM tables in MySQL aren't expected to support foreign key constraints until MySQL 5.2. As a result, you need to code the same logic in your PHP scripts instead.

Once records become orphaned, your data loses much—if not all—of its value. So you need to establish **deletion rules** for your records. The best way to understand what this entails is by looking at an actual example. Figure 14-15 shows the relationships that basin.jpg has in the phpsolutions database. It has direct relationships with the journal and lookup tables, and an indirect relationship with the categories table through the lookup table.

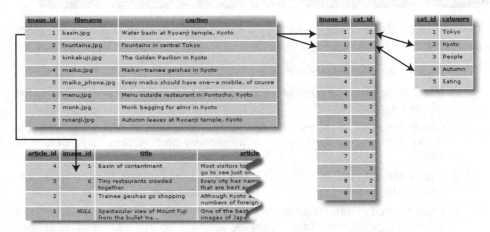

Figure 14-15. When deleting a record in one table, you need to ensure that dependent records aren't orphaned.

Let's say you decide to delete the Autumn category. If you use the categories table only to select images that belong to a particular category, deleting that record alone would probably have no impact on the results you get from the database. However, one day, you suddenly decide that you want to know the categories that a particular image belongs to. When the lookup table tries to find cat_id 4, it's not there. You have broken the referential integrity of your database. So, whenever you delete a record from the categories table, you must also delete all matching references to its primary key in the lookup table.

What if you decide to delete the article associated with basin.jpg in the journal table? The only relationship between the image and the article is that the image's primary key is stored as a foreign key in the article record. Delete the article, and you delete the foreign key, but the image itself is unaffected.

It's a different story, though, if you decide to delete basin.jpg. A reference to the image is stored as a foreign key in the journal table. If you delete the image, the next time you try to display the article, the image will be missing. In other words, article_id 4 is dependent on image_id 1. You need to prevent any record from being deleted if its primary key is stored as a foreign key in a secondary or child table. The deletion should proceed only if there are no dependent records, and it should be accompanied by another DELETE command to remove related records in the lookup table.

To summarize,

- If a record has dependent records, you must delete the dependent records first—or at least remove the dependency by updating the dependent records.

- If there is no dependency, the deletion can go ahead, but you must also delete all references in other tables.

If you're new to databases, this may sound confusing, but it's vital to get right. Otherwise, you'll be faced with a far more tedious and confusing situation when the links in your database stop working.

Before deleting a record that is likely to have dependent records, run a SELECT query on the dependent table searching for any instances of the record's primary key in the foreign key column. So, in the case of the images table, you need to run a search of the journal table like this:

```
SELECT image_id FROM journal
WHERE image_id = (primary key of image you want to delete)
```

For PDO, you need to use SELECT COUNT(*) instead of SELECT image_id.

If the result of the query is 0, you can let the deletion proceed. Any other result should block the process. The code to do this doesn't involve any new techniques; it's simply a question of controlling the flow of the script with if... else statements. You can study the fully commented code in the download files for this chapter in image_delete_mysql.php, image_delete_mysqli.php, and image_delete_pdo.php.

Summary

This chapter began with some basic techniques, but the pace rapidly shifted, and by the end you were dealing with quite complex concepts. Once you have learned basic SQL and the PHP commands to communicate with a database, working with single tables is very easy. Linking tables through foreign keys, however, can be quite challenging. The power of a relational database comes from its sheer flexibility. The problem is that this infinite flexibility means there is no single "right" way of doing things.

Don't let this put you off, though. Your instinct may be to stick with single tables, but down that route lies even greater complexity. If, for example, you were to create columns called article1, article2, article3, and so forth in the images table, it would become impossible to sort the records, and you would have to write complex SQL to search through each column for the information you want. The key to making it easy to work with databases is to limit your ambitions in the early stages. Build simple structures like the one in this chapter, experiment with them, and get to know how they work. Add tables and foreign key links gradually. People with a lot of experience working with databases say they frequently spend more than half the development time just thinking about the table structure. After that, the coding is the easy bit!

In the final chapter, we move back to working with a single table—addressing the important subject of user authentication with a database and how to handle encrypted passwords.

14

15 **KEEPING INTRUDERS AT BAY**

What this chapter contains:

- Deciding how to encrypt passwords
- Using one-way encryption for user registration and login
- Using two-way encryption for user registration and login
- Decrypting passwords

Chapter 9 showed you the principles of user authentication and sessions to password protect parts of your website, but the login scripts all relied on usernames and passwords stored in text files. Keeping user details in a database is both more secure and more efficient. Instead of just storing a list of usernames and passwords, a database can store other details, such as first name, family name, email address, and so on. MySQL also gives you the option of using either one- or two-way encryption. In the first section of this chapter, we'll examine the difference between the two.

Choosing an encryption method

The PHP Solutions in Chapter 9 use the SHA-1 encryption algorithm. It offers a high level of security, particularly if used in conjunction with a **salt** (a random value that's added to make decryption harder). SHA-1 is a one-way encryption method: once a password has been encrypted, there's no way of converting it back to plain text. This is both an advantage and a disadvantage. It offers the user greater security because passwords encrypted this way remain secret. However, there's no way of reissuing a lost password, since not even the site administrator can decrypt it. The only solution is to issue the user a temporary new password, and ask the user to reset it.

The alternative is to use two-way encryption, which relies on a pair of functions: one to encrypt the password and another to convert it back to plain text, making it easy to reissue passwords to forgetful users. Two-way encryption uses a secret key that is passed to both functions to perform the conversion. The key is simply a string that you make up yourself. Obviously, to keep the data secure, the key needs to be sufficiently difficult to guess and should never be stored in the database. However, you need to embed the key in your registration and login scripts—either directly or through an include file—so if your scripts are ever exposed, your security is blown wide apart. MySQL offers a number of two-way encryption functions, but AES_ENCRYPT() is currently regarded as the most secure. AES_ENCRYPT() is not available in MySQL 3.23, but the ENCODE() function should be more than adequate for most websites.

Both types of encryption have their advantages and disadvantages. I'll leave it to you to decide which is best suited to your circumstances, and I'll concentrate solely on the technical implementation.

Using one-way encryption

In the interests of keeping things simple, I'm going to use the same basic forms as in Chapter 9, so only the username, salt, and encrypted password are stored in the database.

Creating a table to store users' details

In phpMyAdmin, create a new table called users in the phpsolutions database. The table needs four columns (fields) with the settings listed in Table 15-1.

Table 15-1. Settings for the users table

Field	Type	Length/Values	Attributes	Null	Extra	Primary key
user_id	INT		UNSIGNED	not null	auto_increment	Selected
username	VARCHAR	15		not null		
salt	INT		UNSIGNED	not null		
pwd	VARCHAR	40		not null		

In Chapter 9, the username doubled as the salt, but storing the details in a database means that you can choose something more unique and difficult to guess. Although a Unix time-stamp follows a predictable pattern, it changes every second. So even if an attacker knows the day on which a user registered, there are 86,400 possible values for the salt, which would need to be combined with every attempt to guess the password. So the salt column needs to store an integer (INT). The pwd column, which is where the encrypted password is stored, needs to be 40 characters long because the SHA-1 algorithm always produces an alphanumeric string of that length.

Registering new users

The basic registration form is in register_db.php in the download files for this chapter. The completed scripts are in register_mysql.php, register_mysqli.php, and register_pdo.php.

PHP Solution 15-1: Creating a user registration form

1. Copy register_db.php from the download files to a new folder called authenticate in the phpsolutions site root.

2. The entire PHP script needs to go in a conditional statement above the DOCTYPE declaration to ensure that it runs only when the Register button is clicked. The first part of the script needs to validate the username and password to make sure they meet your minimum criteria. Add the following code at the top of the page:

```php
<?php
// execute script only if form has been submitted
if (array_key_exists('register', $_POST)) {
```

15

```php
// remove backslashes from the $_POST array
include('../includes/corefuncs.php');
include('../includes/connection.inc.php');
nukeMagicQuotes();
// check length of username and password
$username = trim($_POST['username']);
$pwd = trim($_POST['pwd']);
// initialize message array
$message = array();
// check length of username
if (strlen($username) < 6 || strlen($username) > 15) {
  $message[] = 'Username must be between 6 and 15 characters';
  }
// validate username
if (!ctype_alnum($username)) {
  $message[] = 'Username must consist of alphanumeric characters ➥
with no spaces';
  }
// check password
if (strlen($pwd) < 6 || preg_match('/\s/', $pwd)) {
  $message[] = 'Password must be at least 6 characters; no spaces';
  }
// check that the passwords match
if ($pwd != $_POST['conf_pwd']) {
  $message[] = 'Your passwords don\'t match';
  }
// if no errors so far, check for duplicate username
if (!$message) {
  // connect to database as administrator
  $conn = dbConnect('admin');
  // rest of code goes here
  }
}
?>
```

After removing backslashes and trimming whitespace from the username and password, this series of conditional statements subjects them to a number of validation tests. You have already met strlen(), which gets the length of a string. The username is passed to the function ctype_alnum(), which returns false if a string contains anything other than alphanumeric characters with no spaces.

You could also use ctype_alnum() for the password, but allowing nonalphanumeric characters in passwords makes for greater security. So I've used the expression preg_match('/\s/', $pwd) instead. This checks only for whitespace, including tabs and new line characters.

If any of the tests fail, a suitable message is stored in an array called $message. However, if everything is OK, $message remains empty, and—as I'm sure you remember—an empty array equates to false. So, if no errors are detected, the script that goes in the final conditional statement will be executed. This is the code that connects to the database and inserts the username and password.

3. Before charging ahead with inserting the new record, you need to find out whether the username is already recorded in the database. Because it has been tested by ctype_alnum(), you know that $username doesn't contain any characters that could cause problems with SQL injection or quotes. So you can use it directly in the SQL query. For the original MySQL extension and MySQL Improved, add the following code at the point indicated by the comment in the final conditional statement:

```
// check for duplicate username
$checkDuplicate = "SELECT user_id FROM users
                   WHERE username = '$username'";
```

For PDO, use this:

```
// check for duplicate username
$checkDuplicate = "SELECT COUNT(*) FROM users
                   WHERE username = '$username'";
```

4. Now run the query. For the original MySQL extension, use this:

```
$result = mysql_query($checkDuplicate) or die(mysql_error());
$numRows = mysql_num_rows($result);
```

For MySQL Improved, use this:

```
$result = $conn->query($checkDuplicate) or die(mysqli_error($conn));
$numRows = $result->num_rows;
```

For PDO, use this:

```
$result = $conn->query($checkDuplicate);
$numRows = $result->fetchColumn();
// release database resource for next query
$result->closeCursor();
```

5. The variable $numRows now contains the number of records matching the username. It should be only 0 or 1. Since any number other than 0 equates to true, you can use $numRows on its own as a test. Add the following code immediately after the preceding step (it's the same for all connection methods):

```
// if $numRows is positive, the username is already in use
if ($numRows) {
  $message[] = "$username is already in use. Please choose another ➡
username.";
  }
// otherwise, it's OK to insert the details in the database
else {
  // create a salt using the current timestamp
  $salt = time();
  // encrypt the password and salt with SHA1
  $pwd = sha1($pwd.$salt);
  // insert details into database
```

15

If $numRows is anything other than 0, a message is added to the $message array. Otherwise, it's OK to register the username and password in the database. The first step is to store the current Unix timestamp in $salt. Then pass the password and the salt (joined by a period—the concatenation operator) to sha1() for encryption.

6. Everything is now ready for insertion into the users table. All three values are safe to use without further processing: $username has already been checked by ctype_alnum(), $salt is a Unix timestamp, and the sha1() function encrypts whatever is passed to it as a 40-character hexadecimal number. This means that you can embed the variables directly into the SQL query like this:

```
// insert details into database
$insert = "INSERT INTO users (username, salt, pwd)
            VALUES ('$username', $salt, '$pwd')";
```

You don't need quotes around $salt because it's an integer being stored in a numeric column. Although $pwd is a hexadecimal number, it does need quotes because it's being stored in a text-type column.

> These variables are safe because they have been processed in ways that remove any risk of SQL injection or problems with quotes. However, if you have any doubts about user input, always use mysql_real_escape_string() or a prepared statement. It's extra work, but it's better to be safe than sorry.

7. Execute the query. Use this code for the original MySQL extension:

```
$result = mysql_query($insert) or die(mysql_error());
```

For MySQL Improved, use this:

```
$result = $conn->query($insert) or die(mysqli_error($conn));
```

For PDO, use this:

```
$result = $conn->query($insert);
```

8. An INSERT query returns true if it succeeds, so you can use the value of $result to prepare the final message as shown in the following code. The code goes immediately after the previous step, but before the two closing curly braces and PHP tag at the end of step 2. The new code is shown in bold, with the existing code for context.

```
        if ($result) {
            $message[] = "Account created for $username";
        }
        else {
            $message[] = "There was a problem creating an account for ➥
$username";
        }
    }
  }
?>
```

9. All that remains is to add the code that displays the contents of the $message array. A foreach loop iterates through each element to create an unordered list like this (the code goes just before the opening <form> tag):

```php
<h1>Register user</h1>
<?php
if (isset($message)) {
  echo '<ul class="warning">';
  foreach ($message as $item) {
    echo "<li>$item</li>";
    }
  echo '</ul>';
  }
?>
<form id="form1" name="form1" method="post" action="">
```

10. Save register_db.php and load it in a browser. Test it thoroughly by entering input that you know breaks the rules: nonalphanumeric characters in the username, a password that's too short or too long, nonmatching passwords, and so on. If you make multiple mistakes in the same attempt, a bulleted list of error messages should appear at the top of the form, as shown in the next screenshot.

11. Now fill in the registration form correctly. You should see a message telling you that an account has been created for the username you chose.

12. Try registering the same username again. This time you should get a message similar to the one shown in the following screenshot. Check your code, if necessary, against the download files.

15

Now that you have a username and password registered in the database, let's wire up the login form. Copy the following files from the download files for this chapter to the authenticate folder: login.php, menu.php, and secretpage.php. Also copy logout_db.inc.php to the includes folder. These files replicate the setup in PHP Solution 9-8, allowing you to log in and visit two restricted pages. The code in menu.php and secretpage.php is identical to Chapter 9, except that I have changed the session time limit from 15 seconds to 15 minutes. The include file is also identical, except that it takes you to the authenticate folder, rather than the sessions one, after logging out. All the work is done in login.php.

PHP Solution 15-2: Authenticating a user's credentials with a database

1. The form in login.php is the same as in Chapter 9, but all the code above the DOCTYPE declaration has been removed. Much of the authentication process is similar to working with a text file, but I think it's easier to start with a clean slate. Begin by adding the following code above the DOCTYPE declaration:

```php
<?php
// process the script only if the form has been submitted
if (array_key_exists('login', $_POST)) {
  // start the session
  session_start();
  include('../includes/corefuncs.php');
  include('../includes/connection.inc.php');
  // clean the $_POST array and assign to shorter variables
  nukeMagicQuotes();
  $username = trim($_POST['username']);
  $pwd = trim($_POST['pwd']);
  // connect to the database as a restricted user
  $conn = dbConnect('query');
```

The inline comments explain what's going on. There's nothing new here.

2. Next, you need to retrieve the username's details from the database. Use the following code for the original MySQL extension:

```php
// prepare username for use in SQL query
$username = mysql_real_escape_string($username);
// get the username's details from the database
$sql = "SELECT * FROM users WHERE username = '$username'";
$result = mysql_query($sql);
$row = mysql_fetch_assoc($result);
```

This is a straightforward SELECT query that needs no explanation.

For MySQL Improved, use this:

```php
// get the username's details from the database
$sql = "SELECT salt, pwd FROM users WHERE username = ?";
// initialize and prepare statement
$stmt = $conn->stmt_init();
if ($stmt->prepare($sql)) {
  // bind the input parameter
  $stmt->bind_param('s', $username);
  // bind the result, using a new variable for the password
```

```
    $stmt->bind_result($salt, $storedPwd);
    $stmt->execute();
    $stmt->fetch();
    }
```

This selects the salt and the stored password. The password needs to be bound to a new variable, $storedPwd, to prevent overwriting $pwd, which already contains the version of the password submitted through the login form.

For PDO, use this:

```
// get the username's details from the database
$sql = "SELECT * FROM users WHERE username = ?";
$stmt = $conn->prepare($sql);
$stmt->execute(array($username));
$row = $stmt->fetch();
```

This is a straightforward SELECT query that needs no explanation.

3. Once you have retrieved the username's details, you need to encrypt the password entered by the user by combining it with the salt and passing them both to sha1(). You can then compare the result to the stored version of the password, which was similarly encrypted at the time of registration. For the original MySQL extension and PDO, use the following code:

```
if (sha1($pwd.$row['salt']) == $row['pwd']) {
  $_SESSION['authenticated'] = 'Jethro Tull';
  }
```

Because the results of the SELECT query are already bound to variables in MySQL Improved, the code is slightly different, as follows:

```
if (sha1($pwd.$salt) == $storedPwd) {
  $_SESSION['authenticated'] = 'Jethro Tull';
  }
```

As in Chapter 9, the value of $_SESSION['authenticated'] is of no real importance.

4. The rest of the script handles a failed login attempt and redirects a successful login in the same way as in Chapter 9. It looks like this:

```
    // if no match, destroy the session and prepare error message
    else {
      $_SESSION = array();
      session_destroy();
      $error = 'Invalid username or password';
      }
    // if the session variable has been set, redirect
    if (isset($_SESSION['authenticated'])) {
      // get the time the session started
      $_SESSION['start'] = time();
      header('Location: http://localhost/phpsolutions/authenticate/ ➥
menu.php');
      exit;
      }
  }
?>
```

15

5. Save `login.php` and test it by logging in with the username and password that you registered at the end of the previous section. The login process should work in exactly the same way as Chapter 9. The difference is that all the details are stored more securely in a database, and each user has a unique and probably unguessable salt.

Check your code, if necessary, against `login_mysql.php`, `login_mysqli.php`, or `login_pdo.php`. If you encounter problems, use echo to display the values of the freshly encrypted password and the stored version. The most common mistake is creating too narrow a column for the encrypted password in the database. It must be at least 40 characters wide.

> Although storing an encrypted password in a database is more secure than using a text file, the password is sent from the user's browser to the server in plain, unencrypted text. This is adequate for most websites, but if you need a high level of security, the login and access to subsequent pages should be made through a Secure Sockets Layer (SSL) connection.

Using two-way encryption

The main differences in setting up user registration and authentication for two-way encryption are that the password needs to be stored in the database as a binary object using the BLOB data type, and that the comparison between the encrypted passwords takes place in the SQL query, rather than in the PHP script. Although you can use a salt with the password, doing so involves querying the database twice when logging in: first to retrieve the salt and then to verify the password with the salt. To keep things simple, I'll show you how to implement two-way encryption without a salt.

Creating the table to store users' details

In phpMyAdmin, create a new table called `users_2way` in the phpsolutions database. It needs three columns (fields) with the settings listed in Table 15-2.

Table 15-2. Settings for the `users_2way` table

Field	Type	Length/Values	Attributes	Null	Extra	Primary key
user_id	INT		UNSIGNED	not null	auto_increment	Selected
username	VARCHAR	15		not null		
pwd	BLOB			not null		

Registering new users

The validation process for the user registration form is identical to the one used for one-way encryption in PHP Solution 15-1, apart from the SQL that checks for a duplicate username. The name of the table needs to be changed from users to users_2way.

After checking that the username isn't already in use, you store the encryption key in a variable. I have chosen takeThisWith@PinchOfSalt as my secret key, but a random series of characters would be more secure. The password and key are then passed as strings to ENCODE() or AES_ENCRYPT() in the INSERT query. Those are the only changes required.

> *The following scripts embed the encryption key directly in the page. If you have a private folder outside the server root, it's a good idea to define the key in an include file and store it in your private folder.*

The code for the original MySQL extension looks like this (new code is highlighted in bold):

```
    // otherwise, it's OK to insert the details in the database
    else {
      // create key
      $key = 'takeThisWith@PinchOfSalt';
      // insert details into database
      $insert = "INSERT INTO users_2way (username, pwd)
                VALUES ('$username', ENCODE('$pwd', '$key'))";
      $result = mysql_query($insert) or die(mysql_error());
      if ($result) {
        $message[] = "Account created for $username";
```

The code for MySQL Improved looks like this:

```
    // otherwise, it's OK to insert the details in the database
    else {
      // create key
      $key = 'takeThisWith@PinchOfSalt';
      // insert details into database
      $insert = "INSERT INTO users_2way (username, pwd)
                VALUES ('$username', AES_ENCRYPT('$pwd', '$key'))";
      $result = $conn->query($insert) or die(mysqli_error($conn));
      if ($result) {
        $message[] = "Account created for $username";
```

For PDO, it looks like this:

```
    // otherwise, it's OK to insert the details in the database
    else {
      // create key
      $key = 'takeThisWith@PinchOfSalt';
```

15

```
                      // insert details into database
                      $insert = "INSERT INTO users_2way (username, pwd)
                                 VALUES ('$username', AES_ENCRYPT('$pwd', '$key'))";
                      $result = $conn->query($insert);
                      if ($result) {
                        $message[] = "Account created for $username";
```

You can find the finished code in register_2way_mysql.php, register_2way_mysqli.php, and register_2way_pdo.php in the download files.

User authentication with two-way encryption

Creating a login page with two-way encryption is very simple. After connecting to the database, you incorporate the username, secret key, and unencrypted password in the WHERE clause of a SELECT query. If the query finds a match, the user is allowed into the restricted part of the site. If there's no match, the login is rejected. The code is the same as in PHP Solution 15-2, except for the following section. For the original MySQL extension, it looks like this:

```
                      // prepare username for use in SQL query
                      $username = mysql_real_escape_string($username);
                      // create key
                      $key = 'takeThisWith@PinchOfSalt';
                      $sql = "SELECT * FROM users_2way
                              WHERE username = '$username'
                              AND pwd = ENCODE('$pwd', '$key')";
                      $result = mysql_query($sql);
                      $numRows = mysql_num_rows($result);
                      if ($numRows) {
                        $_SESSION['authenticated'] = 'Jethro Tull';
```

For MySQL Improved, it looks like this:

```
                      // connect to the database as a restricted user
                      $conn = dbConnect('query');
                      // create key
                      $key = 'takeThisWith@PinchOfSalt';
                      $sql = "SELECT * FROM users_2way
                              WHERE username = ? AND pwd = AES_ENCRYPT(?, '$key')";
                      // initialize and prepare statement
                      $stmt = $conn->stmt_init();
                      if ($stmt->prepare($sql)) {
                        // bind the input parameters
                        $stmt->bind_param('ss', $username, $pwd);
                        $stmt->execute();
                        $stmt->store_result();
                        $numRows = $stmt->num_rows;
                        }
                      if ($numRows) {
                        $_SESSION['authenticated'] = 'Jethro Tull';
```

Note that with MySQL Improved you need to store the result of the prepared statement before you can access the num_rows property. If you fail to do this, $numRows will always be 0, and the login will fail even if the username and password are correct.

The revised code for PDO looks like this:

```
// connect to the database as a restricted user
$conn = dbConnect('query');
// create key
$key = 'takeThisWith@PinchOfSalt';
$sql = "SELECT COUNT(*) FROM users_2way
        WHERE username = ? AND pwd = AES_ENCRYPT(?, '$key')";
$stmt = $conn->prepare($sql);
$stmt->execute(array($username, $pwd));
$numRows = $stmt->fetchColumn();
if ($numRows) {
  $_SESSION['authenticated'] = 'Jethro Tull';
```

The completed code for all versions is in the download files login_2way_mysql.php, login_2way_mysqli.php, and login_2way_pdo.php.

Decrypting a password

Decrypting a password encrypted with two-way encryption simply involves passing the secret key as the second argument to the appropriate function like this (using DECODE() for the original MySQL extension):

```
$key = 'takeThisWith@PinchOfSalt';
$getDecryptedPassword = "SELECT DECODE(pwd, '$key') AS pwd
                         FROM users_2way
                         WHERE username = '$username'";
```

For MySQL Improved and PDO, you use AES_DECRYPT() in a prepared statement like this:

```
$key = 'takeThisWith@PinchOfSalt';
$getDecryptedPassword = "SELECT AES_DECRYPT(pwd, '$key') AS pwd
                         FROM users_2way
                         WHERE username = ?";
```

The key must be exactly the same as the one originally used to encrypt the password. If you lose the key, the passwords remain as inaccessible as those stored using one-way encryption.

Normally, the only time you need to decrypt a password is when a user requests a password reminder. Creating the appropriate security policy for sending out such reminders depends a great deal on the type of site that you're operating. However, it goes without saying that you shouldn't display the decrypted password onscreen. You need to set up a series of security checks, such as asking for the user's date of birth or mother's maiden name, or posing a question whose answer only the user is likely to know. Even if the user gets the answer right, you should send the password by email to the user's registered address.

15

All the necessary knowledge should be at your fingertips if you have succeeded in getting this far in the book.

Updating user details

I haven't included any update forms for the user registration pages. It's a task that you should be able to accomplish by yourself at this stage. The most important point about updating user registration details is that you should not display the user's existing password in the update form. If you're using one-way encryption, you can't anyway. If the update form is exclusively for changing passwords, you don't need to check that the username is unique in the database, but you should ask for the old password and check that it matches before updating it. Failure to do so would allow anyone to change another person's password at will. If you offer the opportunity to change a username, you also need to check that the new one is unique.

If the user wants to change other details but not the existing password, you could add a check box or radio button to signal that choice. Your PHP script needs to use conditional statements to execute different UPDATE queries depending on the choices made. If the user selects the option not to update the password, all references to the password need to be left out of the SQL; otherwise, you run the risk of replacing the existing password with a blank one, leaving your site wide open. Another, perhaps simpler approach is to have separate forms for updating the password and other details.

Where next?

This book has covered a massive amount of ground. If you master all the techniques covered here, you are well on your way to becoming an intermediate PHP developer, and with a little more effort, you will enter the advanced level. If it's been a struggle, don't worry. Go over the earlier chapters again. The more you practice, the easier it becomes.

You're probably thinking, "How on earth can I remember all this?" You don't need to. Don't be ashamed to look things up. Bookmark the PHP online manual (www.php.net/manual/en/index.php) and use it regularly. It's constantly updated, and it has lots of useful examples. The search box at the top right of every page (as shown in the following screenshot) takes you straight to a full description of any function that you want to know more about. Even if you can't remember the correct function name, it takes you to a page that suggests the most likely candidates.

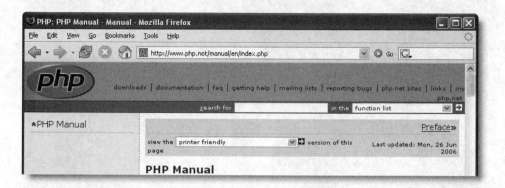

What makes dynamic web design easy is not an encyclopedic knowledge of PHP functions, but a solid grasp of how conditional statements, loops, and other structures control the flow of a script. Once you can visualize your projects in terms of "if this happens, what should happen next?" you're the master of your own game. I consult the PHP online manual many times a day. To me, it's like a dictionary. Most of the time, I just want to check that I have the arguments in the right order, but I often find that something catches my eye and opens up new horizons. I may not use that knowledge immediately, but I store it at the back of my mind for future use and go back when I need to check the details.

The MySQL online manual (http://dev.mysql.com/doc/refman/5.0/en/index.html) is equally useful. Make both the PHP and MySQL online manuals your friends, and your knowledge will grow by leaps and bounds.

15

INDEX

SYMBOLS AND Numerics

You Need the Companion eBook

Your purchase of this book entitles you to buy the companion PDF-version eBook for only $10. Take the weightless companion with you anywhere.

We believe this Apress title will prove so indispensable that you'll want to carry it with you everywhere, which is why we are offering the companion eBook (in PDF format) for $10 to customers who purchase this book now. Convenient and fully searchable, the PDF version of any content-rich, page-heavy Apress book makes a valuable addition to your programming library. You can easily find and copy code—or perform examples by quickly toggling between instructions and the application. Even simultaneously tackling a donut, diet soda, and complex code becomes simplified with hands-free eBooks!

Once you purchase your book, getting the $10 companion eBook is simple:

❶ Visit **www.apress.com/promo/tendollars/**.

❷ Complete a basic registration form to receive a randomly generated question about this title.

❸ Answer the question correctly in 60 seconds, and you will receive a promotional code to redeem for the $10.00 eBook.

2560 Ninth Street • Suite 219 • Berkeley, CA 94710

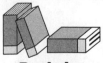

eBookshop

THE EXPERT'S VOICE™

Offer valid through 5/20/07.